THE HOOSIER GAME

By Dr. James L. Brunnemer

DEDICATED TO GRANDPA'S SPECIAL SIX:

Noah Brunnemer
Julia Brunnemer
Nate Brunnemer
Sam Brunnemer
Kaity Brunnemer
Jake Brunnemer

CREDITS

Cover Photograph:
Geoffrey J. Thompson
Geoffthompsonimages.com

Original Illustrations:
Tim Greatbatch
tgreatbatch@att.net

Editor:
R. Peter Noot
delhistage@gmail.com

Contact the Author:
Jim Brunnemer
thehoosiergame.com
or
jimbrunnemer@gmail.com

Copyright © 2013 Dr. James L. Brunnemer
All rights reserved.
ISBN: 1481053426
ISBN 13: 9781481053426

Herb,

Hope you enjoy this walk back it through time — to the real "Hoosier Hysteria."

[signature]

INTRODUCTION

Basketball and Indiana are as inseparable as potatoes and Idaho. No comprehensive history of the Hoosier state can ignore the impact of the game on the Indiana culture. That God ordained the state of Indiana as the capital of His basketball universe is hardly hyperbole to many Hoosiers.

This is a tale of two boys whose lives would intertwine through a shared allegiance to and love for the game in mid-twentieth-century Indiana. One, Josh Seaberg, would pass from his youth to maturity and from high school through college to become a responsible and productive professional educator.

However, his best friend, schoolboy hoops hero Jake Skoon, would be seduced by, then wed for life to, the game of basketball. He became consumed by celebrity as a teen that he would never attain in the adult world.

Skoon's pursuit of glory on the hardwood was a vision common among thousands of Indiana schoolboys. An exceptional talent for tossing a ball through an iron hoop would propel Jake to prominence in a rural community where one could see at least two basketball goals from any backyard in town. Well-intentioned townspeople would unfairly place him atop a pedestal by the time he was fourteen years old. Hometown adulation and statewide recognition became his cocaine.

While most boys left high school glories behind in the normal progression to adulthood, Jake would never develop an identity separate from basketball. His sheltered existence as a small-town teenage icon left him unprepared for the unspectacular routine of adult life. Sadly frozen in his adolescence, Jake's tailspin after the glory days of high school would be cheerless and agonizing. A constant tide of disappointments and rejections awaited him in the game of life that bestowed no extra points for one who could shoot baskets well.

To understand Jake's troubled life is to comprehend the unparalleled, almost spiritual hold that high school basketball had on Hoosiers of his era.

Connoisseurs of the sport know that in the fall of 1891 in Springfield, Massachusetts, Dr. James Naismith, a physical education instructor at the Young Men's Christian Association Training School, was directed by the superintendent to devise a game to be played within the confines of the gymnasium, which would keep the students occupied and fit during the brutal New England winter.

After much experimenting Dr. Naismith created thirteen rules to govern a new sport he would call "basket-ball." (Despite a century of innovative modifications and additions to the rules of basketball for succeeding generations of coaches and athletes, Naismith's original regulations remain as the bedrock of the game.)

The object was to score a goal by tossing a soccer ball into peach baskets that had been nailed by the school custodian to the railing at opposite ends of the second-floor running track that just happened to be ten feet above the court below.

What the invention of "basket-ball" has meant to America and the world has placed Naismith among a short list of sports geniuses for all time.

Unlike many social movements—if sport may be termed as such—that spread gradually outward from the locality of its origin, the game leaped over four states and the Appalachian Mountains, landing in Montgomery County, Indiana, in 1894. A Naismith disciple at Springfield, the Reverend Nicholas C. McKay, had journeyed to the plains of west-central Indiana to become secretary of the YMCA at Crawfordsville. There he taught his students the game that had been in existence for just over two years. Indiana and basketball proved to be an ideal match.

On Friday, March 16, 1894 members of the YMCA at Lafayette, Indiana, traveled to nearby Crawfordsville to challenge their counterparts in the new game. It was the first contest played outside the state of Massachusetts. Avoiding the pot-bellied stove in the middle of the gymnasium floor, the teams engaged in a spirited competition. The Crawfordsville Y won, 45-21.

Hoosier Hysteria was born.

At the turn of the twentieth century, in heavily agrarian Indiana, hundreds of small towns and tiny unincorporated crossroad hamlets had been established to accommodate the commercial, educational, and social needs of those in outlying areas. Farm life was arduous and lonely, especially for youth. The occasional barn dance, quilting bee, or family social provided only periodic relief from the monotony. Naismith's invention rearranged the priorities for entire towns.

In its infancy basketball provided inexpensive entertainment for the masses and became a source of community pride in small Hoosier settlements. Spirited rivalries developed among neighboring villages. Hoosier farmers' social calendars in the fall and winter months came to revolve around two events: church services on Sunday and the boys' high school game on Friday nights. Townspeople developed close emotional attachments to the local team and its players—and to (winning) coaches.

As the popularity of high school basketball grew, the Booster Club of Indiana University decided to sponsor an elimination tournament that would determine which high school in the state had the best team. The inaugural state championship tournament was held in the original Assembly Hall on the Bloomington campus over the weekend of March 10—11, 1911. Before an estimated 1,200 witnesses Carroll Stevenson would score 14 points to lead Crawfordsville over Lebanon, 24-17, to become the first state champion.

The IHSAA's winner-take-all format would become nationally recognized for its scope and drama. The tournament was acknowledged by observers—even beyond Hoosier borders—as the greatest high school sports attraction in the world. Enthusiasm for basket-ball became so fervent in the Roaring Twenties that many Indiana high schools constructed gymnasiums with seating capacities exceeding the town's number of residents. An early example was Martinsville, which had a population of 4,895 in 1924. A spectacular modern structure, holding 5,382 fans, opened just in time to launch the team to its first state championship. Three years later a 17-year-old named Johnny Wooden would lead the Artesians to their second title.

Today, Indiana has thirty-five high school gyms seating 5,000 or more spectators. Nine of the world's ten largest high school gymnasiums are located in the Hoosier state. At the top of the list is the oval stadium at New Castle's Chrysler High School, with a capacity of 9,325 seats.

The opening week of the state tourney became an annual statewide festival. On average, ten to twelve high school teams from the surrounding geographical areas gathered at each of sixty-four sites for sectional play. In most cases, that would be the county seat where the area's largest high school was located.

Entire towns got behind the team. Storefronts, cars, and school hallways would be lavishly decorated in school colors. Hometown newspapers devoted special sections to the team and pages of ad space purchased by local businesses exhorted the local five to "Go! Fight! Win the sectional!"

Rural communities became virtual ghost towns as caravans of students and fans journeyed to the host school to support their favorites. Generations of Hoosiers who experienced the excitement and color of sectional play—prior to consolidation in Indiana—recall the event as among the most memorable of their high school years.

Thirty-four years after inventing the game Dr. Naismith attended the 1925 Indiana state basketball finals, the very special guest of Indiana High School Athletic Association administrators. Along with 15,000 fervent spectators at the Indianapolis Exposition Building the game's creator watched Frankfort defeat Kokomo, 34-20, for the championship trophy. In a post-game interview Naismith told a gathering of Indiana notables, "Basketball had its origin in Indiana, which remains the center of the sport."

Beginning in the 1940s basketball caught on in Indiana's urban areas. With larger pools of athletes to select from, metropolitan institutions had the advantage over rural county schools. Superior training facilities and mega-sized gymnasiums made it increasingly remote for small schools to compete for the state championship. With a student body of only 161, Milan's astonishing upset of powerhouse Muncie Central (student body of over 2,000) in 1954 was inspirational. But it was an aberration.

With a burgeoning number of large city high schools dominating state tournament play, the sectional round gained greater importance to small towns which began to experience little success in advancing to the regionals, semifinals, and finals.

Upsets of heavily favored teams by the underdogs became the stuff of legends. An unheralded, scrappy outfit could even gain glory in losing to a larger school's team, if they came close in a valiant effort.

If a small school team advanced deeply into the tournament they might become the "people's choice." Legions of fans across the state would jump on the bandwagon of a feisty underdog until its inevitable elimination occurred. An under-sized school team advancing beyond the sectional or regional round could cast the team and its players into a special place in a town's history.

Today, driving through tiny Wingate, Indiana, visitors are greeted by a roadside sign, proudly proclaiming:

WINGATE – STATE BASKETBALL CHAMPIONS – 1913, 1914

There has been no high school in Wingate for over fifty years.

During a state tournament in the late 1950s a visitor from Stockholm's national team was astounded by the passion of the 14,983 rooters gathered at

Butler Fieldhouse. The Swede remarked to a veteran sportswriter, "Basketball seems to be another religion in Indiana."

With no hesitation the scribe replied, "I guess it depends upon your definition. According to Webster's, a religious body has a system of beliefs, organized by a body of followers, held to be supremely important, and marked by zealous devotion and conscientious maintenance.

"If it walks like a duck, and quacks like a duck…"

TABLE OF CONTENTS

1. Return to Morgans Awe 1
2. Where Were You, in '62?.. 19
3. Elvis Was in the Building 33
4. *Ich Liebe Dich* 45
5. Blue Eyes Crying in the Rain 55
6. The Greatest Generation 65
7. How Far is it, Dad? 79
8. The Milan Miracle 93
9. Those Halcyon Days 107
10. You Can Play—if You're not Catholic, or Black 119
11. Sittin', Whittlin', and Spittin'.. 133
12. Boys to Men... 145
13. Death by a Thousand Cuts 157
14. Sir Knight 173
15. Dogs Don't Bark at Parked Cars.. 185
16. Don't Call Him a Cowboy 'Til You Seen Him Ride 201

17. Eleemosynary 213

18. Fer a Ten Minute Nap. 225

19. B.O.B. 237

20. Moon River and Me 249

21. Jake's Coon 263

22. He's Not Jimmy Rayl, But— 273

23. Bomp-Ba-Ba-Bomp-Ba-Bomp-Ba-Bomp-Bomp 283

24. Off to Slay the Dragon 299

25. Three Seconds…Two…One. 315

26. What'll I Do Now? Where'll I Go? 329

1

RETURN TO MORGANS AWE

Saturday, February 24, 1962
Jourden Arena, Madison, Indiana
7:15 p.m.

The team arrived at Madison Central High School precisely as Coach O'Ryan had planned. The pre-game itinerary never varied.

Six cheerleaders hurried off the mud-streaked yellow school bus.

Josh Seaberg and his teammates followed, shuffling in single file through the narrow aisle between the rows of passenger seats. Each player carried a black canvas satchel with MORGANS AWE BASKETBALL stenciled in bright orange letters along the side.

Stepping down into eight inches of crusted snow, the team members strolled briskly toward the Thomas A. Jourden Arena nearby. A sprinkling of Morgans Awe fans who had arrived early for the game shouted encouragement to the Raiders team.

The midwinter sky was pitch-dark beneath thick, hovering clouds. During sectionals in the early 1960s, unusually heavy snows and frigid temperatures were common in Indiana.

In just over an hour, powerhouse Madison Central would engage these country boys for the championship of the 1962 Indiana State High School sectional tournament at Madison, Indiana.

Knowledgeable sportswriters gave the Morgans Awe squad no chance to pull off a monumental upset of one of the most highly respected high school basketball programs in the state. In a final poll prior to the tourney, a majority of scribes ranked Coach Saul Fortune's Madison Central Cougars second, behind only defending state champion Kokomo.

This was the second game of the day for both teams. Morgans Awe had struggled to a 61-55 win over the Saints of St. Isadore in the morning semifinal game. Then, in its

THE HOOSIER GAME

first match of the day, Madison Central easily brushed aside Sycamore Creek, 79-44, resting their regulars for much of the second half.

Entering the arena, the Raiders walked courtside to reach the ramp leading to their locker room beneath the stands. The aroma of freshly popped corn always signaled to Josh Seaberg that it was game night.

Morgans Awe rooters arose to welcome their boys with a resounding ovation. Madison fans across the court responded with a low chorus of boos. It was not surprising that the 6,904 seats were nearly filled, an hour before tip-off time.

The team members descended into a dimly lit hallway and found their designated dressing room. Its musty odor was a familiar one. The next eight to ten minutes were routine: find a locker and exchange civilian attire for a basketball uniform.

The collective tension among the players was apparent, their bearing subdued by the seriousness of the challenge before them. Only the snapping of gum chewed by open-mouthed teenagers and brief, muted exchanges between teammates and coaches disturbed the weighty hush in the room.

A man of average height with a muscular frame, head coach Durand Michael O'Ryan was physically imposing at age forty-two. Bright blue eyes blazed beneath heavy brows. The coach's rough-hewn face was splashed lightly by freckles and his closely cropped, rust-colored hair warned of a sometimes volatile temperament.

Though he possessed a quick and clever wit, O'Ryan's general demeanor was that of an intense, no-nonsense disposition. A taut, unsmiling, if not menacing expression dissuaded folly in his presence. The coach suffered silliness grimly, and fools, never. He was not quite cynical about life, but a committed, often blunt realist in all things. O'Ryan told the truth as he saw it, even if it might offend or disappoint the listener.

The family from which he'd sprung had been Irish proud and dirt poor. Michael had worked at odd jobs since junior high school. He possessed the street smarts of one who had come up the hard way.

In high school Mike O'Ryan was an incorrigible rebel with a history of marching to the beat of his own drummer. Independent and undisciplined, he didn't play organized sports in school. Tough and prickly, he never backed down from a fight. He was a guy the school bullies feared.

At seventeen, O'Ryan dropped out of high school and lied his way into the Marines Corps. While in the military, he completed high school and college requirements through the GI Bill.

Coaches who came to tiny towns like Morgans Awe typically were fresh-out-of-college neophytes, seeking to build a reputation for a promotion to a larger school. Or there were the over-fifty lifers, hard men wrinkled and graying from years of coaching at the armpit schools of the state.

RETURN TO MORGANS AWE

O'Ryan fit neither group. He'd coached successfully both at large inner-city high schools populated with mostly indigent kids and at suburban prep schools with students of wealth and privilege. He had borne the pressure of unrealistic expectations; dealt with unreasonable, selfish, whining parents; and tolerated ill-mannered, uninformed media who were critical merely to create controversy. He loathed the rabid winning-is-the-only-thing, barstool critics who pressured faint-hearted school administrators to sack decent, dedicated coaches.

Mike O'Ryan had turned his back at midlife on those chanting his name and recruiting him to win at their school. His ideal was to spend his teaching and coaching career in what he considered a purer environment.

His philosophy was grounded in hard work, self-discipline, and a realistic assessment of his players' talents. He believed that goal-setting and toughness led to success in coaching and in life. Coach O'Ryan taught his players to make reasoned decisions and to be accountable for their actions.

Above all he was a leader. He had learned through bloody fighting on the island of Guadalcanal to take care of each of his men.

His players feared him, and utterly revered him.

Saturday, May 5, 2012
Morgans Awe, Indiana

Someone once said that "when you return to your boyhood town, you find it isn't the town you long for. It's your boyhood."

The wisdom of that adage would become apparent to Josh Seaberg during the tense and cathartic forty-eight-hour period that lay just ahead.

The 67-year-old college professor was returning to attend the 50th class reunion of a high school that no longer existed. Although the school had not graduated a class since 1969, former classmate Sheila Wood had created a Morgans Awe High School website and her call for alumni of the 1962 class to gather had persuaded Josh to return to the site of his youth.

It had been over thirty-five years since he had been to Morgans Awe. He wondered if he would recognize former friends and classmates with whom he was forever linked.

Seaberg had set out this morning from his home in Oxford, Ohio. The landscape was bathed in brilliant sunshine as he drove toward Morgans Awe on US Highway 50, southwest of Cincinnati. Passing through the gently rolling hills of southeastern Indiana, Josh lowered all four windows of his maroon

THE HOOSIER GAME

2010 Ford Taurus. The brisk air of early May flowed through the car. Too accustomed to the artificial sanctuaries of heating and air conditioning, he was invigorated by the freshness and chill of spring.

Turning south at Dillsboro onto Indiana State Road 62 brought him to within twenty-five miles of Morgans Awe. Well-kept barns and vast, newly plowed fields now yielded to a more severe landscape of steep ravines, rocky outcroppings, and forested hills. Pristine rivulets dripped from ancient layers of shale here and there along the roadway.

Although the glaciers of the Pliocene and Pleistocene periods had not reached as far south as what is now Jefferson County, those natural events dramatically influenced the development of the area. About two million years ago, the Ohio River Valley was formed. Frigid waters rushing off melting glaciers laid bare much of the limestone bedrock beneath the surface.

The dense growth of sycamore, ash, cottonwood, pine, black walnut, tulip and sassafras trees, stirred by a lively breeze, swayed rhythmically along both sides of the road. Rosy pink flowers of redbud trees and snow-white blossoms of dogwoods heralded the coming of spring. Sprouting foliage was a reminder that the barren asphalt and the cold brick and steel of cities had not consumed God's *entire* earthly domain.

Josh had come within range of a Louisville broadcasting station and a familiar refrain now caught his attention. Wafting through the car was the velvety voice of Tony Williams:

> *When the twilight is gone, and no songbirds are singing,*
> *When the twilight is gone, you come into my heart.*
> *And here in my heart you will stay, while I pray.*
> *My prayer, is to linger with you,*
> *At the end of the day, in a dream that's divine.*
> *My prayer, is a rapture in blue,*
> *With the world far away, and your lips close to mine.*

Stirred by the haunting melody, Josh recalled a special moment at a school mixer during his freshman year in 1958. The Platters' wistful tale of young love was the #1 hit on the pop charts. This dreamy air had inspired him to invite Judy Wyllis, a cute eighth-grader, to join him in his very first slow dance. A parched throat and sweaty palms betrayed his nervousness as he mumbled his request. Judy, a 14-year-old pony-tailed blonde with a broad smile, accepted.

Josh had held his tiny partner as if she were delicate glass as they randomly shuffled to the unhurried beat of the song. It had been a heady moment.

State Road 250 joined Highway 62 just south of Cross Plains. Exiting a severe curve, Seaberg spotted a curio of the past, six small weathered billboards at the edge of a farmer's field.

Most such wooden testimonials had disappeared decades ago. Josh chuckled as he read the clever jingle promoting a once-popular shaving cream.

> I KNOW
> HE'S A WOLF
> SAID RIDING HOOD
> BUT GRANDMA DEAR
> HE SMELLS SO GOOD
> BURMA-SHAVE

Further south, the crystal-clear sky gave way to ponderous thunderheads boiling above. The vivid colors of the countryside were dulled by the slate-gray shades of an approaching storm. The wind intensified, occasionally jolting the car with blustery gusts.

Arriving at the crest of Mt. Moriah, Josh could see below him the familiar valley of his hometown. From the lofty overlook, the village appeared to have changed but little. The town extended nine streets from east to west, eight from north to south. Even today Morgans Awe was too small for a Wal-Mart or a McDonald's.

The town, fitting snuggly in the bottomland below, had earned its unusual name during the American War Between the States.

In the only significant Civil War military action north of the Ohio River, Confederate Brigadier General John Hunt Morgan and two-thousand cavalrymen entered southern Indiana on July 8, 1863. For six days, Morgan's Raiders terrorized Hoosier citizens, burning and pillaging small towns and settlements along the river.

On the fourth night of the raid, Morgan and his men swept through what is now Jefferson Proving Grounds, a US Army testing site near Dupont. At midnight, the cavalry briefly stopped to rest their horses and to get some much-needed sleep. Three hours later most of the soldiers were back in the saddle as Morgan headed toward his fateful capture in Ohio.

At daybreak about thirty of Morgan's rear guard made an unscheduled sally to a tiny hamlet known as Ecker's Valley. They intended to plunder what they might in the way of fresh horses, food, and personal possessions. The settlement consisted of a sawmill, a clapboard church that doubled as a schoolhouse on weekdays, and about twenty framed houses and log cabins in the surrounding countryside.

The bandits unexpectedly stumbled into a feisty nest of inhabitants who had anticipated such a movement. A coarse abatis had been hastily constructed on a hill overlooking the lone dusty road that led to the settlement. There, the bold band of three-dozen citizens crouched in ambush.

As Morgan's horsemen emerged from the shadows of a grove of trees, a volley of enfilading gunfire met their advance. After a vigorous exchange of muskets and pistols, the bewildered invaders fled. An unsubstantiated report cited the militia's leader, Isaiah Woodburn exulting, "Look at 'em run, boys. Morgan's in awe of our virtuous arms!"

Despite the fact that John Hunt Morgan was nowhere near the skirmish, the settlement was known thereafter as Morgan's Awe. With passage of time, the possessive apostrophe fell away, but the Morgans Awe name stuck.

Flanked on both sides by steep limestone walls, the roadway plunged downward into the town limits. Josh smiled at the sight of the old water tower looming like a sentinel over the village. Soaring ninety feet, the metal structure looked like a teapot on four stilts. It was unlike the sleek, round, modern water basins of suburban America today. No smiley faces emblazoned this pillar of the past.

The landmark was in obvious need of a paint job. Travelers now were welcomed to the **Tow of M g ns we**. Decades of unsympathetic rain, icy winds, and relentless sun had obliterated some of the letters.

Josh arrived more than an hour before his former classmates would gather at the home of hosts Will and Betty Billings. With ample time, he decided to look for sites in Morgans Awe that endured in his mind like sepia photographs.

The town resembled the one where he grew up. But now, the village looked tired and dingy, utterly lacking in character. Morgans Awe had no traffic lights. Locals navigated through a combination of paved and gravel streets.

Driving along thoroughfares he'd known as a child, Josh found that the dearth of stately trees contrasted sharply with his memories. In summers past, a lush growth of overhanging foliage created a green canopy. Looking down the street was like peering through a tunnel. The sun's rays, streaming through fluttering leaves, produced a dappled effect on the pavement.

RETURN TO MORGANS AWE

Morgans Awe, Indiana, "...too small for a Wal-mart or a McDonald's."

THE HOOSIER GAME

A symbol of an earlier era, Williams's grain elevator and feed mill stood prominently, seemingly unaltered by time. Closer examination, however, revealed a decaying structure of rust and wear.

The steeples of both the former Evangelical United Brethren Church (now the United Methodist Church) and Jesus' Disciples Apostolic House of Worship spiraled upward toward low-hanging clouds.

Josh drove to Pearl Street, the main drag of Morgans Awe. Here were found the only sidewalks in town. Once a hive of activity, the charming downtown of his youth also had faded over time.

When he was a boy, weekends were anticipated with glee. Farm families made their weekly sojourn into town to sell eggs and farm produce and to purchase groceries and other necessities. The streets would be rife with makeshift booths displaying a variety of foodstuffs. Downtown was a haven for socializing and catching up on local happenings.

What used to be Hawkins General Store—where families bought everything from fresh meats and vegetables to tools and furniture—had gone through several owners. Its wooden floors had been worn smooth and shiny by generations of shoppers. The U.S. Post Office was no longer housed there. Gone was the pot-bellied stove that warmed customers on winter days. Likewise, the long glass case filled with varieties of tantalizing sweets had been removed. The young Josh had been especially fond of the rope suckers concocted by the Curtiss Candy Company.

He often rode his bicycle to the store with his Mom's grocery list in hand. She always bought meat from Mr. Wynn, the butcher. He would cut the slices requested, wrap the bloody pieces in white freezer paper, tape the package shut, weigh it, and scribble a price on it with a black grease pencil.

Mrs. Seaberg usually gave her son a dime to purchase a six-ounce soda pulled from the icy water in Harlan Hawkins's Coca-Cola dispenser. Or he might go for five pieces of twisted-rope licorice. Another favorite was the miniature Coke-shaped wax bottles of colored sugar water. It was customary to chew the paraffin after sipping the tiny amount of liquid inside.

The store's wood-framed front with two large windows was no longer shaded by a sizable canopy. Local men used to sit beneath it on caned chairs, arguing about politics, the weather, sports, "bin-ness," and the "guv'ment."

Surviving decades of use, however, was the old screen door, decorated with an oval blue-and-red tin sign across the front proclaiming that "RAINBO BREAD is <u>good</u> bread." Familiar to those of Josh's generation was the monotonous cadence—whap……whap…..whap….whap…whap..whap-whap-whap—as a coiled spring returned the flimsy door against the jamb. Mr. Jennisen had a swatter handy for the pesky flies that entered each time the door opened.

Hawkins's store was the closest thing to a hangout teens had in Morgans Awe. Inside, alongside the counter of a soda fountain, were four rounded leather stools. Adjacent to the counter were three small square tables. Each was covered by glossy, red-and-white-checked cotton oilcloth. Teenagers could enjoy exotic refreshments there, like a cherry-chocolate Coke or a lime phosphate. They bought ten-cent bags of Chesty potato chips to dip into mustard, an improvised precursor to nacho chips and salsa.

Josh's personal favorite at Hawkins's was a sundae called a Free Lunch. The hot fudge and melted marshmallow oozing over vanilla ice cream was not a lunch, nor was it free.

A nickel in the jukebox played a Top Forty tune. Spend a quarter and you could choose five songs—and receive a sixth one as a bonus.

The general store had been a monument to the amiable hospitality of small towns in the Midwest. Characteristic of neighborly owners of that time, credit was extended interest-free to families who bought groceries or goods during the week. Bills for the purchases were stored in a cigar box. On Saturday, after payday, people settled their accounts. The process began anew on Monday.

Next to the general store was the Totem Pole Barbershop. A traditional peppermint-striped pole stood on the walkway outside the gray block building. Gone, however, was the wooden totem that had given the shop its name. As a boy, Seaberg had his hair trimmed closely there, every two weeks.

Willard "Dull Knife" Treecat no longer entertained customers. His clientele had endured the Native American's marginal hair-styling skills in order to hear the wildly humorous yarns he spun in his measured, droll delivery.

On this day a young blond man sat alone, one leg over the other, in the single barber chair. He was flipping through a magazine, awaiting his next client.

Ahead, another prominent symbol of the small family business had vanished. Every Friday and Saturday night, Scoop 'n Dollie's Country Restaurant had teemed with locals filling its 42-seat capacity. The building was now vacant.

Outside, next to the front porch, protruding from a decaying wooden platform, stood an old-fashioned well pump and spout. The long pump handle read "Woodford Hydrant Co." and chained to the pump was a tin cup. Beneath

THE HOOSIER GAME

was a bucket of water into which the cup was dipped and poured into the spout to prime the pump.

On hot summer days, kids drank the chilled water from the well far below. Leaning over, a boy placed his mouth against the spout—defying mother's orders—and pumped the handle. The refreshing liquid flowed easily over the tongue and down the gullet.

Across the street was the Morgans Awe Volunteer Fire Department. The 1961 International Harvester fire engine was parked outside the garage. The once-cherry red exterior of the truck had been sun-bleached to a dull rose color.

Adjacent to the MAVFD was a small building where country doctor Richard Gentry had practiced. Folks came to Doc Gentry—or he came to them—for everything from whooping cough to bunion removal. On one occasion he'd responded to a call after 9 p.m. to remove a fish bone from Josh's throat.

Doc died about twenty years ago. No one had replaced him. His passing forced Morgans Awe residents to travel twelve miles south to Madison for health care. A local farrier had purchased the building, selling leather goods and horse tack. The blacksmith tended to horses in a shed built onto the side of the original.

Next to Doc Gentry's old office was a white stone structure that formerly housed the Farmers Savings and Home Loan. Ninety percent of Morgans Awe farm and homeowners had mortgages there. Gordon McGraw—owner of Myers and McGraw Hoosier Farmers Insurance Company—kept an office in the building. Mr. McGraw would come to the Seaberg home monthly to collect the family homeowner's insurance premium. The portly but always well-dressed insurance agent casually sat and chatted about local happenings as he wrote out a receipt for Betty, who handed him a check for the $9 premium.

Morgans Trail Bar had remained in the John Coleman family. It hadn't changed much from former days. Tired, leather-faced farmers would drift into town at the end of sizzling summer days, grimy from their labors. Within the cool recesses of that saloon, the men drank iced beer, the perfect remedy for a parched throat.

Josh now steered his Taurus into Thesdon's Gas and Food Mart. Its predecessor had been "Red" Schoenkoppel's Sinclair filling station. Missing was the one-car garage and grease pit where the former owner-mechanic repaired cars, trucks, and farm machinery.

The first time Josh had fueled the family car, a 1956 Chrysler DeSoto, was November 1960. He'd loved that car. The DeSoto FireFlite Sportsman was a roomy four-door hardtop sedan with the distinctive nine-teeth grille. It had wraparound windows, the small side flap glass for front-seat occupants, tailfin styling, an AM radio, and was powered by the 255-horsepower automatic PowerFlite engine. Curb finders attached to the right front and rear bumpers enabled one to negotiate the curb when parallel parking. The headlight dimmer was on the floor. All windows were hand-cranked. The interior was upholstered in dark velour. It was a time before seatbelts. Josh's father had purchased the sleek black model brand new, for $3,454.

At the station, Sam Chandler, a classmate who worked part-time, would bounce out of the building, offering his greetings.

"Fill 'er up, Josh?"

"No thanks, Sam. Just give me three gallons."

"Reg'lar or ethyl?"

"Gimme the cheap stuff."

Josh could still picture the scene. The young attendant carefully held the handle on the hose as he pumped fuel into the car. After putting the requested amount in the tank, Sam stepped to the side of the vehicle and asked, "Check the orl?"

"Nope, I'm good."

"Warsh the winder?"

"Yeah, Sam, would ja'?"

After Sam had buffed the windshield til it was spotless, Josh handed him three quarters and a nickel for the three gallons of fuel. He received three pennies in change.

Today, as the sky continued to darken, Josh got out of the car, unlatched the safety lock opening the lid on his gas tank, and removed the nozzle. The credit card option was not available at the pump, so after filling the tank, he walked inside to pay the stranger $49.92 for the fourteen gallons. The clerk didn't notice his customer's wry smile.

As he left Thesdon's, Josh glanced at the adjacent lot, where Earl Barnett's used car and truck dealership had been. No trace of that formerly thriving business could be detected in what was now an empty field of crabgrass and scrub brush. It was years ago that Earl moved his business to the outskirts of Madison.

Back in the car, Josh flicked on the wipers as a light rain began to drum against the windshield. With apprehension, he turned onto Brook Drive. It led straightaway to his old neighborhood.

THE HOOSIER GAME

Two blocks from his former home, he encountered the Elysian field of his youth. Berglund's Cooperage was the only industry in Morgans Awe. Barrels and kegs created and assembled in the "bucket factory" had supplied farms and businesses throughout the Midwest.

Stacks of oaken staves had surrounded the huge brick structure, where young architects had built a network of hideouts. Adjacent to the outdoor storage area was a vast, rock-strewn field of grass and sandburs where, in daylong summer games, boys would emulate their baseball heroes—Stan Musial, Willie Mays, Mickey Mantle, and Ted Williams. Crisp and colorful fall mornings would find Josh and friends playing tackle football with nary a pad or helmet in sight. Bike races, track and field events, and sundry other games fed their natural competitiveness.

If there was no one around, a boy often engaged in an especially popular activity: batting rocks. With a sawed-off broomstick or similar length of wood, a kid could pass hours tossing round pebbles from the gravel drive into the air and striking them as he would a baseball. Batting from both sides, he went through the lineup of his favorite teams. Certain landmarks in the field determined whether he had hit a single, double, triple, or homerun, or if he'd grounded out, popped up, or flied out. The games in your imagination, Josh thought now, were preferable to those on TV.

At the bucket factory field, one learned an abundance of valuable lessons applicable to adult life. Bumps and scrapes were of no consequence in these games. The older boys met excessive whining with quick justice. It was quit complaining or go home.

Berglund's Cooperage had long since closed. Squares of cardboard had replaced glass in the windows. The huge roof sagged as if in mourning. Sections of the brick walls had been gashed and toppled by who knows what.

Further on, Josh slowed as he passed 210 Brook Drive, where he'd spent half of the first eighteen years of his life. The former family home was a red-brick ranch with two bedrooms, one bath, a one-car garage, one phone, and one television.

An expansive and well-maintained lawn and garden once covered these grounds. The two-acre lot sloped gently like a natural terrace to the banks of Brushy Fork. Thick hedges, which it was his dubious honor to trim twice each summer, bordered the street.

About twenty lads from the town and surrounding farms devised all manner of games and entertainment in the Seaberg backyard. Endless Wiffle ball contests, wrestling, races, and a variety of other competitions of skill and strength filled the day. At dusk, boys played "slips," a form of hide-and-seek on bicycles.

On one occasion, for about a fortnight, the boys got away with pitching pennies against the front porch steps. But then Larry Burnet's mother called Josh's mom to report that she had discovered a copious amount of change in her son's blue jeans. In short order, the two sleuths figured out that their miscreant sons and their buddies were gambling. Mrs. Seaberg swiftly put the quietus on that nefarious activity.

Another creation of those fruitful adolescent minds was a one-of-a-kind golf course. A posthole digger was employed to excavate small hollows in nine locations around the yard. Campbell's pork and beans cans were inserted into the ground. The Seaberg's boy-powered push mower trimmed the grass for a putting surface. Crude sticks with rags attached marked the hole placements on the greens.

The Waters twins brought over two old clubs—a nine iron and a putter—that their grandpa had purchased at a yard sale. Ray Rounds lifted four scruffy balls from his dad's golf bag. However, before the novelty had worn off this amusement, Josh's mother ordered the nascent PGA hopefuls to re-landscape the grounds. While hanging wash on the clothesline, she'd inadvertently sprained her ankle when she stepped awkwardly into the eighth hole.

But on this day, the battered old homestead stood in stark contrast to the childhood utopia of a half-century ago. Most of the huge maple, cottonwood, sycamore, and oak trees that had lined the narrow lane either had been severely cropped or cut down altogether.

A crude annex, with nothing to augment the reputation of its builder, was clumsily attached to the original house. All was in need of paint, and a new roof would have helped matters. Ragged pieces of cardboard substituted for two missing windowpanes beneath rotting eaves.

Scarred and broken toys were strewn across the once neatly groomed lawn. Here lay a child's rusty tricycle with a rear wheel missing. Over there a broken lawn mower napped. Other assorted trash, including half of a canoe, was scattered haphazardly over the muddy yard of buffalo grass and sandburs. A flower garden that had served as the centerpiece of the yard now was overgrown with knee-high weeds. The final insult was a dated Chevy pickup on blocks, a wheel and a front fender gone from its rusted frame.

It was a disheartening scene.

THE HOOSIER GAME

Driving onward, Josh passed by a vacant field. Gone was Morgans Awe High School, where students of all twelve grades had gathered daily in the three-story brick structure. The building and adjoining gym had been razed years ago. Two other tiny community high schools—Jericho and Mainport—had merged with MAHS. The new educational conglomerate was known by the unappealing designation Mor-Jer-Main Consolidated School System.

South of town arose majestic Tanner's Hill, a monolith unchanged by the vagaries of time. Often, a person revisiting a place of his youth that seemed of considerable size finds the landmark is disappointingly normal in the adult reality. Not so with this awesome natural wonder. Tanner's Hill dwarfed the surrounding terrain.

In winter, boys slogged to the top of the snow-covered promontory, pulling rickety sleds behind them. Plummeting steeply—extending the length of two football fields—was a snowfield designed for young boys by God himself. Intrepid youths shouting "Geronimo!" careened wildly downhill. Sled and boy would be launched skyward periodically from the small moguls strewn naturally across the hillside. Approaching the bottom, it was prudent to bail out before pin-balling off the trees lining the banks of Brushy Fork.

The landowners were rarely seen, giving tacit approval to the boys' antics. That is, until Pee Wee Reynolds catapulted headfirst into a sycamore tree. Those arriving quickly at the scene weren't certain at first whether the boy or the tree suffered the most damage. But it was evident after a rudimentary examination of his shattered sled and prostrate, limp form lying in the snow that Pee Wee had lost the encounter.

Speaking through tiny gasps, the young Reynolds uttered, "Think—broke—ribs."

Donny Walbrook replied, unsympathetically, "What 'chu whinin' about, Pee. You still got twenty-two more."

Although liability lawsuits were foreign words in those days, Pee Wee's misfortune ended sledding at Tanner's Hill for a time.

Just ahead was Memorial Park. A Civil War-era mortar guarded the entrance. Attached was a plaque honoring the sons of the area who'd given their lives in American wars.

Josh steered into the park. There he first noticed the paved basketball court. It was like seeing an old friend. He and his peers had honed their basketball skills on that asphalt throughout their high school years. Along one side was a natural amphitheater. Crowds had gathered there regularly to watch local prospects compete with one another.

Drawing nearer, he noticed dry, amber-tinged crabgrass sprouting through the cracks of the weathered surface. From each of the two backboards at the ends of the court hung iron rings in varied states of conspicuous disrepair. The rims bent downward, attesting to attempts by players to perform that most admired play in contemporary basketball—the spectacular slam-dunk. Worn shreds of seine twine straggled from the baskets. Evidently, the nets hadn't been replaced for some time. Behind each backboard stood two rusted light poles, their bulbs shattered or missing.

He felt a sad twinge with the realization that playing hoops was no longer a chief priority for local teens. Five decades ago "the Game" was paramount to Morgans Awe youth. It had been a high honor to represent the town in its black and orange basketball uniforms.

Next his eyes rested on the playground equipment that had been a delight to the girls and boys of the town. Corroded stanchions supported remnants of broken swings with detached chains that sprawled on the dirt below.

The cherished old shelter house, where his family held celebrations and reunion picnics, was clearly in an advanced state of decay. An unfriendly, weather-bleached sign nailed to the door warned, "SHELTER CLOSED. DO NOT ENTER."

Seaberg now decided to call on an old friend. It would be a one-sided conversation.

He turned south onto Highway 62. The sycamore-lined road roughly paralleled Brushy Fork on its winding way to Madison. The shale bottom and rapid clear waters of the stream flowed into Indiana-Kentucky Creek, which poured, miles away, into the Ohio River.

About two miles down the road, Josh turned into Gilley's Cemetery. Row upon row of aged gravestones stood guard over the remains of Morgans Awe citizens. Many had been lying in peace here since antebellum days.

THE HOOSIER GAME

Tanner's Hill, "...a snowfield designed by God himself."

It was only yards from his parked car that Josh found the gravesite of his former best friend, basketball hero Jake Skoon. His throat constricting and his eyes misty, Josh read the inscription etched into the granite block of stone:

Marvin Jacob "Jake" Skoon
November 27, 1944 – November 9, 1975

Warm spring rain, fall softly here,
Verdant sod, lie lightly here,
Autumn leaves, be bright, be bright,
Goodnight, my son, goodnight, goodnight.

Though Jake would not be attending the reunion, his would be a prominent presence, nonetheless. Eighteen days before his thirty-first birthday, Jake Skoon had blown his brains out.

2

WHERE WERE YOU, IN '62?

Jourden Arena
7:34 p.m.

This week, 660 Indiana high school teams began play at sectional tournament sites all over Indiana. Like many host schools, Madison Central dismissed Wednesday afternoon classes to accommodate the games held in the gymnasium. The elimination drama would intensify throughout the week until a champion was crowned. After tonight, only sixty-four teams would advance to the regional round, a ninety-percent casualty rate.

A few players moved toward the training table where assistant Coach John Barnhard taped ankles and attended to mild aches and pains the players brought to him.

Josh traded his jeans for short basketball trunks, which descended to mid-thigh. Next he slipped over his shoulders the sleeveless jersey of burnished orange with black trim and numerals. Inscribed across the chest in bold script letters was "RAIDERS."

Reaching into his satchel he pulled out a fresh pair of white athletic socks. He had packed two pairs, anticipating that the team would be playing in the championship game.

Josh stretched the distinctive black knee-high socks with orange pinstripes over his calves. Each player wore a black silken warm-up jacket trimmed in orange. A few players chose to wear knee pads for protection against floor burns—or for style points.

He tightly laced his low-cut, canvas "Chucks." The rubber-soled, white Converse All-Star basketball sneaker was favored by nearly every high school in Indiana. The shoe was developed by Columbus native and former standout player Chuck Taylor.

With his athletic ensemble now complete, Josh was ready to play ball.

Other members of the squad lined up at the water fountain, went to the bathroom, or simply milled around until the coaches called the team together. Sitting quietly, Josh took note of a large inspirational sign on the locker room wall.

THE HOOSIER GAME

> It is not the critic who counts, nor the man who points how the strong man stumbled or where the doer of deeds could have done them better. The credit belongs to the man who is actually in the arena; whose face is marred by dust and sweat and blood; who strives valiantly, who knows the great enthusiasms, the great devotions, and spends himself in a worthy cause; who, at best, knows the triumph of high achievement; and who, at the worst, if he fails, at least fails while daring greatly, so that his place shall never be with those cold and timid souls who know neither victory nor defeat.
>
> *President Theodore Roosevelt*
> *Paris, France, April 23, 1910*

Josh had been in the arena where there was a clear winner and a loser. He knew of the risks and rewards inherent in competition. It was a dear price one paid to attain excellence. Untold hours spent on dusty or muddy or frozen dirt basketball courts had prepared him for the severe test awaiting on the floor above. Would he and his teammates have the ability and strength of resolve to defeat a team that by all measures appeared to be hugely superior to the Raiders?

Coach O'Ryan was himself considering that very notion. Generally, in moments before the starts of games, coaches had to suppress their own inner demons. While exuding a confident manner, a coach faced a nagging paradox.

As Hall of Fame coach Pete Newell once observed, "A coach is pessimistic by nature. He knows every mistake his players are capable of making. He has analyzed the strengths of the opponent. As the game approaches he talks positively while his inner thoughts reflect this negativism."

While maintaining a sunny equanimity toward his team, the coach likely is thinking, "How in the world can we beat this team? What if we can't stop them from scoring? My God, what if we don't score a point?"

As O'Ryan considered the enormous odds against his players actually beating Madison Central, his duty was to be a model of fearlessness, encouraging his players as if he had no doubt they would win.

It was now time to take the floor for the pre-game warm-up session.

Coach was composed as he addressed the team in a voice barely above a whisper. His comments were brief and uncomplicated. With tension building within his players, the coach intentionally projected a tranquil aura. The objective was to create a serene, confident front before they jogged to the court to loosen up. When the team returned to the locker room afterward Coach O'Ryan would get down to serious business.

It was already serious to Josh Seaberg. As they left the locker room, he felt the familiar logjam in his throat.

May 5, 2012
Morgans Awe

As Josh walked up the path, red brick chips crunching underfoot, the front door of the Billings home swung open forcefully. Filling the doorframe was a hulk of a man dressed in a plaid shirt, blue jeans, and scuffed boots. Shunning formalities, he roared out his profane greeting.

"Helly-be-damned! If you ain't the same scrawny shit you was in high school!"

The voice was an echo from the past. Despite a puffed face, beefy jowls, and thick white hair, the sparkle in the man's eyes and the impish grin were unmistakable. Mark Danner engulfed Josh in a suffocating bear hug, lifting him off the porch step.

To the man who had put on at least seventy-five pounds since Josh had last seen him, he replied, "Who's been feeding you? Zookeepers?"

In high school Mark had been an angular, raw-boned farm boy standing six-feet-four with 210 pounds on a muscular frame. With his auburn shock of hair, he resembled an oversized Huck Finn. Mark's was a free spirit, too, just like the original. Now his fleshy face and portly waist conjured up an image of a genial and indulgent grandfather. Above the din of people enthusiastically conversing, Mark roared, "Hey, guys. Look whut-ta cat drug in!"

Several people turned to see who the most recent arrival of the Class of '62 was. Josh heard his name called out in simultaneous acknowledgment by a number of these ostensible strangers. He stepped into a living room crowded with men and women who, it appeared, might be comfortable in a Senior Center. Josh struggled to envision these sexagenarians as they were when he last saw them as teenagers.

"Who are these old people?" he thought to himself.

A few of those present were exceedingly thin, but most were stout to rotund. Double chins were the norm and most faces showed the prominent wrinkles of advancing age. Sagging flesh on limbs or weight collected on torsos and buttocks testified to a shift in the center of gravity. Natural white and graying hair and balding heads contrasted with a few noticeable dye jobs. Several canes and

THE HOOSIER GAME

one aluminum walker held some of the most infirm of the group steady and upright. Betty Billings rushed to take Josh's hands in her own. "Will and I are so happy you're here, Josh. It's good to see you again."

Recalling her sweet voice and gentle demeanor, Josh replied, "It's my pleasure to be here, Betty. You have a lovely home."

It was the same farmhouse that Will Billings had grown up in, albeit having undergone several renovations and additions over the years. It was spacious, but warm, with burning logs crackling in the fireplace and a grandfather clock—handed down from his great-grandfather—tick-tocking next to another antique, his father's old roll-top desk. Of course, the house was filled with modern appliances and furniture, including a 42-inch flat-screen TV attached to a wall in the living area.

Betty proceeded to pin a nametag on the lapel of Josh's blazer. The makeshift ID included a copy of the grad's high school senior photo.

Calling her husband by his high school nickname, Josh asked Betty, "Where's Bear?"

"He's in the kitchen pouring drinks. Will was so excited when he saw your name on the reservation list."

Playing in the background, faintly blending with the Babel of classmates' conversations and sounds of peeling laughter, were tunes of their youth. The old 45-rpm disks were long gone, of course. Oldies now were purchased on CDs.

You're only sixteen, but you're my teenage queen.
You're the prettiest, the loveliest, girl I've ever seen.
Sixteen candles, in my heart will glow,
Forever and ever, for I love you so.

As they arrived, members of the 1962 Raiders basketball squad had gravitated toward one another. A spontaneous mini-reunion within a reunion broke out among former teammates. Josh hadn't been in the company of these men—most now drawing Social Security—for nearly forty years. They shared the bond of brotherhood developed by playing on the finest Morgans Awe basketball team ever.

Approaching him with a broad smile from ear to ear was a short, plump, balding man. The buck-toothed grin of his youth obviously had been altered by serious dental work. His was a round face with a prominent forehead and large, sleepy eyes.

"Moon?"

"Josh! Hey, man, good to see you!"

Josh stifled a chuckle, recalling an unforgettable incident that occurred in a long-forgotten game. Jamie Ross had been a perpetual scrub for MAHS, possessing minimal basketball talent. Nonetheless, he had a huge heart and unfailing commitment to the team. On a night when the regular players had established a healthy lead, Coach called Ross to enter the game. In his haste to report to the official scorer, Jamie leaped from the bench and yanked downward to remove his warm-up pants. Unfortunately, he dug one layer too deeply into his basketball wardrobe. The woolen leggings dropped to his ankles along with his basketball shorts. To his mortification, Jamie was now attired only in his jock strap, his bare butt shining toward the home crowd. He quickly recovered, but not until a legend was born. From that moment forward, Jamie Ross would be known forever as "Moon."

The real punch line, the ironic twist, was that Dr. Ross became a noted proctologist in St. Louis. He was easily the wealthiest of those gathered here, having turned a small medical practice into one of the largest consortiums of surgeons in Missouri.

Delighted to see his old friend, Jamie shouted, "Sonny! Look who's here!"

Josh's eyes now fell upon Sonny Watkins, a classmate who had left a leg in the jungles of Vietnam. Bronze-skinned with a prominent cleft chin, Sonny's countenance bore a sober but alert expression, as if he were perpetually on a mission. The former soldier's close-cropped hair was snowy white, his frame was slender and his carriage vertical. His perfectly pressed attire and burnished black shoes bespoke of the self-discipline that a thirty-year military career had ingrained in him. Hidden beneath his perfectly-creased trousers was the prosthesis attached to what remained of his thigh.

Sonny had enlisted in the Marines right after high school. His courage and leadership had resulted in several combat promotions, ultimately advancing him to the rank of captain. During the Tet Offensive in February 1968, he stepped on a land mine. Sonny returned to his country a legitimate war hero stunned by the bewilderingly vile treatment that many Vietnam veterans received from a politically torn American public.

Following the war, Sonny had served on the faculty at the Marine Military Academy in Harlingen, Texas, until his recent retirement. Sonny and Josh embraced robustly. Both men's eyes began to mist.

"You look great, Josh," Sonny offered.

"So do you, buddy. I'm so proud of you."

Mark chimed in to contain any further show of sentimentality.

"What're you doin' here, anyways, 'Wats?' You wouldn't show up to see a mouse eat a bale a-hay, use'ly."

"I just came to see if you were as fat and ugly and rich as everyone told me. I see they got two out of three right."

Josh was comforted to hear again the nasal Kentuckiana twang of his youth. Delivered with a lazy, drawn-out tempo, Ohio Valley dialect oozed slowly, like sorghum from a jar. Slurring over words and essentially altering the rules of proper grammar was characteristic of Hoosier-speak in Indiana's southern counties.

Feeling conspicuous with his more stilted, collegiate delivery, Josh began to adapt his conversational style to the regional rhythms and elisions of these friends, rounding off words like "something" to "somethin'." One time he even used "them" for "those."

From the front entrance a new voice intruded on the laughter of the ex-teammates. Approaching the circle was a diminutive man dressed in a garish Hawaiian shirt, bright yellow Bermuda shorts, flops, and a Panama hat.

"I see I got here just in time to raise the intellectual average of you buncha' yay-hoos."

A loud chorus of "Fries!" announced the arrival of Arnie Packard, the witty former student manager for the Raiders. At five seven and no more than 155 pounds, he looked much as he did the last time Josh had seen him. Arnie's crooked grin and shuffling gait were unmistakable. His deep tan was evidence of his year-round residence in Sarasota, Florida. Hazel eyes were squeezed onto a thin, ferret-like face.

Arnie was smothered with hugs, handshakes, and hearty pats on the back. The men also showered him with a rowdy mixture of disparaging remarks about his heritage and questionable character.

"Where the hell's the nurse?" Arnie shouted. "I'll be openin' a mortuary tomorrow. Lookin' at this bunch, I'll be rich within the month. Exceptin' you fine- looking ladies, of course." He smiled coyly at the women nearby.

"Hey, Fries, love that haircut with a hole in the middle."

"Now don't be petty, boys," Arnie responded. "We cain't all be studs. Guess it's my burden to bear alone in this collection of im-potent has-beens."

"Fries, you haven't changed a bit," marveled Jamie.

Arnie Packard had acquired his matchless nickname at a drive-in movie. Outdoor theatres were a popular destination for teens in the 1950s and 60s.

WHERE WERE YOU, IN '62?

For twenty cents apiece a carload of young friends could descend on the drive-in to watch the movie and ogle girls.

You pulled alongside a metal pole four feet high. The detachable speaker had a flange to hang on the car window. By pressing a button you could talk to a person at the refreshment stand. If you didn't mind waiting for your order, a young female carhop would deliver food to the car.

Arnie was a clever and mischievous prankster. Often his antics exceeded his discretion. One summer evening Josh drove Mark Danner, Moon Ross, and Arnie to watch *The Longest Day*, a film about the D-Day landings on Normandy. Arnie sneaked his mom's *mammillaria grahamii* into Josh's DeSoto, hidden in a paper bag. This flower—commonly known as a "pincushion cactus"—was about five inches in height, maybe three in diameter. The tips of the mass of protruding spines were razor sharp. Arnie quietly awaited an opportunity to make use of this prickly plant.

As usual, Mark ignored the speaker's order button, immediately heading to the concession stand located in the middle of the lot. As Danner walked away Arnie switched off the overhead light that shone on the car's interior when a door was opened. Next he placed the cactus in Mark's rear passenger seat.

Danner returned moments later with a large Coke and French fries. With both hands occupied, he swung into his seat. Instantly he vaulted upward when he sat on the *mammillaria*.

"HOT DAMN!" Danner yelled as his head hit the car ceiling. Cokes and ketchup-soaked French fries showered Mark and his fellow rear seat occupant, Moon.

Naturally, the front seat guys roared at the sight. Mark was doing a slow burn while Moon was bitching about being a victim of collateral damage. It was at this point Arnie couldn't leave well enough alone. He began to sing his own version of a child's ditty:

"Oh, there ain't no fries on me. No there ain't no fries on me. There may be fries on summa' you guys, but there ain't no fries on—"

Splat!

It was now Arnold wearing what remained of the beverage and soggy French fries. Vengeance was sweet for the occupants of the rear seats.

He was rarely addressed as Arnie after the incident.

As Josh giggled to himself in recalling the scene, a distinctive, high-pitched staccato laugh returned him to the present. Only one person in Josh's memory ever snorted in that particular fashion. It could only be Grover Willburn, who'd been a gangly back-up center on the '62 squad.

"Eye-God, Hyeenie," Mark said, "Whut-da hell you cacklin' about?"

"M-M-Mark," Hyeenie countered, "Y-Y-You used to j-j-jus' be d-d-dumb and uggg-ly. N-Now yer' dumb, ugly, and f-f-fat!"

"Grover, you fornicatin' hilljack. You wuz ten years old fore you found out yer name warn't 'Git Wood.'"

Jamie jumped in again. "I hope you married a woman who can do your laundry, Hyeenie. You guys remember Grover only washed his practice gear twice a season. That stuff was so smelly and stiff, his socks entered a dance contest on their own."

"F-F-Finished s-s-second, t-t-t-too," Hyeenie added.

Josh weighed in, recalling the time Coach O'Ryan made Grover bring his birth certificate to practice.

"He was on you hard. Yelled that you moved slower'n a glacier. Coach said he wanted to make sure you were alive. He broke up when you actually brought it with you!"

Josh was amused at how seamlessly his former teammates segued into the inane locker room banter characteristic of teenage athletes. Crude, offensive humor aimed at teammates was a rite of passage into a tight circle.

How one handled derisive remarks about those things of which he was most sensitive revealed a lot about his character. The barbs were whimsical and absurd, usually wrapped around a touch of truth, yet greatly exaggerated for effect. A prominent physical feature, a peculiar trait, or a certain idiosyncrasy could bring a torrent of insults meant to embarrass and humble the target. Although the teasing could be brutal, its leavening effect brought teammates closer. The bond and respect among players was tempered in the fire of competition. It was comforting to know that the same guys who rode you the hardest would be the first and most steadfast in closing ranks in support should any teammate be threatened.

As the old friends talked, Josh learned that over half of the team members still lived in Morgans Awe, or nearby. Only Josh, Jamie, and Sonny had earned college degrees. Mark spent one year at Morehead State College in Kentucky. He dropped out to take over the family farm when his dad died in a tractor accident. He now owned the 3,000-acre farm up near China.

By virtue of his position as a former college professor Josh had earned a measure of deference from these less-educated men. Some had even read the books he had authored.

WHERE WERE YOU, IN '62?

Moving forward from the rear of the circle, a smiling, somewhat bashful-looking man emerged, offering his extended hand to Josh. Elmer Freebolt was dressed in an ill-fitting suit and a wide, decades-old tie. His hands were rough, his nails bitten to the quick. The creases of his palms were stained with the grime of a working man.

Elmer had been among the poorest of Josh's teammates. The Freebolts had lived in poverty as long as he had known them. By the time the boy was in junior high school his father had run off, leaving the family destitute. They were forced to live on handouts from neighbors and poor-relief checks. Josh's mother often sent to Mrs. Freebolt used clothes and other items for her eight children.

Josh recalled the time in the middle of winter when Elmer came to school in a short-sleeved, gaudy shirt that had a beach scene with a palm tree on the back. His mother had purchased the cheap material at a church rummage sale. She inadvertently reversed the pattern as she sewed the pieces together, resulting in the palm tree being positioned upside down. Though humiliated, Freebolt ignored the snickering of classmates and continued to wear the shirt until it fell apart.

Elmer and his three sons now owned one of the largest disposal companies in southern Indiana. Josh felt such a sense of pride for the poor kid who grew up to own a successful business. Disdaining the handshake, Josh hugged his former teammate while congratulating him on his accomplishments.

"Anybody ever hear from Si-Si?" Sonny Watkins asked.

"Last I knew he was out in California," Arnie offered.

"Yeah," added Bobby Mack Deal. "I heard he was prez'dent of some big lumber comp'ny out there."

"You guys remember his mom?" said Moon, with a suggestive smile.

At that several of the party grinned wolfishly. Mention of Si-Si's mother conjured up visions of a goddess.

At age thirteen, Cristobal Caesar "C.C." Aguirre and his family moved from Mexico City to Morgans Awe. The boys immediately nicknamed him "Si-Si."

He was the son of a quiet, gentle-natured father, Olivio, and a fiery, stunningly attractive Brazilian mother, Yara Bermudez Rodriguez. With midnight-dark eyes, flashing white teeth, long black hair, and flawless, bronze-tinted skin, Mrs. Aguirre was outrageously beautiful. Libidinous teenage boys would gawk at her with mouths agape.

Whenever possible the lads chose Si-Si's small back yard for summer Wiffle ball games. If they were lucky, they might catch glimpses of his mom hanging wash on the clothesline. If they were truly blessed she might be seen as she lay out to tan.

It didn't take Si-Si long to catch on to his new buddies' interest in his mother.

"You guys are sick," he would say. The thought of his teenage friends lusting after his mom was an abomination.

Sonny picked up the story.

"I'll never forget the first time Hyeenie went with us to Si-Si's. Mrs. Aguirre came out to hang up the wash just as we got there."

Moon interrupted to describe clearly what they all remembered.

"She was wearing a white blouse tied up in a knot above her waist. You could see her belly button—"

"An outie," interrupted Bobby Mack.

"Yeah, and oh lordy, them skin-tight yeller short-shorts not leavin' much for the 'magination."

Deal, again. "I lost my breath every time her chest heaved."

"Well, I looked at Grover and he was just standin' there, his tongue hangin' out," added Moon.

"Wonder he didn't git a sun burn on that sucker," Sonny chortled.

"When she finally finished and went inside, Hyeenie, his eyes wide as saucers, says to no one in particular, 'D-D-Did y-y-you guys s-s-s-see them b-b-b-boozums?'"

That story had been told many times over. Today the participants laughed with the same gusto as they had a half century ago.

Bobby Mack Deal stepped forward to offer his hand to Josh. Still ruggedly handsome, Deal's mahogany eyes complemented his thick brown hair and bronze skin. He was trim and moved with the grace of a much younger man.

A natural raconteur, Bobby Mack had an infectious laugh that gave no warning of its approach, but simply exploded into full-faced joy as he emitted a hardy guffaw escaping from somewhere deep inside. As his mouth flew open and his eyes disappeared, his whole body shook with involuntary spasms of hilarity.

"Hey, Josh, 'member the time Sonny did a haidstan in-nat rainstorm? With that huge nose upside down, he almost drown-ded."

"Tell us about it, Dumbo," Sonny answered, chuckling, referring to Bobby Mack's protruding ears. "Do little kids still ask if they can use you as a kite?"

WHERE WERE YOU, IN '62?

At first Josh didn't recognize Joe Cotter. He was standing on the periphery of the gathering, looking self-conscious through darting, beady eyes. His sallow complexion and sunken cheeks suggested sickliness. A rumpled, well-worn suit sagged on his bony frame.

"Hey, Joe, how ya' doin'?" Bobby Mack asked, noticing his former teammate.

Cotter looked up, conspicuously uneasy.

"Great, great. Got a new job just this week."

Lying, of course.

Joe Cotter's loud, slurred speech and trouble with balance confirmed he had been drinking before coming to the reunion. Time, alcohol, and drugs had taken their toll.

Josh was both sad for Joe and annoyed by him. His presence forced the group to acknowledge him, pretending he was okay, as if he weren't among the dregs of society. Josh felt guilty for feeling that way, but he couldn't help himself.

Others simply refused to look at him, as his condition increased their discomfort. Always kindhearted and sympathetic, Jamie Ross talked quietly with Joe for several minutes to help the outcast feel welcome.

"Have any of you guys seen Coach O'Ryan? Whatever happened to him? Is he still alive?"

"Didn't he die of a heart attack?"

"I heard he had a heart problem," Mark piped up. "But when they looked, he didn't have one."

"He d-d-didn't have n-no ulcer, n-n-neither," Grover added. "But he was a c-c-c carrier."

The men chuckled lovingly at the memory of a man who, leatherneck tough, had influenced each of them in positive ways.

Josh knew the real story.

"No, he passed away back in '83. We traded Christmas greetings every year, so when he died of cancer his daughter called to tell me."

Josh and Jamie were the only members of the '62 squad to attend Coach's memorial. Dr. Ross made the trip to Terre Haute from St. Louis and Josh from Ohio to pay their respects.

Josh credited the influence of Coach O'Ryan for his success as a student, teacher, and citizen. Michael O'Ryan was one among a handful of adults—besides his parents—who contributed significantly to Josh's outlook on life.

THE HOOSIER GAME

With the consistency of the sun rising, the coach challenged the boys who crossed his path over the years to be better than they thought they could be. Josh was one who had listened.

The men had a store of humorous remembrances of their beloved mentor.

"You guys 'member when Coach gotsa mad at us at halftime over at Mainport?" Mark grinned.

Jamie picked up the story: "Yeah, he was yellin' at Bobby Mack for some basketball sin—"

"An' he kicked in the brass screen at the bottom of the lockerroom door," Mark continued.

"He tried to pull his foot out," Jamie noted, "But he was caught in the screen and—"

"He couldn't get loose," said Mark. "He was cussin' somethin' furious when Coach Barnhard led us up to the floor for the second half. We're about to go out for the tip when we look up and here's Coach walkin' toward us with only a sock on one foot!"

The men reacted with spasms of laughter as Jamie continued the story.

"It was halfway through the third quarter when the janitor brought his shoe to the bench. Coach slipped it on and we never heard him mention it again."

"Mark, didn't you try to tease him about it at practice that week?" Josh asked slyly.

"I did. But I didn't git too far. I ast 'eem since we won, was he gonna leave one of 'ees loafers home next game. Said 'the only loafer I'll leave behind is you, Pea-brain.'"

Mark shared another tale of him and Coach O'Ryan crossing wires.

"It still pisses me off that time Sonny stole Coach's fedora after practice. 'Course I was the usual suspect. Tried to tell Coach it weren't me. He knew I knew who done it, though. But I wouldn't tell. He run me so many laps the next day I coulda stepped on a coin with my Chucks an' tole you whether it was a nickel or a dime."

"He was one of a kind, that's for sure," Jamie sighed.

Sonny began anew. "Bond sure learned a lesson when he moved in. It was the first scrimmage and Bathwaite was dribblin' all over the place. Coach blew the whistle and asked Bond if he ever intended to pass the ball. O'Ryan told him 'If you can beat a thrown ball down court, I'll never again say anything to you about dribbling too much.'"

"Yeah, Coach put Bond on the baseline at the end of the court," Deal remembered. "He told 'eem to dribble as fast as he could to the far basket. Bathwaite took off, lickety-split. Bond had just reached half-court when Coach threw the ball over his head to Josh at the other end."

"Bond got the point on the first trip. But O'Ryan had him try another ten or twelve times—"

"So he wouldn't forgit."

"Hey, Willburn, can you still spell 'cat'?"

"That was the best," said Sonny, anticipating the story.

"I d-d-didn't th-th-think it w-w-was so d-d-damn f-f-funny," Grover deadpanned.

Josh chimed in, asking, "What was it? Didn't you get called about four times for too much time in the lane against Hillcrest our senior year?"

Jamie quickly set the stage. "Coach was so mad at Wilby. The next day's practice he asked you if you'd been sleepin' in the three-second lane. You said 'No,' and he said, 'Son, you only got three seconds in there.'"

"Coach tells Grover," Sonny continued, "'Next time you're in the three-second area, count one-Mississippi, two-Mississippi—'"

Watkins doubled over at this point.

Now Jamie again: "You started up, 'Wa-wa-one M-M-Missuss—'" before Coach realized his mistake."

"He couldn't hardly contain himself," Mark added. "Coach just said, 'Grove, whenever you're in the lane, just spell cat and get the hell out of there.'"

Arnie turned the spotlight on his favorite target.

"Hey Shamu, I can tell by that fat ass a-yours that you finally stopped runnin' tours."

Every man in the group knew to what Fries was referring. While Coach O'Ryan occasionally used salty maxims to make a point, he disdained swear words from his teenage players. Cursing was punished immediately by the coach, requiring the potty mouth to run laps around the gym and up the bleachers. He called them "tours."

Most caught in the act were immediately contrite. The guilty felt morally lacking, sure to go to Hell, for muttering "daa-yum" under their breath. Coach could do that to you.

Mark was bred to his colorful, irreverent vocabulary. His profanity was a family trait. Mark tried but never could control his bawdy tongue. The habit was part of him, like mustard on a hotdog. In an attempt to curtail Mark's

THE HOOSIER GAME

coarseness, Coach O'Ryan made the burly teen run tours around the gym whenever he lapsed.

However, the constant stoppages during practice to discipline Mark drove the coach crazy. Finally, after endless delays at practice, Coach changed tactics. He would endure the accumulation of Mark's profanity and then discipline him afterward, two tours for every curse word. The student manager, Arnie, was directed to keep a tally sheet of Mark's verbal indiscretions. Sometimes he needed more than one page. At the end of practice, Coach O'Ryan would turn to ask, "How many today, Arnold?"

"Thirteen, coach."

"Okay, Mark, twenty-six tours."

Usually Mark would still be slogging around the gym after the rest of the team had showered and was heading home.

"Damn Fries cheated me," muttered Mark. "He counted ever 'goddam' as two, and a 'sonuvabitch' fer four!"

As the laughter at this latest tale ebbed, Josh broached a subject the men in the room had avoided up to this moment.

"Jake's been gone nearly forty years now. He would've loved being a part of this."

An awkward pause in the levity followed this reference to the man most felt was a victim of his success as a teenage basketball hero. In high school Jake Skoon had been the sun around which the rest of his mates orbited. Each had his own separate memories of the man they followed, envied, protected, and marveled at on the basketball floor. The requisite responses of "So sad," "What a shame," and, "I still can't believe he killed hisself," were mumbled within the group.

"I'd sell my soul to see Jake shoot one more jumper," Bobby Mack offered.

"So would Jake," Mark quipped.

3

ELVIS WAS IN THE BUILDING

Jourden Arena
7:40 p.m.

As the Raiders rushed onto the playing floor the Morgans Awe crowd hailed them with a rousing ovation. A sea of contrasting colors marked the respective student cheering sections sprinkled around the grand hall. The orange and black-clad Raiders' supporters faced directly across mid-court from the huge contingent of Madison Central fans dressed in red and white.

The Madison Central team had not yet appeared.

Jake Skoon led his teammates onto the court. The team formed two oblique lay-up lines. Each player jogged toward the hoop to meet a pass from a teammate, leaped, and laid the ball off the square outlined on the backboard.

With a subtle glance, Josh Seaberg found his girlfriend, Pat Sargossa, among her fellow Pep Club rooters. As their eyes met they exchanged brief smiles. He knew she would be awaiting him after the game, win or lose.

As per his ritual, Mark Danner left the line and trotted over to the second row under the basket where his fourteen-year old sister, Abby, was seated next to their parents. Abigail Jane Danner had been born with one extra chromosome.

Her head was unusually large, her face wide, and her nose flat. A squat, stunted body and the creased palms of her hands marked her as a child with irreversible Down Syndrome. Abby's sweet disposition, angelic smile, and perpetual courage always inspired her older brother. The strapping teenager bent over gently, smiled, and placed a soft kiss on Abby's forehead.

As he turned to go back to the playing floor, he heard Abby's signature request demanded before every game: "Dunt it, Mawk! Dunt it!"

THE HOOSIER GAME

Dunking the ball in 1962 was not a common act in high school play. Unlike today's game of rim-rattling, outrageous dunks, very few high school players could throw the ball down back then.

In the final game of the regular season, in honor of his sister, Mark had "dunted it" five separate times. Abby's face wouldn't surrender her joyful smile for hours afterward.

As tipoff time approached, the SRO crowd crammed into Jourden Arena numbered well over 7,500 fans. Some were standing shoulder to shoulder alongside Madison Fire Marshal Louis Rucker. He had the authority to remove fans who were sitting in the aisles or standing in places ordinarily not allowed; but to do so would trigger a small riot. Instead, he kept his eyes glued to the action on the floor, cringing inside at the possibility of a catastrophic fire.

The mixture of sights, sounds, and smells produced the familiar sensory transformation within Josh. The hairs on his arms and neck tingled. His heart throbbed. Breathing became a series of hurried, barely sufficient pants. The parched feeling in his throat and on his tongue—a.k.a. "cottonmouth"—contrasted with the profuse sweating of his hands. A steady, dissonant murmur buzzed in his head.

"Calm down, Josh, calm down," he whispered to himself.

The surge of adrenalin coursing through Josh's veins was deceiving. He felt as if the height of his vertical jump had multiplied but his hand-eye coordination seemed to have stayed in the locker room. His first lay-up attempt slammed hard against the glass, bounding embarrassingly over the hoop.

The excess nervous energy that would propel Josh through the rigor of the game now had to be brought under control. Usually, once the action began, muscle memory would engage to quell his body's instinctual response to the pressure of the moment.

Brilliant arc lights accentuated the kaleidoscope of color from all points of the hall, creating a dazzling scene. The sea of faces encircling the court melted into a blur of roiling humanity. Heat generated by the over-capacity throng of basketball fans packed tightly into the bleachers had raised the temperature on the court noticeably.

Adapting to the panorama presented by the vast arena was a challenge. The Raiders were accustomed to playing in claustrophobically tiny gyms, where the architecture generally featured a brick wall at one end of the playing area and a curtained stage at the other. MAHS rarely played before crowds in excess of 700 people.

Here at the Jourden Arena, bleachers holding hundreds of spectators extended far beyond the ends of the court. Viewed through the transparent backboard, the erratic motions of the crowd were distracting.

As the shooter moved farther from the basket, his perspective was altered considerably. The orange ring on which he focused seemed to be suspended in air. Jake noticed his normally dependable jump shots were falling short. As with all natural shooters, he adjusted the arc and distance of his attempts accordingly.

Yell leaders of the opposing schools were stoking the fervor of their rooting sections. The girls—and the occasional male with a megaphone—led the pep clubs and other fans in cheers for their favorites.

No cheerleader rested tranquilly on her knees under the basket; each was in constant motion on the sidelines throughout the game. Their freelance leaps and vigorous gestures with pom-pons during the action on the floor inspired spontaneous crowd support.

Josh and his mates settled into the pre-game warm-up routine, as Raiders backers sang along with the Pep Club:

> "Our boys will shine tonight, our boys will shine.
> Our boys will shine tonight, all down the line.
> They're all dressed up tonight, don't they look fine.
> The sun goes down and the moon comes up,
> Our boys will shine!"

Madison Central High's student cheer block of more than 500 teenage girls and boys dwarfed that of the Raiders, whose entire student body numbered 218.

Morgans Awe's comparatively tiny contingent of rooters was reinforced, however, thanks to a phenomenon observed only during tournament time. Other schools that had been eliminated earlier in the sectional typically switched their allegiance—for one or two games only—to back the team they disliked the least. On this night, students from each of the high schools not playing threw their support to the underdog, meaning that the Central Cougars were villains in their own gym.

With an energy similar to the fervor of a political convention floor with delegates announcing their nominees—"The great commonwealth of Kentucky casts its eight votes for the next president!"—the other schools provided spirited support to their enemy's enemy. The ritual began with the smallest schools' cheer sections. Then the larger schools weighed in, swelling the noise.

"Hey, Morgans Awe. Say, Morgans Awe. Jericho's for ya!"

Loud cheers erupted from both the Jericho and Morgans Awe cheer blocks. The grateful response followed: "Hey, Jericho, say, Jericho, Morgans Awe says 'Thanks!'"

"Hey, Morgans Awe, say, Morgans Awe, Mainport's for ya!"

The noise swelled as the accumulation of fans joined in cheering with the Morgans Awe backers.

THE HOOSIER GAME

Suddenly, an explosion of thundering sound evoking the 1812 Overture reverberated throughout the hall. The startled Morgans Awe players reflexively turned to find the source of the ear-piercing noise.

The Cougars had arrived.

May 5, 2012
Morgans Awe

Additional guests arrived in the Billings's congested living room. Josh excused himself from his teammates to mingle with others. Vaguely familiar faces sparked dim images of past events, like details of a hazy dream recalled. Half a dozen former classmates stood around a kitchen table paging through editions of Morgans Awe yearbooks from 1958 through 1962. With a smile, Seaberg blended into the group. Each greeted him by name.

"I'm embarrassed," Josh admitted sheepishly, as he leaned toward others to have a glance at nametags. It was helpful that women's maiden names were included.

"Everyone is familiar but your names just won't come to me."

"You're no different from the rest of us, Josh," replied Mary Gierke, his former lab partner in Mr. Baker's biology class. "At least you can see well enough to read the print on these horrible photo-tags."

Knowing little or nothing of former schoolmates' adult lives, his recollections were limited to teenagers he once knew, of singular shared incidents, of flirtations, of old resentments, of bullies, or of students he had held in high esteem.

"Josh, you look about the same as you did back in high school," said Donna Jo Hirndon, an object of his puppy-love in junior high.

"We were just saying how we're in the autumn of our lives," offered Susan Jonquin, with whom Josh had endured the mumbled history lectures of Mr. Greyholden. "That makes old age seem poetic, sort of."

Now intruding on the conversation were the rousing lyrics of a song everyone knew by heart:

Good golly miss Molly, sure like to ball.
Good golly miss Molly, sure like to ball.
A-when you're rockin' and a rollin',
Can't hear your mama call.
From the early, early mornin'

ELVIS WAS IN THE BUILDING

To the early, early night,
When I caught miss Molly rockin'
At the house of blue lights,
Good golly miss Molly, sure like to ball.

Little Richard was a wild and funky rock 'n' roller, a singer of such inane hits as "Keep a-knockin' (But You Cain't Come In)," "Good Golly Miss Molly," "Tuiti Fruiti," "Long Tall Sallie," and "Lawdy Miss Clawdy" in the mid-1950s.

"My Lord, I haven't heard that song in ages," Mary sighed.

Dale Lammer chimed in, "Elvis is still the King. I bet he would still be rockin' in his jump suit in Vegas today if he had'na O-D'd."

Susan joked, "I read where a woman in Tennessee claimed she saw him eating a peanut butter and banana sandwich in a Denny's last week."

"If he was still kickin, they'd hafta' oil him up like the Tin Man and whisper the lyrics in his ear."

"I'd still scream for Elvis," gushed Rita Wells. "He's still the one-and-only 'U.S. Male.'"

Perhaps the most enduring legacy of the fifties and sixties was the first truly original American music that teens could claim as their own. Anyone who was an American high school student between 1955 and 1965 lived during what is generally known as the Rock 'n' Roll Era. Captured in gentle ballads or hard-hitting rock rhythms were themes of teen angst: the pain of unrequited love; the daily drama of peer social acceptance; rebellion against unreasonable restrictions of parents; teen depression and thoughts of suicide; and the perceived unfairness of life.

Epitomizing the rebellious new wave of rock singers was a twenty-year-old truck driver who rose to nationwide prominence following an appearance on Ed Sullivan's "Toast of the Town," the most popular variety show on television at the time.

On Sunday evening, September 9, 1956, fifty-two million viewers—one-third of the American population—watched and listened as the Tupelo, Mississippi native, Elvis Aron ("I don't sing like nobody") Presley, performed four songs. The pulsating beat of *Hound Dog* and *Don't Be Cruel*, along with Elvis's sexually suggestive gyrations created an immediate storm of controversy. Many adults and clergy were outraged at what they perceived to be a vulgar display by a licentious hillbilly who threatened the moral ruination of an entire generation of young people.

Presley became an instant legend.

"Isn't it funny that you hear our music everywhere these days?" said Sheila Wood. "All the Golden Oldies radio stations, at Starbucks, restaurants, and malls."

"My favorite singer of all time was Paul Anka," June offered. "He was just the best."

"What about Ricky Nelson?"

"Chuck Berry was the *o*-riginal rocker," asserted Roger. "That guitar he played would get so hot he'd hafta drop it right on the stage till it cooled off!"

"We all thought he was a white guy until we saw him on American Bandstand."

"I loved those 'beach-blanket' movies with Frankie Avalon and Annette Funicello," said Donna Jo.

"Yeah. 'Venus' was a great song to cha-cha to."

Roger cracked, "Doesn't Avalon have 'bout a hundred grandkids now?"

"For me, no one could top Concetta Rosa Maria Franconero," Dale Lammer teased.

"Who?"

"He means Connie Francis. Dale's just showin' off," Mary Jo offered.

"Ah, yes. 'Where the Boys Are,' one of *the* all-time best slow-dance songs," recalled Roger.

"Don't forget Brenda Lee. Wasn't she about fourteen when she had her first number-one record?"

"Remember when 'doo-wop' music first came on the scene? I just loved Dion and the Belmonts."

The mention of "doo-wop" music conjured up in Josh's mind images of wistful teens—white and black—who gathered evenings on the corner of a narrow inner-city Philadelphia street, standing around a barrel filled with burning wood and trash to keep them warm. There, harmonizing *a cappella*, songs were composed on the spot. In three minutes or less, the doo-wops told a story of love and loss, of bliss and misery.

"And there's Motown. They say Berry Gordy borrowed about 600 bucks from his uncle or somethin' to start a recording studio. Man, did he make a mint."

"Soul music was a whole new thing, straight out of the black culture. Diana Ross and the Supremes were my favorites."

As the group discussed the various styles of fifties music, a frivolous tune sung by Dodie Stevens caught their attention.

ELVIS WAS IN THE BUILDING

He wore tan shoes with pink shoelaces,
A polka dot vest, and man, oh, man,
He wore tan shoes with pink shoelaces,
And a big Panama with a purple hat band.

"Tan shoes with pink shoelaces!" Max Williams chuckled. "The wildest clothes I ever wore was argyle socks and pegged pants."

"Yeah, you guys looked like you were poured in 'em," smiled June. "And you had those big belt buckles."

"Worn buckled, you was goin' steady. Unbuckled, you wasn't."

Donna Jo could still recall what she had worn on the first day as a freshman at MAHS.

"I had on a skirt with a big white poodle on the front. Underneath I had about four layers of crinoline. I tied a pastel scarf around my neck, wore a big black belt, and my saddle oxfords with red rubber soles, and bobby socks turned down three times. I thought I was really cool—or 'neato,' as we used to say."

"The more layers you had, the better it was. The skirt bounced when you walked. Sitting down was a whole 'nother thing."

"Remember when Sue Wright and Virginia Wilfong intentionally wore skirts with the hem above the knees? They didn't last even one period before Mrs. Gates, sent them to the girls' dean."

"When Sue and Ginny came into her office, Miss Mitchel told them to get down on their knees. Neither of the hemlines of the girl's skirts touched the floor. She sent them home immediately to return in appropriate clothing!"

"We could wear loose jeans or slacks off the school grounds, or if we were doing something extracurricular, like decorating for a school dance. Or clam diggers!"

"With a hem half-way down the calf," Sheila specified.

"Wearing shorts to school was taboo. Unless it was an after-school event."

"Even then, the hem couldn't be higher than the midpoint between hip and knee."

"Can you be-*lieve* that some communities actually had laws keepin' girls from wearing short-shorts?"

Todd Paul recalled a classmate who caused a mini-scandal while decorating for the senior prom. He lowered his voice as he related the incident, because the leading player was now chatting with classmates in the adjacent room.

THE HOOSIER GAME

"Sherry O'Neal come to the gym wearin' a pair a-them short-shorts with the cheeks of her tokus leakin' out. All the guys loved it!"

"She was packin' ten pounds-a spuds in a five-pound sack," Roger chortled.

Sue noted that "The administration didn't much care for it. 'Bad Girl' Sherry was suspended from school for two days."

The discussion turned to the most bothersome but crucial statement of a teenage girl's personal appearance: her hairstyle. Most girls endured the agony and time-consuming process necessary to turn shoulder-length hair into curly permanents.

"You guys had it made with your hair," Donna Jo said. "We girls had to cope with all the crap it took to look beautiful for you."

"Yeah, you guys all had flattops or burr cuts."

"Except for the 'greasers.' They slicked back their long hair with Brylcreem and combed it into ducktails—"

"It was 'ducks ass' in impolite company," Roger laughed.

Each of the women had a horror story about the barbarity of curlers and bobby pins.

"Oh, God. Perms were the worst. My mom would always do my hair in the kitchen. There was that awful odor. And the rollers. I hated having to go to bed with those things around my head."

"One time when I took the rollers out, I had a big old mass of frizz. My mother put lemon juice on it to make my hair look shiny and squeaky-clean."

"I mostly wore a pageboy cut in high school," offered Rita. "I could hardly sleep 'cause the bobby pins that held the curls would stick you when you laid down."

"When my hair would get longer, I'd try a pony tail with short bangs for a few weeks. We'd get those grow-grain ribbons at Newberry's in Madison. You pulled your hair back real tight. When you took the rubber band off, it hurt!"

"Remember we'd all wear an updo at formal dances?"

"Yes, except for the holy rollers. They'd stack all that hair up, clamp it in place with bobby pins, then didn't wash it for weeks."

"Donna Jo! Be careful. Patty Morrow's coming today!"

"Pentecostal Patty's comin'?" Roger practically shouted. "She's the last person I'd guess would be at a reunion. She was so uptight she wouldn'a kissed a boy if he was Tab Hunter."

Max chimed in, "She was about five-four unless you counted the hair. That made her about six-three."

"You haven't seen her yet, have you, boys?" Rita asked slyly. "Just wait."

Roger brought up the Lover's Lane of Morgans Awe, Honeysuckle Road, which was little more than a gravel pathway that wound around behind Tanner's Hill.

"Remember takin' your girl out there for, uh—"

"Petting," said Mary, completing Roger's sentence for him.

"Whoever came up with 'pettin' or 'neckin' anyway? We was *makin' out*."

"Weekends, if you didn't get to the Hill before nine o'clock, you couldn't find a place to park."

"Funny," said Donna Jo coyly, "I never was out there."

"Oh, pa-*leeze*, Jo," Mary commented sarcastically. "You and Max were out there so often they named a tree after the two of you!"

"Back then, you girls were in charge of keepin' our hormones in check," Max noted, with a grin. "We guys all talked a lot about sex. But very few of us had any bona fides, so to speak."

"MAX! Shame on you!" Donna Jo chided her husband.

Josh offered his first comments on the subject.

"The worst thing you could do to your parents was to embarrass the family in the community. That alone was reason enough to scare you into behaving."

Roger added, "Yow, ever' once in a while a girl would quietly disappear from class. Nobody said much. You just knew she was off somewhere to have a baby."

At this point, Arnie joined the group. Max greeted him with "Hey, Fries. You still one a-them rich snobs from south Florida?"

"I don't know, Max-a-million. Yesterday my broker bought four hunnerd shares-a futures in telephone booths. Don't think that'll turn out too well."

Todd turned back to the subject. "I knew for sure times had really changed when my youngest, Kelly, brought home her high school newspaper. Imagine my surprise when I read a graphic article on 'Facts You Should Know About Oral Sex.' It had stuff about birth control, abortion, and so forth. Couldn't believe it."

"You people know what the best-kept secret from teenagers was when we were in high school?" Arnold asked. "When the Food and Drug Administration approved the first birth control pill in 1960."

THE HOOSIER GAME

"I'm guessin' I missed that memo," Max remarked.

Todd chimed in, "I think the school administration and parents embargoed the news release. I didn't know about it till I was in college. Couldn't afford a girlfriend by that time, anyway."

Pointing to a yearbook photo of the 1961 Christmas Dance, Mary noted the "up close and personal" slow-dancing style of Max and Donna Jo.

"Yeah," said Max, "That was the night we fell in love."

Donna Jo smiled broadly at the memory.

"Good thing ole Miss Mitchel didn't see you two. She'd a throwed you both out for fornicators," Dale joked.

Max recalled a subject that had had the class of '62 up in arms.

"Weren't we the first class not allowed to write on our cords?"

It was traditional for seniors to write messages and sign their names in permanent ink on their pale yellow corduroy pants and skirts. Some would create clever drawings and other artwork.

However, several members of the previous senior class had written ribald humor and traced obscene cartoons on their cords. The miscreants were duly punished by what the students termed the school Gestapo. From that time forward, only plain cords were allowed.

"Student Council complained to Mr. Oberfeldt, but he wouldn't budge. I was really put out about it."

Laughing at the absurdity of the generational rift of the time, the banter turned to memories of former teachers.

"Teachers looked much older then, and more serious," Margaret Lammer commented. "I realized later they really weren't. But it certainly seemed like it."

Those in the small group recalled certain peculiarities of their former mentors.

"Do you remember Mrs. Rousch, the art teacher who always had her hair up in a bun? And she wore that same faded, moth-eaten green sweater ever' day."

"Miss Himmelfennig wore hers in a tight bun, too. Looked like her eyes was buggin' out of her head."

"And she had that heavy German accent. She always blurted out 'Ach!' when she was frustrated."

"I thought she was a Nazi."

Roger spoke of the attention-getting tactics of his health and safety teacher. "Old Coach Spillner, he'd chuck erasers or chalk at you if you wasn't payin' attention in class. Bounced one off-a my head more 'n once."

"Miss McGinn was always clearin' her throat. You felt like she was doin' it because you were up to somethin' wrong and she'd caught you," said Max of his former social studies teacher.

"I'll never forget Mrs. Tansing making Rhonda Smith stand in the wastebasket because she was giggling in class. She said, 'Act like trash, you'll be treated like trash!' Can you imagine if teachers tried to get away with that today?"

"Remember that dorky Mr. Ezzard, tryin' to motivate us with his corny, 'Get outta' the mustard and ketch-up' line?"

Tim Doring recalled a paddling administered to him by the notorious "chairman of the board," Mr. Callisey.

"In seventh grade, we'd just come in from the playground. We was always squirrelly before class started, and he'd git all mad. To get our attention that day he pounded his fist on the desk and hollered, 'Quiet! The next peep I hear from anyone, you're gonna get it!'"

Tim went on. "I swear I didn't think, didn't plan it or nothin'. My lips, on their own, hollered 'Peep!' I was in the first row so the paddlin' machine jerked me outta my seat, told me to bend over and whacked my butt so hard I still cain't sit down right.

"Ever'body got dead silent. But they all had a good laugh at me later."

Josh was intrigued by the peaceful, mellow feelings gripping him now. Sharing memories of the past had revived in him agreeable sentiments for those days long ago. It was like wistful times as a child, lying on his back in the grass as a gentle breeze of a warm spring day feathered over him. Beneath an azure sky, he'd imagined seeing shapes and faces in the brilliant white cumulous clouds floating above.

Each successive conversation affirmed the goodness and simple decency of these people with whom he had grown up so many years ago. He had forgotten friends like those gathered here today, along with the quiet, unheralded teachers and coaches, who had contributed in both pronounced and subtle ways to his development as a youth. Josh felt a new appreciation for how special growing up in Morgans Awe had been.

However, by the very nature of the beast, a reunion such as this limited meaningful discussion. As he drifted among his classmates, Josh noted that most conversations regarding any topic beyond the memories of school years were meandering and shallow. Attempting to condense fifty years of life into a fifteen-minute chat proved to be futile.

THE HOOSIER GAME

Judging by the superficial exchange of social pleasantries, Josh sensed that his classmates hadn't traveled from places far and near only to renew relationships with one another. Beneath the laughter and propriety lay an undercurrent of sadness. As adults, these familiar strangers appeared to be collectively mourning a time now gone, never to return.

Excusing himself, Josh moved into the dining room to encounter another cluster of classmates. He offered his hand to thrice-married and divorced Sherry O'Neal, who instead pulled him close, saying, "None of this shakin' hands for me, Josh. I come from a long line a' huggers."

"Have you seen Pat, yet?" Sherry asked, right on cue. Josh had already spotted the person with whom he most wanted to visit.

"I just noticed her over there. Would you folks excuse me for a minute?"

4

ICH LIEBE DICH

Jourden Arena
7:44 p.m.

The Madison Central team entered the arena like the Earp Brothers and Doc Holliday striding through the streets of Tombstone. The players exhibited a confident, intimidating air as they trotted unhurriedly onto the court. Looking into the steely eyes of scowling faces, Josh felt as if every one of them had a personal grudge against him. Like you had stolen their girlfriend or beaten up their little brother.

Through their self-assured demeanor the Cougars warned opponents that this was their turf and that intruders would not be treated kindly.

The Madison cheer block blustered:

> *"That's our team,*
> *The best in the land.*
> *Come on fans,*
> *Let's give 'em a hand!"*

Madison Central had earned the right to be arrogant. Few high schools in Indiana matched the Cougars' basketball legacy. Three-time winners of the state tournament and once a runner-up, Central had been a consistent top-ten team over the years.

During the past decade, no Indiana high school had a higher winning percentage than the Cougars. In his eleventh season at Madison Central, Saul Fortune's record—220 wins, 33 losses, an 87 percent success rate—ranked among the best of Hoosier high school mentors. This year MCHS had beaten all twenty-two of their regular season opponents including several of the better teams in the state.

THE HOOSIER GAME

While Morgans Awe had posted a 20-2 regular-season slate, there was no comparing the difficulty of the two teams' scheduled competition. Despite impressive wins over two ranked squads—Seymour Jefferson and Indianapolis McCormack high schools—most of the Raiders' victories were over opponents considered mediocre by state standards. Although MAHS was among the highest-scoring units in the state—averaging more than eighty points per game—the team was untested in a game of this magnitude. Besides, Morgans Awe had never won even one sectional championship.

A statewide consensus of sportswriters had selected Madison Central as the favorite to win the state championship. Among that number were two veteran observers of high school basketball, Will Peck and Merle Hollings of WKIN radio, Louisville, who would be bringing the play-by-play account from courtside to their listeners in the Kentuckiana area.

"Welcome, Indiana High School basketball fans," began Peck, "to the championship game of the 1962 Madison sectional from historic Thomas Jourden Arena on the banks of the Ohio River. I'm here with my sidekick for the contest and the voice of the Louisville Cardinals, Merle Hollings. Merle, we have the makings of a classic confrontation so familiar to Hoosier hoops fans tonight in this meeting of the highly-favored Madison Central Cougars and Coach Mike O'Ryan's spunky little Raiders from Morgans Awe."

"Right you are, Will," Hollings joined in. "The matchup of the city boys of Madison—population 12,335—against the darkhorse from the small farming community of 680 embodies the charm and allure of the Indiana State tournament. This game has the aura of the David versus Goliath theme so beloved by Hoosier basketball fans."

Continued Will, "Another intriguing aspect of the impending clash is the contrasting styles of the two coaches. On one hand you have Saul Fortune, a product and advocate of the 'Hinkle System' against the 'hell-bent-for-leather,' fast-break style of Morgans Awe Coach Mike O'Ryan. The two coaches couldn't be more different in their approach to the game."

Standing five foot seven, his swarthy complexion accented by heavy facial stubble, Saul Fortune stalked the MCHS sideline. A darkly handsome man, Fortune's neatly coiffed hair and prominent eyebrows complemented sparkling black eyes that became slits, virtual weapons, when focused on the misdeeds of his players. Well groomed and stylish in his dress, he always coached games wearing a well-tailored suit, white shirt, and tie.

Fortune was a disciple of his former Butler University coach Tony Hinkle. A living legend, Hinkle had a surpassing influence on Indiana basketball in the 1950s and 60s. Many of the best high school coaches across Indiana employed some facsimile of the "Hinkle system."

Because his Butler teams generally lacked the size of their opponents, the wizened coach emphasized pattern basketball. Hinkle employed a relentless variety of cuts, screens, and multiple passes to create drives to the basket or space for open jump shots. His structured offense required players to excel in the fundamentals of the game.

Coach Fortune stressed patience, discipline, and adherence to his conservative offensive strategy. His approach relied on low-risk decisions by the players to minimize turnovers. "Basketball is simply a game of turns," he was fond of saying. "You get a turn, we get a turn. The team that makes the most of its turns wins the game."

Combining rugged rebounding strength and a furious, lock-down man-to-man defense, the Cougars severely tested the will of their foes. Opponents had averaged only thirty-four points per game against the stifling Madison Central gauntlet.

In contrast, Coach O'Ryan was an advocate of the Branch McCracken "Hurryin' Hoosiers" school of basketball. Emphasizing quickness, rebound positioning, sharp passing, and accurate, on-the-run decision-making, McCracken's teams consistently led the Big Ten Conference in scoring.

The fast break was key to the Raiders' success. In fifteen years of coaching high school basketball, O'Ryan's attacking style had resulted in 248 wins in 300 games.

O'Ryan's offensive patterns provided organization; but he taught players to recognize when to depart from the system as opportunities developed. Basketball, in his view, was a game of constant motion with continually changing circumstances within the ebb and flow of action. He believed that too much order resulted in automatons blindly repeating rehearsed movements.

Departing from the set offense involved risk-taking. Essential to O'Ryan's coaching philosophy was developing players who were not afraid to fail. The offensive scheme was not for timid boys who dreaded embarrassing themselves, those who feared the hazards of making mistakes. The coach would excuse errors of commission but railed at errors of omission, of not being bold and aggressive.

Notwithstanding the heavy odds against his squad, Michael O'Ryan was as certain as he had ever been as a coach that on this night, in this place, the biggest upset of the tournament was about to happen.

May 5, 2012
Morgans Awe

Patricia Sargossa and Josh had been steadies during high school. Following graduation, it became evident when they went off to college—Pat attending Indiana University and Josh, Berea College in Kentucky—their relationship

THE HOOSIER GAME

would change. Both had aspirations well beyond Morgans Awe. They remained in close touch for a time. But as diverging paths widened, their correspondence waned.

A few years ago Josh and Pat ran into each at O'Hare International in Chicago. They talked for over two hours, Pat nearly missing her flight. The two hadn't been in contact since.

Pat was chatting with classmates June Brillig and Martha Jane Coster when Josh approached from behind.

"—and I couldn't believe my eyes!" June exclaimed. "We'd flown to Dallas in the fall of '95 to visit with George's sister and to watch his nephew, Gary, play linebacker for the Longhorns. We drove to Garland where they lived. At around six, we were sittin' in the living room. I looked up and there you were, Pat, in living color on the TV screen!

"I jumped up, screaming, 'I went to high school with her! She was in my graduating class!'"

Confused, sister Clara asked, "Who?"

"Pat Sargossa! Only your name was Randell. They all thought I was nuts 'til George recognized you, too. You were so pretty and professional. I almost got in the car and drove down to the studio to see you."

"If I knew you were that close, June," Pat smiled, "I would have driven to Garland to connect with you, too."

Pat had retired in 2006 as newscast co-anchor for WHTX-TV in Plano, Texas. She had arrived during the television era when attractive female journalists were being sought as co-anchors with the seasoned male commentators who had traditionally dominated anchor positions.

While her good looks may have gotten her in the door, Pat had risen to her lofty position through intelligence, hard work, and persistence. She was an esteemed member of her profession.

Martha Jane commented, "I'd heard or read that you were a broadcast news anchor—maybe it was in the Madison paper—but I never knew where you were. How was it that you got into television?"

"Honestly, it was the weekend that John Kennedy was assassinated," Pat replied. "My roommate and I were watching TV in the dorm suite on our floor. Like everybody else in the country we were shocked when Walter Cronkite came on to announce President Kennedy hadn't survived. I still remember Cronkite slowly removing his glasses, sighing, and then saying, 'President Kennedy died at 1 p.m., Central Standard Time.' Of course, we all just collapsed in tears.

"It was that moment that I was inspired to be a female Walter Cr—"

"Josh Seaberg!" shouted June.

Josh blushed, not knowing for certain who the woman was.

"Hi!" he quickly answered.

The women greeted him glowingly.

Looking over her shoulder, Pat recognized Josh immediately. Delighted, she stood and lifted her arms toward him. The two shared a warm, albeit brief, embrace.

"Hi, Pat. How are you?"

"Fine, Josh! You look great. It's so good to see you!"

The years had been agreeable to Pat. She appeared much younger than sixty-seven. Her thick, once-naturally raven hair was now entirely silver, trimmed neatly in a moderately short bob. Always poised and dignified, Pat wore a stylish navy blue jacket and pants.

High cheekbones and shimmering black eyes accentuated her classic beauty. Her gentle smile was enhanced by the brilliant white of her perfect teeth. No cosmetic surgery had disturbed Pat's unblemished face. Slight wrinkles at the corners of her eyes suggested a mature but not an elderly woman. Kind eyes and a genial sense of humor provided a window into her caring disposition.

In high school she had stood five-ten. Girls who weren't petite in that era generally were uncomfortable with their height. Invariably those girls would subtly stoop or slouch, hoping to be inconspicuous in a crowd. Pat always stood erect, calm and self-assured. Even today she was strikingly well-proportioned, at ease in her statuesque frame.

With her grace and peaceful bearing, she appeared almost regal. A teacher who had both Pat and Josh in class as seniors, noting their close relationship, paid her a tribute he'd not forgotten. Speaking to Josh between classes, Mrs. Chamblee said of her, "Pat wasn't high-born, but she's well-bred."

Her familiar gestures, expressions, and vocal inflections seemed little changed from those of the admirable person Pat had been as a young woman. After greeting Josh, June and Martha Jane subtly moved away, sensing that the former high school sweethearts might wish to talk alone.

"We'll catch up with you two later."

Josh and Pat moved to a nearby sofa. Their conversation was comfortable and flowed easily. Josh handed Pat a photograph of his one grandchild, Carrie, and Lisa, his daughter. Josh and wife Amanda had divorced in 1998.

"They're lovely," Pat said softly. "Where are Lisa and Carrie now?"

THE HOOSIER GAME

"Lisa lives less than twenty minutes from her mother in Milwaukee. She's an attorney for the Mander Charitable Foundation."

Josh felt keenly the failure of his only marriage. He and Amanda Karnes met at Berea when Josh was a senior and she a sophomore. They had wed shortly after her graduation, but had parted not long after their thirty-first anniversary.

"You know, Pat, the day of our high school graduation I kind of offhandedly asked my dad for his advice about the future. Dad looked at me and said, 'Life's hard, son.' I said, 'C'mon, Pop, you gotta give me more than that!'"

Josh shook his head and with a wry grin, said, "I didn't realize at the time how profound that simple wisdom was."

"We couldn't have known how really naïve we were then, Josh."

Pat hadn't married until she was almost thirty. She had found stability and contentment in southwest Texas where she lived with her rancher husband of thirty-five years, Daniel Randell. Together they'd reared three children and now enjoyed the rewards of being grandparents to girls Susannah, Rebeccah, and Hannah, and grandsons Danny, Doak, and Derek.

She adored her husband.

"Dan's honest, sincere, hard-working, and holds his faith and family as his top priorities. He has a well-balanced, serene view of the world. I just have so much admiration for Daniel and how his parents raised him."

"That's great to hear, Pat. Tell me about your kids and grandchildren."

At that moment, above the noise of chattering classmates, the opening lyrics of a song well known to both caught their attention:

Wise men say,
Only fools rush in,
But I can't help falling in love with you.

Both smiled warmly in recognition of a love song that was once special to them. In December 1961, Josh and Pat had driven to Madison to see the movie *Blue Hawaii*, starring Elvis. Holding hands in the flickering dark of the theater, they had adopted the song as their own.

In recalling their past relationship, there would be no unseemly effort at stirring up a fantasy from their teenage years. Theirs was a shared, heartfelt esteem for one another. Each delighted in mutual memories of an age of fun and innocence.

"Pat, I never told you how embarrassed I was when I picked you up on our first date."

"What do you mean?"

"Well, first I was intimidated by the large, lovely home you lived in. When I knocked on the door, this scowling, six-foot-five muscle man answered. I was afraid he was going to body-slam me just for having the gall to ask his daughter out on a date."

"You weren't the first guy my father scared like that," Pat chuckled. "He invited me in. But it was like he'd asked a known felon to sit at the dinner table. Your mom was so beautiful and warm and welcoming. While we waited for you, I sat down on the couch. And then it happened."

"What?"

"My stomach began to growl. It wasn't any ordinary, momentary, after-lunch rumble. This was a full-blown, Niagara Falls-over-an-amplifier kind'a roar. I used my stomach muscles pushing in and out to try to stop it. It just kept going on. I'd rather have had acupuncture on my eyeballs than endure that humiliation.

"Your parents smiled—even your dad—to try to make me feel less self-conscious. What a nightmare!"

"I didn't know that! But I do remember the time when you were the maddest you ever were with me."

Josh clearly recalled that bizarre evening with Pat.

"*Nein. Nein.*" he responded, using one of only two Deutsche words in his vocabulary. (The other was *Gesundheit.*)

"We spent an entire evening together and you never spoke a word of English. Drove—me—nuts!"

Pat had enrolled in an after-school class in conversational German taught by Miss Himmelfennig. To help her students develop confidence in the language the old frau had instructed each to speak nothing but German when in each other's presence.

"*Entschuldigung. Verstehen Sie? Wieviel Uhr ist es?*" Pat asked Josh, giggling.

"Yes, I got no bananas," he answered mockingly. "I don't suppose you're telling me I won the Clearing House Sweepstakes?"

"*Nein*, Joshua. I was so proud of myself that I stayed on task the whole evening. I made mistakes with the language, but you didn't have a clue when I did."

"Dirty trick. Most frustrating date I ever had. I went to kiss you goodnight and you said 'I'll feeder shame,' or something like that."

THE HOOSIER GAME

"*Auf Weidersehen! Gute Nacht, Bis Morgen.*"

"What does that mean?"

"Look it up," Pat added, her lilting laughter pleasant to the ear.

"What you didn't hear, Josh, was what I said as I closed the door. '*Ich liebe dich.*'"

"I know that one. 'You got zits on your nose.'"

"Nice try."

"You've got to admit, though, I had a pretty clever comeback," Josh said proudly.

"That you did. At my seventeenth birthday party. Mom and Dad, my older sister and her husband, and two of my girlfriends were there. You handed me a gift and a card, then tried to say '*Herzlichen Gluckwunsch zum Geburtstag!*' What came out was something like 'Hers lickin' Gluckwench zoom get burger stag.' To this day, that was the most pathetic attempt at speaking German that I've ever heard."

"Well, you should have given me some credit for trying to say 'Happy Birthday.'"

"I have to admit it was cute."

A new cadre of former schoolmates gathered around Pat and Josh, greeting both enthusiastically. Before consigning themselves to visiting with others, Josh and Pat agreed to sit together at the reunion dinner.

Jake's ex-wife, Jill Harrison Skoon, abruptly appeared at Josh's side. They embraced for several seconds before he offered, "How are you doing, Jill?"

Jill had been the cutest of the Morgans Awe High School varsity cheerleaders with a petite, curvaceous body built to stir the hormones of teenage boys. Naturally, she and Jake—the spunky cheerleader and the team star—gravitated toward one another. They were like royalty in the high school society of the sixties.

Their marriage had lasted eight tumultuous years until finally Jill gave up her attempts to raise Jake from his persistent adolescence into adulthood. With his identity wrapped solely in the game of basketball, Jake never could get beyond his days as a high school hero. Nothing ever fulfilled Jake's self-regard as high school basketball had. He clung to past glories in the absence of any meaningful success as an adult.

After the divorce, neither had remarried. They'd remained close until he died.

Her once shiny blond curls had returned to their natural brunette color and were now trimmed to a very short length. As is often the case with the most attractive and popular girls in high school, the adult Jill was plump, her body altered by time and genetics. The wrinkles in her roundish face and a somewhat sad, subdued smile were a testament to a worried life.

Jill's two adult children had accompanied her to the reunion. She introduced Jennifer, now in her mid-forties, who bore a striking resemblance to her dad. Deep-set brown eyes and her broad, toothy, dimpled smile was unmistakably Jake's. Jason, her younger brother, looked more like his mom, his face punctuated with penetrating blue eyes and a pug nose. Josh had not seen them since the funeral, when both were in elementary school.

Eyes welling up with tears, Jill dabbed at her eyes with a tissue. As she began to speak of her former husband, her pain seemed just as raw as the last time Josh had seen her, three decades ago.

"Oh, Josh—" was as far as she got before her throat involuntarily constricted and she fell into his arms, sobbing softly.

5

BLUE EYES CRYING IN THE RAIN

Jourden Arena
7:56 p.m.

Now back in the locker room, Jake Skoon sat calmly, a basketball in his abnormally large hands. He alternated between spinning the ball on one finger and shooting phantom shots into the air. His detached expression belied a competitive spirit and obstinate resolve.

Jake had prepared for this moment. How often had he played alone on a compact dirt surface, imitating his heroes against imaginary foes? Dribbling, feinting, pivoting, then shooting a worn rubber basketball at the hoop nailed to the barn, the young Skoon had hit thousands of game-winning shots in his imagination.

The contest against Madison meant so much to Jake. Perhaps too much. To win would bring personal glory and lifelong approval from citizens in Morgans Awe for as long as basketball was played there. The consequences of losing were grave beyond the actual importance of the game.

All season long he had faced defenses designed to frustrate and provoke him. Opposing coaches had double- and triple-teamed Jake, employed box-and-one and triangle-and-two zones, and used half- and full-court pressure to disrupt his rhythm. Larger and more physical defenders were assigned to bump and bruise him, and smaller, quicker boys to harass him constantly.

None of those approaches had completely hindered Jake for an entire game. Coach O'Ryan's superb capacity for devising clever ways to counter those defenses enabled Skoon to display his remarkable shooting touch.

Observing Jake's jump shot was to appreciate all the fundamentals of form that coaches tried to teach their players. He had developed his smooth shooting motion as a youngster, tossing a tennis ball into a wire-mesh sieve he had swiped from his mom's kitchen.

From fingertips directly above his head, Jake released his shot at the apex of an impressive vertical jump. It was at this point that his inexplicable, near-perfect hand-eye coordination set him apart.

The ball arced high into the air, its trajectory in perfect accord with the basket. With stunning regularity, the basketball settled softly into the net with the barely audible "pop" characteristic of the faultless shot.

Morgans Awe resident Conrad Oliver had been blind for more than half of his sixty-six years. A lifetime season ticket holder, he never missed a Raiders home game. He contended that the most pleasing sound was just as Jake would launch his deadly jumper. Conrad could tell it was Jake because the supporters of both teams would become deathly silent for seconds, holding their breath in anticipation. If the ball went in, the Morgans Awe crowd would react with unified bedlam. A miss was followed by a drawn out "Awwwww," mixed with shrieks of disbelief. Despite never actually having seen Jake shoot, Oliver claimed, "Skoon could throw a basketball through a donut hole."

On this evening Jake Skoon was wired. His normally expressive eyes were hard and focused. He lived for the opportunity to measure his skills against top-flight players, to prove he belonged with the basketball elite in Indiana.

The last time Josh had seen his best friend so intense was earlier in the season prior to the game against Jeffersonville Manning High, a school three times the size of Morgans Awe. A veteran player on that team had openly questioned Skoon's abilities in the city's local newspaper.

"Skoon's like a lot of those small-town guys who score a bunch of points against other Podunk schools," the brash teen was quoted. "We'll see how he does against a real defense."

Jake exploded for 42 points that night, most coming against the player who had made those reckless comments. Sensing the confidence and passion of his teammate sitting next to him, Josh thought privately, "What Jake will do tonight even I would pay admission to see."

Coach O'Ryan signaled his players to gather at the chalkboard. Across the top of the green slate, written in bold white letters, was this:

NEVER BE HAUGHTY TO THE HUMBLE.
NEVER BE HUMBLE TO THE HAUGHTY.

BLUE EYES CRYING IN THE RAIN

Below that was the Madison starting lineup.

F	#23	Hankins
F	#45	Weatherford
C	#50	DeVreaux
G	#3	Miller
G	#10	Wells

Coach O'Ryan took his seat on a stool adjacent to the chalkboard. His head panned slowly from player to player, making eye contact with each boy in turn.

Breaking the silence, O'Ryan spoke in a calm unwavering voice.

"Men, I need your advice."

A pause of about ten seconds seemed like minutes to the players.

"If you doubt that we can beat this team, tell me now. If you're satisfied to be in the championship game but you don't expect to win, then say so now and I'll coach you to finish second."

The teenagers didn't know how to react. What was he saying?

Michael O'Ryan had a consistent record of beating seemingly superior teams, but it wasn't trophies or the praise of a fickle public that appealed to him. O'Ryan embraced the role of underdog, a man against the odds. Coach welcomed the valiant struggle of battling a worthy foe in a fair contest. His greatest reward in coaching was developing young men to reach beyond their perceived abilities to experience improbable success.

He also knew the pain of falling short, inches from victory, losing out in the waning moments. Though each loss permanently tore away a piece of him, it stoked the fires of resolve to strive anew.

The coach continued. "Morgans Awe history is against you. The teams that the townspeople remember best—the ones that almost beat River Forest in 1944 or came close to upsetting Central in '52, or would have gone to the state if Dolan hadn't fouled out in '58—were still losers.

"If Madison wins tonight—especially if you come close—you'll have all the excuses you need. Locals and family members will tell you how great you are, how the referees robbed you, or that you had an off night and would have won if you'd played your usual game. Then they'll forget you and start talking about next year.

"Lads, it's the winners who are remembered, not the 'come-close-ers.' So what's it gonna be? Do you believe in yourselves?"

A few players stirred and answered, "Yes!"

"Will we win this game?"

The entire team yelled in unison, "YES!"

THE HOOSIER GAME

Jake Skoon (4) "...could shoot a basketball through a donut hole."

"So you don't mind if I coach to win the sectional championship?"

A raucous response and grins all around at Coach O'Ryan's mock request assured him they were ready.

May 5, 2012
Morgans Awe

Regaining her composure, Jill apologized to Josh for losing control of the raw emotions lying just beneath the surface.

"Even though Jake's been gone all these years, I still think of what we missed together," Jill lamented. "If I'd just hung on, maybe Jake would've found a doctor that could've helped him."

"Jill, really, you did all you could."

"He was a troubled man, Josh. But he did leave me with two great kids. Jennifer married a good guy. Paul has provided well for his family. They have two girls, Leah and Jessica. Jen is a maternity ward nurse at Methodist Hospital in Indy. Loves her job.

"I hate to admit it, but I didn't encourage Jason to play sports. From little on, people in town expected him to be a star player like his dad. But he just never had the interest. Jason got his architectural degree from Ball State. He's with the Gormes architectural company in Louisville. Jake would've been so pr—"

Josh pulled Jill close as her voice broke. She again dissolved into tears.

It was then Josh recalled that brisk autumn day in 1975 when his old friend showed up at his office.

Saturday, October 11, 1975
Oxford, Ohio

Josh was an untenured associate professor of history at the university in Oxford. He had been teaching a weekend course the afternoon Jake Skoon appeared unexpectedly at his door.

"Dr. Joshua Seaberg!" Jake cried as he swept into the small room, embracing his former teammate with an enthusiastic hug.

Both stood there, momentarily grasping for words equal to the occasion. Grinning widely, they simultaneously blurted out an animated "How are you?"

Josh was shocked to see Jake appallingly overweight, at least seventy pounds heavier than since he had last seen his high school friend. Jake's fleshy double chin and bloated cheeks were so uncharacteristic of the man who once carried 145 pounds on a six-two frame. His cheeks and bulbous nose were tarnished by acute rosacea. Jake's eyes were rimmed in red from a recent hangover or insomnia—or both. His midsection hung grossly over his belt and his thinning hair was prematurely gray.

Josh noticed bits of Jake's breakfast dried onto the lapel of his out-of-style Nehru jacket. His arms protruded from sleeves far too short. Mismatched trousers and scuffed shoes completed the ensemble.

After an awkward interlude of trivial chitchat, Jake suggested the two go across the street to Reinie's Bar and Grill. As they slipped into a booth, Josh asked in a lowered voice meant to seek a serious conversation, "How is life, Jake? Are you doing okay?"

His corpulent companion responded with a shrill, overly enthusiastic and utterly fabricated, "Couldn't be better, Josh. Everything's just great!"

Jake's false front of self-confidence and too-friendly manner was sorrowfully transparent. He had not called, written, or spoken to Josh in many years. It was evident to Josh that Jake wanted something.

Former teammates had alerted Josh to his friend's insensible lack of responsibility. Jake was still trying to trade on a name recalling past glories of high school, a name that was now more infamous than acclaimed. He was deeply in debt, always looking at the next opportunity to make easy money.

The people around Morgans Awe who had loaned him money, or employed him until he eventually failed as a result of his frequent absences, had learned to avoid him. Jake's life had become a continuous loop of missed appointments, empty promises, and banal betrayals. He found solace in local bars where so-called friends sat for hours drinking next to Jake and recalling his glory days as a Raider.

Nowadays, Jake was mostly in search of his next shot of Jack Daniels or seeking cash for his latest get-rich-quick scheme.

"What did you think of the state championship game?" Jake interjected, failing to consider that Josh hadn't seen an Indiana high school game in years.

Reaching for something to relate to this veritable stranger, Josh asked, "How are Jill and the kids? They are what now, ten, eleven?"

"Jennifer was twelve last month. She's a beauty. And Jason will be ten in December. He starts Cub League basketball in a couple weeks. He can fire it up there. I think he's gonna be just like me."

Actually, Jake hardly knew his kids. Since he and Jill had divorced Jake rarely came around. He steadily missed child support payments. It was not that different from when they were married. Jake's shiftlessness had caused Jill and the children to be constantly on the edge of poverty. He had always been more engrossed in himself than in them, anyway.

Jake steered the conversation back to high school days, a time when he was on top of a teenager's world. Josh listened politely, though cheerlessly, as his former best friend scrambled to find something the two had in common besides high school memories.

Not long into his third Killian's Red, Jake abruptly began to enthuse about a project he was working on, one that "can't miss."

"Josh, things are really turning around for me. I've got this great opportunity I just gotta tell you about."

He was on the verge, he claimed, of breaking ground on Skoon's Motel in Morgans Awe, which would be a shrine dedicated to the exploits of past Raiders basketball teams and heroes—especially that great '62 squad—and Jake Skoon.

For courtesy's sake, Josh listened with feigned interest. The notion was so absurd it might have been laughable had it not been so pathetic. If a trustworthy, discerning person proposed a serious project, Josh might have asked relevant questions and offered genuine encouragement. But it was fruitless to reason with the impractical dreamer Jake had become.

Even if Morgans Awe could support such a venture, Jake had no proven business instincts. He had never created a business plan, nor did he have the capital necessary to launch such a project.

But he clumsily asked Josh for a loan nonetheless. Josh was not positioned to make such an investment, even one that had promise of success. It was an act of desperation for Jake to impose on his former best friend.

"I only need another $50,000 or so to make it go, Josh."

It might have been Josh's silence and unintended expression of pity that brought Jake back to reality. Jake seemed to recognize in that brief moment how low he had sunk. Both men were embarrassed—Josh for Jake, and Jake for himself.

As Seaberg groped for an appropriate response to politely decline his friend's request Jake quickly reverted to his smiling, jovial persona of only minutes ago. He made a few shallow, inane comments in an effort to regain his dignity. With a brief acknowledgment of his delight in seeing Josh again, he left as quickly and surprisingly as he had come.

It was the last time he saw Jake alive.

THE HOOSIER GAME

Just one month later, Josh had received a telephone call from a distraught Jill Skoon. Heart-broken, she could barely be understood through her sobs. Jake was dead.

Before Josh could gather any further information or offer condolences, Jill hung up.

Wednesday, November 12, 1975
Morgans Awe

Josh arrived late for the funeral service that had drawn him back to Morgans Awe on that raw November day. The dreary gray backdrop was fitting.

Stepping out of the car into a chilly drizzle, Josh leaned bareheaded into the wind. He pulled the collar of his trench coat tightly around his neck.

A startling flash of lightning split the sky, a sinister hiss warning of its immediate proximity. The deafening crackle of the thunderbolt followed instantly. A low rumbling sound like that of kettledrums gradually retreated from the area. Then stillness, save for the rustling of the trees and the plip-plop of raindrops all around.

The memorial service had already begun. A small blue tent stood beside the gravesite, periodically buffeted by abrupt gusts of wind. A handful of folding chairs within the cramped space were reserved for family and close friends. Jill Skoon sat in front, weeping silently as her young children sat by her side. Beside the tent, a dark mahogany casket, Jake's final earthly abode, sat suspended over the burial site.

Quietly Josh melded with three dozen sober-faced mourners who had come to witness the interment of a man once applauded by throngs of people. Spotting Jamie Ross, he moved to his former teammate's side.

Bobby Harrison, Jill's brother, was playing guitar and singing Willie Nelson's mournful ballad.

In the twilight glow I see her,
Blue eyes crying in the rain.
When we kissed goodbye and parted,
I knew we'd never meet again.
Love is like a dying ember,

BLUE EYES CRYING IN THE RAIN

And only memories remain.
And through the ages I'll remember,
Blue eyes crying in the rain.

The lyrics seemed eerily suitable for the occasion. Jill Skoon—she of the ice-blue eyes—and Jake had parted two years ago. The effects of Jake's unbearable self-loathing, fueling his chronic depression, had finally driven Jill to sue for divorce.

Josh was barely conscious of the pastor's graveside homily and the muffled sobs around him. He felt his breast constricting as he thought about his friend's wretched adult years.

"Yea, though I walk through the valley of the shadow of death, I will fear no evil, for thou art with me. Thy rod and—"

Tears fell and sniffles were audible as the minister concluded the rite. The memorial service had been especially somber, lacking the usual celebration of the life of the deceased. The shocking circumstances of Jake's death made palpable the grief of those assembled around the gravesite. Jake's tormented, sometimes pathetic life's journey was at an end.

Those who knew Jake best told of his increasing despair in the latter months of what he perceived was a failed life. Dying at his own hand in such a swift and unexpected manner, Jake left behind an especially tortuous grief for his bewildered loved ones.

Jill had encouraged him to seek professional help for his feelings of desperation and hopelessness. But Jake was too proud to confide in a stranger about his emotional exhaustion. Finally, seeking ultimate relief, Jake chose to leap into an unknown oblivion rather than tolerate any longer the constant repetition of his own personal hell on earth.

Suicide was rare in small, intimate, tradition-minded communities like Morgans Awe. Jake's family and friends were burdened with unwanted—and unfair—self-introspection. Jill was left to confront her indescribable heartache, guilt, embarrassment, and anger. The unanswerable questions haunted her. *Should I have acted sooner or more forcibly as his moods turned darker? How could he do this to me? To our family? How will I explain this messy, inexplicable act to well-meaning but curious friends?*

Following the brief graveside service, Reverend Collins announced on behalf of the Skoon family that all were invited to a luncheon at the nearby United Methodist Church.

Josh and Jamie greeted one another with subdued but genuine warmth. Chatting in lowered voices, the two men agreed to drive together to the wake.

"Man," Jamie said wistfully, "What a shame."

"It is sad. But Jamie, it really doesn't surprise me that Jake took his own life."

Steering through the cemetery gates, Josh told his former classmate about the recent visit he'd had with Skoon.

"I couldn't shake the feeling that he was in severe emotional stress and a danger to himself. When he asked for an investment in his motel project, you could just sense the desperation he felt in lowering himself to hit up an old friend for money. I hadn't even given him an answer when he suddenly changed back to his mask, all self-confidence and optimism. Now I feel like I let him down, Moon. I didn't take the opportunity to offer help, to try to reason with him. I was just glad to see him leave."

Painfully saddened, Jamie merely shook his head in sympathy, adding, "It sounds as if nothing could have helped him at that point."

Arriving at the church, Jake and Jamie descended the stairway to the social room where the meal would be served by the Methodist women's auxiliary group. Here the men met up with Jill.

Hugging both tightly, she thanked them for coming so far to be at the service.

"You always meant so much to him, Josh," she said, shedding bitter tears. "You became what he wanted to be. Jake just despised himself. I couldn't help him anymore."

"Jill, it wasn't your fault. Jake had his demons."

After a short conversation, Josh and Jamie left without eating. Neither said anything on the drive back to the cemetery. Departing for home, the disconsolate pair wished one another good luck and good health.

On the return to Oxford Josh stared vacantly as the miles passed, trying to make sense of Jake's tragic end.

6

THE GREATEST GENERATION

Jourden Arena
7:59 p.m.

Coach O'Ryan now focused on defensive assignments.

"We've worked toward this day for a year now. You will be the best-conditioned team on the floor tonight. The key for us is to be as tough mentally and physically as they are."

The coach turned toward his only junior starter, Bond Bathwaite.

"Bond, you'll take Wells, number 10."

Cole Wells was the Cougars' captain and chief ball-handler, the playmaker on offense. He darted about the court like a hornet in a bad mood. The stocky 5-10 senior didn't score often. But his gift for penetrating an opponent's defense, then passing to an open teammate, was exceptional.

"Get in his jersey as soon as he crosses mid-court," O'Ryan continued. "Try to force him to the middle where you'll get help. Wells looks to pass first, but he can shoot it. You have to play him tight, okay?"

"Got it, coach."

"Sonny, you'll guard number three. You've seen how Miller favors his left hand on the dribble, so overplay him, force him to his right. He's always looking for his corner jumper. He doesn't drive the baseline very often so stay tight on him on the outside."

Despite standing only 5-11, Watkins often drew the opponent's best offensive player. At 6-4, Marty Miller held a decided height advantage over Sonny.

Wells's backcourt mate was deadly accurate with his push shot. His range of fifteen to twenty-five feet gave the Cougars a consistent weapon from the outside. Unlike the jump shooter who released the ball at the apex of his vertical leap, Miller pulled the trigger with both feet on the hardwood. While Miller's shot was easier to defend, Coach Saul's

THE HOOSIER GAME

Hinkle-style offense provided a series of screens to get the slender, left-handed sharpshooter open looks at the basket.

Marty, handsome and of slender build, was a "flapper," characteristic of the cocky or self-absorbed player. After making a basket or a good play on offense, flappers return to the defensive end with an exaggerated pumping of the elbows, resembling a bird fluttering its wings. This tended to draw attention to the player, as if to say "Look at me, see what I did!"

Opponents resented a flapper's show-boating and felt the sting of his implied taunts. It often provided the motivation to press even harder to shut him down. In a culture that encouraged modesty and selfless play, Miller's self-aggrandizement provoked dislike by anyone not a Cougar fan.

"Miller doesn't like people in his face, Sonny," Coach O'Ryan emphasized. "When he's got time to square up he'll drain that jumper from anywhere. So you be on him like fleas on a junkyard dog. He's a hothead, so if you get to him early he can get rattled and take himself out of the game."

Sonny nodded, nodded, and nodded again at each point the coach made, stressing with his grim silence that he got the message.

Josh's concentration had been diverted by the muffled sounds of foot-stomping and pre-game cheering that penetrated the walls of the bunker in which the team was assembled. Wooden joists groaned and construction beams creaked amid the chaos in the arena. A tremendous roar burst above, causing the coach to pause in his instructions. An even more piercing explosion of sound followed the first one.

Josh surmised that the two schools' fans were competing in their versions of the familiar chant:

> *"Two bits, four bits, six bits, a dollar,*
> *All for Morgans Awe stand up and holler!"*

He was jolted back to the locker room at the sound of Coach's voice: "Josh, you're on number 50, DeVreaux."

The darkly-tanned, powerfully built Karl DeVreaux was 6-5 and outweighed Josh by fifty pounds. His frigid blue eyes and intimidating scowl forewarned of his rough style of play. Josh anticipated a grueling time of it. He would have to counter DeVreaux's nasty temperament and brute strength with a level head and clever play.

"DeVreaux's a load. He'll try to bully you under the basket. He'll foul someone hard early to mark his territory. Be smart. Use his aggressiveness against him. He'll bite on the head-fake, so use it, Josh. You'll be shooting some free throws tonight."

"Yeah," Josh thought ruefully, "If he doesn't tear my head off first."

As the Raiders' weakest defender, Jake Skoon was assigned to guard the opponent least likely to be an offensive threat.

"Hankins is your man, Jake, number twenty-three. On offense, he sets screens and rebounds and goes hard to the boards, but rarely takes a shot from more than five feet from the hoop. Be ready to sag off him and double-team Weatherford like we worked on in practice. But don't lose Hankins when a shot goes up because he gets a lot of garbage buckets on tips and second shots. Put a butt in his waistline, Jake."

The crucial match-up would be Mark Danner against DeWitt Weatherford. Coach O'Ryan turned to his strongest player.

"You know Weatherford's their best athlete, Hoss. He's listed as center but their offense gives him plenty of space to roam in the post. We won't stop him completely. But we have to force him out of his comfort zone in the key."

Lithe, with a muscular body, Weatherford moved with the grace of a deer. At 6-6, 185 pounds, Weatherford was among the best players in the state. Though fiercely competitive, he nonetheless was quiet and reserved, rarely changing expression during a game. He had an assassin's heart.

"Mark, you have to front him. Fight him for position. Avoid silly fouls and look for help from Jake and Josh on the backside. Sonny, sag in on Weatherford when you can. But don't drift too far off Miller."

It was a gamble putting Danner on Madison's star. Mark was the only Morgans Awe player physically equal to Madison's big men. If Danner got into foul trouble the Raiders had no one to contend with Central's towering front line.

Carrying two hundred and ten pounds on his 6-4 frame, Danner was the proverbial big ol' farm boy. Off the court he was jovial, with a devilish, dimpled grin and sparkling blue eyes beneath a thatch of reddish-orange hair. Between the lines, he served as the team's emotional leader and enforcer.

Mark Danner was tough and unflinchingly loyal. During his first game as a sophomore on the Morgans Awe varsity he'd made an indelible impression on his teammates and coaches.

A veteran player from Hillcrest High School, Roy Hall, was defending Jake with very physical, even dirty, play. When Hall knocked Skoon down on a drive to the basket Mark made a mental note of the incident. The next time Jake brought the ball up the floor, his hacking, clawing nemesis matched him step-for-step. Danner stationed himself at the ten-second line to set a pick to help Jake shed Hall. The Morgans Awe star drove the ball straight at Danner. Hall, unaware that a cold stone pillar was in his path, crashed full bore into Mark's stationary body. The collision resulted in an audible "OOOOOFF" from the defender as he slumped to the court, gasping for breath.

THE HOOSIER GAME

DeWitt Weatherford (45), "Six-foot-six, with the grace of a deer—and the conscience of an assassin."

The ref's whistle screeched. The official had detected the faintly disguised forearm Danner had thrust into the opponent's throat at the point of impact.

"Intentional foul," screamed the ref.

Pivoting toward the official, Mark looked him squarely in the eye and sneered, "That was a chicken-shit call, Stripes. An' you know it sure's there's balls on a bull."

Sorely offended by the impertinence of the 16-year-old, the ref brought his hands up in the classic "T" sign, assessing a technical foul.

Mark cracked, "You got me, Stripes. But it sure's hell weren't for lyin'."

Stammering, spittle spewing from his lips, the ref shrieked, "Y—You—You're disqualified number 50!"

Mark had gotten a ticket to the locker room for the balance of the game and a place in the hearts of his teammates for all time.

Wednesday, November 12, 1975
Oxford, Ohio

Arriving home that evening, Josh couldn't sleep. He arose from his bed at 2 a.m., went to the den, and turned on the TV. A mindless sci-fi movie crawled across the screen; but Josh neither saw nor heard it. He was engrossed in thought, half-grieving and half-cursing Jake Skoon. Jake's youth had expired, but he never grew up. He was a man so saturated in the glory of Indiana basketball that his life was meaningless without it.

"Why?" Josh spoke aloud. "Why?"

Tuesday, November 28, 1944
Southport, Indiana, and Morgans Awe

Today, neighbors in Southport drove a pregnant Betty Seaberg to St. Francis Hospital on Indianapolis's south-eastside. At half past nine, Joshua Charles Seaberg entered the world, his tiny cry spreading joy and relief to his exhausted mother. Marine corporal Marshall Seaberg would learn of his son's birth four days later on the Tarawa atoll where he was engaged in the desperate struggle for possession of that key strip of rock in the Pacific during World War II.

At that same hour, ninety miles southeast, Marvin Jacob Skoon was born to Norval and Hannah Skoon at the family farmhouse near Madison. The expectant father had paced anxiously through much of the thirteen hours that his wife had labored.

THE HOOSIER GAME

Mid-1940s to early 1950s
Southport and Morgans Awe, Indiana

The post-war America in which Josh and Jake grew up was a time of renewed hope and opportunity. Returning soldiers, young and energetic, sought the American Dream of home ownership and of the material goods not available to them before.

As one of those soldiers, Marshall Seaberg had survived three years and two months of fighting in the Pacific theatre. Following the furious battle for the island of Guadalcanal, he had received a Bronze Medal for conspicuous bravery, exposing himself to withering enemy fire as he identified strike zones for American Naval pilots.

Mr. Seaberg was a robust man, over six feet two inches tall, weighing a solid 200 pounds. He had premature flecks of gray in his dark hair, likely the result of enduring the horrors of war. Josh would never hear his dad speak of that experience or of the heroism for which he had earned his combat medal. His father hid his memories of that time somewhere in a place deep within, never to see the light of day. Quiet and studious, Seaberg was eager to begin anew the life that had been put on hold for the four years of war.

His wife, a gregarious, curious woman, was an inveterate seeker of conversation. Betty Seaberg seemed to know everyone in the neighborhood, along with the names of their children and pets. Strangers would not stay that way long in her presence. She loved to tell and listen to stories, true or embellished. Betty had a throaty, throw-back-her-head laugh that was engaging. A pretty woman, she was slightly plump, with rosy cheeks, large brown eyes, a warm smile, and a positive attitude that never flagged, even in the darkest and loneliest hours.

Among Josh's earliest memories was of his mother singing to him this childhood ditty as he lay on the bed with a burning fever.

> *"Jimmy crack corn and I don't care,*
> *Jimmy crack corn and I don't care,*
> *Jimmy crack corn and I don't care,*
> *The master's on his way."*

After the war, the Seabergs had moved into the first floor of a two-story frame house on the outskirts of Indianapolis. Their neighbors, John and

Molly, a loud and quarrelsome couple, lived in the upstairs apartment. The two families shared a single bathroom on the second floor. While inconvenient, the tiny bathroom was preferable to using an outdoor facility, as many others in the neighborhood had to do. Bathing in the cast-iron tub supported by four tiny legs, with a rubber stopper in the drain—and very little hot water available—was a constant irritant.

In the crowded living room, the central light source was a single, soft-glow bulb at the end of a long black electric cord dangling from the twelve-foot ceiling. Both the carpet and wallpaper were gaudy, mismatched patterns of flowers and swirls.

An overstuffed sofa and chair provided a sitting area where Mr. Seaberg read by the light of a floor lamp. A bulky Philco console radio with a 78-rpm record-player stood between Betty's sewing machine and a small table for the plain, black telephone.

Betty cooked meals three times daily on a relatively modern gas-burning stove. The kitchen sink had one large basin with hot and cold water spigots delivering well water from an underground spring. Unlike many young couples, the Seabergs also enjoyed the luxury of their Frigidaire.

The family clothes were laundered weekly in another newfangled appliance, the electric washing machine. Clothes swished around in a vat of detergent and water, then were rinsed in a galvanized tub of clear water (the same tub that Josh bathed in twice a week). After squeezing excess moisture from the garments with the attached wringer, Betty toted the basket outdoors and using wooden pins, hung the wash on the line to dry. During winter, Betty hung laundry on a makeshift line in the kitchen.

The residence was heated by a coal oil furnace that pushed warm air through floor vents along the walls. The pungent odor of burning kerosene evoked memories of Josh's youth that followed him well into his adult years. The warmth associated with that aroma triggered scenes of blissful, frosty winter days.

Of course, the Seabergs had no air conditioning, and in summertime, open windows and a small fan provided their only relief against the often-brutal heat and humidity of central Indiana.

As a child attending Cowan Elementary School in Southport, Josh walked three blocks from school to home for lunch. His mother was invariably listening intently to "Pick-a-Pocket," with Jim Shelton as host on Indianapolis's WIBC radio station. The flamboyant Luke Walton provided sports news. The show played music, too. "Little Jimmy" Dickens, for one, plucked a banjo and sang in his nasal twang the latest in country-western tunes. Josh loved to hear Little Jimmy whine his heart-rending lyrics of love and woe.

"It ain't no use in dreamin', cause I gotta wake up and find you." Or "He's got a way with women, and he just got away with mine."

On occasion, Betty allowed herself to listen as the host of "Queen for a Day" showered a lucky member of the audience with gifts and praise, and to dream that she herself might someday be chosen queen.

One chilly day in the fall of 1952, Josh observed a curious incident during his lunch hour. In the years after the War, it was common to see transients traveling alone—hitchhiking when possible, walking when necessary—searching desperately to find work. The unshaved, unwashed, shabbily dressed vagrant—often a veteran—sought any menial job with which he might earn enough for his next meal.

On this day, Josh was surprised to find a wretched sparrow of a man tapping on the Seabergs' back door. Nodding wordlessly to the despairing stranger Betty returned with a sandwich and a glass of milk in hand. After gulping down the lunch, the man offered to work to pay back the kindness. Josh's mother found a small chore the beggar could do, more to salve the poor man's dignity than to have the task done. It was a scene that was repeated in Josh's home several times over the years and in countless other homes as well. Government subsidies were bad words in those days, even to the poverty-stricken, and most people felt bound to help others in need.

Every August during his elementary school years Josh accompanied his mother to Washington Street in downtown Indianapolis to purchase new clothes for the coming school year. The previous year's clothing no longer fit the growing youngster. Jeans bought last summer now barely reached his ankles. The knees were frayed or patched. Slender arms protruded from long shirt sleeves that ended well above the wrists.

The itinerary never varied. First, Mrs. Seaberg window-shopped at various department stores, scrutinizing fashions and price tags for future forays on her own. If she found an appealing outfit, Betty would use a store's layaway plan. For a semi-expensive $18 dress, a down payment of three dollars reserved the garment. After paying that amount each of the next five weeks, she returned to the shop to pick it up.

THE GREATEST GENERATION

The highlight of her day was lunch, sipping Chicken Velvet Soup at the elegant L.S. Ayres Tea Room. Then it was off to Robert Hall's, where middle-class housewives brought their young to outfit them for school.

Josh knew the jingle by heart:

> *When the values go up, up, up,*
> *And the prices go down, down, down,*
> *Robert Hall this season,*
> *Will show you the reason,*
> *Low overhead, low overhead.*

His reward for being patient at the department store was a short walk down Washington Street to the White Castle. Even as a boy, Josh could devour five of the mini-burgers with extra pickles—at seven cents each—along with fries and a Coke.

Evenings found Josh playing on the living room floor as the Philco radio played in the background. His dad sat in his soft chair, his mother on the couch, reading and sewing, respectively. The family tuned into episodes of "The Inner Sanctum" ("*Creeeeeeak*") and "Fibber McGee and Molly," with the inevitable clamorous collapse of McGee's overloaded closet. The creepy voice of Lamont Cranston warned his listeners that "Only the *Shadow* knows."

Marshall took Josh to see his first basketball game when the boy was seven years old. After Homecroft Community High School had won the sectional tournament, father and son lingered to join students and other fans of the Redwings to commemorate their triumph. Josh watched, amazed, as excited high school students dragged wooden fence slats, railroad ties, and even outhouses to a hillside to be stacked and ignited. The flickering flames of the giant celebratory bonfire cast an amber glow over the crowd and on the bare branches of surrounding trees and shrubs. Spirited speeches by the victorious players and the coach, cheered hardily by the crowd, created a scene Josh would never forget.

While the Seabergs represented the conventional middle class, Jake's mother and father faced more difficult circumstances. Jake's dad, able seaman Norval Skoon had been aboard the *USS Enterprise* in August 1942 while under attack by the Japanese near the Solomon Islands. During the battle he permanently lost use of his left arm, the result of an explosion on deck. He was awarded the Purple Heart and honorably discharged after recovering from his wounds.

His sinewy, reed-like frame was encased in sun-dried skin as tough as the leather of the belt that held his trousers up. Norval's complexion was sallow; his countenance sad-eyed, if not stoic. He rarely looked up when speaking, usually employing terse, one- or two-word responses. The elder Skoon tended to mumble, barely parting his lips, because of the crooked and missing teeth in a mouth that lacked even cursory dental work. Norval's recurrent rattling cough and raspy voice betrayed a lifelong habit of heavy smoking.

A harsh life had diminished the natural loveliness and buoyant spirit of Hannah Skoon. Yet a bright smile occasionally transformed her careworn face, providing a hint of the sparkling beauty she had once been.

A very bright woman, Hannah privately mourned her lack of formal education. She had been an excellent student throughout her youth, but was forced to quit high school in her junior year to help her ailing parents. She therefore had missed her opportunity for the high school diploma that might have led to a different, perhaps less difficult existence. She came to accept, without complaining, the unremarkable daily grind of being Mrs. Norval Skoon.

The Skoons scratched out a living on fifty acres of bottomland along Brushy Fork. Norval worked the land with a weathered 1928 Farmall tractor he'd purchased at a farm auction.

After the war, most farming families could afford only the necessities. "We'll just have to make do" seemed to be the mantra for joyless survivors like the Skoons.

Norval supplemented his meager income through odd jobs—towing vehicles, hauling trash, plowing snow. He had been an accomplished mechanic before losing the use of his left arm but his disability was no cause for special treatment because so many others had equally or even more devastating injuries.

On Saturday afternoons, Skoon could usually be found at Morgans Trail Bar, sipping beer for hours and joshing with fellow drinkers until he was pretty well potted. More than once his friends drove him home or followed him until he arrived there safely.

Hannah cooked on a stove fueled by wood chopped from the small grove of trees behind the house. Well water poured into the metal kitchen sink as she labored over a hand-operated pump. Heating water was a matter of filling pails on the kitchen stove. She washed and rinsed the family's clothes in a converted metal barrel, then hung the garments on a rope stretched between two posts. She was a skilled seamstress who made most of her husband's and Jake's clothes, and all of her own.

THE GREATEST GENERATION

A small table with four mismatched chairs hugged a wall next to the ice box. Twice weekly a truck pulled into the Skoons' driveway, a large man emerging with a bulky leather pad fashioned to cover his shoulders. Armed with a pair of oversized pincers he would seize a hundred-pound block of ice, tote it to the kitchen, and place it gently inside the ice chamber.

The little farmhouse was heated by the kitchen stove and a coal-fired, pot-bellied furnace in the living room. In winter, heavy woolen blankets warded off the cold of the unheated bedrooms. Jake often woke up mornings to find his bedspread with a light cover of snow that had blown in through cracks in the window casings.

An outhouse about twenty yards from the back door of the residence served as the bathroom. Traversing those sixty feet seemed an endless journey during the brutal cold of the Hoosier winter.

Their austere possessions included no radio, let alone a TV, and the Skoons had no telephone, either. If an emergency call needed to be made, Hannah walked two miles to use a neighbor's wall phone and delivered the urgent news through the small megaphone receiver held close to her ear. Colds and fevers, measles, upset stomachs, bee stings, and sprains were not crises in the Skoon residence. One had to break a limb or at least suffer a stitchable gash before Dr. Gentry would be summoned to the house or fetched in the family vehicle, a rusted-out 1935 Ford pick-up truck in need of constant repairs.

Like many farm wives, Hannah gathered her weekly supply of eggs from a brood of chickens kept in a small coop in the yard. Most Sundays, Hannah would select an unfortunate fowl from the henhouse, grasp the flapping, squawking fryer by its legs just above the clawed feet, step on its neck, and jerk. The headless bird flopped around the yard spewing blood until its involuntary dance of death ended. The carcass was dropped into a galvanized bucket of scalding water to make it easier to remove its sharp quills. Jake held the chicken by its legs while his mom artfully plucked the bird clean of its feathers.

On weekly trips to the market in Morgans Awe, Hannah's shopping list would usually include a loaf of Wonder bread (19 cents); a ten-pound bag of granulated sugar (65 cents); a half-gallon glass bottle of Maplehurst vitamin D milk (36 cents); a pound of bacon (41 cents); five pounds of General Mills flour (27 cents); chili powder (8 cents); a regular box of Wheaties cereal (30 cents); two pounds of fresh ground hamburger (50 cents); and Morton Salt in a cylindrical cardboard container (28 cents). Rarely did her available cash exceed the necessities that she purchased. If there happened to be a bit of spare change, Hannah purchased a cake mix to provide an occasional sweet treat for the family.

Coming to town was her chance to gather news and juicy tidbits from other farmers' wives. Hannah enjoyed the monthly gathering of women quilters on those occasions when she had time and energy to attend. Catching up on neighborhood news at a quilting table provided the social interaction she longed for.

Local clerks were another source of scuttlebutt for Hannah. Women behind the counter at the general store were like relatives, sharing items of interest gathered from others around the community. If Flossy Windhorn had an abscessed tooth; if Joseph Jones suffered the DTs from his habitual drunkenness; if Pastor Marsdon was spending an abundance of time at the widow Sanders' home; or farmer Cronen hurt his back tossing a hay bale onto the wagon, the women behind the cash registers knew it.

Hannah's favorite clerk was Nellie Kellner, a sassy, sixty-year-old widow who checked groceries at the general store. Regular customers were acquainted with her quick, and sometimes stinging, wry wit. Squat and plump, Nellie had a heart of gold but had little patience with complaining clients who entered her check-out lane.

On one occasion a grumpy local, finding the Sunday newspaper not delivered on time, carped a bit too loudly to suit Nellie. "Well, I guess the Madison paper's late again," whined the elderly man.

Nellie shot back, "Either that, or nothin' happened yestiddy."

The cheeky clerk and an equally brash former high school classmate, Ford Mullins, had an ongoing friendly feud. They would argue about anything. Once, Ford brought three bananas to the cashier that he thought were on sale.

Mullins placed the bananas on the counter. Nellie added the total up and said tartly, "Twunny-one cents, Ford."

"Wait a minute, Nellie. Them bananas are on sale."

"Huh-uh."

"Yer wrong, Nellie. Thar on sale fer a nickel apiece."

"No they ain't. Ever one of um's seven cents."

The pair traded barbs a few more times before Nellie ended the dispute. She picked up one of the bananas, peeled the fruit—exposing about half of it—then took a hearty bite. What was left of the banana she placed in the sack with its mates, and announced to the exasperated customer, "That'll be fi'teen cents, Ford."

THE GREATEST GENERATION

As a boy, Jake was introduced to hard work early on. Despite his small stature, he assumed the typical farm boy's daily chores. By the time he was twelve, Jake drove the tractor, plowing and planting corn and beans in the parched acres of the Skoon farmland. In summer, he lifted heavy bales of hay onto a wagon to be put up in barn lofts. He chopped and stacked cords of wood for use in winter. He would regularly accompany his dad to local job sites, lifting heavy bags, raking or shoveling as the job demanded.

And he learned to shoot a basketball. Jake's father had played on the Morgans Awe high school five as a senior in 1941 before enlisting. Now Norval followed the local team faithfully. He took Jake to most of the home games.

Jake was only six when his father nailed a rusted hoop above the barn door. From that time forward, the son would spend long hours shooting a worn rubber basketball through the net-less goal, hoping one day to be a star player for the Raiders.

Neither Marshall Seaberg nor Norval Skoon considered himself part of what newscaster Tom Brokaw would one day label the "Greatest Generation." The war was a distant memory (except in occasional nightmares). Both men were focused on providing a living for their families through honest labor for fair pay. Frills or risky ventures were for another guy. They didn't expect a handout—only a chance to improve the lot of their respective families.

In the summer of 1953, Betty Seaberg's uncle, Lane Medwin, offered Marshall the general manager's position at Medwin's Mill in Madison. The business was thriving. Farmers from southern Indiana brought grain to Medwin's to be transported to markets along the Ohio River. Josh was nine when the Seaberg family moved from Indianapolis to Morgans Awe, about ten miles north of the county seat.

Josh and Jake would be brought together by happenstance; over time theirs would become a friendship like that of two brothers.

7

HOW FAR IS IT, DAD?

Jourden Arena
8:02 p.m.

A knock on the door preceded a brief exchange between student manager Arnie Packard and an official. Turning to face O'Ryan, Arnie whispered, "One minute, Coach."

It was time to take the floor. With the last few seconds, the coach reminded his team of the Cougars' lethal tactic. "Remember, they like to intimidate you from the start. They'll press us full court like their hair's on fire. Keep your poise. Don't let their early bluster knock you on your heels. Toughness goes both ways, boys. Don't back down.

"On offense, let's dance with whut brung us. Take care of the basketball. Mark, Josh, have a solid base on your screens. Jake, Bond, Sonny, make sharp cuts off the pick. Work for a good shot, then crash the boards."

Grasping a slice of chalk, Coach O'Ryan quickly reviewed the opponent's pressing defense with a diagram on the green board.

"When they press, execute what we've worked on. They'll pick you up man-to-man and try to force you into a double-team trap anywhere on the court. Don't panic! Josh, Sonny, be alert to help the guards if they get in trouble. Mark, stay near the half-court center circle for the outlet pass. When we break down the defense, be alert for opportunities to drive to the hole. Above all, stick to the plan. Protect the ball!"

Coach paused.

Tension was etched into the somber expressions of the players. Nervous energy was flowing out of Mark Danner through the involuntary, frenetic shaking of his right foot and leg. Coach locked onto Mark's widening eyes.

"Nervous, Mark?"

"More'n a whore in church, Coach."

THE HOOSIER GAME

The burst of laughter from the team and the mock surprise preceding Coach O'Ryan's sly grin reduced the stress in the room. The players were breathing again.

The team members now stood and gathered around their coach. Reverend Sharter moved to the perimeter of the huddle as the boys lowered their eyes.

"Lord above, we ask that your light shine on, and your love surround, all the boys on the playing floor this evening. Help us to remember that our prayer is not that you will be on our side, but that we will be on yours. As Paul told the Corinthians, 'In a race, all the runners run, but only one gets the prize. Let us run in such a way as to get the prize,' for it is for your glory that we have prepared for this challenge. Watch over each of us, guide and protect us, through your Son, Jesus Christ. Amen."

With arms extended and fingers interlocked, the team members tightened the ring around Coach O'Ryan. His final words were brief.

"Men, I didn't notice any cowards in that locker room over there. And there aren't any wearing orange and black, either. You've earned the right to play the best. And so did Madison. But I know something ole Saul and his lads don't. You ARE the best team on the floor this night. And you WILL win this game! LET'S GO!"

Shouts and screams erupted as the team burst through the door and up to the court. In a matter of minutes the Morgans Awe Raiders would compete in the most significant public event of their young lives.

Saturday, July 11, 1953
Moving to Morgans Awe

On this pleasant summer day the Seaberg family was enroute in their 1949 Ford Custom Sedan to their new home. Traveling south on U.S. 31, the Seabergs hauled their few household appliances and items of furniture, plus the family's clothes and other personal property, in a borrowed trailer. Marshall and Betty had purchased a three-bedroom home in the tiny community in southeast Indiana for the princely price of $9,855. The family would sleep this evening in the first house they had ever owned.

The ninety-mile trip led them through the heart of south central Indiana. At Columbus, rear to the popular Bobolink Restaurant, Marshall turned onto State Road 7. Passing over raised rubber expansion seals between the fifteen-foot-long slabs of poured concrete, the familiar blip-blip-blip of the tires droned on monotonously. To Josh, passing through the ten- to twelve-foot-high cornstalks flanking the highway was like navigating a small canyon.

HOW FAR IS IT, DAD?

Betty Seaberg was czarina of the car radio. She favored the music of popular vocalists of the day. Her personal favorite was the smooth style of a young Jewish tenor, Eddie Fisher.

Any time you're feelin' lonely,
Any time you're feelin' blue.
Any time you feel down-hearted,
That will prove your love for me is true.
Any time you're thinkin' 'bout me,
That's the time I'll be thinkin' of you.
So any time you say you want me back again,
That's the time I'll come back home to you.

"How far is it now, Dad?" came the periodic refrain from the back seat.

"It won't be long, Josh," replied his father. "Another half-hour and we'll be there."

Entering the small village of Scipio, Marshall saw just ahead the distinctive round orange-and-blue sign of a Gulf filling station. Mr. Seaberg pulled next to a gas pump where the attendant filled the tank, checked the oil, and cleaned the windshield. Gas cost twenty-one cents per gallon.

After paying, Marshall pulled across the roadway and steered into the parking lot of Weisenbach's Wayfarer Grill. Among the few pleasures the Seabergs indulged in while traveling was stopping at one of the hundreds of pastoral family restaurants that dotted Hoosier roadways. Since most meals were prepared at home, eating out was a special treat.

Mr. Seaberg steered the car to a spot beneath the covered walkway that extended from the main restaurant. Here, customers who preferred eating in their car or taking the meal with them were greeted by a carhop, who took the food order. A cute teenage girl hustled to the driver's window, offering a menu with a smile and a friendly, "Hi folks. What can I getcha?"

Within minutes the server brought a tray with two cheeseburgers, a barbecue sandwich, two orders of fries, cole slaw, two Cokes, and a malted milkshake. Mr. Seaberg handed the young lady two dollars and two quarters, instructing her to keep the change. After subtracting the meal cost of $1.95, the girl beamed at receiving the very fair tip of fifty-eight cents.

THE HOOSIER GAME

Weisenbach's Wayfarer Grill "...two cheeseburgers, fries, and a chocolate milkshake for ninety cents."

HOW FAR IS IT, DAD?

Josh had ordered a cheeseburger deluxe, fries, and the chocolate malted. He always felt as if he had received a bonus with the shake, for the cold metal serving container that came with it held more of the creamy liquid than the glass did. That chilled, extra half-cup was saved until the last, completing a very satisfying meal.

Returning to the highway, Marshall turned east onto a county road at Wirt. Crossing over U.S. 421, Josh noted a farmer's barn with *SEE 7 STATES FROM ROCK CITY ATOP LOOKOUT MOUNTAIN* painted on its sideboards.

At China, veering north onto S.R. 82, they entered Madison County, arriving at Morgans Awe just minutes later. Approaching the town limits, Josh noted two farmers standing in a field near the side of the road. Each was covered in dusty blue denim bib overalls, with red bandanas tied around their necks. Packets of Mail Pouch tobacco protruded from side pockets. Ruddy faces beneath sweat-stained Farm Bureau caps watched curiously as the Ford and trailer passed by.

About a quarter of a mile further was a white rectangular sign, announcing:

MORGANS AWE
POP. 881
(Unincorporated)

Proceeding into the village the Seabergs found the small commercial area to be swarming with people. In the 1950s Morgans Awe was considered a safe haven, removed from the stress, drugs, crime, pollution, and other headaches of large cities. The pace of the farming culture tended to be more tranquil than that found in urban areas.

Predominantly white and archly conservative Anglo-Saxon Protestants, Morgans Awe residents considered established institutions, long-standing traditions, and conventional thought to be virtues of a Christian culture. They held patriotism, faith, modesty, honest work, fair play, and obedience to the law to be the keystones of a successful life.

Divorce and babies born out of wedlock were stigmas of disgrace. Standing in a welfare line was considered shameful.

The primary job of married women was to keep the family running smoothly in the traditional way: cooking, cleaning, and raising the kids. Women working outside the home were mostly teachers, nurses, grocery and drug store clerks, or clerical staff for male professionals.

THE HOOSIER GAME

Men were expected to earn the money and take care of outdoor maintenance, cars, and other mechanical things. The only industry of any type in Morgans Awe was Berglund's Cooperage, employing thirty-seven workers from the area. Those who didn't farm generally held jobs in Madison or commuted to the many limestone quarries found in southern Indiana. Several drove sixty miles one way to the grand quarry at Oolitic, where limestone for the Empire State Building had been excavated and cut.

The child was not the center of the family. Children were required to be quiet in the presence of adults and any rights and opinions were allowed at the pleasure of the parents. Choices weren't dictated by kids. Mothers didn't ask, "What would you like to eat?" Children ate what was placed on the table or went without. If a child stubbornly refused what was offered, it was a long wait until the next meal.

Tantrums were dealt with without delay. Bad behavior usually didn't reach public places. If a child did "show out" in a local market or store, parents did not hesitate to confront the unruly child, applying a hot hand to the posterior if necessary. No one worried that they might be brought up on charges of child abuse. Parents did what they felt was necessary to teach children respect.

Morgans Awe residents were typical of the Hoosier society of the mid-twentieth century. White newcomers were welcomed with uncommon courtesy and warmth. Everyone greeted strangers with a smiling "Hello." However, move-ins would learn that they had to earn their place in the community pecking order. Older, homegrown natives dominated the social and political scene.

Consistent with most of Indiana at that time, ninety-seven percent of Madison County's residents were Caucasian. While not all Hoosiers were unwelcoming of blacks in their communities, a substantial number of the people of the Hoosier state were uncomfortable, if not openly hostile, in the presence of Negroes.

African-Americans—the "colored population"—were well aware of the notorious "sundown towns" in the Midwest. "Be out of town by sundown" was the unspoken mantra of white people who wanted no blacks settling in their communities. Through a combination of legal formalities and intimidation, blacks were discouraged from moving to rural locales. Years later, Dr. Martin Luther King, Jr. would speak of going "up south" to Indiana.

Despite a rapidly changing culture fueled by technology, the people of Morgans Awe remained skeptical of "newfangled things." Advocates of any departure from accepted mores often resulted in a backlash from the protectors of the "way things are."

Josh's mom and dad would come to understand that worrying about Josh's safety was less of a concern in Morgans Awe than in the outskirts of the capital city. Parents were comfortable allowing kids to be on their own for hours at a time. With bicycles, youngsters had the freedom to explore, create, and learn in a healthy atmosphere.

Arriving at his new home, Josh found an abundant yard teeming with mature trees. A shallow creek bordered a portion of the Seaberg property. Josh would later recall the unforgettable piercing song of swarms of locusts that day. The cicadas hung on bushes and the leaves of trees during their brief adult lives before littering the ground with their dry empty shells. They would return, as ordained by nature, in seventeen years.

Marshall had wisely placed Josh's bike at the rear of the trailer. It was the first item removed when they reached the residence. During his cursory exploration of the neighborhood, Josh would learn that within a three-block area of his home there lived two dozen lads in his age range.

The balance of that summer of 1953 would be a time of making new friends and engaging in all the normal activities of which youngsters pursued fun and adventure. Josh, Sam Chandler, Larry "Smiley" Burnett, "Pee Wee" Reynolds, twins Larry and Gary Waters, "Ray Boy" Rounds, and "Frog" Nelson became inseparable comrades.

The Morgans Awe youth found competitive outlets in just about any activity. Kids regularly played tag, marbles and Andy-over. Everyone knew what "Olly-olly-oxen-free" meant. They scrapped like hungry pups to be the best in bicycle races, climbing trees, jumping from garage roofs, holding their breath under water, and finding the most four-leaf clovers. They even held a contest behind Donny Waithen's dad's tool shed to see who could pee the farthest.

Josh especially relished long bike rides through the surrounding country. Regular stops included Tanner's Hill, where kids would roll themselves downward through the grass until gloriously dizzy, stumbling and falling, giggling uncontrollably as they tried to rise. The boys would fish for bluegills in Brushy Fork while keeping a close eye out for blue racers slithering through the grass.

At Aufderhaagen's Orchard, luscious apples could be had for free when Herr Auffie wasn't looking. The lads would skin up the trees and heist the treasure after closing hours. Josh recalled the amazing bellyaches that accompanied eating too many of the tart green Granny Smiths.

THE HOOSIER GAME

Toward evening the lads amused themselves playing hide-and-seek. When the porch lights came on it was time for the reluctant lads to return home.

"Josh," Betty would call out in no specific direction. "Supper's ready. Come on in."

Minutes later she shouted the same request into the darkening shades of dusk. Naturally, Josh ignored the summons. However, the third time she punctuated the urgency of the moment by yelling, "Joshua CHARLES, GET in this house!" When his mom used his given names together he beat a hot trail to the back door.

On rainy days the boys fought furiously over the usual collection of board games like Monopoly and Chinese checkers, and a host of card games such as "I Doubt It," "Rummy," and "Starve Dog." Many a time a losing player would toss the cards angrily or tip the board in frustration, ending the game to the howling dismay of the others.

Josh never heard any of his buddies utter, "I've got nothin' to do. I'm bored." To even hint at such a thing, particularly in the presence of one's parents, could result in a boy being immediately assigned to the business end of a garden hoe, to a pair of shears to trim hedges, or an old-fashioned muscle-powered lawn mower.

Baseball was the common denominator for boys of all ages. Almost every morning Josh and friends would leave home to play all day long at the area adjacent to Berglund's Cooperage. The clay field was invaded by splotches of wire grass and sprinkled liberally with sandburs, and pebbles, and shards of broken glass. From the right field foul line to dead center loomed the prodigious brick wall of the bucket factory. In all the games played that summer only two batted balls had cleared the tar-covered roof. Josh had hit one of those.

In one game, Iggy Conrow struck a towering drive that shattered the glass of a window on the third story of the building. The day foreman, Boss Skinner, dashed outside to scold the crowd only to see the elbows and backsides of youths fleeing the scene.

Most of the bats the lads used were cracked, because no one had money to buy new ones. Small nails bound the split pieces together, which were then wrapped in black electrical tape. When baseballs were battered until unraveling in a spray of string and fuzz, the game would be temporarily suspended and everyone went looking for discarded soda bottles. The local grocer paid two cents for each bottle returned. When a sufficient number was collected, a player would bike to Hawkins's store to buy another cheap ball.

HOW FAR IS IT, DAD?

There were only five mitts available—all right-handers—for the numerous boys in the game. The gloves were dropped on the field at the change of innings for use by older members of the opposing team. Younger boys looked forward to the day when they moved up the ladder of seniority to claim one of the prized mitts.

Kids played ball with no adults interfering. Loud exchanges of disagreement often followed a disputed play. Generally, democracy resolved the problem. If not, the eldest and/or toughest kid in the game would play benevolent dictator, making the call to end the argument.

During pauses in the daylong games, the boys quenched thirsty throats by taking turns drinking from a garden hose. Once in awhile, a guy might have enough change to buy a six-ounce Coke, Nehi grape, or Cho-cola drink to share with the multitude. Sizes of sips were monitored closely as the bottle was passed around the circle. Anyone drinking more than his share was immediately censored by having Homer Redman—he of the vice grips on the ends of his huge arms—squeeze him around the middle until the glutton promised never to do it again. Or until he puked.

As August turned to September, these random weekday adventures ended. On the morning after Labor Day, 1953, Josh and his fellow fourth graders showed up for the first day of school.

Morgans Awe Community School—an aging, three-story, neoclassical structure typical of school buildings constructed in the 1920s—looked like a brick fortress with windows. Inside, creaky wooden floors were buffed to a dazzling shine. Fresh enamel paint gave the walls a wax-like sheen. Portraits of Lincoln, Washington, Jefferson, and Franklin hung intermittently along the corridors in ornamental frames.

Narrow lockers lined the hallways. Each senior had a locker of his own. Students from fifth grade up had to share with a partner. Classrooms had high ceilings from which two mounted light fixtures hung, plus a transom was over every door. The American flag in each room had thirteen stripes and forty-eight stars.

Standing before their designated classrooms, beaming teachers—the men dressed in narrow ties with jackets and the women wearing wool skirts or print dresses and heels—greeted students.

Principal Lawton, a tall, intimidating figure, followed the practice of *in loco parentis*, essentially meaning that principals and teachers were students' legal guardians while at school. Corporal punishment was not considered cruel but

THE HOOSIER GAME

a necessary tool used occasionally to enforce rules. That practice was generally accepted and supported by parents.

Josh entered room 103 where a slender, pretty young woman welcomed her pupils with a pleasant smile and warm eyes. The bell had not yet rung, but most of the students were already in their seats. The familiar lined, black chalkboards were mounted on each wall. Across the top of one were the letters of the alphabet, written in both lower- and uppercase cursive. On another, in neatly inscribed characters, was "Welcome to Fourth Grade! Miss Harriet Stoneham."

Spotting the seating chart, Josh found his desk in the back row. It was one of those vintage, turn-of-the-century wooden desks with a hole in the upper right corner for an inkwell that was never used, a pencil slot carved into the top-center, and a black cast-iron base supporting the flip-up seat.

Occupying the desk next to his was a taller, thin boy with protruding ears and a congenial expression on his face. Since teachers customarily assigned seats alphabetically, Joshua James Seaberg and Marvin Jacob Skoon would sit side by side throughout elementary school.

The boy sitting spoke first.

"Hi. My name's Jake."

"I'm Josh. We just moved here."

"Where'd ja move in from?" the young boy asked, since he had not seen Josh before.

"From Indy'naplus."

"I live on a farm—"

The bell sounded to begin the school day, interrupting their brief conversation.

"Hello, boys and girls, and welcome," the teacher said with enthusiasm as she called the class to attention. "My name is Miss Stoneham and I'm so happy to see you!"

Miss Stoneham's first duty was roll call. All of those on her list answered. Next the boys and girls who had brought money for book rental and school materials lined up at the teacher's desk. When it was his turn Josh handed over a sealed envelop with the six dollars it cost for both semesters.

Delivering instructions regarding class rules, handing out textbooks, reviewing library procedures, and conveying her expectations on assignments consumed the balance of the morning. It was now time for the students to line up in the hallway for the march to the lunchroom.

Both boys had brought lunches packed in brown sacks. They sat together as they would nearly every day afterward.

Josh soon became a regular visitor at the Skoon farm, usually covering the three miles from home on his bike. Jake introduced his new friend to country life. The boys climbed trees, made forts out of hay bales, hunted mushrooms, and climbed all through the crossties of the old barn.

One weekend Jake had invited his new friend to go hunting. It was a time-honored ritual in rural Indiana, and nearly every boy of ten years and older owned a shotgun. Fathers gave sons a firearm, taught them how to use it, and expected the boys to handle the weapon responsibly.

It was a crisp and clear fall Saturday morning when Josh arrived at the farm. Norval Skoon was just then driving out of the barn on his tractor. Over the rattling noise of the engine, Josh hailed Jake's father.

"Hi, Mr. Skoon. How are ya doin'?"

"I'm busier'n a billy goat with two peckers, son. Jake's over in them woods squirrel huntin'. If yer goin' thataway, be careful. He might shoot you fer a deer."

Hearing a loud report, Josh found Jake in the nearby trees. He whooped emphatically to make sure his sharp-shooting friend didn't fill him full of buckshot.

Jake loaned his friend a .410 shotgun. After Josh took a few practice shots at a tin can mounted on a fence, the two began to comb the woods to stalk rabbits, or perhaps to bag a pheasant in the cornfield.

The first hunting venture of Josh's life did not go well.

Barely five minutes had passed when the host spied a rabbit and downed him with a clean shot. Josh felt a little nauseated as he watched Jake slip the bloody carcass into his hunting jacket pocket. Jake bagged four more rabbits, each artfully shot in the head, while Josh hadn't even raised his gun.

When Jake spied a rabbit hunched down in a copse he whispered to Josh, "See that rabbit sittin' over in nat brush?"

Josh shook his head. To his unpracticed eye the perfectly still rabbit was indistinguishable, camouflaged in the natural growth surrounding it.

"See 'is head? No, right there in front a-you."

The next sound was a blast from the shotgun at Josh's shoulder. The boys plodded through briars and fallen limbs to where the rabbit lay. It had rolled over on its side.

"You got 'im, Josh!" Jake shouted gleefully as he peered at the bloody animal. "Didn't zactly hit dead-center, but you gotcher first rabbit."

THE HOOSIER GAME

The truth was Jake had peppered the body of the small rodent with so much lead that it would be inedible.

Looking down at the quivering animal that was still alive despite the lead pellets in its dying body, Josh looked sadly at its frightened eyes. As Jake continued to celebrate, tears burned in Josh's eyes. He turned away, not wanting Jake to make fun of him.

Jake never mentioned his friend's queasiness about killing that small game animal. But he wisely never asked him to go hunting again.

The months passed routinely. The winter of that year would become associated in Josh's mind with a bouncy hit song made popular by Patti Page.

How much is that doggie in the window?
The one with the wagglely tail.
How much is that doggie in the window?
I do hope that doggie's for sale.

Christmas came with the usual excitement and pageantry. Along with the new clothes under the tree, Josh would find a tinker toy set, a Fort Apache with miniature cowboys and Indians, and the games Tiddleywinks, Cooties, and Pick-Up Sticks.

Marshall Seaberg had a special surprise for his family. On Christmas Eve, a Sears delivery truck had pulled into the driveway. As Josh's mother and father beamed, two men lugged a new RCA console television set with a 16-inch, round, black-and-white screen into the living room. It had a mahogany veneer cabinet accompanied by the "rabbit ears" antenna. Once the TV was plugged in, Josh excitedly twisted the dial on the set, trying to decide among the three channels available in the greater Louisville area.

TV opened up a whole new world to eager viewers. Sports, soap operas, variety shows and news programs, had captured the American public, and millions purchased the electronic miracle that was mass-produced following the World War.

Favored offerings in the Seaberg home included "The Jackie Gleason Show," featuring Gleason, the unparalleled genius of physical comedy; "Gunsmoke," with characters Matt Dillon, Miss Kitty, and Chester; "I Love Lucy," highlighted by the zany antics of Ricky and Lucy Ricardo, and Fred and Ethel Mertz; the variety show, "Toast of the Town," with host Ed Sullivan; and both the "Ozzie and Harriet" and "Father Knows Best" family comedies that portrayed middle class life in the fifties.

HOW FAR IS IT, DAD?

Betty's best-loved half-hour on TV was "Hit Parade," on Saturday nights. Snooky Lanson, Russell Arms, Dorothy Collins, and Gisele MacKenzie performed the latest pop tunes.

On Friday nights Josh and his dad watched a "wrasslin'" show, as stars Eduoard Carpentier, the Baron Leoni, Mitsu Arakawa, and the hated, preening Gorgeous George pummeled one another in sold-out arenas filled with shrieking, blood-thirsty crowds. Josh and his friends were inspired to try the flying dropkick, the Chinese sleeper hold, the scissor lock, and full- and half-Nelsons on one another.

Nineteen-fifty-three had been an eventful year for young Josh Seaberg. He had been uprooted from his birthplace and replanted in a tiny town near the southern border of Indiana. New friends and new adventures were abundant in Morgans Awe. His parents seemed happy and content.

Mr. Seaberg welcomed the New Year with a tradition widespread at the time. At midnight on New Year's Eve, Josh walked outside with his dad into the crisp winter air. Marshall raised his Browning automatic shotgun skyward and fired one blast to mark the beginning of the New Year. The night sky echoed with the din of reports fired simultaneously as other men across the town followed the odd ritual.

Life was good in Morgans Awe on January 1st, 1954.

8

THE MILAN MIRACLE

Jourden Arena
8:08 p.m.

On the court the starting fives of both teams engaged in the final warm-up session. Starters had peeled off their jackets and sweat pants. As the Raider reserves gathered outside the perimeter, Josh, Sonny, Mark, Bond, and Jake followed their routine. Each had a ball, alternately practicing free throws and shooting from the floor. Jake rehearsed jump shots from far out on the perimeter. As usual, Josh divided his practice attempts between medium-range jumpers and drives to the hoop along the baseline. Mark went through his variety of hook shots and lay-ins near the basket. Sonny and Bond shot free throws.

The blare from the timer's horn signaled the teams to return to their respective benches. It was time to introduce the ten players who would square off on the opening tip.

Clustered together in their huddle the boys united in shouts and hugs and slaps on the back and rump, all intended to get suitably fired up. Beneath that facade of optimism and self-assurance each individual hid his fear of the unknown. If things did not go well early in the game, doubt could strike suddenly and then swiftly leap to panic. Calm leadership from the veteran players and the coach were critical if a team began to go wobbly.

Coach O'Ryan hadn't seen his team panic the entire season.

The Raiders five were presented first. Booming through the loudspeaker above the court, Josh heard his name.

"For the Morgans Awe Raiders—in black uniforms with orange numerals—at one forward, a senior, standing six-feet three inches tall, number 31, Josh Seaberg!"

The Morgans Awe cheer section responded in unison, with, "GO-OOO-OOO-OOO, JOSH!"

Seaberg trotted to the foul line and faced the opposite end of the court.

"At the other forward, senior, at five-feet eleven, number 25, Sonny Watkins!"

THE HOOSIER GAME

"GO-OOO-OOO-OOO, SONNY!"

As Sonny joined his teammate on the floor, he acknowledged Josh with a handshake and a pat on the rear.

"At center, a senior, standing six-feet four, number 51, Mark Danner!"

"At one guard, a junior, at five-ten, number 11, Bond Bathwaite!"

"And at the other guard position—"

As Jake Skoon was introduced, frenetic Morgans Awe spectators overwhelmed the public address announcer. As the deafening ovation washed over his best friend, Josh's eardrums tingled. This kind of applause was reserved for a special player only. Jake was one who struck fear and loathing in his opponents.

"—a senior, six-feet two, number five, Jake Skoon!"

Surely the thunderous applause for the Raiders' star could be heard at Scoop 'n Dollies back in Morgans Awe.

"And now, for the Madis—"

The Cougar rooting contingent was on its feet. The salvo of cheers rivaled that of the Raiders'. In contrast to the muscular, hirsute Cougar men the Morgans Awe boys appeared conspicuously smaller in stature, paler in color, less mature. The disparity in height and bulk was obvious. Madison Central's front line of Hankins (6-4), Weatherford (6-6), and DeVreaux (6-5) was among the tallest in the state. To have even one good player standing as high as 6-4 was a defensive challenge for opposing coaches. Facing three exceptional players that big was frightening.

In the backcourt, the sharp-shooting Miller and the clever leader Wells had out-played every opponent all season long. The Morgans Awe guards looked to be overmatched against the imposing duo.

As the two squads stood facing one another, spectators were asked to remove their hats and stand for the national anthem. Only moments before the gathered horde had resembled a giant cauldron of writhing heads, arms, legs, and torsos. Now, a respectful hush engulfed the mass of fans jammed into the bleachers.

Scoreboards at each end of the court read the same: game clock, 8:00 minutes. Score, Morgans Awe 00, Madison Central 00. Five amber lights noted each team's number of timeouts. Only the first of the four red lights signifying quarters was lit.

A trumpeter sounded the opening notes as the crowd sang in unison,

"O, say can you see, by the dawn's early light—"

Josh Seaberg stood erect, right hand placed respectfully over the 31 on his game jersey. He peered at the Stars and Stripes hanging high above center court. His four Morgans

THE MILAN MIRACLE

Awe High School teammates flanked him along the foul line at the north end of the arena.

"O'er the land of the free—and the home—of the—brave!"

A steadily rising tempest of noise from the restless crowd drowned out the final notes of the Star-Spangled Banner. Both teams returned to their respective huddles for last-second instructions. In less than sixty seconds the combatants would become embroiled in the maelstrom of a Hoosier sectional championship game.

May 5, 2012
Morgans Awe

Sympathetic classmates nearby noted Jill's brief surrender to pent-up emotions. She now gathered herself, drying the tears from her eyes. After a quiet exchange of reminiscences, Josh excused himself. He ambled over to greet his old locker partner and the house bartender.

"Hey, perfessor! What are ya drinkin'?" bellowed the garrulous Will Billings.

Bear's round cheeks, meaty jowls, and squinty smile lit up at the sight of his old classmate and friend. The two shared a handshake and hug.

"Mr. Barkeep, I'll have a Coors Light, if you please, with a big dose o' happy!"

Will, who had played in the school band, was an ambassador for good cheer and laughter. In Bear's company one would have to try very hard to be gloomy. He was six feet tall and 260 pounds. His infectious smile and positive nature endeared others to him.

They talked of the old days, of family, and mutual friendships.

"How long have Betty and you been married, Bear?" Josh asked, referring to Will's lifetime companion.

"Bet and me got married on July the fourth, 1962. It'll be 50 years in a coupla' months. And we just landed our twelf' grandchild. Peggy and Adam, our youngest, had their third child last Tuesday."

"Jesus, Will. How do you afford your Christmas gift list?"

"Well, I leave all that up to Betty. I jist go out'n git me a job in December to pay for all that stuff she buys."

"You'd make a great Santa Claus! Hey, Bear, I remember that time you were so sure you saw a UFO over Morgans Awe. Did you ever get to meet the pilot?"

THE HOOSIER GAME

Will grinned. "Naw, Joshua. But I bleeve I've met a few of his cousins over at the Trail Bar."

Billings began to sing along with an old favorite playing in the background—Ben E. King's "Stand By Me.

When the night has come,
And the land is dark,
And the moon—

As Bobby Mack Deal, Arnie Packard, Mark Danner, and Jamie Ross returned to the bar, they joined in, with "—is the only light we will see."

Then altogether, "No, I won't be afraid, oh, I won't be afraid, just as long as you stand, stand by me. And darlin', darlin'—"

With half of the self-styled crooners singing off-key, the song was abandoned in laughter.

"Hey, did all you guys see *Hoosiers*?" Bobby Mack asked.

"Are you kiddin'? I've watched that bout a hunnerd times. Best movie ever," declared Jamie.

"Does it always turn out the same, Bobo?" Josh teased.

Featuring Gene Hackman as Hickory High School head coach Norman Dale, *Hoosiers* had roughly portrayed what many old-timers still recall as the greatest game in Indiana basketball history: tiny Milan High School's epic upset of Muncie Central to win the state tournament championship in 1954.

Bobby Mack now seized center stage with his spot-on impersonation of actor Dennis Hopper's character, Wilbur "Shooter" Fletch, in the 1986 movie.

"Yer playin' Cedar Knob tomorra," dead-panned Bobby. "Ain't nobody knows 'em better'n me.

"I been watchin' how you been breakin' the colts," he continued with his word-for-word interpretation of Hopper's lines.

"But my fren', you cannot play them all the way man-da-man. They got no head-toppers. Cedar Knob? A buncha' mites.

"You gotta' squeeze 'em back in the paint. Run ya off the boards. Make em chuck it from the cheap seats. Watch that purgatory they call a gym. No drive, twelve foot in.

"That'll do," he concluded.

The gray-haired and no-haired men surrounding their former teammate cheered and clapped. Even a few of the women standing nearby laughed at Bobby Mack's amazing simulation of "Shooter".

Josh recalled the legendary Milan-Muncie contest well. As ten-year olds, he and Jake had watched the televised game from a front row seat on the family couch.

Saturday, March 20, 1954
Morgans Awe

Seven-hundred fifty-one Indiana high schools had begun sectional play three weeks earlier. Every team began the single-elimination state playoff on an equal basis. All faced the same odds of winning the state championship: 1.3 chances in a thousand.

Muncie Central, Elkhart, Terre Haute Gerstmeyer, and Milan high schools were the final four surviving teams who would fight for the state title at Butler Fieldhouse.

Back in Morgans Awe that chilly Saturday morning, Josh was up early. He jumped on his bike, a rubber outdoor basketball under one arm, and pedaled the five-minute ride to Memorial Park and the outdoor basketball courts.

Every weekend, in good weather or bad, a dozen boys between the ages of twelve and eighteen played pick-up games there. Their team having been eliminated in the sectional tournament three weeks ago, a few of the Morgans Awe varsity players organized the games.

Josh hung around the fringes, shooting on an adjacent court, in hopes that he might get a chance to play. Being tall for his age, he would sometimes be invited to sub. Over time, Josh had impressed the leaders with his developing skills. He became a regular fill-in when needed. Besides, he was a polite kid who didn't say much, accepting his place in the pecking order.

He learned a valuable lesson early in his development as a basketball player: whenever possible, get into the games with older boys. Even though they dominated the action—Josh might play an entire scrimmage without getting to shoot—by competing with taller, stronger, and more experienced guys he was forced to improve his game. If you couldn't keep up, you wouldn't play.

Returning home early that afternoon Josh caught the last half of the second game of the tourney on TV. Attendance was always the same for the state finals: a sellout crowd of 14,983.

THE HOOSIER GAME

Josh was surprised that tiny Milan High School was beating Howard Sharpe's vaunted Black Cats of Terre Haute Gerstmeyer. The Cats' high-scoring Arley Andrews was stifled by the small but quick Milan defenders. Bobby Plump was on his way to scoring 26 points to lead the Indians to a 60-48 win.

The championship game would pit the heavily-favored Muncie Central Bearcats—who had beaten Elkhart, 59-50, in the first game—against Milan.

After supper, the doorbell rang. Since the Skoons had no television Jake's dad dropped him off to watch the game with Josh. Marshall and the two boys eagerly took their places in front of the family's Philco as the 8:15 p.m. tip-off neared. Betty sat quietly sewing in her chair with little apparent interest in the sports event that had replaced her preferred show, "The Hit Parade," in the Saturday night viewing list.

After Josh flipped the ON switch the black-and-white screen slowly came to life. A white dot appeared in the middle of the dark screen, then the horizontal line of light would expand until fuzzy images came into focus, the TV warming up after about 45 seconds.

Josh heard the acknowledgment of Indiana Bell Telephone Company, which sponsored the telecasts during the state finals. The familiar, stentorian voice of young Carl Lee Kenagy—better known by his broadcasting name of Tom Carnegie—filled the living room. As did countless others, Josh appreciated Carnegie, also, for his dramatic commentary of the Indianapolis 500-mile race, for which he had gained international fame.

Milan, located in the rolling hills of Ripley County in southeastern Indiana, had only 161 students in its high school. Representing the fifth-largest Hoosier city, on the other hand, Muncie Central was nearly ten times the size of Milan and the Bearcats were the only four-time state champion at the time, earning trophies in 1928, 1931, 1951, and 1952. Few followers of basketball gave Milan a chance to win.

Muncie's daunting front line of Jim Hinds (6-5), Gene Flowers (6-2), and John Casterlow (6-6) dwarfed that of the Indians, who started only one player over six feet tall. Milan was not a complete unknown, having gone to the Final Four the previous year when they had lost in the afternoon session to eventual state champion South Bend Central, 56-37.

"I doubt if this'll be much of a game," Marshall observed as Carnegie began the pre-game show. "Muncie Central is just too big up front for Milan."

"Boy, them Muncie guys are sure tall," Jake agreed.

"Plump and Craft are pretty good players," Josh responded. "If they just get hot—"

THE MILAN MIRACLE

"Yeah, but Jimmy Barnes and Phil Raisor'll be on them like ducks on a June bug."

Milan controlled the opening center jump. Senior guard Plump immediately traveled. Muncie's leading scorer and all-state player Gene Flowers sank a one-handed set shot from 20 feet away. Bearcats, 2-0. The first two plays of the game seemed to confirm that the Milan lads were in over their heads.

Acknowledging that his undersized five likely would not stand a chance in an up-tempo game against Muncie's tall and talented team, Coach Marvin Wood utilized what sportswriters labeled a "cat and mouse" offense. Employing screens and sharp cuts along with accurate and multiple passes on the offensive end, Milan began to find holes in the Bearcats defense.

Surprisingly, Wood's Indians took the lead midway through the first quarter.

As Milan stuck to its conservative game plan the Muncie players became frustrated. When the Bearcats did get their hands on the ball they often rushed up the court, taking hurried shots or turning the ball over in their haste to catch the wily Indians.

With under three minutes to go before the halftime break Plump drove from the left wing for an easy lay-in. Milan's shocking 22-13 advantage would be the widest for either team during the game. Gene Flowers nailed two long shots before the end of the half, bringing Muncie Central back to within six, 23-17.

At the arena the usual halftime pilgrimage to the concession stands and restrooms was lighter than normal. Fans stood at or near their seats—some stunned, others deliriously hopeful—disbelieving what was taking place on the playing floor.

Veteran sportswriters and broadcasters were dumbfounded by the turn of events. The radio voice of the Bearcats, Don Burton, was trying to explain to the thousands listening back in Muncie how the team had gotten themselves in this pickle.

Betty had moved to the kitchen to pour a quantity of popcorn kernels into a pan of hot grease. Soon the familiar sound of the grains of corn pattering the underside of the lid could be heard. Minutes later she delivered an abundant bowl of the tasty snack that was topped with a healthy dose of melted butter. As Betty reached into the freezer to get ice cubes from the tray to cool glasses of lemonade, the Seaberg telephone rang.

A neighbor, Mort Mirland, was calling Marshall to ask if he was watching the game. Josh listened to one side of the conversation.

THE HOOSIER GAME

"I know. I can't believe it either.

"Muncie'll get back in control in the third quarter, you wait'n see. When they get the lead Milan'll have to come outta that stall offense. Milan's raisin' a ruckus. But you don't win the 500 drivin' a John Deere tractor."

"Naw, it won't happen. Okay, Mort, see ya Monday."

Jake spoke up. "Mr. Seaberg, I think Milan's got a chance."

"Slim to none, son. McCreary is in that locker room right now, lightin' a fire under Hinds, Flowers, and Casterlow. Milan'll be lucky to get a rebound in the second half."

The Muncie five started the third quarter determined to put the Indians away. Two free shots by Joe Crawford and yet another long outside field goal by Flowers brought Muncie to within two, 23-21. Since Ray Craft's free throw late in the second quarter, the Bearcats had scored eight straight points.

With less than five minutes remaining in the third quarter big Jim Hinds nailed a 15-foot shot from the baseline to bring Muncie to within a single point.

Betty was now drawn into the drama unfolding on the oval TV screen. Though she admitted her lack of understanding of the game, she became absorbed in the colorful play-by-play account by Carnegie and the intense excitement of the crowd.

"What's the score?" she implored.

"25-24, Milan."

"Oh, my goodness!"

Milan ran its resourceful offense to perfection. On their most recent possession the Indians had exchanged twenty-two passes before Craft was fouled by Muncie's Leon Agullana. With Craft's successful free throw Milan inched ahead, 26-24. But as the third quarter came to a close Muncie tied the score on a drive by Agullana.

"See, I told ya. It's all but over now," Marshall remarked, knowingly.

Betty scolded her pessimistic husband.

"Marshall! Stop talking like that. You're so negative! I bet Milan wins."

The elder Seaberg scoffed at such a fantasy.

"I'm just tellin' ya what the Lord knows. Milan's got the chance of a one-legged man in an ass-kickin' contest."

"Hush!" Betty answered in disgust.

The final eight minutes would begin with the teams exactly where they had started the game—dead even.

Casterlow controlled the fourth quarter tip for the Bearcats. Ron Truitt fouled Hinds in attempting to block a close-in shot. The junior forward swished both free throws. It was now 28-26, Muncie.

"All's right with the world now," taunted Marshall.

Betty scowled harshly at her husband, tiring of his disparaging attitude toward the underdog boys for whom she was rooting. Mr. Seaberg responded with a devilish sparkle in his eyes and the grin of a Cheshire cat.

Bearcat backers breathed a collective sigh of relief. It appeared that Milan had missed its chance. There would be no stopping the mighty Muncie machine now.

Coach Wood had other ideas. He knew the Bearcats could break the game wide open if the Indians faltered now.

So Wood stopped Muncie from playing.

From the 7:45 mark in the fourth quarter until they called a timeout with only three minutes and twenty-eight seconds remaining, Milan made no attempts at the basket. In fact, in accordance with the rules of the day, there was no dribbling or passing. Plump stood near mid-court, simply holding the ball.

Muncie's Coach McCreary instructed his players to stay between their man and the basket, but not to pressure Plump, so Jimmy Barnes, never taking his eyes off the Indian guard, moved no closer than five feet from his opponent.

What Josh would always remember was the crowd response while the ten players on the floor were virtually motionless. A continual roar, like that of millions of tons of water cascading over Niagara Falls, provided the background as Plump remained glued to his chosen spot just inside the center line. Occasionally a Bearcat would hop in place to keep loose. Once, Jim Hinds could be seen doing jumping jacks.

"Dad, what is he doin'? They're behind!"

"It's a smart move, Josh. Wood thinks if he can keep it close they might win it on a shot at the end."

Finally, Wood signaled time out. Less than 3½ minutes remained in the game.

Milan broke the huddle ready to resume the offensive. But Plump missed an 18-foot jumper. Barnes retrieved the ball. Things didn't bode well for the Indians.

Then a turnover by the Bearcats' Flowers led to a shot from the right wing by Milan's Craft, tying the game at 28-28.

THE HOOSIER GAME

Flowers missed an open jump shot and Barnes fouled Plump on the rebound. The first free toss spun agonizingly around the rim before dropping into the net. Plump swished the second. Milan was back in front.

When Milan's Ron Truitt stole a pass that Barnes intended for Hinds under Muncie's basket, Milan had possession of the ball and the lead. Indians backers could hardly breathe. Bearcat fans slumped in despair.

Expecting Milan to return to its stalling game the crowd was aghast when Ray Craft found an opening in the Bearcat defense and drove to the hoop. A basket would put Muncie in an even more precarious position.

He missed the wide open lay-up.

Betty Seaberg gasped. She scolded Craft as if he were a naughty son of hers.

"RAY, how could you?"

An agitated Marshall, now openly rooting for the gritty Indians added, "That was just plain dumb!"

Hinds snared the rebound and fired the ball to Jimmy Barnes. Barnes fed Flowers, who laid it in, tying the game at 30 apiece. The clock showed 00:48 left to play.

"Oh, glory be to gracious!" Betty moaned.

Milan carefully brought the ball across the line, Plump controlling the ball and dribbling watchfully but making no advance toward the basket. With just eighteen seconds to go, Wood signaled his senior captain to call timeout. The Seaberg household sat captivated by the inconceivable events unfolding before them.

Meanwhile, the delirious fans in the Fieldhouse and the hundreds of thousands watching or listening to the game could never have guessed what was taking place in the Indians huddle. Inside the tight circle, Coach Wood was diagramming the final play for an attempt by Plump. Suddenly, senior Gene White spoke up.

"Why don't we get everybody else out of the way and get them over to the side of the floor?"

Wood thought it an excellent idea. He adjusted the play.

As the scoreboard clock began to wind toward zero, Craft passed the ball to Plump, then joined the rest of the Milan players on the left sideline.

Alone at mid-court with only Jimmy Barnes between him and the basket Plump continued to hold the ball as the scoreboard clock ticked toward zeroes: 18—17—16—15—14—13—12.

"Come on, son, you can do it," Marshall whispered to himself.

THE MILAN MIRACLE

With six seconds remaining, the 5-10 Milan star made his move toward the basket. The speedy Barnes impeded Plump's progress to the hoop but was careful to avoid fouling him.

Plump reached the right side of the foul circle. There he put on the brakes, sprung straight upward, and deftly released the ball. Caught flat-footed by the suddenness of Plump's move, Barnes recovered to leap high with his right hand extended. He was too late.

Bobby Plump's jump shot settled softly into the net with two seconds showing on the scoreboard. Amid the chaos, from the scorer's table an official fired the gun signaling the end of the game. The crack of the blank cartridge could hardly be heard over the pandemonium of the nearly 15,000 now standing in Butler's hallowed fieldhouse.

He probably didn't know it at the time, but Bobby Plump had just become a Hoosier icon.

Betty jumped from the couch shrieking, "They won! Milan WON!"

Josh and Jake remained fixed on the TV, watching as ecstatic fans stampeded the fieldhouse floor. The court was like a swarming ant hill as the Milan faithful engulfed their teenage heroes.

Outside, in Morgans Awe, sounds of an impromptu celebration of the tiny school's unexpected state title win were mounting. Horns were honking and shouts of triumph replaced the quiet of the sleepy village. The deafening bleat of the steam whistle atop the Berglund bucket factory reverberated through the frosty air.

People spilled out of their homes to gather at the high school parking lot. Exhilarated by the outcome, locals assembled to share the excitement of the historic game they had just seen.

Marshall and Betty grabbed winter overcoats and rushed outside, Jake and Josh following close behind, to join friends and neighbors in the manic scene. Within half an hour more than 400 people from in and around Morgans Awe arrived at the school to share vicariously in the David-slays-Goliath morality play.

Similar reactions were occurring simultaneously in hundreds of small towns across the Hoosier state. The raw display of emotion for the unlikely heroics of a handful of teenage boys illustrated, at a visceral level, Indiana's inexplicable passion for the game of basketball.

The spontaneous festival of joy continued into the wee hours of Sunday morning. Milan players, coaches, student managers, and cheerleaders were

THE HOOSIER GAME

led to an Indianapolis Fire Department truck for a joyous ride to the center of the city. There, the driver bowed to a request by the team to round Monument Circle on the *wrong* side of the road.

Next morning, the young champions left their hotel at 10 a.m. and, riding in five cars provided by Milan businessman Chris Volz, the victorious coaches and players led a lengthy caravan of cars, buses, trucks, and even motorcycles down U.S.-421 toward home. Large crowds had gathered in towns like Shelbyville, Greensburg, Napoleon, and Osgood, lining the roadway to salute the Milan team as they passed through. Remnants of high school bands were hastily assembled for musical salutes to the young Davids of Indiana.

The Milan-Muncie Central game in 1954 is still considered by oldtimers to be the greatest upset ever in the Indiana State Tournament. The Indians' astonishing victory over the perennial powerhouse epitomized the tale of a tenacious, cagy underdog toppling the giant from its throne.

The famous box score stands as everlasting verification of the most acclaimed game in Indiana basketball history:

Milan (32) | Muncie (30)

	FG	FT	TP	PF		FG	FT	TP	PF
Truitt	2	1	5	2	Hinds	3	4	10	3
Engel	1	0	2	0	Flowers	5	1	11	0
White	0	1	1	2	Casterlow	0	0	0	1
Plump	3	4	10	1	Raisor	0	0	0	2
Craft	4	6	14	0	Barnes	2	1	5	2
Cutter	0	0	0	0	Crawford	0	2	2	0
Wendelman	0	0	0	0	Agullana	1	0	2	3
Totals	10	12	32	5		11	8	30	11

Shooting averages: Milan: 10-32 FGA, .313, 12-13 FTA, .923
Muncie: 11-42 FGA, .262, 8-9 FTA, .889
Officials: Referree, Marvin Todd; Umpire, Cyril Birge

THE MILAN MIRACLE

At tournament time every year since, the Milan Miracle is recalled by sportswriters and followers of Indiana high school basketball. Fans are always looking for the next people's choice to remind them that the size of the school matters less than the size of the hearts of its players.

In Morgans Awe, two boys were inspired by the events of the third Saturday in March, 1954. The notion that they, too, might one day stand where Bobby Plump and Ray Craft had was planted that night in Josh Seaberg and Jake Skoon.

9

THOSE HALCYON DAYS

Jourden Arena
8:14 p.m.

Up in Row F, Seat 12, Katy O'Ryan engaged in the superstitious ritual she followed before the start of each of her husband's games. Surrounded by family and friends, she first hugged each person in turn. Katy then kissed the cross worn around her neck and closed her eyes for a brief prayer, ending by tracing the sign of the cross on her chest. She gripped her rosary beads tightly in her palms, enduring the endless angst of a coach's wife.

Scanning quickly her game program, she noted, apprehensively, the marked difference in the height and weight of the Cougar squad and her Raider boys.

Dressed in their distinctive home uniforms, with white, T-shirt style jerseys and trunks of solid cherry red with white trim, the Madison players broke their huddle, shouting in unison, "Pride!"

The Raiders lingered, forming a tight circle around Coach O'Ryan. His final words were almost always brief and inspirational rather than instructional. With a wry grin the coach said simply, "Ain't no bronc never been rode. Ain't no cowboy never been throwed."

Jake and his mates burst from their huddle with an enthusiastic chorus of "Team!"

Starters of the opposing teams met at center court for the traditional handshake. Players were sweating profusely already, a result of the heat radiating from the arc lights above and from the capacity crowd crammed into the arena. And, of course, from the nearly unbearable tension.

The murmuring of the spectators had grown steadily into a crescendo of sound as players of the two squads reached the center circle. A prolonged, continuous din reverberated throughout the arena as cheerleaders incited seven thousand ardent rooters to higher and still higher levels of intensity.

THE HOOSIER GAME

MORGANS AWE "RAIDERS"

Colors:	Orange and Black
Head Coach:	Michael O'Ryan
Asst. Coach:	John Barnhard
Athletic Dir.:	Rufus Gottschalk
Principal:	Mr. Otis Oberfeldt

Player	Ht.	Wt.	Cl.	Po.	W—C
Bobby Mack Deal **	5-9	135	Sr.	g	2—3
Jake Skoon ***	6-2	155	Sr.	g	4—5
Bond Bathwaite	5-10	160	Jr.	g	10—11
Jamie Ross *	5-9	140	Sr.	g	12—13
Orson Mannheim *	5-9	145	Sr.	f	20—21
Sonny Watkins **	5-11	160	Sr.	f	24—25
Josh Seaberg **	6-3	175	Sr.	f	30—31
Elmer Freebolt	6-0	165	Sr.	f	32—33
Joe Cotter *	5-10	150	Sr.	f	40—41
C.C. Aguirre	5-7	155	Jr.	g	44—45
Mark Danner **	6-4	210	Sr.	c	50—51
Grover Willburn	6-5	180	Jr.	c	52—53

MADISON CENTRAL "COUGARS"

Colors:	Red, white, and blue
Head Coach:	Saul Fortune
Asst. Coach:	Luke Prizendine
Athletic Dir:	Rob Laurence
Principal:	Dr. Warren Brown

Player	Ht.	Wt.	Cl.	Po.	W-C
Marty Miller*	6-4	170	Sr.	g	3
Roosevelt Dime	5-8	145	So.	g	5
Cole Wells**	5-10	180	Sr.	g	10
Henry Fields*	5-10	160	Jr.	g	13
Clay Childs	6-2	205	Sr.	f	20
Jerry Hankins*	6-4	175	Jr.	f	23
Augie Andriss	5-11	170	So.	g	25
Charley Clendon*	6-2	165	Jr.	f	30
Darrell Bratton*	6-3	170	Jr.	f	33
Donel Satterwhite	6-6	190	So.	c	43
Karl DeVreaux**	6-5	225	Sr.	f	45
DeWitt Weatherford**	6-6	185	Sr.	c	50

108

Except for the officials at the scoring table, everyone was standing.

The two referees, faces taut, proceeded to center court. Each was dressed in black and white striped shirts, pressed gray pants, white shoes, and a whistle on a cord around the neck. The taller of the two carried the orange Spaulding basketball beneath one arm.

As he lined up beside a Madison player, Josh's tongue felt like a dry stick in a mouth of dough. He knew that after the opening tip his pounding heart, labored breathing, and those twelve monkeys jumping around in his stomach would subside. Once the game began, it was as if a light switch turned off the nerves and the trained athlete kicked in.

The arena lights over the spectators were dimmed.

The head official stepped between Mark Danner and DeWitt Weatherford, ready to toss the ball high into the air. Players around the circle jostled for position.

Tip-off time.

It was about to get personal.

Spring, 1954
Morgans Awe

With Memorial Day came the end of the school year. The annual swim in Brushy Fork following the final day of school tested the gang's mettle. No matter how chilly the weather and frigid the water, the boys hurled themselves into the swimming hole with gusto.

Morgans Awe had no youth baseball program. When tryouts began in Madison's Little League, Sonny Watkins's father, who'd never played organized ball, drove him there in hopes his son could make one of the teams.

First, however, Sonny needed a ball glove. A lefty, Sonny had never owned a proper fielder's glove. In sandlot games in Morgans Awe, only mitts made for right-handed players were available; so in order to throw with his dominant arm, Sonny had become adept at catching a ball with the fingers of his right hand jammed awkwardly into a wrong-handed glove.

On the day of tryouts, Sonny's dad took him to the Western Auto store in Madison to buy his first mitt. As Sonny scanned the rack of some twenty fielder's gloves he realized that none were made for left-handers. His dad, having no idea which arm Sonny threw with, eagerly encouraged him to pick out any glove he wanted. Sonny seized the bird in the bush. He grabbed one of the right-hander's mitts. Mr. Watkins paid the $12 price and off they went to the ball diamond.

The volunteer coaches randomly placed boys in positions around the diamond, hitting grounders and fly balls to assess the skills of each of the

THE HOOSIER GAME

players. Sonny was assigned to third base. Not wanting to be embarrassed in front of his peers, he placed his new glove properly on his left hand and awaited his first grounder. He scooped the ball cleanly, but made an awkward wrong-handed throw that barely traveled half way to first base.

Instructing Sonny to "really throw hard, not like a girl," the coach hit two more balls at him, each with the same result. When the coach pointed to right field, Sonny asked if he might have one more try. He then switched the glove to his right hand. Sonny easily snatched the hot grounder the coach hit to him. He blazed a throw to the boy playing first base, who wasn't expecting the high-speed missile now coming straight at him. Sonny's throw hit the boy full in the chest. The coaches rushed to aid the sobbing first baseman. Assured that the boy was okay, the coach turned to the Morgans Awe lad, exclaiming, "Son, you're left-handed."

"Yes, sir," Sonny meekly replied.

"And durn fast, too. Boy, git over there with them pitchers."

After that incident, with his overwhelming fastball, Sonny became the best hurler in the league.

Sunday, July 11, 1954
Cincinnati, Ohio

On this day, Mr. Seaberg and Mr. Arney piled Josh, Sonny, Drake Arney, and Jake in the Arneys' station wagon for a trip to Cincinnati to watch the Redlegs face the Brooklyn Dodgers. It would be the boys' first time at a big league game. Crossing over the old iron bridge on Hopple Street, the excited boys could see Crosley Field in the hazy distance.

Finding their seats in the Sun Deck in right field, the youths were captivated by the lush emerald grass of the vast ball field. The grounds crew smoothed the reddish-brown soil of the infield and marked the baselines with brilliant white lime just before the start of the game. The sights, sounds, and smells of the ballpark melded into an image each would carry into adulthood.

As the home team trotted onto the playing field, Josh's baseball cards sprang to life. There, in person, were the Reds' Ed Bailey, Roy McMillan, Johnny Temple, Gus Bell, Wally Post, and slugger Ted Kluszewski. Unlike his teammates, Big Klu eschewed the red undershirt beneath the sleeveless Reds jersey, displaying massive shoulders and biceps.

Josh was a devoted Dodgers fan. Among his favorites were the burly catcher, Roy Campanella; Carl Furrillo, the rightfielder with the rocket arm; the fiery Jackie Robinson; and the Duke of Flatbush, home run smasher Duke Snider. If Paradise had truly been lost, Josh had found it at Crosley Field.

In a slugfest, the Dodgers beat the Redlegs, 12-9. Furrillo's seventh inning grand slam provided the winning margin.

After the game, the adults led the boys to a gate where they could get a close look at the Dodger players walking to the team bus. Hoosier native Carl Erskine paused briefly to sign Marshall Seaberg's game program. Marshall then placed the precious memento in Josh's eager hands.

As Brooklyn's splendid first baseman, Gil Hodges—another star from Indiana—hurried to the bus Josh had a creepy thought. With his black, slicked-back hair, squinting eyes, and aquiline nose, Hodges resembled Bela Lugosi, the frightening Dracula of late night TV movies.

Summer, 1954
Morgans Awe

Summer vacation provided the unencumbered boys with time and space for the high jinks common to adolescents. No one wore helmets while roller-skating or riding bikes. Skinned knees and bumps and bruises, colds, and other normal childhood maladies were handled with homemade potions or a sympathetic kiss on the wound.

One day Timmy Dole scrounged up an old pair of pillow-like boxing gloves from the family attic. A flimsy boxing ring was constructed, consisting of clothesline wrapped around a tree, a rake, and two broom handles rammed into the ground. The bouts were spirited, consisting mostly of pushing and shoving and headlocks. Wild punches rarely connected. The cotton-stuffed gloves ensured that no one would be seriously injured even if a wayward blow found its mark.

The boys thought they had witnessed their first real knockout in one match when Pee Wee Reynolds smacked Iggy Conrow flush on the schnozzle. Iggy staggered, then dropped like a stone, lying there with a slight strand of blood leaking from his nose.

Iggy became a hero for being the first to be rendered unconscious in combat. But later that day he confessed to taking a dive and acting close to death to hide his embarrassment at being tagged by the littlest guy on the block.

THE HOOSIER GAME

Naturally, when he came clean, Iggy was the target of merciless taunts and teasing.

Every kid was familiar with kick-the-can, a form of hide-and-seek with a different twist. A tin can was placed at home base. A boy was chosen to be "it," and while he counted to twenty-five the others scattered to conceal themselves. The object was to emerge from hiding and kick the can before the defender did. If you lost, you were now "it" and the game started over.

Gabby Weathers was the prototypical chubby tenderfoot in the neighborhood, rotund and slow of foot. If Gabby strayed even ten yards from the base most of the boys could run the length of a football field and still beat him to the can.

One time, Arnie Packard, who was no Jesse Owens himself, lost the race as Gabby lumbered to the can first. Gabby finally would get to hide instead of being "it."

However, the devious Arnie had set Gabby up. As Arnie began counting, all the lads found safe hiding. The portly Gabby chose to conceal himself behind an obstacle nearest to home base. That fact was confirmed when Arnie stole a furtive glimpse and saw Gabby's ample butt protruding from a maple tree twenty feet away.

Arnie began to move farther from home base. Peering from his hiding spot Gabby believed Arnie was far enough away that he might have a chance to reach home first. So he left the safety of his refuge and began trundling toward the can. As the other boys watched, Arnie turned suddenly to begin his sprint toward the base. It would be close.

Amazingly, Gabby beat Arnold by a few steps and the portly lad swung his leg forward to kick the Doles pineapple tin with as much force as he could muster. On impact, however, the can failed to move. Gabby fell forward in a heap, yelling in confused agony.

He wasn't aware that as he had shuffled off to his hiding place Arnold had used the hammer he had hidden under his jacket to pound a wooden stake into the ground—at the exact height of the can—and then placed the can atop it.

Gabby's mother called Mrs. Packard that night after her sobbing son reached home. Arnie was confined to the homestead brig for a week, while Gabby nursed his sore big toe.

Among other memorable antics was the time Larry Marker un-stole an item that he lifted from Hawkins General Store. That day, while a dozen of the gang stood in a circle playing mumblety-peg with their pocketknives, Larry's older brother, Dean, drove up in his '49 Willys Jeepster to fetch Larry for dinner. Like many teenage boys old enough to drive, Dean had attached a suicide knob to the steering wheel of the car, allowing him to drive with one hand while wrapping his other arm around his girlfriend. These small Lucite knobs were considered ultra-cool.

Larry decided that such an attractive doodad was just the thing he needed on his bicycle handlebars. Of course, he didn't have a dollar to buy one. He decided to go into Hawkins's to cob it. Sure enough, the next day he rode up brandishing a steering knob on his handlebar, which had a gaudy yellow rose within the transparent acrylic base.

The young Marker's glory lasted less than a day. His guilty conscience and fear that someone had seen the dirty deed and would report him to the police had gnawed at him since committing the high crime. Afraid to go to the clerk with an apology, he atoned for the theft by returning to the store and slipping the knob back into the bin. His act of contrition was no doubt unusual—not many proprietors have stolen merchandise snuck back onto their shelves.

Donny Waithen was a committed and adept maven of such offbeat skills as walking on stilts or on his hands. He especially enjoyed using tin cans for shoes. Wearing tennis sneakers, Donny would stomp on soup cans with each foot. The tin folded around the soles and he would walk about as if it were stylish to wear cans on his feet. Once he tried to play baseball on his unique cleats. He got a hit, but as he rounded first he threw a can and sprawled in a patch of sandburs. Picking out the spiny stickers proved to be the least of his problems. The rest of the players comforted him until his parents arrived and took him to the hospital to tend to his broken ankle.

Collecting baseball cards became a competition for the boys who could afford the ten cents to purchase a pack of eight rectangular trading cards and a flat piece of bubble gum. A picture of a Major League player graced the front, with his statistics on the reverse side. All the boys envied Murray Oldham, as he had a card for every player in the starting line-up in both the National and American leagues.

The cards served a dual purpose. To make their bikes sound like motorcycles, boys would fasten a baseball card or two to one of the forks on the front wheel. As the bike gathered speed, the cards would flap against each of the spokes, producing a rat-a-tat sound.

THE HOOSIER GAME

Fall, 1954
Morgans Awe

Summer break ended with the annual Labor Day celebration. A popular quartet, the Crew-Cuts, was at the top of the pop music charts with their hit, "Sh-Boom."

> *Hey nonny ding dong, alang alang alang,*
> *Boom ba-doh, ba-doo ba-doodle-ay,*
> *Oh, life could be a dream (sh-boom),*
> *If I could take you up in paradise up above (sh-boom),*
> *If you would tell me I'm the only one that you love,*
> *Life could be a dream, sweetheart,*
> *(Hello, hello again, sh-boom and hopin' we'll meet again).*

The next morning, Josh took his seat in Mr. Mohrer's fifth grade classroom to begin the new term. At the beginning of each school day, Principal Oberfeldt came on the intercom to direct faculty, staff, and students to rise to recite America's Pledge of Allegiance. Today the announcement was delayed so that teachers could explain the addition of two words to the national oath of loyalty. On the chalkboard Mr. Mohrer had written in neat cursive the Pledge that now included the words "under God." On June 14 President Eisenhower had signed the clause into law, the result of a national campaign by the Knights of Columbus to thwart a growing movement to separate church and state in public references to Christianity.

In the ensuing months, Josh, Jake and their friends would delight in playing the first organized basketball of their young lives. During the summer, a new head coach, Michael O'Ryan, was hired to replace 62-year-old Rufus Gottschalk, the Morgans Awe mentor for the past eleven seasons. The boys learned that Mr. O'Ryan was a stern taskmaster who intended to bring his own brand of discipline and attention to fundamentals to the basketball program.

Coach O'Ryan had started a youth league on Saturdays for Morgans Awe's fifth and sixth grade boys. After a couple of days practice, the youngsters were divided into six teams of seven players each.

Of all those competing in the league Josh was among the taller players. Having competed with older boys and men, he also was more skilled than most of his peers.

Despite being a skinny runt of a kid, Jake, meanwhile, regularly filled the basket with his deadly one-handed push shot from distances on the court that few of the others even attempted.

The varsity coach was present every Saturday to watch the games, and his steady encouragement inspired confidence in the youngsters. Coach O'Ryan insisted on fair play, teaching the boys to be gracious in both victory and defeat. He would become the most influential person in Josh's life, outside of his family.

The Seabergs purchased season tickets for Morgans Awe high school home games. Young Josh was captivated by the colors of contrasting uniforms, the pep band, the cheerleaders, the noise of the crowd, and the heroics of the players.

Each Saturday afternoon, Josh tuned in to the Big Ten Game of the Week, listening to the smooth, baritone voice of broadcaster Jack Drees and his excitable partner, Lindsey Nelson. Major network televised sports coverage was limited to that telecast and a small segment of the nightly news.

Indiana University's games reached Morgans Awe via independent television station Sarkes-Tarzian, originating from Bloomington. Josh followed the exploits of Coach Branch McCracken and his Hurryin' Hoosiers through the partisan voices of Bob Cook and Paul Lennon.

The telecasts were sponsored by Chesty Potato Chips. Betty's weekly grocery list always included a 25-cent bag of the Chesty chips and a half-dozen six-ounce Cokes. During the Monday night IU games, Josh was allowed to consume the entire bag of chips and one of the Cokes.

In November, on his tenth birthday, Josh opened a very special gift from his parents. Unwrapping a colorful, checkbook-sized box, Josh found three tickets to attend the Hoosiers' season opener on the fourth of December. That evening, along with a capacity crowd of 10,000 in the old IU fieldhouse, Josh reveled in IU's 77-66 victory over Valparaiso. His favorite player, 6-10 center Don Schlundt, tallied twenty points.

Jake fell asleep that night with visions of one day playing for the Crimson and Cream-clad Indiana University team.

Friday, Christmas Eve day, 1954

Enticed by the aroma from his mom's brownies baking in the oven, Josh entered the family kitchen, only to find his mother quietly sobbing over the

THE HOOSIER GAME

sink. Grampa Stines had died a week before last Christmas and Betty Stines Marshall was still grieving his passing. Only moments before, she had been singing carols and laughing during her favorite season of the year. But then Josh heard the tenor voice of his mom's favorite singer, Eddie Fisher, on her small Philco, vocalizing his latest pop hit, *O My Papa*. The lyrics struck Betty where raw feelings were kept.

Oh, my pa-pa, to me he was so wonderful,
Oh, my pa-pa, to me he was so good.
No one could be, so gentle and so lovable,
Oh, my pa-pa, he always understood.
Gone are the days when he would take me on his knee,
And with a smile he'd change my tears to laughter.
Oh, my pa-pa, so funny, so adorable,
Always the clown, so funny in his way.
Oh, my pa-pa, to me he was so wonderful,
Deep in my heart, I miss him so today.

Monday, December 27, 1954
Augusta, Georgia

Since Christmas vacation lasted until January 5, Josh accompanied his mother on a road trip that would take him farther from Morgans Awe than he had ever traveled. Betty's younger sister, Mary, had given birth to her first child that week at the Ft. Gordon military post near Augusta, Georgia, where her husband served in the Army. Betty and Josh climbed aboard a Greyhound bus in Louisville that would carry them on their journey south.

Living in rural Indiana, in a town with no blacks, Josh had had little exposure to prejudice and the unfair treatment of Negroes. On this trip he would witness for the first time the institution of segregation in the Southern states.

Changing buses at the depot in Knoxville, Tennessee, Josh encountered separate drinking fountains and bathrooms marked, "Whites Only" and "Colored Only."

As he and his mother traveled deeper into the South, the bus driver halted numerous times to take on passengers waiting at designated stops along the route. At one point, a tired-looking, dark-skinned woman, holding her belongings in a brown sack, stepped onto the bus. Josh noticed she moved directly to the rear of the bus without pause or comment.

Even for a young, naive boy like Josh, unaware of the culture's Jim Crow rules for blacks, the indignity of treating a group of human beings that way seemed mean. Something wasn't right about that, he thought.

At that same time in the north, a group of teenagers were making their own statement for the advancement of their race. Led by a quiet but resolute coach, a basketball team from a segregated Indianapolis high school was breaking down barriers in the sacred basketball gyms of Indiana.

They were known as the Crispus Attucks "Flying Tigers."

10

YOU CAN PLAY— IF YOU'RE NOT CATHOLIC OR BLACK

Jourden Arena
8:15 p.m.

Mark Danner and the stoical DeWitt Weatherford were coiled in anticipation of the game-opening toss. Cradling the ball, the ref quickly flipped it high above the two. Both players sprang into the air.

Weatherford jumped quicker and higher than the thick-legged Morgans Awe center, tapping the ball forcefully toward the backcourt and into the hands of guard Cole Wells.

Madison had first turn.

Wells whipped a brisk pass up court to forward Ned Hankins. Spotting Weatherford flashing through the key, Hankins flipped the ball to his teammate. Mark was a step behind the play, so Raider forward Sonny Watkins moved to cut off the Cub star's thrust to the basket. Weatherford used his left forearm to fend off the player a half foot shorter, his elbow slapping forcefully onto Sonny's forehead. The ball nestled softly into the net as the referee's shrill whistle stopped play. With his upraised hand clenched into a fist, the official pointed at Sonny.

"Foul on number twenty-five! Basket is good."

Coach O'Ryan sprang from the bench, emphatically calling for an offensive foul against Weatherford. The ref coolly ignored O'Ryan's protest. Standing in front of the scorer's table, he raised two fingers of his left hand and all five of the right. Sonny raised his hand as required.

The Raiders coach continued to plead his case as the man in charge moved to his position beneath the Madison Central basket.

THE HOOSIER GAME

Weatherford's free throw completed the three-point play. The sequence of events had taken only four seconds.

Josh retrieved the ball from the net and stepped out of bounds to begin play for the Raiders. Expecting an easy toss-in to a teammate, he saw instead the two Madison guards Saran-wrapped to Jake and Bond. Josh looked frantically to pass the ball inbounds.

After slashing the air with his right hand five times, the man in stripes again brought a halt to the action.

"Five-second violation. White ball."

Sonny had committed his first mental mistake of the game. Trotting across the ten-second line, he'd forgotten to remain in the backcourt as an outlet should the guards be covered.

Coach O'Ryan had warned his players that the Cougars would start the game with hard-nosed, full court pressure.

Saul Fortune's emphasis on defensive mayhem was in fact the centerpiece of his coaching philosophy. Madison's players attacked opponents end-line to end-line with skin-tight defense that resulted in a lot of slight but bothersome contact. Bodies collided, knees gouged thighs, and wrists and arms were slapped by wanton swipes at the ball. Madison Central's exhausting display of strength, quickness, and will wore opponents down. Fortune constantly badgered the refs from the bench, whining that "You can't call a 'ticky-tack' foul like that! C'mon, ref. Let 'em play!"

The draining monotony of his team's physical play usually influenced the referees to overlook all but the most explicit fouls. Officials found that attempting to call every incident of contact constantly interrupted the flow of play. Tonight they were allowing the two teams to mix it up, giving Coach Saul's bigger and stronger squad a decided edge.

Following the turnover, Cole Wells signaled the out-of-bounds play. The Cougars lined up in a box formation at the free throw lane. Hankins screened for Weatherford, then suddenly spun halfway around to receive Wells's pass. The play worked perfectly. Mark stayed with DeWitt. Sonny was caught in the pick, leaving the 6-4 Hankins wide open for an easy basket.

Madison 5, Morgans Awe 0.

As the ball slipped through the cords Sonny snatched it and hurriedly passed to Bathwaite. Bond made a quick move laterally, received the ball and confidently started up court. A look of bewilderment crossed his face when the lightning hands of Wells slapped the ball cleanly from behind toward Marty Miller. Catching it in stride, the lanky guard took one dribble toward the goal. An easy two.

The Raiders trailed by seven only twenty-four seconds into the quarter.

YOU CAN PLAY— IF YOU'RE NOT CATHOLIC OR BLACK

On the subsequent possession, Josh in-bounded the ball to the tightly-guarded Jake Skoon. As the Raider guard turned and began dribbling along the sideline, Weatherford darted into his path. Miller closed to harass him, digging at the ball as he bumped knees with his adversary. Jake dribbled the basketball off his foot and out of bounds.

Miller received the in-bounds toss at the top of the free throw circle and in one fluid motion launched his high-arcing left-handed push shot over a flailing Sonny Watkins. Nothing but net. Nine-zip.

Madison continued to pressure the ball. Bond managed to dribble by his defender and spotted Josh unguarded about fifteen feet on the right side of the Morgans Awe hoop. The junior guard's hasty pass landed in the lap of a fan in the third row of the bleachers.

Before the stricken Raiders could retreat to defend their basket Wells hurled a baseball pass to Miller at the centerline. Marty fed Ned Hankins hustling down the middle. Hankins lofted an alley-oop pass to a wide-open Weatherford near the Cougar basket. Stretching at the apex of his leap, the Madison star snared the ball in both hands and laid it lightly over the rim and into the net.

The Central crowd erupted while Morgans Awe rooters cringed at the withering onslaught.

The Raiders' first four offensive possessions had resulted in turnovers. Morgans Awe had not attempted even one shot. Madison hadn't missed one.

The Cougars led 11-0 with a brutally efficient display of picture perfect basketball. Josh's worst nightmare was occurring in front of the largest audience he'd ever played before.

Coach Ryan calmly arose.

"Time out!"

May 5, 2012
Morgans Awe

Returning to Will's makeshift bar, Josh found his former teammates in a spirited debate about the best Indiana high school teams of all time. Mark offered his opinion that the 1961-62 Manual Redskins, led by identical twins Tom and Dick VanArsdale, both of whom became All-Americans and NBA stars, could have handled the best of their era.

"That Manual team our junior year was the best I ever seen," Mark proclaimed. "Them VanArsdell twins just dominated."

"C'mon, Markus," Moon retorted, "You do remember they never even won the state!"

"Referees screwed 'em in the champeen-ship game against Kokomo," Danner argued.

"Are you tryin' to tell me they coulda beat Greg Oden and Mike Conley at Lawrence North? Those guys won three titles in a row!"

"Hey, Don't forgit," Orson Mannheim replied, "The Marion Giants won three straight, too. Eighty-five, eighty-six, an' eighty-seven. Bill Green ended up coachin', how many champs? Five?"

"He won six, actually. Those at Marion and one other. Can't remember where—"

"It was that 1969 Indin'aplis Warshington team," Bobby Mack Deal offered. "They didn't lose a game that year. McGinnis and Downing made All-Americans at IU and both of 'em played in the pros, too."

Sonny chimed in, "The best team to ever come out of these parts was Madison in 1950. Twenty-six and two, won the state. With Spence Schnaitter, Bud Bunton, and Ted Server they were the highest-scoring team ever at that time."

"That's prob'ly true."

"You guys must be losin' touch in your old age," said Fries, entering the fray. "Any fool who knows Indiana basketball knows that the Attucks teams of '55 and '56 were the best ever. Even if Oscar'd never been born they woulda won the state. With him, nobody could touch 'em. They only lost *once* in sixty-two games those two years."

"Yeah, think of all the championships Attucks mighta won if they hadn't been barred from the tournament all those years."

Indiana High School Athletic Association
Indianapolis, Indiana

During the first three decades of Indiana high school basketball tournament play, not every Hoosier boy could aspire to be a member of a state championship team. Generally, if you were not white and Protestant you were not eligible to play in the event. During that time, Hoosier Catholic and segregated, all-black high schools shared an ignoble parity. The Indiana High School Athletic Association had denied membership to both.

Universal anti-Catholic bias was exported to America from its earliest beginnings. Insoluble differences in religious beliefs and discrimination against Catholics by the Protestant majority forced the Catholic Church to develop a scholastic system for its brethren separate from public schools.

YOU CAN PLAY— IF YOU'RE NOT CATHOLIC OR BLACK

From 1928-42, Indiana private Catholic high schools—like Indianapolis Cathedral, Ft. Wayne Central Catholic, Anderson St. Mary's, and Evansville Memorial—held a championship basketball tournament apart from the annual IHSAA extravaganza.

Like Catholic schools, all-black high schools in Indiana were discouraged from playing basketball against sanctioned member schools—and were banned from state tournament play—because of the policies of the IHSAA Board of Control.

Interestingly, because they chose to assimilate into American public schools, Jews were less likely than Catholics and African-Americans to be the subject of official discrimination in high school sports. Fearing that Jewish Day Schools would create an unhealthy division between Hebrew and Gentile communities, Jews preferred that their children learn American culture and language through public schools. Religious instruction for Jewish students was provided in Synagogues.

The history of racial discrimination in Indiana has been well-documented. Although slavery had been outlawed by an act of the territorial government in 1816, the revised Indiana Constitution of 1851 forbid "further immigration of blacks and mulattoes to the state" and further directed "those already resident in the state to emigrate elsewhere."

Following the Civil War, in response to the humiliating and often brutal policies of Reconstruction, a number of former Confederate officers organized the Ku Klux Klan to, according to its founders, "protect its women and the Southern way of life." In practice, that meant terrorizing and disenfranchising blacks. What historians call the "second wave" of the KKK originated during and just after the First World War.

At that time, Indiana was alleged to have the most powerful Klan organization north of the Mason-Dixon Line. Politicians sympathetic to and supported by the Klan rose to high positions in Indiana government. The KKK demonstrated its influence with the 1924 election of Edward Jackson as governor. His campaign was eagerly advanced by Grand Dragon D.C. (David Curtiss) Stephenson, a rabid racist, and his followers.

The migration of five million poor African-Americans from the South, seeking a better life in northern cities, reached its peak in the early 1920s. America's largest minority settled in urban areas, where heavy industry sought cheap labor.

The saturation of blacks in the inner city of Indianapolis created a problem of providing education to the growing population of black children and teens.

THE HOOSIER GAME

Confronting this dilemma, the Indiana General Assembly passed an act requiring school trustees of communities with a sufficient number of African-Americans to organize separate, segregated schools.

Despite protests from many in the community, Crispus Attucks High School was constructed in 1922 exclusively for black students and faculty, making segregation in education official policy in the capital city.

Two other Hoosier cities with high numbers of African-Americans quickly followed the Indianapolis model. Evansville Lincoln (1927) became the second blacks-only high school in Indiana, followed by Gary Roosevelt (1929).

Although these three high schools were built specifically to isolate blacks from the greater white student population, to say that Indiana public education was completely segregated by race in those days is not entirely accurate.

Many small communities, like Franklin, Indiana, had been part of a secret network of abolitionists and sympathizers—the so-called "underground railroad"—during the 19th-century who provided safe houses for black slaves escaping to free states and Canada. Descendants of blacks who remained in predominantly white communities could gain acceptance, particularly if a black teen could help the high school basketball team win games.

The state athletic association recognized that barring those athletes from playing would arouse the wrath of many citizens of integrated towns. The IHSAA quietly accepted the fuzzy hypocrisy that allowed a handful of high schools to play minorities on their squads.

The first great black athlete to play for a state champion was Dave DeJernett, star player for the state champion Washington Hatchets in 1930. A mere five months following the IHSAA tourney—August 7, 1930—two young black men, Thomas Shipp and Abram Smith, were hung on a tree seventy miles northeast of Indianapolis at Marion, Indiana. Lynching was still alive, and not just in the Southern states.

Monday, December 8, 1941
Washington, D.C.

On Monday, following the attack on Pearl Harbor, President Roosevelt and the Congress of the United States declared war on the Empire of Japan. Lost in the fervor of America's entrée into the worldwide conflict was an historic action by the Indiana High School Athletic Association that would hardly be noticed outside the Hoosier state. However, the effect of the legislation would be immeasurable to a society bound to the game of basketball from its roots upward.

Saturday, December 20, 1941
Indianapolis, Indiana

Twelve days following Roosevelt's historic speech, the IHSAA announced a resolution to allow all schools to participate in the organization's sanctioned events:

> *Membership in the Association shall be open beginning August 15, 1942 to all public, private, parochial, colored, and institutional high schools of the state offering and maintaining three or four years of high school work, provided they meet the requirements of the Association and also subscribe to its rules and regulations.*

The 1943 tourney would be the first in which all high schools, public and private, black and white, would be invited to participate.

From the beginning Crispus Attucks administrators confronted two severe challenges in seeking to provide an athletic program for its teenage boys. In building the new high school, Indianapolis school board members provided only a nominal sum in construction costs for a gymnasium. Attucks's tiny gym was little more than a practice facility, seating fewer than fifty spectators. As a result, Tiger teams were forced to play all of its games on foreign courts.

Additionally, the Tigers' athletic director encountered great difficulty in putting together sports schedules. Public schools in Indianapolis and scores of others throughout the state refused to play Attucks's squads, forcing them to travel to compete with high school teams in surrounding states.

In the summer of 1950, Crispus Attucks High School principal Russell Lane hired a relatively unknown junior high school teacher named Ray Crowe to coach the varsity basketball team. The result would be seven years of unparalleled basketball excellence.

Under the leadership of Ray Crowe, Crispus Attucks teams would become among the best known and most-feared fives in the history of Indiana basketball. Coach Crowe and his talented teenagers would revolutionize high school

THE HOOSIER GAME

basketball. In contrast to most teams' deliberate, controlled tactics, the Tigers rolled over opponents with their fast-paced tempo, selfless teamwork, and aggressive defense.

Unforeseen by those who refused to play Attucks were the many smaller high schools in rural areas that began to make room on their schedules for the Tigers. Curious white fans in small towns came out in droves to see the athletic black teens play the game with their high-energy style.

In Crowe, Principal Lane had found an ideal partner to carry out his agenda for racial harmony. Lane insisted that his students—players and rooters—behave "appropriately" at the games. That meant acting in ways acceptable to whites. Lane himself would accompany the team to other schools on game night, making certain to greet and shake hands with as many of the opponents' officials, board members, and fans as possible.

Like Lane, Crowe was a disciplinarian. He allowed his players no arguing with referees, no disrespecting other players or fans, and no overzealous celebrating, lest they offend their white counterparts. Crowe had been exposed early on to the injustice and bigotry of elements of white society. He would deal with racial discrimination with dignity, hard work, wise decisions, and utter respect for himself and others, regardless of color.

After advancing deep into the state tourney from 1951 through 1954, Attucks finally broke through to the championship in 1955.

Josh remembered the thrill of seeing Oscar Robertson and the Flying Tigers play, in person, for the first time.

Saturday, March 12, 1955
Morgans Awe to Indianapolis, Indiana

Of all the teachers in the one-building Morgans Awe School, Mrs. Eva Felling was among the most favored by her students. Two generations of Morgans Awe graduates had passed through her fifth grade English class. Mrs. Felling was equally adept at teaching manners and other life skills to feral eleven-year-old lads as in parsing compound sentences.

Her husband, Harold, was superintendent of schools at nearby Jericho.

The Fellings never missed a Morgans Awe game, home or away. Mrs. Felling had taken a fancy to her students Jake, Josh, and Sonny. Several times during the season the couple had treated the boys—with parents' permission, of course—to Raiders' games outside of the county.

YOU CAN PLAY—IF YOU'RE NOT CATHOLIC OR BLACK

Among Mr. Felling's close friends was the superintendent of the Rushville school system. It was through his former IU roommate that he had purchased five tickets for the 1955 Indianapolis semi-state tournament. When the Fellings invited the three boys to attend, the youngsters were overjoyed.

Today, Josh, Jake, and Sonny—scrubbed up and dressed in their Sunday clothes—squeezed into the rear seat of the Fellings' 1955 Ford Fairlane for the hundred-mile trip to the state capital. To them, traveling to Butler Fieldhouse in faraway Indianapolis was tantamount to receiving a pass through the Pearly Gates to survey Heaven.

Arriving at Meridian Street on Indianapolis's south side, the car passed through a seemingly endless gauntlet of stoplights as they headed north. Finally Mr. Felling turned left onto 49th Street in the Butler-Tarkington area. Ahead of them, rising out of the ground, appeared an immense brick structure.

Josh, Jake, and Sonny had their first look at the holy cathedral of Indiana basketball, Butler Fieldhouse. On entering the building, the utter size of the arena was a jaw-dropping sensation.

"I never seen a barn this big," Sonny whispered to his mates. The Fellings chuckled softly at the wide eyes and open-mouthed amazement of their young charges. They delighted at the unspoiled wonderment of the lads.

While the vast building ran lengthwise, east to west, the court inside was positioned north to south. The wooden bleachers climbed gradually upward, row after row. At the top of the cavernous arena, players on the court looked like miniature people.

Contributing to the distinctive aura of the legendary basketball arena were the massive clerestory windows high above the court. During afternoon games, brilliant rays of sunshine blended with dazzling vapor lighting to create an unforgettable visual effect.

Its sonorous sound system reverberated into every nook and cranny of the hall, accentuating the feeling of immensity.

The Felling party passed along the sidelines as they walked toward their seats in row five. The players benches were located about a foot and a half below the raised court.

"Mr. Felling," Jake asked, "How many people does this place hold?"

"About 15,000," was the casual reply.

Actually, attendance for today's semi-final match-ups would be identical to that of every state final since the tournament first came to the Butler Fieldhouse

THE HOOSIER GAME

in 1928 (with the exception of a three-year hiatus during World War II, when the event was held at the Indianapolis Coliseum). Every one of the 14,983 available seats was filled by fans to watch Columbus challenge Attucks in the first game of the morning session, followed by Rushville against Muncie Central in the afternoon contest.

Tension was building as the 11:45 a.m. tip-off time loomed.

Crispus Attucks and Columbus were into their final pre-game warm-up. The newly polished playing surface glistened. The echo of bouncing basketballs and squeaking shoes clashed with clacking typewriters of newsmen, the chattering of radio commentators speaking excitedly into their microphones, and the spirited fight songs from school pep bands, creating a dizzying cacophony at courtside.

Josh was eager to see the Tigers from the school he had called "Christmas Attics" as a six-year-old. His father had to explain to him that the high school was named in honor of the first American killed in the Revolutionary War, a Negro named Crispus Attucks.

Attucks had won 28 of its twenty-nine games played to date. A junior named Oscar Robertson was the Tigers' best player. Listed as a forward, the 6-5 Robertson played outside or inside with equal skill. While the boys had never seen him play, none would ever forget how #43 performed that day.

Oscar's gift for seeing the whole floor and his instincts for making split-second decisions was beyond the realm of his high school counterparts. There was nothing fancy about his game. His head feints, cross-over dribble, accurate passes, and superb timing as a rebounder set him apart from the others on the floor. He scored on tip-ins, strong drives to the hoop, short turn-around jumpers, fifteen-foot fadeaways, and high-arching shots at ridiculous distances from the basket. Deadly accurate at the free throw line, Oscar lofted the ball, one-handed, from a spot just over his forehead.

Even without Robertson, the Tigers were a formidable collection of high school players. The Attucks kids were mostly poor and several had moved to Indianapolis with their families from the South as youngsters. Bill Scott (Alabama), Sheddrick Mitchell and Bill Hampton (Mississippi), Willie Meriweather, and Robertson (both born in Tennessee) were part of the flight of black families to northern states in the early decades of the twentieth century.

In their shiny green and gold uniforms, the lanky Tigers were imposing. Each was sinuous, athletic, and fundamentally sound. Eyes alert and intense,

YOU CAN PLAY—IF YOU'RE NOT CATHOLIC OR BLACK

they played with little outward emotion, approaching their opponents with respect but absolutely no fear.

Deadly serious from the outset, the Tigers of Coach Ray Crowe dispatched the Bulldogs with ease, 80-62.

The second contest was similar to the first as Muncie Central dominated a scrappy but under-manned Rushville five, 65-48. Coach Jay McCreary's lads were seeking to avenge their stunning loss to Milan in the title game one year ago. All five starters had returned—Hinds, Flowers, Casterlow, Barnes, and Raisor—senior veterans with height, strength, deadly shooting, and stifling defense. The Bearcats were consensus favorites to win the state championship.

Following the Muncie-Rushville rout, the Felling coterie returned to the car and drove south to Monument Circle for a bit of sightseeing. The brief tour of downtown Indianapolis was capped with the boys slogging up the 330 steps of the Soldiers and Sailors Monument for a bird's-eye view of the sprawling city.

The Fellings now treated the boys to a meal at Shapiro's Deli. Corned beef piled high on a home-baked sesame-seed bun and a liberal slice of dill pickle on the side was a new treat for Josh.

It was now time to return to the Fieldhouse. Arriving thirty-five minutes before tip-off the Fellings and the boys found the stands to be nearly full. Indiana's two best teams would meet head-on in tonight's Indianapolis semifinal game in what most sportswriters felt would be the *real* state championship game.

From the beginning of the 1954-55 season, Muncie Central and Crispus Attucks had been rated numbers one and two, respectively, in sportswriters' weekly polls. As they prepared to face one another for the Indianapolis semistate championship, the two squads had combined to win fifty-five games, while losing only once each.

There was some resentment by Attucks players and their fans at their second-place ranking. The Tigers had raced through the sectional and regional rounds of the tourney, defeating the opposition by an average margin of thirty-one points per game.

Many Hoosiers were not happy to witness an all-black high school intrude upon what had once been almost exclusively a white tradition. Though it went unnoticed by the boys, the Fellings sensed an undertone of racial unease in the crowd when white cheerleaders in the uniforms of other Indianapolis high

THE HOOSIER GAME

schools joined their teenage counterparts from Attucks to spur on Tiger rooters. While they did not detect any overt racial epithets, it was evident to the Fellings that numbers in the crowd were dismayed by the too-close mixing of white and black young people.

The Attucks cheer block began to sing their famous "Crazy Song," with half the students echoing the other half's lyrics:

> *Oh, Muncie's rough (Oh, Muncie's rough),*
> *And Muncie's tough (And Muncie's tough).*
> *They can beat everybody (They can beat everybody),*
> *But they can't beat us (No, they can't beat us).*
> *Hi-de-hi-de-hi-de-hi (Hi-de-hi-de-hi-de-hi),*
> *Hi-de-hi-de-hi-de-ho (Hi-de-hi-de-hi-de-ho).*
> *That's the skip-bob-beat-um (That's the skip-bob beat-um),*
> *That's the Crazy Song (That's the Crazy Song.)*

Play was fierce from the start. The score seesawed throughout the game with numerous lead changes and ties. While the Bearcats ran their deliberate offense to perfection the Tigers punctured Muncie's defense by continuously storming to the basket with its vaunted fast-break attack.

With less than ninety seconds left in the game, Attucks had surged to a 71-65 lead. Seemingly beaten, the Muncie team responded with the fury of a wounded animal.

Two free throws by Hinds and another by Casterlow cut Crispus Attucks's lead to 71-68. Another missed attempt by the Tigers led to a basket at the other end by Gene Flowers, bringing the Bearcats to within one point, 71-70. To win, Attucks had only to control the ball for the final twenty-five seconds.

To the horror of the Tigers' fans, Muncie Central's pressure defense forced a turnover by guard Bill Hampton. The Bearcats now had the ball with twelve seconds left to score the winning basket. After a timeout, Muncie's Phil Raisor attempted to throw the ball to Jim Hinds near the basket. Anticipating the pass, Oscar Robertson leaped in front of Hinds to steal the ball, dribbled twice, then tossed the ball high in the air to snuff out the remaining seconds.

Josh and his future varsity teammates had witnessed two great high school teams battle to exhaustion before Crispus Attucks finally won the contest.

YOU CAN PLAY— IF YOU'RE NOT CATHOLIC OR BLACK

Moreover, the boys had seen the future of basketball personified in the man who would become known as the "Big O." Robertson's competitive temperament, court savvy, leadership, and surpassing basketball skills would one day earn him a place among the elite athletes ever to play the game of basketball. Watching Oscar Robertson control a game with his scoring, rebounding, playmaking, and defense was to observe a true master at work.

One week later, Coach Ray Crowe's Flying Tigers left no doubt as to which was the best high school team in Indiana. In the state championship game, Attucks put on an overwhelming exhibition of unbreakable will and devastating efficiency. Robertson played as expected—better than anyone else. His thirty points led Crispus Attucks to a 97-74 victory over another all-black Indiana high school, Gary Roosevelt.

The IHSAA had crowned its first champion from a segregated high school. By winning the 1955 state title, Attucks had proved it could compete with the best of its white teenage counterparts.

Crispus Attucks's rise to prominence in Hoosier high school basketball paralleled pivotal events in the burgeoning movement of African-Americans' struggle for equal opportunity. While Attucks's achievements on the court were impressive, it was the impact on race relations in Indiana that set the team apart from all other tourney champions.

Despite both camouflaged and baldly overt racial taunts and slights, the Attucks team—combining great coaching, superior talent, and "proper" attitudes—began to gain the grudging respect of basketball-loving Hoosiers. As Attucks grew in basketball stature, the general white population could no longer ignore the talent and character of Crowe and his teenage stars.

The Tigers coach and players had compelled reasonable people in Indiana to confront, in earnest, issues of discrimination, justice, and fair play. Emboldened black leaders surfaced to challenge the status quo.

Months later—on December 1, 1955—Josh was seated on the couch reading the latest edition of a new magazine called *Sports Illustrated*. His dad pored over the daily newspaper. As usual, Walter Cronkite was delivering the six o'clock news on CBS-TV. Marshall lifted his eyes to the television upon hearing of an incident that helped change the face of America forever.

Cronkite reported the story of a twenty-year-old seamstress who had refused to give up her seat to a white man on a crowded city bus in Birmingham,

THE HOOSIER GAME

Alabama. Rosa Parks's defiance of the established custom and her subsequent arrest galvanized civil rights leaders—black and white. The indomitable young woman defied the laws of Alabama and in doing so became the symbol of black resistance in America. Miss Parks's courage in the face of utter hostility and personal danger inspired an entire generation to demand equal treatment—a crusade that would be relentless throughout Jake's and Josh's high school years.

11

SITTIN', WHITTLIN', AND SPITTIN'

Jourden Arena
8:19 p.m.

Madison's dominance at both ends of the court had completely unnerved the Raiders. During the two-minute, thirteen-second debacle, the Cougars had exposed the uncertainty in the minds of the Morgans Awe players.

As the official signaled a break in the action, the pumped-up Madison five strode with conviction toward Coach Fortune. Saul would offer restrained praise for their initial efforts. There would be, however, no hint of premature celebration or disrespect for their opponents. Saul was too wise and seasoned to allow his team to fall prey to overconfidence.

O'Ryan's players trudged to their bench like boys returning home from a humiliating showdown with a bully. Shoulders stooped and stunned expressions on ashen faces, they anticipated a severe scolding.

Now was the time for O'Ryan to demonstrate why he had been so successful in his coaching career. His team was in real danger of caving in.

Standing on the outer perimeter of the huddle was assistant coach Barnhard, affirming why he was content to be a poorly paid volunteer. He was sympathetic to the boys' plight but had no clue as to what he would say or do under these traumatic circumstances.

O'Ryan's immediate challenge was to halt the momentum Central was riding. The cumulative effect of the onslaught had resulted in the Raiders playing scared, focusing on avoiding mistakes at the expense of losing their aggressiveness.

It was a fine line the coach would tread. He had to challenge his team sternly to redirect their collective attention to the game plan while not breaking their already bruised spirits. It was crucial that he dispel their growing doubts about their ability to compete with Central.

Huddled together, the players leaned forward toward the kneeling coach as he spoke above the din surrounding them.

"Listen, boys. We've got 'em right where we want 'em. A hog that shits fast don't shit long."

Surprised team members chuckled. Their taut expressions softened. Coach O'Ryan's coarse barnyard maxim served to distract them from the disaster taking place on the court.

"We've just got to get back to doing what we do best."

O'Ryan turned first to Mark Danner. Coach often singled out his tough-minded senior center when the team wasn't playing well. Mark could handle criticism. His ego wasn't fragile like those of some of his teammates, so the coach would send his scolding of the squad through Danner's strong shoulders.

"Jeez-us Petes, Hoss! What's the matter with you? How many rebounds you got?"

Before Mark could open his mouth, Coach answered the question for him.

"I'll tell you how many. The next rebound you get and four more and you'll have five! Get that wide fanny of yours in front of Weatherford and get the ball. NOW!"

Of course, Coach O'Ryan had conveniently ignored the fact that Madison hadn't missed a shot so far.

He addressed the Cougars' bewildering full-court man-to-man pressure.

"Guards, you know they're pickin' you up right at the baseline, denying the entry pass. We prepared for this! Twice you haven't gotten the ball in play in time or you've thrown it away.

"When we do get it in play, Wells and Miller are trapping you along the sideline. Either Weatherford or Hankins leaves his man and when you try to pass it back to the other guard they're suckin' it right out of the air!

"Sonny, you didn't break back to help the guards on the press. What were you thinking? Jake, you and Sonny switch positions on the press.

"Next time they score, Bond, you take the ball out of bounds. Sonny, you step out of bounds at the other side of the basket along the end line. Pass the ball to Sonny, Bond, then jump in bounds and run a diagonal toward him. Get the ball to Bond on the run, Sonny. They'll be caught off guard, at least the first time. Don't panic. You've got five full seconds to run the play.

"Bond, beat the guards and find Mark at center court. DeVreaux is hanging back to protect the basket. Hoss, when you get the ball, look for Josh or Jake breaking into the front court. We'll turn this press into a lay-up line."

SITTIN', WHITTLIN', AND SPITTIN'

Coach O'Ryan continued to plead with his players who wanted to believe but were still reeling from Central's intimidating performance. Heads nodded, but sullen expressions made plain that they were not yet convinced.

"Look, men. Why have you all of a sudden turned into five statues on the defensive end? Defense is all about what?"

"Grit," several responded in unison, aping what the coach had repeated over and over again.

"Damn straight! It's the will, the determination, the courage to beat the other guy, play after play after play. It's wearin' him down by being in his face every time he tries to dribble or pass. It's havin' your rump in his gut on every rebound! A hand in his face on every shot! Make him know that you'll be in his shorts every time he tries to move!

"Sonny, a guy wearing your uniform used to be my best defender. Where did he go today?"

Sonny glumly looked downward.

"The game started two minutes ago. Are you ready to start playing?"

Watkins nodded slightly, his eyes mere slits below heavy eyebrows. Coach knew Sonny hardened his focus when scolded.

"Listen. We're changing to our switching-zone. Remember, guard the man in your area just like our man-defense. Call out switches. Double down every time you get the chance. If they flood your area, you'll get help."

The buzzer interrupted Coach O'Ryan, signaling the end of the break. He continued without pause.

"Now this won't do us a bit a' good if you don't talk. Move your feet. Every guy in that other uniform who penetrates our defense ought to see a double-team. And cut off the passing lanes."

One official now leaned into the huddle.

"Time to play, coach."

O'Ryan's final instruction was aimed at sending a message to the Cougar five. He leaned to within inches of Mark Danner, meeting him eye-to-eye.

"Mark, Mr. DeWitt Weatherford is makin' easy money off you in the lane. Next time he drives let him know a man's in there and that you intend to control traffic the rest of the night."

Danner knew precisely what coach meant. He didn't have to be told twice that he was to take a measure of Weatherford's fortitude.

May 5, 2012
Morgans Awe

As the debate about the best Hoosier high school five dwindled, Jamie asked about the barbershop where the Morgans Awe boys had gone regularly for a trim.

THE HOOSIER GAME

"I drove by the old Totem Pole in town. There was a young guy sitting in the chair waiting on customers. Anyone know what happened to that rascal Dull Knife?"

Mark, who still patronized the shop there, spoke up. "The ole Indian croaked 'bout five years ago. I heard they barried him with a rusty pair of clippers he used right up to the end."

Josh recalled the barber as the "funniest man I ever knew."

"God threw the mold away when he built the Chief," Arnie added. "If there'd been a Politically Correct Police in those days they'd a-had to send in a whole strike force to clean up the barbershop crowd."

Faded memories of that theater of the absurd flowed back into the present, Josh chuckling as he recalled his trips to see the Chief.

Saturday, March 17, 1956
Morgans Awe

In Morgans Awe, as in all bucolic Hoosier towns in the 1950s, men assembled at the barber's for more than just a haircut or shave. The Totem Pole served as a gathering place, a hotbed for social commentary, political debate, and arguments about sports.

This morning, as he did every other Saturday, Josh had ridden his bike to the Totem Pole Barbershop. The bell attached to the door tinkled as he entered. The boy silently took a seat to await his turn. Small thatches of silver-gray, black, blond, and reddish trimmings were strewn around the base of the lone hydraulic swivel chair.

There was a large wall mirror behind the barber's chair. All the necessary equipment—an electric hair trimmer, a straight razor for shaves, combs, towels, tonics, and other tools of the barber trade—were spread out on an old chest of drawers. The barber carried an abundance of Butch wax to stiffen hair so it would stand up for flattops and Hollywood burrs.

The walls were adorned with faded, sepia-toned photos of past Morgans Awe basketball teams. A piece of net from the 1931 Scottsburg holiday tournament championship and a faded jersey worn by a former Raider star were among the memorabilia hanging here and there.

Two smoothly-worn church pews, saved long ago from a fire at the old Baptist church outside of town, hugged opposite walls to accommodate clients and the usual cast of local "uptown coaches." A coffee table, with multiple nicks and scratches, held copies of hunting and fishing and sports magazines along with issues of today's *Madison Daily Correspondent* and the *Louisville Courier-Journal*.

SITTIN', WHITTLIN', AND SPITTIN'

The Totem Pole "...where locals argued with the civility of a Congressional hearing."

THE HOOSIER GAME

Two pool tables in the back room were in constant use. All day, men passed through the opening into the rear parlor to shoot a game of eight ball or straight pool. There stood a faded red Coca-Cola dispenser, a dime a bottle. An acrid cloud of cigarette smoke filled the dimly lit room.

The proprietor and grooming specialist were one and the same: Owen "Dull Knife" Treecat, or "Chief," as some called him. A natural raconteur, the Native American was the ringmaster of the circus of characters who frequented his establishment.

Haircuts were one dollar and twenty-five cents. Haircut was a relative term. Dull Knife was generally adept at his trade except when a lively discussion occurred, which was the norm in the Pole. If he was expounding on this or that or arguing some fine point Dull Knife might nick an ear or cut a swath in the otherwise smooth surface of the hair. This was a predictable hazard when Treecat was on the stump.

A sizeable, hooked nose took center stage on his ruddy, weathered countenance. The dour-faced Chief rarely smiled despite his propensity for uttering outrageously funny quips and yarns. His often biting humor was delivered in a droll monotone, always eliciting responses from the victims of his anecdotes. All of his regular customers had been humbled at least once by the Chief's caustic wit.

For thirty years Dull Knife had groomed men's hair while providing a haven where the men could argue, laugh, boast, and espouse their own brand of wisdom. He knew all the whims, quirks, and vagaries of his Morgans Awe clientele. There was no need for surnames, for Treecat created a gruff but affectionate nickname for practically every local who came through the barbershop doors.

Monikers were not assigned blithely or by whim. One earned the privilege of receiving the Chief's colorful nicknames in a sort of right of passage into his personal club. The Treecat badge of dishonor might be a reminder of an odd habit or behavior, unusual dress, a noticeable physical trait, or an unfortunate incident so outrageous as to provide the inevitable insulting label for the client.

Of course, women and children, teenagers, and strangers who occasionally entered the premises were excluded from such vulgar foolishness.

"Corntassel" Humphrey, whose ample tuft of stringy yellow hair hung loosely to his shoulders, was a frequent customer. So were "Slow Eye," "Kettle Gut," "Hook Foot," "Hog Eye," "Loppy," "Beyond Ugly," "Pukie," "Rat's Ass,"

SITTIN', WHITTLIN', AND SPITTIN'

"Moose Mug," "Cornpone," "Muck," "Drain-Brain," "Gizzard," "Balloon Butt," "Greasy," "Canyon Mouth," "Huggy," "Burrhead," "Fish Grin," "Two tooth," "Skillet," "Frogwart," "Crudd," "Buzzard Body," "Wiffy," "Roach poacher," and "Gutter Rumpus."

The patriarch of the only Chinese family in the county was known as "Slowboat." "Two Fingers" Watkins had lost his digits in a corn combine. "Shine" Winslow occasionally brought a few quarts of his homemade brew for an after-hours session in the Pole pool room. Jake "Crumb" Wakeland was seen in Scoop 'n Dollie's Restaurant once, brushing cornbread morsels from the table into his bowl of ham and beans. Morvel Sparks was a man of high character who once changed gears in his truck from "drive" to "reverse"—while traveling forty miles an hour—scattering engine parts all over Tickbird Road. When Morvel showed up at the Pole with two black eyes and a broken nose, he became "Shifty" forevermore.

Testosterone levels were lofty in the Totem Pole crowd. The raucous clientele—including several idlers who camped in the shop daily just for the fun—were experts at needling one another.

Tasteless personal insults—delivered playfully to soften the edge—obliterated every barrier of propriety. Sexual and racial jokes abounded. Hints of vanity, pomposity, pretension, or haughtiness by individuals were subjects for ridicule and humorous scorn. Victims could expect an assault with all the civility and dignity of a congressional hearing.

It was here that the self-proclaimed "uptown coaches" gathered, passing judgment on the local basketball team—especially the coach—and the Indiana Hoosiers. (There was one known Purdue grad in the entire county. He showed up only when the Boilermakers beat archrival IU.)

Arguments about hoops in general and the Morgans Awe team in particular raged day-in, day-out, throughout the year. As soon as basketball season ended, locals speculated about the prospects for next year.

Regulars referred to the Totem Pole as the "butcher shop." It was rumored, but never confirmed, that Owen Treecat was a direct descendant of Little Turtle, the great Miami warrior who led Indian resistance against white settlers in Indiana during the 1800s. It was only natural that Dull Knife became a barber, according to a local sage.

"Knife's got the bloodlines," Frogwart Fenn once observed. "His ancestors was experts at removin' hair."

THE HOOSIER GAME

Treecat advertised shaves for $1.50. But no one in memory had had the fortitude to let the Chief get that close to his throat with a razor.

Today, two elderly farmers in bib overalls sat at opposite ends of a pew, chatting casually. One whittled idly at a short piece of pine wood, the shavings falling on the floor at his feet. The other occasionally directed a spew of tobacco into the brass spittoon.

Earl "Wheezer" Barnett, owner of Earl's Affordable Used Cars and Trucks, was in the barber's chair covered with the white, striped linen sheet tied snugly at his collar. Dull Knife clipped away at the middle-aged man's three-week old growth of graying hair.

One of the old-timers, Harlan "Hick" Brice, held a thin paper strip in one hand while pouring tobacco from his packet with the other. After folding the paper, then licking the seam, he lit the roll-your-own cigarette. Hick began to appraise the dubious deer-hunting prowess of a skittish local rube.

"Ja-hear Ole Ollie Hornbeck, he hunted fer more'n two hours out at Mason's holler last week. All he got was a apple tree fer 'ees trouble."

The small audience chuckled at the friend all knew as a nervous, excitable character.

Dull Knife added, "If you put together all them trophy trees he's bagged in his life he'd have a right fine forest."

"Ollie ain't hurt the deer population none, that's for sure," laughed Earl.

The whittler, Possum Trot Williams, noted a new addition to the décor of the shop. Over the doorway was a shiny, mounted largemouth bass of significant size, landed recently by the Chief. Or so he claimed. Trot swore Treecat had bought, not caught, the trophy fish.

"Knife, you couldn't ketch a cold if you was nekked in a blizzard. I seen nat same feesh at a flea market over to Dupont last month."

With a melodramatic, pained expression the Chief retorted, "You're just jealous, Trot, cause you cain't outsmart a fish that's got a brain the size of a breadcrumb. All you do on the water is drown worms."

Clarence Thibault made his entrance, interrupting the feuding fishermen. Thibault, afflicted with a lisp that drew comparisons to Sylvester the Cat, was known as Tooney. Despite his speech impediment, even he was not off limits to the crass verbal abuse.

As the lanky Thibault found a seat in the Totem Pole sanctuary, Hick Brice mimicked his good friend. "Hey, Tooney! Howth trickth?"

Responding in kind, Tooney smiled and retorted, ""Better'n the lot of you thorry thlackers."

Hick Brice shot back, "Eathy for you d' thay."

"You buncha' drunkth and derelicth can teethe me 'bout my lithp. I can thtill take thpeech training but all'a you cain't do nothin' 'bout that ugly all over your puth."

All those indicted laughed as heartily as Tooney, who then "took hith theat, with a thatithfied thmirk on hith faith."

From the poolroom came the voice of Chalk Carter, eight-ball champion of Morgans Awe.

"Hey, Chief, you still got that flimsy tennis racket in the closet. There's a fly in here bigger'n a buzzard."

Chief retorted, "Ketch him in your hat. You can have him for supper tonight."

The crowd continued to swell as Crumb Wakeland and Kettle Gut Harper slipped into the shop.

Hick greeted the young Wakeland with a wave of the hand. "I see yer still gittin' up at the crack a' noon, Crumb."

"You look like five miles a' bad road," added Earl.

"Boys, I feel like I been rode hard and put up wet. I woke up this morning, jumped outta' bed, an' I run outside 'n kissed the bus. Came back in and hopped on the old lady and went to town."

His crude rejoinder was acknowledged with hearty laughter.

Dull Knife continued the interrogation of the roundish Wakeland. "You still on that three-month diet you started a year ago, Crumb?"

"Nah. Had ta give it up. It called for two jiggers of Metrical mixed with two jiggers a' whiskey. I lost five pounds and my driver's license."

"I had a weight problem once't," Chief shared. "Ever time I went in the doc told me I had ta lose fifteen, twenty pound.

"I got ta lookin' closer an' re'lized he was one of them marathon runners, skinny as a runt suckin' the thirteenth tit. So I went out an' got me a fat doctor. He never made mention of my fat ass onc't."

Earl Barnett spoke up with sad news of a former Raider player.

"Ja hear Root Wells died last week?"

"Iz'at so? Now there was a real hustler. He'd skin his knees, bark his shins, dive on his belly and crawl like a snake to git a loose ball. Hell, they didn't have to sweep the gym floor after games he played in."

THE HOOSIER GAME

"Little feller. He had to stand on a concrete block to kick a duck in the ass."

"Ole Root could shoot it, though. I seen 'eem go twenty-eight fer thirty-two one night," deadpanned Brice.

"You kiddin', Hick? Did he really make twenty-eight baskets?"

"Not egg-zactly. The boys passed Root the ball thirty-two times," he deadpanned, "an' he shot it twenty-eight."

The crowd chuckled at the joke.

"I said he could shoot, not that he could make any. He didn't wear out no nets in high school."

Wheezer Barnett went on. "They say he had a heart attack playin' ball over't the YMCA in Scottsburg."

"Too bad. Wudn't he only 'bout thirty?"

"That's right. But Ole Root's still playin' baska-ball," Trot claimed.

"The man's dead 'n gone, Trot. Colder'n a mackerel," Barnett challenged.

"Nope, Wheeze, yer wrong. He's still playin'—in the six-foot-'n-under-league."

They all laughed, so he told it again.

Keeping things lively, Dull Knife said, "Hey, did you all see the *Courier-Journal* yesterday and the story 'bout a hold-up at the Liz'bethtown National Bank over in Hardin County, Kentucky?

"A one-armed guy with a mask on come in wavin' a pistol and made everone hit the floor. While he wuz coverin' 'em all he pointed his stub at the clerk and tole her to put all the hunnerd-dollar bills in a bag and hand it over. He got the money an' run.

"Well, the robber wuz dumm'ern a day-old pig. Soon as the cops got there and got the description of the bandit, they went straight to the guy's house, found the cash, an 'rested 'eem. He was the only cat in Hardin County with one arm a-missin'."

The listeners let out a collective groan.

"I swear!" Knife claimed. "Read it right there in the *Journal*."

"That dog won't hunt," Earl retorted.

"Yer out like a fat woman stealin' second, Indian," Trot added.

"That's why we call you Chief Walkin' Eagle, Treecat," Wheezer claimed. "Yer so full of it, you cain't fly."

Feigning shock and hurt at the insinuation that he might tell a stretcher, the Chief defended himself.

142

"Eye-god, you magpies wouldn't bleeve a one-legged duck swims in a circle if you counted laps all day."

"Sorry, Chief, but that'n's too rank even for this buncha' fools."

A slight trace of a grin from the normally taciturn Chief betrayed the tale as the hoax that it was.

The door swung open. In shuffled octogenarian Whitey Evans, stooped and wizened. A bulbous nose spread across his deeply creased and sunburnt face. Only his alert, glistening eyes betrayed the youth within this old man.

Kettle Gut Harper greeted him first.

"Hey, Whitey. Good to see you. I heard you were down with the croup. Ya' okay?"

"I'm still standin', Gut. But I figger 'bout one more clean shirt'll do me."

"I don't bleeve that fer a minute, Whitey," Tooney chimed in. "I thaw you thniffin' aroun' the widow Chalmerth over at the Trail Bar lath night. Thee din't look like thee rethented the attention, neither."

"Lordy, that woman's uglier 'n a passport photo," Knife moaned. "Looks like her face 'ud been set on farr and put out with a golf shoe."

"You-all know Whitey. He don't fret about good looks. He likes his wimmin nude, lewd, and tattooed."

"Whitey, is it true she can speak five langeeges but cain't say 'no' in any of 'em?"

"The widda only wants to git into that dusty old money you got stashed in the barn loft, anyway, Whitey."

"I heard that ole gal is a great housekeeper. She's divorced three suckers and every time she kept the house."

"Yeah, but the ole harpy'll hafta wait a spell. I don't think Gabriel's ready to blow his horn fer Whitey jist yet."

"Well, I never figgered you boys to be jealous of a fine ole gentleman like me," Whitey chuckled. "Lookin' over you boys proves there's one advantage to bein' stupid. None of you'll ever git lonely."

At the jingle of the bell on the door, talk of the homely hussy ended. Mrs. Holbein entered with her grandson in tow. The double threat of a female and a child's presence compelled the men to temper their coarse conversation.

Dull Knife applied the perfumed astringent he called "panther pee" to the back of Barnett's neck. As he grabbed his broom to sweep up the growing pile of hair around the chair, he called out, "Nex!"

THE HOOSIER GAME

Josh dutifully hopped into the worn leather chair for one of the scores of trims he would receive at the hands of Chief Treecat. Time spent in the Knife's lair proved to have a secondary benefit for the dollar and a quarter he paid each visit. That price included a full-tuition scholarship to the school of the unsophisticated but memorable homespun wisdom provided to him by members of the Totem Pole faculty.

12

BOYS TO MEN

Jourden Arena
8:20 p.m.

In the stands, many fans wearing orange and black were slumped in gloom. Most MAHS supporters had believed the team could derail the Cougar machine. Those hopes were being crushed already by the shear annihilation of their Raiders in every facet of the game.

Her head in her hands, Katie O'Ryan was suffering on an even more personal level. Watching the destruction of her husband and his team was excruciating.

Now breaking their huddle with a spirited "Raiders!" the team returned to the court re-energized by Coach O'Ryan's rousing pep-talk.

Bond received the ball from the referee to resume play. Madison Central was coiled to attack with the same savage intensity that had exposed the Raiders' weaknesses.

But this time Sonny surprised his defender by stepping out of bounds at the end line. Simultaneously Bond whipped a pass to him, then rushed into the playing area. Wells and Miller were momentarily confused as Sonny returned the ball to his teammate.

Cougar fans who were not aware of the rules for in-bounding the ball after a made basket howled at the refs.

"They cain't pass a ball to another guy standin' outta bounds, idiot," screamed one leather-lunged Madison fan near the action.

Racing up court Bond dribbled by both Madison guards. He flipped a lob pass to Mark near the centerline. Weatherford, slashing between Mark and the ball, nearly stole the timid pass but his grasp closed on nothing but air.

Mark fed the ball to Josh, who was breaking to the hoop. DeVreaux deftly cut off his path. Hankins slid back to cover the basket. Josh turned to find Jake, who returned the ball to Bond. He set up the half court offense.

THE HOOSIER GAME

Mark had moved into the high post. Bond bounced a pass into the big man. With a powerful burst, Mark turned his shoulder into Weatherford's chest and knocked him off his feet and onto his backside on the hardwood.

The official's shrill whistle halted play.

Placing his left hand on the back of his head and thrusting a fist forward, the referee vigorously signaled an offensive foul on number 51, Danner.

"Charging. No basket."

Weatherford lay sprawled on the court, with blood already oozing over his lips. The Cougars' players reacted with surprise and rage. Incensed that their star player had been abused, DeVreaux walked menacingly toward Mark. Danner matched his scowl as he moved to meet the burly Madison lad. A referee stepped between the two, sternly warning both to back off.

Other players approached the budding scuffle. Sonny purposely bumped Miller, who retaliated by pushing the Raider guard's chest with both hands. Josh stepped between the two.

"C'mon, Sonny. We can't afford to lose you. Cool it."

Watkins and Miller traded looks of contempt, then turned away.

Mark's bold play redefined the terms of battle. Until that moment the Raiders had submitted to Madison's roughhouse approach. Central's instinct to intimidate and destroy a team's confidence and cohesion had worked from the outset—until Mark responded to his coach's challenge.

After cooler heads prevailed, action resumed with Cole Wells receiving the inbounds pass. He immediately recognized that the opponents were now playing zone defense. The quickest man on the court, Wells dribbled sharply into the web of the Raider defense. As he drove to the basket Seaberg slid into his path. Wells left his feet, as if to shoot, then tried to dish the ball off to Hankins along the baseline. Sonny didn't bite on Wells's move to the hoop, and, stepping into the passing lane, he stole the ball cleanly.

Bond reacted swiftly, racing ahead of everyone toward the opposite end of the court. Sonny deftly lofted a long pass beyond Miller's reach. Bond caught the ball in stride, dribbled twice and pushed the ball off the backboard and into the basket. MAHS was on the scoreboard at the 6:26 mark.

Central hustled back, Miller launching a hurried fall-away jumper over Watkins's fully extended arm. The ball nicked the underside of the iron ring, where Danner eagerly snared the missed attempt.

In one fluid motion, Danner rifled a two-handed, over-the-head pass to Seaberg near the sideline. Josh fed Bond as he scurried up the court. Bathwaite dribbled at top speed as the Madison players retreated unevenly. To Bond's right was Jake, while Sonny filled the left lane. It was a textbook execution of the three-on-two break.

Watkins made his oblique cut to the basket. Bond, looking to the right at Jake, flipped the ball behind his back—ala Bob Cousy—to Sonny, whose left-handed lay-up settled softly into the net.

Josh and his mates were moving freely, their earlier nervousness now under control. Unimpeded by the fear of failure, their bodies were reacting with abandon. They were playing Raider basketball again.

Challenged by the awakened gusto and sagging zone employed by the Raiders, the Madison team began to rush their shots and grew careless handling the ball.

While Madison failed to score on its next two possessions, Jake Skoon turned the first quarter into his personal shooting clinic. As the Cougars struggled, Jake began to drain rainbow jump shots.

Weatherford missed an eighteen-footer from the side. Retrieving the wayward shot, Josh passed to Jake down court, who launched a jumper from outside the free throw circle. Splash! The Morgans Awe crowd jumped to their feet.

Bathwaite's tight defense forced Wells into a traveling violation.

Sonny set a perfect screen on Wells, freeing Jake for a 17-footer. The net snapped as the shot went through. Raiders fans remained standing, roaring with every Skoon score.

Weatherford slowed the Morgans Awe rally, hitting a fadeaway jump shot as Mark slapped his wrist. His free throw was good. The score stood at MCHS 14, MAHS 8.

On the ensuing trip down the court, Wells closed up tight on Jake at the ten-second line. Bond set a firm screen on Cole. Jake raced into the key where he was hacked by Hawkins on his shot attempt. Jake was true on both free throw tries.

Josh tied up Hankins along the baseline, then controlled the tip to Sonny. With Wells frantically chasing Jake over and under a maze of screens, the Raider star received a pass just a hair inside the out-of-bounds line in the left corner. A flick of the wrist from twenty-three feet and the ball zipped through the seine twine.

A crack in their previously unrestrained arrogance now having been exposed, Madison's players began to argue among themselves, pointing fingers at one another at each breakdown. They had discovered the opponent was not only worthy but dangerous. Grudging respect had been earned.

On the Cougars' next possession, Weatherford threw a pass behind Wells, the ball skipping out of bounds. The Raiders failed to capitalize. Josh had set a pick for Jake, then rolled toward the basket to receive a well-placed bounce pass but his shot rimmed out.

Miller failed on a short jumper. Weatherford outmaneuvered Mark, tipping the ball once, twice, but the ball bounded into Danner's big hands.

THE HOOSIER GAME

"No lay-ups," the burly Karl DeVreaux (50) reminds a flattened Raider guard Bond Bathwaite (11).

At the other end, Bond drove past Miller and sliced into the lane. DeVreaux saw an opportunity to avenge Mark's earlier hard foul on Weatherford. As Bathwaite left his feet, the burly Cougar center fouled him hard, knocking him to the floor. The Raider guard's teammates rushed to help him up, while DeVreaux sneered at the players in black and orange. Both referees rushed in to avert further feuding. Both teams held their tempers. The hard foul was simply tit-for-tat. Shaken, Bathwaite missed both attempts.

On the next trip down the floor, Watkins fouled Hankins, who missed the free throw. Josh smothered the rebound, then bounced the ball to Bond.

Dribbling behind his back, Bathwaite made a sterling move toward the hoop. When Wells left Jake to cut Bond off, the Raider guard made a nifty pass to his sharpshooting teammate. Skoon didn't disappoint. His basket with less than a minute remaining in the first quarter drew the Raiders into a tie, 14-14.

Wells then fed DeVreaux under the basket. Karl missed the gimme.

Skoon and Josh now executed a perfect pick-and-roll. As DeVreaux switched off to defend Jake, Josh spun, received Skoons pass and laid it in, giving the Raiders their first lead of the game.

Leaping from the bench waving his arms frantically was Madison's coach. It was Saul Fortune's turn to call timeout.

With only forty-two seconds remaining in the first quarter, the veteran mentor was not waiting for the break between periods. He had to stop the bleeding.

Friday, May 25, 1956
Morgans Awe

As Josh and the rest looked forward to the end of the school year, Elvis had yet another Top Ten hit, "Heartbreak Hotel," beginning with the yearning lyrics:

> *Well, since my baby left me, I found a new place to dwell,*
> *Its down at the end of Lonely Street, at Heartbreak Hotel,*
> *You make me so lonely, baby,*
> *I get so lonely,*
> *I get so lonely, I could die.*

The Old Settlers Festival on Memorial Day weekend marked the beginning of summer break for school kids in Morgans Awe. The two-day event featured booths with vendors selling various enticements. There was a hog roast;

THE HOOSIER GAME

displays of farm machinery and agricultural products; horse racing duels; music from local fiddlers and pluckers; a turkey shoot for local marksmen; and a special salute to vets who fought in American wars.

The capstone of the weekend was a reenactment of the townsmen's courageous 1863 stand against Morgan's Raiders. The few folks with ancestors from the small band who faced the Rebel invaders were held in reverence for that one day of the year. A slight dilemma for the event planners was that Homer Woodburn, the town sot, was a direct descendant of the group's leader, Isaiah. To ensure Homer wouldn't show up and cause an embarrassing scene, town council member Alten Gernich was assigned to transport Homer to his favorite bar in Louisville for the day.

Periodically, Betty Seaberg drove to the riverfront town of Madison to shop at the numerous quaint boutiques along Main Street. On occasion, she allowed Josh to invite a carload of his friends to see a movie at the Ohio Theater. Mrs. Seaberg would drop the boys off and return later to pick them up.

The movie routine was a familiar one. As they found their seats, a fifteen-minute newsreel was playing. Next came a cartoon (sometimes, if they were lucky, a second bonus animated feature appeared). Favorites were Bugs Bunny ("What's up, Doc?"), Elmer Fudd ("Kill the wabbit, kill the wabbit!"), Daffy Duck ("You're dith-picable"), Yosemite Sam ("Dead rabbits tell no tales"), and Sylvester the Cat ("Thufferin' thuccotash"), the voices of each provided by the amazing Mel Blanc.

Among the Western movie heroes of the day were "The Singing Cowboy," Gene Autry; the Cisco Kid and Pancho ("Oh, Seez-co"); Hopalong Cassidy; and Roy Rogers and the Queen of the West, Dale Evans. The bad guys always got it in the end, of course. Despite the frenetic gunfights the boys never questioned why no wounds or blood appeared on a victim, or how six shooters could blaze away indefinitely without reloading. Sonny did mention once the oddity of loud clops of horses' hooves as they raced lickety-split over dirt roads. And Jake always wondered why the wheels on the wagons turned backwards as they traveled along at high speeds.

On this Saturday Betty delivered the boys to the theater, as usual. In the mischievous minds of the four 13-year-olds a plot had been hatched to provide added entertainment for the audience.

Each boy had hidden a bag of marbles on his person. They had settled into seats in the back row awaiting a propitious moment to discharge the colorful glass orbs onto the gradually descending concrete floor. When the marbles were released simultaneously, an annoying racket resulted as they rolled toward the front, pin-balling off the bases of the tin metal seats.

The theater manager appeared with a flashlight at precisely the moment that the boys launched the last of the marbles. To the perpetrators' surprise he shined his light on them and ordered each to follow him to the lobby. He didn't appear to be amused.

Josh and friends tried to deny they had anything to do with the crime. How could the man possibly suspect the four in the last row of the theater, who were wearing jackets on one of the hottest days of the summer? Four crushed brown paper bags at their feet had provided additional evidence of the mischief.

When Josh's mom showed up, she found the by-now contrite pranksters quarantined in the manager's office. Upon hearing the account and viewing the sheepish expressions on the faces of the offenders, the mortified Mrs. Seaberg made each boy, in turn, apologize for his misdeed. Then, with a glare that could have melted a shot-put, she ordered them to the car. The excruciating silence on the return trip was broken only by occasional growls condemning the four scamps to a yet-to-be-decided penalty.

It turned out not to be a hanging offense and the incident made a special memory for the boys.

That summer the close friends began showing up at the Skoons' farm to play basketball. Nailed over a door to the barn was a regulation hoop. The court consisted of compacted earth, the grass having long since been worn away. Whether they raised dust on dry days or slogged in mud after a rain the boys played on. Sweltering Indiana temperatures and humidity were ignored. Blistered feet were commonplace on the brutally hot summer days, as were skinned knees and elbows. Shorts and T-shirts and fraying tennis shoes were the standard uniform.

When cool weather set in, the players dressed in ragged jeans, torn sweatshirts, and those same tattered sneakers. During icy conditions the slick, grimy rubber basketball became hard as a rock, contracting until it hardly bounced.

The chafing effect of the gritty basketball and cold on rough hands caused cracks to appear in the palms. Players ignored the stinging pain while wrapped up in the competition. However, when the boys returned home and washed those raw frigid hands, the piper was paid. Doused in hot water, their hands revealed bloody creases that opened in the skin and smarted as if they'd dunked their hands in Morton Salt.

THE HOOSIER GAME

Thunderstorms occasionally forced the boys to postpone the outdoor games. So Norval Skoon devised a new makeshift playing area by clearing a 20-by-15-foot space in the barn hayloft.

The distance from the peak of the roof to the rough-hewn floorboards was about 16 feet. Screwed into a heavy cross beam were a backboard and a goal. The players had to be constantly vigilant to avoid falling down the rectangular ladder well by which they had clambered up to the second-story court.

Many Hoosier basketball fans would claim that the flat trajectory of the jump shot that was characteristic of Indiana boys bred on the farm was developed in the cramped conditions and low ceilings of similar barn lofts all over the state.

Now entering seventh grade, Josh and his peers looked ahead eagerly to October try-outs for the Morgans Awe junior high team. Thirty-five boys—80 percent of the males in the class—showed up in hopes of earning one of fifteen uniforms reserved for those boys who made the squad. The seventh-grade coach was Jerrod Jaggers, a 6-8 giant of a man who played his college ball at a small school in Tennessee.

Practice consisted of rehearsing the fundamentals of passing, dribbling, shooting, defense, and rebounding. Full-court scrimmages—shirts against skins—were intended to weed out the lesser players from the promising prospects.

Although he was among the better players, Josh took nothing for granted. He nervously approached the daily cut list posted on a bulletin board outside the coach's office. Would this be the day his name would be missing from the roster of survivors?

After two weeks, the final cuts were made. There, in alphabetical order, between the names of Redmon, Homer, and Skoon, Jake, was Seaberg, Josh. Josh was handed an oversized blue jersey with a red block numeral 6 on the back.

The uniforms were old varsity hand-me-downs, too large and ill-fitting for the bodies of undeveloped adolescents. The warm-up jackets were made of coarse, Lindsey-woolsey fabric that chafed skin wherever it touched. Nonetheless, no uniform he wore afterward as a player would ever generate more excitement and pride than that frayed, musty-smelling, and sweat-stained garment he received that day.

The seventh grade schedule consisted of eleven games against county schools. The season opener—a 43-27 victory over the Mainport Riverboys—would be indicative of subsequent contests. The Raiders won every game by a comfortable margin. Jake proved to be the team's most impressive player, twice scoring twenty-eight points in a single game. On both occasions his individual total exceeded that of the opponent's entire team. Locals would take note of the squad's undefeated record. Their success boded well for the future.

On a daily basis Josh, Jake, Mark, and Sonny typically skipped lunch. They headed straight to the gym to spend the entire twenty-five-minute break playing pick-up basketball. Sides were chosen and the team that scored five baskets first remained to play the next team in line. Jake's team rarely lost.

While observing one of the noon-hour scrimmages, Coach Jaggers noticed a diminutive boy with whom he was not familiar, scoring basket after basket. The towering coach approached the scrawny lad, peering downward at a boy who was a foot-and-a-half shorter than he.

"Son, you shoot that thang purty good. How 'bout a game 'a H-O-R-S-E?"

"Cain't. Gotta go to class," the sprite curtly replied.

"Don't worry about that. I'll write you a pass if you need it. What'cher name?"

"Romy Carr."

Romy won the game handily. The coach quickly demanded a rematch. He shouldn't have.

The junior high boys and girls who were spread out around the gym turned their attention to the shootout taking place on the court. They clapped and hooted when Romy beat the coach again, H-O-R-S-E to H-O. Several in the mini-cheering section stayed beyond the bell that announced the start of class.

"Let's go again," the by-now red-faced Jaggers demanded.

Romy proceeded to hit each of his five shots while the abashed coach missed every time. Exasperated, but curious, Coach Jaggers asked, "Young man, we could've used you on our team this season. Why didn't you try out?"

"I did," the sober-faced boy replied.

"You did?"

"Yeah. You cut me."

As Romy turned away, the stunned coach realized that he had dismissed the second-best shooter in the seventh grade, behind only Jake.

The Carr family moved the following spring. Morgans Awe never got to see how good Romy Carr might have been in a Raiders uniform.

It was during the summer of 1957 that the nucleus of what would later prove to be the most successful basketball team Morgans Awe High School

THE HOOSIER GAME

would ever put on a court began to bond. Josh would always associate the Everly Brothers' hit song with that time.

Bye, bye love, bye, bye sweet caress,
Hello, emptiness, I feel like I could die,
Bye, bye my love, goodbye,
There goes my baby, with-a someone new,
She sure looks happy, I sure am blue,
She was my baby, 'til he stepped in,
Goodbye to romance that might have been.

Basketball became the year-round passion of Jake, Josh, and other members of that undefeated junior high squad. Traditional summer activities gave way to their increasing devotion to the Hoosier game. Celluloid cowboy heroes were replaced by current stars of the hardwood, such as Oscar Robertson at the University of Cincinnati and anyone wearing an Indiana University uniform.

Each of the boys was aware of what the game meant to basketball-crazy citizens of Indiana. Having witnessed the amazing triumph of the farm boys from Milan three years before, the seed of a mutually shared vision had been planted.

The effect the local high school five had on the Morgans Awe community was not lost on them, either. Hometown Raiders heroes like Griffin Cordway, Homer Linzinger, and Johnny Bob Schmitt inspired the boys with their play on Friday and Saturday evenings.

When the school term ended, Jake Skoon, Josh Seaberg, Sonny Watkins, Bobby Mack Deal, and Mark Danner made a pact with one another. The five boys agreed that each would show up to play basketball every Saturday afternoon at Memorial Park and evenings during the week as often as possible. It would require sacrifice, especially for Mark and Jake, whose work on the farm often lasted until well after dark.

Basketball for the five became a quest to achieve greater goals. Varsity Coach Michael O'Ryan had told them that they could become a very special group in the future if they stayed together and dedicated themselves to doing what it takes to be champions.

Coach O'Ryan had advised the boys that competing against older and bigger players would help them improve. Jake, Josh, and their mates began to challenge the older players in games at Memorial Park. They regularly competed with freshmen and occasionally the junior varsity players. Some members of the upper classes viewed the upstarts with disdain, resenting the intrusion of the eighth-graders-to-be onto their turf. By the end of the summer, Josh, Jake, Mark and the others were beating the freshmen with regularity and once even whipped the JVs.

With increasing frequency Jake was summoned to the court where the varsity members competed against one another and a few former college players. He became a regular fill-in, earning his chance to play with the older boys because of his uncanny shooting.

When Josh and his buddies returned to school for eighth grade, socio-cultural events of enormous magnitude were playing out in the United States. On September 24, over the defiance of Arkansas Governor Orval Faubus and violent protests by segregationist government officials, nine African-American students integrated Little Rock Central High School. President Eisenhower had federalized the state's National Guard to escort the courageous youths to classes.

The boys were heedless of the internecine war being fought in the country, and the scariest thing on the minds of Josh, Jake, and their comrades was memorizing and then reciting the 271 words of Lincoln's Gettysburg Address. Vlad the Impaler, otherwise known as Mr. Goss, the history teacher, required his students to recite Lincoln's famous oration in order to pass his class.

Speaking for two minutes, sans note cards, and enduring the focused attention of the entire class was agony beyond words. Let-me-die-now panic seized those whose brains froze and forgot the words of the address.

For Josh, Jake, Mark, Sonny, and Bobby Mack, the highlight of eighth grade was another spotless record on the basketball court. The young Raiders defeated all fourteen of the scheduled opponents by an average of nineteen points per game. Hundreds of local fans began to show up to see this exciting bunch dominate other schools.

The closest contest was a high-scoring battle between Morgans Awe and a spunky Sycamore Creek squad. The young Raiders scored their highest point total of the season to hold off the Eagles, 66-57. Jake Skoon was brilliant, scoring thirty-eight points on a variety of jumpers and drives to the basket. In addition to twelve field goals, he sank all fourteen of his free throws.

Old-timers who had followed Morgans Awe basketball for decades could not recall any eighth grader who had ever racked up that many points in one game. Jake inspired a buzz among the Morgans Awe faithful.

It was just the beginning.

13

DEATH BY A THOUSAND CUTS

Jourden Arena
8:28 p.m.

The clearly shocked Cougar players plodded to the sideline, dreading the inevitable chewing out from their livid coach. Inside the huddle, Coach Saul unleashed his fury toward his dispirited teenagers.

Glaring at each one by one, Fortune screamed, "What in the world is going on out there?"

Quickly responding, the coach's chief representative on the court, Cole Wells, began, "Coach, if—" Saul flashed an icy stare at the team captain that could have frozen hell itself.

"Yeah, son," Saul sneered, "And IF your grandma had balls, she'd be your grandpa."

The scowling coach had transformed into a menacing combination of intimidation and outrage. He tolerated no excuses.

Motivating a team is at the core of a coach's profession. In some fashion all coaches are thespians, calling on all manner of emotions to lift players to better performance. An oft-used tool in the coach's repertoire is feigned anger. Most teenage athletes responded to a severe dressing-down by the head man with a heightened sense of urgency and effort.

But now Saul's wrath changed the atmosphere surrounding him. There was a darker, more sinister undertone to his passion and he appeared to be on the edge of some unbridled, frightening action.

"Who decided we'd play this crappy, 'do-si-do' defense tonight? Wells, since you seem to have the answers, let me ask, who's your man?"

"Uh, number five, coach."

"That's funny. I thought so, too. But he's scored ten straight points and you don't seem to have a clue how to guard him. Now, you have two choices, son. Either you get

THE HOOSIER GAME

your ass in gear and stop that boy—or you get your ass in gear and stop that boy. Take your pick."

"Yes, sir," the captain mumbled.

"Listen! This game isn't about what you've done this season or that we're favorites to beat these hicks by twenty points. Hell, it's simple, men. It's about heart! Right now, their pulse is about a hundred and ten beats a minute while you guys are comatose! It's about time you woke up.

"Get your heads on straight now and show this other team that they're boxing way above their weight class!"

With their team now leading, Morgans Awe fans began a familiar challenge to their counterparts on the opposite side of the fieldhouse.

"We've got spirit, yes we do,
We've got spirit, how about you?"

The chant echoed back and forth, the sound rising with each countering salvo.

Inside the Raider huddle, Coach O'Ryan sensed that behind his players' outward jubilation was a lingering uncertainty about their capability to actually beat Madison Central. O'Ryan had seen underdog teams fold when the favored opposition bounced back with renewed intensity. He would be watchful for further signs of doubt among his key leaders.

After attending to a couple of defensive adjustments the coach sent his excited underdogs back onto the floor with this directive:

"I guess you've figured out by now those boys in the red and white are not ten feet tall and bullet proof. You're drivin' the bus now, men. Keep it on the road."

O'Ryan sensed the frustration of the Cougars' players, so he ordered his team into a full-court press, hoping to turn a hurried or careless mistake into yet another fast break.

The Madison five, thoroughly embarrassed by Saul's hard-edged challenge, returned to the playing floor without their earlier swagger but with a firm resolve noticeable in their stern expressions.

Wells found Weatherford on the inbounds pass, who quickly returned the ball to his captain. As he crossed the center line, he recognized that Morgans Awe was again playing man-to-man defense. Cole raised a fist to signal his mates. Central's players positioned themselves in their regular offense.

Hankins broke toward Wells on the left side to receive a bounce pass. Cole followed the ball, cutting closely off Jerry's hip as Hankins faked a hand-off, then took one dribble toward the middle.

Only steps behind Wells, Marty Miller followed his path. Hankins handed the ball to Miller while scraping Sonny off his man with an effective pick.

Miller drove hard to the basket. Josh slid over to cut off his path but arrived late. The two collided in mid-air on the Cougar guard's shot attempt. The ball skipped off the rim.

Up came the ref's arm and closed fist.

"Foul on number 31. Two shots."

Marty's first attempt was true, but his second caromed off the back of the rim, bounding high into Danner's grasp. Mark initiated another fast break with a sharp pass to Bathwaite, who found Watkins sprinting up the left side of the court. Sonny dribbled to the foul line, stopped, then returned the ball to Bond who sunk a reverse lay-up to put the Raiders ahead, 18-15.

With only eight seconds left in the quarter, Central hurriedly moved the ball upcourt. Miller's soft lob intended for DeVreaux was deflected by Seaberg toward Sonny. He whipped the ball to Bond, who sighted Jake running free toward the Raiders' goal.

Receiving the pass, Jake covered the half-court rapidly. Two quick dribbles brought him to the top of the key. With one second showing on the game clock, Skoon disdained a try for a lay-up. His twenty-foot jumper split the net just at the sound of the buzzer, ending the first period. From the crowd came an ear-splitting eruption of joy.

Raiders 20, Cougars 15.

Saturday, May 5, 2012

"Hey, Fries, d'you remember losin' your pants at the carnival the summer before our freshman year?"

Others laughed at the memory of Arnie's embarrassing midway encounter with a group of upperclassmen intent upon carrying out the traditional initiation of freshmen entering high school.

"Yeah. And I don't recall any of y'all rushin' to my rescue, neither," Arnie countered.

"It was just too much fun," Josh needled. "Watching those seniors strip you down right in front of half the county."

"All the girls were sure enjoyin' it—until they saw your spindly legs and huge butt—"

"I was s'prised them pins didn't have a message tied to 'em."

"—they was hollerin', 'Put 'em back on, pah-leeze!'"

"Admit it boys. You were just jealous of my God-sculpted bod."

THE HOOSIER GAME

Saturday, June 7, 1958

Every June, Josh and his friends looked forward to the carnival that came to Madison. Josh and his pals were especially excited this year, because, instead of their parents, Arnie's older brother, Patrick, would be driving them. The lads made plans to meet several of their female classmates there.

Patrick parked the car and went off to his own pursuits, as Josh, Jake, Arnie, Mark, Sonny, and Bobby Mack strode toward the midway. Ambling around the grounds, they passed others their age from schools around the county. Mark ogled a striking blonde teenage beauty who wore white Capri pants and a lavender terrycloth blouse.

"Get a load a-them jugs," he whispered to Josh. "Those 'ud make Sophee Lorr-in jealous."

Danner veered toward the slender and smiling girl, who was with four friends.

"Hey, gorgeous. You married yet?"

Without breaking stride, she looked icily at Mark and replied, "No. But I'm in great demand. Nothing here for you, though, cowboy."

Her girlfriends burst into giggles at her put-down of the stranger.

A group of Morgans Awe girls appeared. The guys joined them and Arnie invited Rae Jean Chiles to ride with him on the Ferris wheel.

At the end of the ride Rae Jean begged Arnie to win her a teddy bear. She was eyeing the adorable panda hanging by the basket-shooting booth. As the pair approached, the barker began his spiel.

"Step right up here, young man. You can win the pretty young lady that bear she's got 'er heart set on. Fitty-cents. Make three-outta-three, the big bear is hers. Two-outta-three, pick a prize off the lower rack. A winner every time."

Arnie had never won a major prize in any of those rigged games of chance. He usually ended up with one of those woven Chinese toys that your fingers got stuck in and wouldn't come off. Or a plastic Jew's harp.

Everyone knew the hoop was so small a basketball could barely fit through. Arnie was reluctant but Rae Jean kept up the pressure until he laid down two quarters and lined up his first shot.

Every attempt rattled around the rim and bounced away. Determined to win, he went through three of the five dollars his parents had given him for the night. He finally gave it up.

As the couple walked away empty-handed, Arnie was startled to see a group of five seniors wearing Morgans Awe letter jackets approaching him. With a feeble smile, he made an attempt at conversation.

"Hey, guys, how ya' doin'?"

Harassment of freshmen was a time-honored tradition among members of the senior class. With a few exceptions, the stalking, capture, and humiliating de-pants-ing of the victim was light-hearted, rather than mean-spirited.

Laughing, the senior men whisked the frightened frosh to a spot behind the funhouse trailer and relieved him of his jeans. Arnie cowered in the darkness, clad only in white jockey shorts, a Morgans Awe T-shirt, and tennies. His fellow freshmen were nowhere to be seen.

Waving the prize for all to see, the seniors dropped Arnie's trousers on the ground at the ticket booth near the Tilt-a-Whirl.

Arnie's dilemma was clear. He had to retrieve his pants without being publicly exposed before the horde of teenagers strolling along the rows of rides. The beet-red Arnie snuck from behind the trailer to a grove of trees that flanked the grounds. Stealthily he crept in the shade of the tents adjacent to the rides and amusement booths. Here he peeked from behind his cover and tried to get the attention of one of his friends.

Unfortunately, Arnie drew the notice of that same cluster of upperclassmen. It was pointless to flee. Two of the antagonists lifted Arnie up by the arms and escorted him, to the delight of the gathering crowd, to retrieve the pants left crumpled on the grass. As other teens laughed hysterically, Packard quickly pulled his pants over his skivvies and hurriedly departed the scene.

Mark, Josh, Sonny, Jake, and Bobby Mack were watching from the safety of Pat's car, where they had fled when Arnie was taken into custody by the senior "frosh patrol." Although they were sympathetic with their classmate's predicament, they'd decided discretion was the better part of valor, slinking off like wet cats, abandoning Fries to his fate.

That evening Josh and his mates retreated to their favorite sanctuary to consider the big questions of life. As dusk turned into night, Josh and his friends ascended a ladder—forbidden to public use—to a narrow platform girdling the village water tower fifty feet above the ground. As they sat with legs dangling beneath the flimsy guard-rail, Sonny, Bobby Mack, Josh, and Arnie were comparing the merits of the day's rasslin' stars.

Without fail, the boys followed the hokey pro wrestling shows every Thursday night on TV. To them there was no disputing the legitimacy of the hand-to-hand

THE HOOSIER GAME

combat. Blood streaming down the faces and chests of the grapplers captivated the naïve lads. The mock dirty tricks of the villains of the ring—fingers poked in eyes, kicks to the groin, rabbit punches to the neck and kidneys, illegal choke holds, all committed before the unseeing eyes of simple-minded referees—were infuriating.

Arnie opened with an unflattering commentary about Killer Kowalski, a favorite of Bobby Mack Deal.

"Jeezus, Bobo, Kowalski's all hat and no cowboy."

Bobby Mack indignantly defended the Killer.

"Arnie, if it was rainin' rattlesnakes, you'd be outside with a bucket. Killer Kowalski kicked the crap out of Chief Don Eagle. And Eagle put your boy, Gorgeous George, down with the Indian Deathlock, easy as pie."

The bickering about who was the toughest of all the wrestlers began to heat up.

"What-chu laughin' at, Sonny?"

Sonny Watkins considered himself the final authority on this subject.

"You two pesticles don't know berry-pickin' from goosin' angels. Nobody beats Verne Gagne and the sleeper hold."

"What about the match with Tojo Yamamoto? He run around that old man like soap down a drain. Gagne hardly laid a hand on that Jap. He was beggin' fer mercy when Tojo pinned 'eem."

"Shows what you know, nitwit. B'fore that match, Tojo's trainer slipped a mickey into Verne's water bottle. Made 'eem sicker'n a dog. That's the only way that sneaky Toe-jam could ever beat Gagne."

"Anybody'd b'leeve that crap is dumber'n a doornail. Why cain't you just admit Tojo whipped that feeble ole fart, fair'n square?"

"I ain't argyin' with you, spastic."

"Birdbrain!"

"Cow Pile!"

"Doosh-bag!!"

"Peckerhead!!!"

"Hog's heiny!!!!"

Neither Sonny nor Arnie would concede one inch on the matter.

Josh usually stayed above the fray, using the voice of reason to soften stalemates that inevitably occurred. He offered this food for thought:

"Alright, you guys. People who know still think Lou Thesz was the greatest rassler of all time."

"Yeah, Lou was tough in his younger days. But he's old now. Dick the Bruiser'd whup him like a ugly stepchild."

"Now there's the toughest hombre in the ring," Bobby Mack offered.

"The Bruiser?" Sonny chimed in. "Hell, Bobo, he couldn't find his ass if he had four hands."

"Myself, I hate the Bruiser," Arnie said. "He was doin' a interview on TV las' Christmas, and the guy ast 'eem did he want to wish a Merry Christmas for all the little kids watchin'."

Imitating the the Bruiser's gruff, raspy voice, Fries growled, "'I'll tell ya what I wish for all the little kids out there. I wish I could break all their little fingers, that's whut I wish!'

"Well, if I coulda, I'd a bought a ticket and went to Louisville that night to boo him myself!"

"That old gasbag tried to—"

"SHHHHHH!"

Josh was the first to see the sheriff's cruiser, headlights off, rolling slowly up the gravel lane beside the tower. The boys froze. No one breathed.

The county sheriff and his deputy, out to nab reprobate teenagers breaking the law, aimed the car's spotlight at the catwalk above.

Sonny hissed to his buddies to scat to the opposite side as the car drew nearer. The lads had become adept at scurrying around the water tank like rats when the occasional lawman appeared.

As Arnie rose slowly from his sitting position, his foot brushed a wrapper from the hamburger he had been eating. None of the boys saw the paper as it wafted slowly downward like a feather, landing on the windshield of the police vehicle. Excess mustard on the paper caused it to stick fast before the lawmen's eyes.

The squad car slowly circled the tower. The frightened lads managed to stay in the shadows just ahead of the officer until slow-footed Arnie's backside appeared in the bright glow of the officer's light.

Shining the powerful beam directly at the miscreants, the cop bellowed the dreaded words: "Halt! Git down from there, all a' youze! NOW!"

Busted!

As the four boys slowly descended the shaky ladder, three were snarling at the clumsy Packard for their dilemma, having spied the evidence on the windshield.

"I swear, Arnie, if—"

THE HOOSIER GAME

Busted! And an unpleasant ride home
in the Jefferson County Sheriff's cruiser.

"That's enough!" the annoyed man in brown yelled, "I wanna see soles hit the ground."

After a stern lecture, ending with a promise to "run you in" if he ever caught them on the catwalk again, Police Chief Oren Ladysmith directed each into the backseat of the cruiser for a ride home knowing that the sight of their child exiting a police cruiser would be enough to cause parents a conniption fit. He escorted each boy to the family's front door and provided a brief summary of his misdeeds.

The following day, each of the wrongdoers shared stories of the punishment angry parents had imposed. None received the death penalty, although Arnie's dad apparently gave it some thought.

They were back on the tower the following Saturday at dusk.

As they had pledged, the five boys met at the Memorial Park courts nearly every day that summer. Each continued to grow physically but it was the developing bond of mutual respect and trust that made the group special.

From time to time, the players spotted Coach O'Ryan leaning against the huge sycamore tree at the top of the slope, casually watching in silence, then disappearing as fast as he appeared. IHSAA rules prohibited coaches from any direct contact with, or organizing practices for, their players in the summer.

As the boys played on, dreaming of the day they would wear the orange and black varsity colors, dramatic events were taking place in the state capital, unbeknownst to the general public. That August, members of the state legislature were studying a new educational initiative that would alter high school basketball in Indiana for all time. Officially, it would be entitled the School Reorganization Act of 1959. To Hoosiers it was known simply as "consolidation."

Saturday, May 5, 2012

If a Hoosier version of Rip Van Winkle woke up today following a fifty-year slumber, his first question might be "Have I really been asleep all these years?"

His second? "What happened to the Indiana state high school basketball tourney?"

After all, when Indiana Rip lay down for his lengthy snooze, the popular tournament ended with one champion earning the coveted crown.

Among former high school players and fans who'd lived during the single-champion era, no conversation could continue long without discussion of the

THE HOOSIER GAME

lost treasure of their generation. The contrast between the current state of Indiana high school basketball and that of the game these 1962 graduates knew was deeply disappointing to them.

It was Dr. Ross who innocently opened the door to a subject still bitterly debated, especially by passionate elderly Hoosiers.

"Who won the state championship this year?" Jamie asked.

An unsmiling Orson Mannheim replied somberly, "We don't have just *one* champion anymore, Moon."

"You wouldn't believe the difference in high school ball nowadays, Moon," Bobby Mack hissed.

"Th-th-there ain't n-no H-H-Hoosier Hyst-t-t-teria no m-m-more," Grover added.

"The powers that be at the IHSAA really screwed up the state tourney," continued Orson. "It's nothin' like it use'ta be. There's *four* state champions now!"

"Ack-shully, there's eight, if you count the girls."

"Class basketball ruined the greatest high school sports playoff ever. It's nothin' but a watered down holiday tourney now. They even eliminated the semifinals."

"What was they thinkin', anyways? The tourney was just fine back then."

"A lot better'n today, I tell ya."

"Sh-shame on the I-I-IHSAA an' them other j-j-jerks who ch-changed it."

Scowling, Mark fairly spat out, "It wasn't the IHSAA that killed basketball in Indiana. It was them damn politicians. The legislature started it all back in '58."

Danner was referring to Indiana lawmakers—most of whom were dead now—whose actions led to the inevitable demise of what many considered to be the greatest high school athletic event in America.

During the mid-1950s, the Indiana state legislature cast its eyes on a Hoosier educational system that appeared to perpetuate inequities between large urban schools and small, rural county schools that predominated in an agricultural-driven society. The concern was that areas of dense population—with more industry, higher assessed property valuations producing greater revenues, access to more modern facilities and equipment, a broader curriculum, and better-paid teachers—created an imbalance in learning opportunities for students attending small, rural schools.

Their assumptions were that by merging smaller school corporations with others in the area the consolidations would operate more efficiently, save taxpayers money, and afford a higher level of service to students and parents.

DEATH BY A THOUSAND CUTS

The intentions of members of the General Assembly to improve Indiana's elementary and secondary education were honorable. However, the edict ultimately transformed, dramatically and irrevocably, Indiana high school basketball and its revered single-elimination, winner-take-all state tournament, slowly, relentlessly strangling the format Hoosiers held sacrosanct.

A state senator who was highly instrumental in leading the charge for educational reform was Birch Bayh Jr., whose father, Birch Bayh Sr., was a longtime and highly esteemed basketball official. The senior Bayh had refereed the 1927 championship game, and also each final game from the 1929 through 1934 state tourneys.

Beginning in 1958, educational leaders fanned out across Indiana to hold hearings to solicit opinions and comments from the general population. After explaining the lawmakers' concerns about the perceived disadvantages of students in rural schools, the representatives proposed a solution to ensure fairness and equal opportunity to all students in the Hoosier state. The smaller school systems would merge with their nearest counterparts to create a better, more equitable educational experience.

Wary citizens immediately recognized the inevitable outcome of such a far-reaching plan. At stake was an essential source of pride in small Hoosier towns. Losing its local high school—and its basketball team—was tantamount to destroying a community's identity.

Characteristically, Hoosiers resist change. The Indiana culture is rooted in custom and tradition. The conservative nature of the majority of the citizenry makes them suspicious of any newfangled ideas. But to even consider tampering with the sanctity of high school basketball was beyond innovation. It bordered on heresy.

During most community hearings, strident exchanges characterized acrimonious discussions between the reformers and the general public. Townspeople felt that the education of their youth within the more personalized environment of rural schools, especially in teaching community values, was preferable to the impersonal atmosphere of mega-schools.

Citizens against consolidation claimed such a drastic move actually would result in fewer kids participating in athletics, student government, drama productions, and school newspaper staffs, for example. Many students would be forced to travel inconvenient distances to attend.

An angry delegation from Morgans Awe traveled to the meeting held in Madison to strongly protest the proposal. Chosen as spokesman was Maury

THE HOOSIER GAME

McDonald, a member of the town council and a fierce supporter of traditional ways. When it came his time to stand before the state's agents promoting the plan, he scolded those who would even consider such an outrage. The educational reformers in charge of the meeting eyed Maury stonily while listening to his derisive accusations.

"You people have a 'ready, fire, aim' approach to this thing. As I read it you've already made up your minds, typical of you big city 'do-gooders.' We farmers know somethin' about fallow fields. Well, that's how your bosses' brains are. This whole thing is ridiculous!"

Despite such vehement protests by the citizenry, legislators voted to adopt the School Corporation Reorganization Act of 1959. It mandated that each school district with fewer than 1,000 pupils submit a plan to the state board of education to consolidate with nearby school corporations.

At the time the Indiana legislature compelled high schools to merge, each of 710 member schools in the IHSAA fielded a basketball team. During the first decade following the enactment of the Reorganization Act, about one of every three disappeared from IHSAA membership. By the turn of the twenty-first century that number had decreased further to fewer than four-hundred.

Morgans Awe was one of hundreds of small Indiana towns that fell victim to consolidation. The proud tradition of the Raiders had vanished forever.

The colloquial charm of the state tournament lay in its little crossroads towns. Even today, old timers remember the glory days of now-defunct high schools. Teams like the Roll Red Rollers, Cory Apple Boys, Monroe City Blue Jeans, Winslow Eskimos, Amo Aces, Kennard Leopardcats, and Ashboro Shamrocks now exist only in dusty yearbooks and the yellowing pages of newspaper archives.

Gone are the Plainville Midgets, Twelve Mile's Milers, Warren's Lightning Five, the Ireland Spuds, and the Swayzee Speed Kings, who defeated Liberty Center's Lions in a record nine-overtime game in the 1964 regional round.

The Marengo Cavemen, Mulberry Berries, Colfax Hickories, Cynthiana Annas, and Smithville Skibos are no more. And gone, too, are the Fairmount Quakers, which had a starting guard in 1949 named James Dean. American hero Ernie Pyle once played for Dana's Aggies.

Farmersburg had its Plowboys, Bunker Hill its Minutemen, and Cadiz its Spaniards. Hometown pride boosted Chili's Polar Bears, Miltons's Sharpshooters, and the Tomahawks of Battle Ground.

DEATH BY A THOUSAND CUTS

Cambridge City fans rallied to the support of their beloved Wampus Cats. There were the Wildcats from Ging and the Cobras from Buck Creek. The French Lick Red Devils produced a star named Larry Bird, who averaged 25 points and 22 rebounds a game his senior season. Even three-time state champion Crispus Attucks high was reduced to a middle school in 1986.

In the mid-1990s, the traditional state championship tournament received its second and, to devoted fans of Indiana high school basketball, fatal blow. At that time talk of moving to a multiclass tournament format began to gain serious traction. After years of study by the Board of Control of the IHSAA, school administrators statewide, and assorted other opinion makers, the tournament was divided into four classes dictated by the size of school enrollment.

A groundswell arose among a considerable number of frantic basketball traditionalists who vigorously voiced their objections. Opponents of the change to class basketball—led by Milan hero Bobby Plump—pleaded passionately to keep the tournament as it was. The introduction of class basketball, it was argued, would kill Hoosier Hysteria and the tournament as they knew and loved it.

Alas, their remonstration was about forty years too late. Apparently those behind the movement to retain the traditional one-winner-only tourney hadn't perceived that the war had already been lost, that the essence of the Indiana state tourney had been quietly eroding over the previous forty years.

The death knell of the one-class tournament had sounded in the 1960s and 70s, but no one seemed to be listening. What advocates of retaining the traditional single-class tourney failed to acknowledge was that the soul of the single-class tourney of the past—the sectional round—had been declining in numbers and relevance as consolidation of small rural schools came to its natural conclusion. It was evident that when communities lost their high school teams, many former supporters failed to transfer loyalty to the new consolidated school.

On March 22, 1997, at the RCA Dome in Indianapolis, Bloomington North High School defeated Delta, 75-54, and thus became the last school to win a single-elimination Indiana state championship. Only 382 teams participated in the final IHSAA single-class basketball tournament.

The next year, four divisions competed in the realigned format for the first multiclass tournament. Ninety-six teams, representing schools with the largest enrollments, contended for the Class 4-A title. In descending order, classes 3-A (95), 2-A (97), and A (105) vied for separate championship honors. The numbers in the high school girl's tournament, played weeks earlier, mirrored the boys'.

With the conclusion of high school play that March, trophies were awarded to girls' and boys' champions in each class.

Attendance and revenue generated by the tournament fell steadily after the four-division arrangement was established. Gymnasiums once filled to capacity for the sectionals played to slim crowds. In 2001, for example, New Castle's Chrysler Fieldhouse, renowned for having the largest high school gymnasium in the world with more than 9,000 seats, averaged 1,709 in attendance for its sectional round. Locals ruefully recalled the day when Steve Alford and his New Castle teammates played to sold-out crowds every game of the regular season.

For younger generations, winning a state title in a four-class tournament would not diminish the pride and feeling of accomplishment earned on the hardwood. Teenaged male and female players, coaches, and their supporters no longer viewed a state championship as an impossible dream.

But to those who witnessed the state tourney in its heyday before consolidation and class basketball, its luster had faded irreparably. The four weeks of high school basketball that had enthralled thousands of Hoosiers fans every February and March was now a shadow of its former self. Never again would the annual version of Hoosier Hysteria produce a David versus Goliath matchup.

There would be no more Milan Miracles.

To be sure, consolidation wasn't the only cause of the downfall of the tournament. Inevitable cultural changes in an ever-dynamic world gnawed at convention.

Cable television and the explosion of the number of college and professional teams altered the viewing habits of a sports-loving nation. The proliferation of sports at all levels has had an enormous effect in trivializing traditional offerings like high school games. A multitude of other modern attractions available to Hoosiers made passé the Friday night walk or drive to tiny high school gymnasiums to witness long-held, intense rivalries of the local squad.

The growth of the Amateur Athletic Union especially damaged the significance of high school basketball. AAU has replaced high schools in developing elite basketball stars in the United States. No longer are high school coaches the primary influence on promising teenage players. AAU coaches, outside advisors, college recruiters and even professional scouts have altered the balance of authority over outstanding high school players and their parents.

The ascendance of girls' and women's sports offerings at every level undoubtedly contributed to forcing changes to the Hoosier state tournament. To its everlasting credit, Title IX legislation, enacted in 1972, led to a host of new athletic opportunities and educational diversity for young women everywhere. That females, who previously did not receive equal opportunities and rewards in athletics, could now perform on national and international sports platforms speaks volumes for the wisdom of those who fought for the historic change in the athletic landscape.

Many lesser factors contributed to the evolution of basketball to what it is today. But unquestionably, the School Corporation Reorganization Act of 1959 had the most deleterious effect on the attraction, spirit, and statewide popularity of high school basketball in Indiana.

Representing the viewpoints of many longtime sportswriters, old hand Charlie DeMertin wrote of the recently completed 2012 state tournament, "The IHSAA awards championship trophies in four separate classes for both girls' and boys' basketball. I would tell you who they are but I can't remember any of them."

The depth of hostility that remained within these alumni of Morgans Awe regarding the decline of the tournament was not surprising. Even after a half-century, the destruction of a monument of their youth—by what they perceived as unnecessary tampering by government officials—lingered like bile.

"Ya' know," Orson continued, "if them buncha hon-yocks had just listened to the people this mess prob'ly would'na ever happened."

"Yow, and if a flea had money he'd buy his own dawg," answered Mark.

"Well, one thing never changes. There'll always be change."

"I reckon."

"But their highfalutin' notions sure killed Indiana basketball."

"A-A-Amen t-to th-that."

14

SIR KNIGHT

Jourden Arena
8:31 p.m.

Jubilant fans of Morgans Awe cheered wildly as the Raider players raced back to the bench.

In the Cougars huddle, Coach Fortune stared fiercely at his downcast five.

Through clenched teeth, he began, "I got three words for that quarter of basketball. Sick-en-ing!"

Barely hiding his contempt for the poor showing of his starters, Saul dismissed them to the Cougar bench. The abashed members of the starting five drifted aimlessly to the perimeter of the circle of players.

Turning to his reserves, the disgusted coach mechanically rattled off their names: "Bratton! Dime! Satterwhite! Clendon! Fields!"

With a jerk of his thumb, he signaled to them to report to the scorer's table. The subs surrounded Saul, eager to take the floor. Their coach gave each boy his defensive assignment, then directed the new five to a change in tactics.

"Forget the full-court press. Pick 'em up tight at the ten-second line. Dime, pressure Skoon. Get in his jersey. When we get the ball, Ed, take it straight at fifty-one. Challenge him to foul you. Play him tough at the defensive end. He'll get frustrated and commit a silly foul, just wait'n see.

"Okay, let's go!"

Ten players met again at the center circle. This time, Danner controlled the tap.

Working against the tight Cougar defense, Josh, Sonny, Mark, and Bond handled the ball deftly. Constantly moving, Skoon sought screens to find an opening for a shot. As Jake sliced off of a pick by Sonny, Darrell Bratton was whistled for grabbing the jersey

THE HOOSIER GAME

of the Raiders star. A ninety-two percent free throw shooter for the season, Jake buried both of the one-and-one free shots.

Cougar guard Roosevelt Dime made an ill-advised pass into a closely defended Donel Satterwhite. Sonny slashed in front of the 6-6 sophomore, stealing the pass. At the opposite end, Bond's bounce pass to Josh led to another fast break score.

The Raiders had extended their lead over Central to nine, 24-15.

On the sideline, Saul squatted, facing a dejected Hankins, Weatherford, DeVreaux, Wells, and Miller. He delivered a scathing assessment of their poor play. Benching them had achieved the desired effect. Each was eager to get back on the court.

Charlie Clendon was fouled by Mark Danner as he attempted a shot. The junior forward missed badly on his first attempt.

The original starters for Madison Central hustled to the scorer's bench to report back into the game. Hankins waited at the scorer's table. Clendon's second shot was good. The ref waved Hankins in.

As champions will do, Madison fought back with a vengeance, stalling the Morgans Awe drive. DeWitt Weatherford started the Cougar comeback with a turnaround jumper over Danner. A drive by Cole Wells and subsequent free throw completed a three-point play, cutting the Raiders' lead to 24-20. Miller's long push shot and another Weatherford close-in basket continued the Cougar charge. Seaberg tipped-in a miss by Skoon, putting the Raiders' margin to 26-24, with 4:18 remaining in the first half.

Weatherford countered with a sharp drive to the hoop for two more.

Coach O'Ryan calmly rose to call his second timeout of the half.

The rejuvenated Cougars returned to the sideline to meet Coach Fortune. Saul could read in their deliberate expressions a determination to crush the country upstarts. Overconfidence had resulted in a humbling setback. The Central players had recovered from the train wreck.

Madison rooters were confident that the people's favorite had had its fun. Even ardent Morgans Awe fans felt that the boys in orange and black had missed their chance.

Despite seeing the Raiders' lead melt away, O'Ryan remained calm. His players trusted their coach. Each listened intently as he assessed the situation.

"Now that he feels he's back in control, Saul will go to a zone to try to slow Jake down," the coach predicted. "Let's go to our 'Tar Heel' set. They won't be expecting it."

Michael O'Ryan had attended a basketball clinic last summer at Chapel Hill, featuring North Carolina's new coach, Dean Smith. Smith was developing a semi-stall attack he named the "Four Corners." Two players were positioned along the baseline in opposite corners of the offensive half-court. Two were stationed near the sidelines at the free-throw line extended. The team's best ball handler controlled the ball at the top of the key.

The team running the offense would seek to score, but only on high-percentage tries. The success of the Four Corners depended upon error-free ball handling. Each player was in constant motion, guided by the movements of the player with the ball. Above all, the offense called for patience and discipline.

Generally used late in a close game, it was designed to reduce time on the game clock. By spreading the floor, the Four Corners forced the trailing team to chase the ball in hopes of getting a steal, which often resulted in easy drives to the basket. Many times, frustrated defenders committed ill-advised or deliberate fouls.

Smith used this offensive set effectively until the NCAA rules committee adopted a shot clock to prevent stalling.

O'Ryan was taking a calculated risk. Although the Raiders had rehearsed this spread offense throughout the year at the close of every practice, this would be the first time Coach would employ it in a real game.

The Cougars had switched from the man-to-man to a 2-3 zone defense, just as Ryan had foreseen. Saul saw that O'Ryan had again changed his offensive set. Now, Fortune wasn't certain how Morgans Awe intended to attack his defense.

Imagine Fortune's surprise when the Raiders didn't attack!

As Bathwaite dribbled across the half-court line, his teammates rushed to their appointed spots. Bond maintained his dribble, but made no move toward the hoop. Wells and Miller were sagging back on opposite sides of the foul circle.

Twenty seconds, then half a minute ran off of the scoreboard clock. Coach Fortune leaped from his seat to counter O'Ryan's clever move. He directed his squad to return to their man-to-man defense and press the Raiders tightly, hoping to force them out of this semi-stall.

The last four minutes of the second quarter would be marked by a nearly flawless exhibition of high school basketball play. However, it was the Raiders, not the Cougars, who would put on an amazing display of dominance. No one in the arena would have believed that DeWitt Weatherford's previous field goal would be the last points the Cougars would score the rest of the first half.

Saturday, May 5, 2012

As the debate on consolidation heated up, Bear Billings began to reminisce about state championship games of the past.

"Most people think Milan beatin' Muncie was the best game ever. For my money, when Damon beat Con-curd High School all by hisself, that was the best final game ever."

THE HOOSIER GAME

Grover agreed. "Sh-sh-sure was a g-great wo-wo-wone."

"Over forty-thousan' people was at the Dome that night. Guess it showed onc't and fer all that no place loved ther basketball like us Hoosiers," Bobby Mack added.

The 1990 IHSAA championship featured undefeated and top-ranked Elkhart Concord High School against underdog Bedford North Lawrence, led by 18-year-old prodigy Damon Bailey. The largest crowd ever for high school basketball in America—41,046 people—witnessed the game.

Bailey wrote a fitting conclusion to his prep career in a thrilling, come-from-behind victory over the Minutemen, 63-60, by scoring all eleven of his team's points in the final three minutes of the game. His 30-point total pushed him past Marion Pierce of Lewisville for Indiana's prep career scoring record, with 3,134 points.

"That wasn't the biggest crowd for a basketball game in Indiana, though," Elmer Freebolt reminded them. "That record was set when Knight coached the 'lympic team."

In preparation for the 1984 Olympic Games, Indiana's Bob Knight had been selected to coach the USA team for the Pan-American tournament in Puerto Rico. Knight arranged an exhibition game matching his Olympians, featuring Michael Jordan and Steve Alford, against a team of NBA All-stars, led by Hoosier superstar Larry Bird. More than 67,000 fans crowded into the Hoosier Dome in Indianapolis, the highest attendance for any indoor basketball game ever played up to that time.

In Indiana, to create an immediate conversational firestorm, one need only invoke the name of Robert Montgomery Knight.

Joe Cotter spoke up for the first time, offering, "Damon Bailey coulda been one of the all-time greats if Knight hadn'a ruin't 'eem."

"What are you talkin' about, Joe?" Bear countered. "Knight was the best coach ever at IU. Hell, he's the best coach of all time."

Coach Knight's removal as basketball coach by President Myles Brand and the Indiana University Board of Trustees in 2001 remained a sore subject for bitter Knight supporters. His three national championships and numerous Big Ten titles were reason enough for his ardent followers to defend him. Adding into the mix his quiet, non-publicized charity; love and concern for his players before and *after* graduation; his absolutely clean program and his players' extraordinary graduation rate; his selfless proclivity for assisting colleagues—especially younger coaches—in very personal ways; and his record of

SIR KNIGHT

meaningful contributions to the game of basketball qualified him as a living legend to Hoosier followers.

"I'm just sayin' he treated his players like dirt. I wouldn't want no kidda mine playin' for 'eem."

Bobby Mack jumped to the former IU coach's defense.

"Lemme see. Knight never cheated in recruitin'. Almost a hunnerd percent of his players graduated. None of 'em ever went to jail."

"An' why do almost all of 'em stand up for him ever'time he's in some tiff or another?" added Mark. "I hear they still go to him for advice, even when ther fifty years old."

"Knight practically built that library they're so proud of up there," claimed Jamie. "He raised most of the money for it and the coach and his wife made a major contribution to the effort."

Added Bear, "I'm told he did a lot of charity work and helped people without lettin' anyone know it. He didn't want no glory."

"He'd show up in kids' hospital rooms without a buncha slimeballs from the press aroun'."

"Yeah, how about Landon Turner after he was paralyzed. He couldn't help Coach Knight then, but Knight took care of him personally in all kinda ways. He was a helluva lot more than just a basketball coach."

"But you cain't win Knight's way no more. Kid's today won't take the abuse he puts out."

"That don't make a lick a' sense, Joe. When he went to Texas Tech, that school hadn't won anything in twenty-five years before he got there. He's won over twenty games ever' year but one. An' yer sayin' kids won't play for him?"

"He passed up Dean Smith to be the all-time winningest college coach, too. The guy who beat Knight's record played for him at Army. The man's a genius."

At this point, a veteran who rarely spoke of his war experiences hinted at his opinion of Bob Knight's coaching style. None of the guys questioned Sonny Watkins's courage in battle. He was esteemed by all for his heroic service to his country. Examples of his leadership and care for his men in combat were legendary. When he spoke of warfare, men listened deferentially.

"I was in basic training at Camp Lejeune in '63, before shipping overseas. Part of the daily routine was carryin' a 200-pound sack of gear to the top of a hundred-foot sand dune.

"You don't really know what you're capable of doin' until a drill sergeant is screamin' in one ear and pissin' in the other, while you think you can't go any

THE HOOSIER GAME

farther. Because of that type of coachin' I was able to carry wounded and dying men in Vietnam to safety, when everything in me told me I couldn't do it."

The obvious reference to Coach Knight's style was not lost on the men. They all nodded in respect for their honorable companion.

"Well. I still don' like 'eem," Joe muttered.

Josh steered away from the increasingly heated discussion by sharing an anecdote about one of Knight's adoring admirers.

"When Bob Knight was still coaching at IU, I was drivin' along I-74 about thirty miles east of Indianapolis. At a farm on the side of the highway was a private fishing pond with a fence around it. On the gate was a sign that said, 'If your name ain't Bob Knight, don't even THINK about it!'"

"Yeah, and you member—"

At that moment, Arnie interrupted the conversation, blurting out, "WHHHOA!"

A shapely woman had just then appeared at the door, wearing a burgundy cocktail dress, the hemline at mid-thigh. Her V-neck bodice revealed ample breasts above a slim waist and hips. Her ivory skin showed no substantial wrinkles in contrast with the rest of the crowd. Long blonde hair, highlighted with silver streaks, lay softly on her shoulders. Her face was tastefully touched with rouge. Lips were outlined in cherry-red lipstick. Long false eyelashes and carefully plucked, arched eyebrows surrounded dark-brown eyes. Her teeth were straight and white.

"Who the hell's daughter is that?" Mark said to no one in particular.

"Roll your tongue back in, Mark," Arnie hissed. "Yer embarrassin' us."

Several of the female classmates stepped forward to greet the latest guest. Most were curious as to who she was. The ladies were seen quizzically whispering to one another at the sight of this incongruently attractive classmate. To them, she seemed like a forty-something who'd wandered into this old people's party by mistake.

As the woman made her way further into the room, an impish grin spread across Bear's face.

"That, my friends, is 'Pentacostal Patty.'"

"N-n-n-o wa-wa-wa-way!" Grover blurted out.

So this is who Rita Wells had teased us about earlier, thought Josh.

Patty Morrow's father had been a lay minister for the Jesus Disciples Apostolic House of Worship that many kids derided as the "Holy Rollers." His eldest daughter carefully adhered to the strictly conservative dress code and severe social restrictions of its members through her high school years. Patty was often ridiculed by Morgans Awe girls for her beehive hairdo piled high, plain face with no makeup, and reputation for "speaking in tongues."

Escorted by a man twenty years her junior, Trish, as she now called herself, was a "cougar" before the term was invented. She glided nonchalantly from person to person, smiling sweetly. Too sweetly. Pentacostal Patty was no doubt enjoying the attention of the men and the clearly evident surprise and envy of her former female classmates.

Take *that*, women of the class of '62.

Lowering his voice, Arnie turned to Bobby Mack Deal.

"Hey, Bobo, didn't you ast her out on a date onc't?"

"Yeah. Said she'd have to pray bout it first," Deal replied, his eyes like saucers as he stared, laser-like, at the sexy woman who had crashed the party.

"That's when you started prayin', too," laughed Mark. "Lord, git me outta here, fast!"

As he poured drinks and opened cans of beer, Bear slyly broached a subject that was certain would bring a spirited response from Dr. Jamie Ross. With an impish grin, the bartender asked, "Hey, Moon, whatever happened to that babe you went goo-goo over in high school? Annie, wasn't it? I figured you two'd git married and have a passel 'a cross-eyed kids."

As a junior, a very shy Jamie had had a brief run at going steady. Annalee Kichler was his first real girlfriend, a pretty, well-built classmate. Because he began to spend more time with his girlfriend than with the gang, Ross endured constant teasing.

"Go away, Bear," Jamie answered, knowing what came next.

"Yeah, you two were really in love, weren't cha'?" Deal chimed in.

"In lust," Josh corrected.

"Just good friends," Moon countered, hoping the conversation would veer into a different direction.

"Good frens', my toke-eye," Bear mocked, keeping the momentum afloat. "You was so moon-eyed around her, yer eyes looked like two fried aggs, sunny-side up!"

"Ah, it was never like that," Jamie retorted, hoping to change the subject.

Bobby Mack continued the harsh interrogation. "Don't give me that bull, James! She dropped you like a lead balloon the first time you puckered up that ugly mouth and tried to kiss her."

THE HOOSIER GAME

"I do remember that time Dean Mitchel called you two in for holding hands between classes," Josh offered.

"In ole lady Mitchel's eyes," Bear claimed, "any boys and girls nuzzlin' in the hallway were on a sure 'n steady path to perdition."

Surprisingly quiet to this point, Arnie asked the rhetorical question: "You know the real story, don'cha' boys?"

The good doctor interrupted, sneering, "I swear, every time we get together, he tells this same old stale lie. Don't you have any new material, Fries?"

"Ah, Doc. This one's just too fine ta die."

While a very cute girl, Annalee had a noticeable flaw. She had a "lazy eye" that often drooped and appeared to be looking in a different direction than the steady one. It was a shortcoming that normally went without comment.

"Remember that time you 'n Annalee was sittin' in the bleachers at the baseball game? You thought she was makin' love eyes at you. But then you noticed she was flirtin' with me in the third row with her wayward eye. Pissed you off, didn'it?"

Fries was already dodging when Jamie lunged at him, playfully threatening violence and chasing him around the sofa until Arnie fagged out. Fries dropped into a defensive fetal position as Jamie whaled away with harmless blows.

"Be careful, Doc. You don' wanna injure them surgeon's mitts, 'specially on a worthless good-fer-nuthin' like Fries."

Tuesday, September 2, 1958

As the new school year began, teens were singing or humming Ricky Nelson's latest hit, "Poor Little Fool."

> *I used to play around with hearts that hastened at my call,*
> *But when I met that little girl I knew that I would fall.*
> *Poor little fool, oh yeah, I was a fool, uh huh.*
> *She played around and teased me with her carefree devil eyes,*
> *She'd hold me close and kiss me but her heart was full of lies.*
> *Poor little fool, oh yeah, I was a fool, uh huh.*

Josh and his freshman buddies quickly learned the rules, written and unwritten, of their new environment. They had joined the upperclassmen on the top floor of the high school building. There they would be introduced in science classes to such teaching aids as slide rules, Bunsen burners, microscopes, and a contraption depicting planets on wire stems whirling around the sun. Drafting class required students to wield a T-square and a triangular architect's ruler.

Initial lessons in typing class usually resulted in students having to constantly separate the snarls of entwined, spiny metal fingers, the result of striking multiple keys simultaneously on their Corona typewriters. Changing the spools of ink ribbons also was a pain.

Other advanced educational technology included short newsreels and reel-to-reel tape recorders, which broke down with regularity. Most classroom teachers had little familiarity with the most basic mechanical idiosyncrasies of the machines, so they usually turned to a student for help when things went amiss.

The fingers and hands of Mrs. Redbank, the librarian, were constantly stained purple by the messy malfunctioning of the mimeograph as she made copies of tests and other documents for teachers.

Hanging on the wall of Miss Luden's geography classroom was the latest in world maps. She possessed the only globe in the school.

By far the favorite class for rambunctious boys was gym. Every day began with each student scaling one of the two thick hemp ropes hung from the rafters of the gymnasium. Climbing hand-over-fist with legs intertwined in the rope, most lads could reach the knot marking the ten-foot level. Stronger and more athletic boys advanced to the tape fifteen feet above the floor. Sonny could even climb to the I-beam from which the rope was strung.

Boys looked forward to spirited games of bombardment, a spin-off of dodge ball. The game was mass mayhem. A rubber ball the size of a grapefruit left welts on various parts of the victim's body.

While most freshmen rode the bus, upperclassmen were too cool for that nonsense. Those lucky enough to own a car picked up their buddies for the ride to and from school.

Underclassmen generally brought lunch pails or brown sacks from home, filled with sandwiches and snacks. Seniors were allowed to leave the school grounds at noon to buy lunch, usually at Scoop 'n Dollies, or Hawkins General Store. The leather-jacketed hoods in the school would congregate at Schoenkoppel's gas station—they called it St. Red's Mission—to have a sandwich, a candy bar, and a surreptitious smoke.

The array of extracurricular activities was diverse for a small school. After-school clubs included service organizations like Hi-Y and Future Farmers of

THE HOOSIER GAME

America for boys and the Sunshine Society and Future Homemakers of America for girls (along with the rare male student who had the courage to endure the teasing he would face).

Band, Choir, Pep, and Dramatics clubs drew the interest of different groups in the school. Both the weekly *Awe-Struck* student newspaper and the school's annual yearbook, *Memories*, were published by the Future Journalists.

Josh and Pat were elected to Student Council as freshman representatives. Both would earn membership in the National Honor Society.

Periodically, the last class of the day would be suspended for band concerts, pep sessions, and convocations featuring various speakers and performers.

Along with student mixers following ballgames, various clubs would sponsor dances for Sadie Hawkins Day, Christmas, and Homecoming. The Junior-Senior Prom was a highlight for upperclassmen in the spring.

Utmost on the minds of Jake, Josh, and friends were basketball tryouts in early October. Unlike junior high, when coaches kept fifteen or more players on the roster, the freshman team would be limited to twelve spots. The basketball version of Darwin's Law began in earnest at the frosh level.

Twenty-three eager teenagers showed up for tryouts. After a brief warming-up period, Coach Tom Davison called the boys together. His message was succinct and unmistakable:

"A black line surrounds the playing area where the best of you will prove you belong on this Raider team. Once you step across that black line, you'd best be ready, 'cause everybody starts out equal. On the court it doesn't matter who your daddy is, if you're rich or poor, or how good you think you are. No one—I repeat, no one—has made the team as of now. The twelve boys who make the final cut will prove to my satisfaction, over the next ten days, that they will give us the best chance to win.

"Okay, form two parallel lines for passing drills."

Practice was spirited but sloppy that day as the nervous players went through a variety of fundamentals. Competition was fierce as every boy put forward his best effort. Davison and his two volunteer assistants were in constant motion, yelling instructions and encouragement along with the necessary corrections as each boy tried to demonstrate why he should make the team.

Five-man squads were picked at random for lengthy scrimmages. Following a series of brutal wind-sprints and agility drills at the end of practice, the exhausted boys were released to the locker room.

One by one, the players plopped heavily onto benches, chests heaving as each gasped for air. Thighs and calves cried out, and blisters on the soles of feet smarted like the stings of yellowjackets.

As the hopefuls were recovering, one showoff emerged who seemed not to have expended all of his energy on the court. Calling his exhausted buddies "wimps," Maurice Brown decided to do chin-ups on the water pipes hanging above the players' heads. The result was not as he intended.

Vaulting upward, he grasped the pipeline with both hands. Unfortunately, that section wasn't wrapped in protective asbestos material as scalding water coursed through the pipes. The shocked teen howled in pain as he released the searing red-hot tube. Maurice quickly rushed to the cold water spigot in the basin across the room. By the time he got there, ugly red lines had already begun to show on his palms.

At that moment, Coach Davison entered the room. He stood over the very contrite Maurice, examined the wounds, then uttered, stonily, "Burn and learn, son."

The rest of the players broke into uneasy laughter.

As practice trials continued, players constantly compared their strengths with those of the competition. How do I stack up against the others? Who is the main threat to my position? What do I do better than the others? Why can't I shoot like he can? Will I make the starting five? The team?

Athletics stripped individuals of all pretenses. Contrary to what many had been led to believe—"You can be anything you want if you try hard enough"—desire alone did not guarantee a spot on the roster. Hard work was necessary to be a good player; but high energy and passion for the game rarely closed the gap between the marginally skilled boy and the athlete with superior talent.

It was not surprising that, following the first week of repeated drills, shooting practice, and scrimmages, Jake, Josh, Mark, and Sonny emerged as the cream of this crop. After Friday's practice, Jake was called into head coach O'Ryan's office. It was there Jake learned he would practice on Monday with the varsity squad. The sharp-shooting freshman would have the opportunity to compete for a starting guard position.

That same day, Seaberg, Danner, and Watkins were informed by junior varsity coach Barnhard that they would be joining the nine sophomores who had made the JV squad. While they didn't know it at the time, all three would open the season as starters, much to the resentment of some of the displaced sophomores' parents.

THE HOOSIER GAME

The junior varsity lost only twice during the year as the freshmen trio of Josh, Sonny, and Mark played leading roles. JV coach Barnhard emphasized defensive fundamentals and conditioning to prepare his charges for future varsity play under head coach O'Ryan. That season the young Raiders limited the opposition to twenty-four points per contest, while putting up an average of forty-five on offense.

Barnhard approached the head coach following an impressive JV win over St. Isadore to remark,

"This is a special group of kids, Mike. I've never coached a more talented and saavy bunch than these guys. Throw in Jake, and—"

"I just hope we're still around to coach 'em next year," was O'Ryan's droll reply.

15

DOGS DON'T BARK AT PARKED CARS

Jourden Arena
8:36 p.m.

The Raiders were playing like a well-oiled-machine. As Morgans Awe calmly looked for openings in Madison's defense, the Cougar players moved up tightly onto their men. As Jake dribbled along the sideline, Miller slashed in from behind, flicking the ball off Skoon's fingers and out of bounds.

"White ball!" yelled official Warden, pointing toward the Madison Central goal.

The ensuing play led to a controversial call against the Cougars. Cole Wells was cited for a violation that was rarely called.

As Cole casually started to inbound the ball to Miller, Sonny Watkins darted in front of Marty, cutting off Cole's passing lane. Reacting to Sonny's surprising defensive move, Wells shuffled his feet as he abruptly checked the throw. The ref immediately blew his whistle, calling traveling on the Cougar guard. Madison fans went berserk.

A particularly loud Cougar rooter bellowed, "How can you call travelin' on a man outta bounds, stripes!"

Livid, Coach Fortune exploded from the bench, with arms spread and palms up, with a look of incredulity on his face. He stomped onto the court to protest the call to official Norm Blaise.

"That was a horse-apple call, Norm! What did he do?"

"You know the rules, Saul. Your boy clearly took two steps. When the throw-in spot is designated, it's the same as if the ball was inbounds. Traveling!"

"I've coached over thirty years, Norm, and I've seen that call made exactly one time!"

"Make that twice, Saul."

THE HOOSIER GAME

With a piercing glance at the veteran official, the coach uttered, "Ah, bullshit," and turned back to the bench.

Fortune's crude comment tipped the scale of the veteran official's patience. Saul didn't see the "T" sign that the referee flashed to the scorer. Reacting to the shrieks of the Central crowd, the livid coach leaped skyward when he realized he had been assessed a technical foul.

Bitterly protesting the perceived injustice, Saul glared defiantly at Blaise. Returning an equally menacing scowl, the ref strode briskly in the direction of Central's coach. If his authority was challenged any further, Blaise was prepared to tack on an additional penalty.

Madison's assistant coach Luke Prizendine quickly stepped between the irate coach and the approaching official, guiding Fortune away from a potential confrontation that might result in his second, and disqualifying, technical foul.

Jamming the fingers of his right hand into his left palm, Saul called timeout.

Jake stepped to the line to shoot the technical free throw. It slid through perfectly.

The Cougar players gathered mechanically into a huddle. The players stood uncomfortably, expecting a stern reprimand. No one dared say a word.

However, their volatile coach moved back to the team's bench and took a seat. Seizing Prizendine by his coat sleeve, Coach Fortune yanked his assistant down beside him.

Fortune's frustration with his team had reached a level of fury beyond his customary indignation. As seconds ticked by, the seething coach sat stoically, with no hint of moving from his spot on the bench.

The awkward situation became intolerable as the end of the timeout period approached. Finally, captain Cole Wells leaned inward to address his confused teammates.

"Okay, guys. Let's quit screwin' around with these farmers! No way they're gonna beat us. Marty, I'll take Skoon now. You switch over to Bathwaite."

The horn sounded, ending the break. As Coach Saul sat expressionless, twenty hands joined in the center of the huddle. The boys broke formation with a half-hearted, "Go Cougars."

As MCHS players turned back to the court, the subs retreated to the bench, avoiding eye contact with their furious mentor.

Thus far, O'Ryan had made no substitutions in the Raiders lineup. He now called on 6-3 Grover Willburn to replace Mark, who had fortunately avoided committing a third foul. Mark was the one player the coach could not afford to lose.

Morgans Awe put the ball in play. From the top of the key, Bond reset the spread offense. With Miller guarding him tightly, Bathwaite faked a shot, then sped by him. As he dribbled freely down the middle, Weatherford jumped into the path to the basket,

DOGS DON'T BARK AT PARKED CARS

leaving Josh alone along the baseline. Bond cleverly dumped the ball off to Seaberg, who made the easy lay-in. Fouled by Hankins, Josh made good on the free toss for a 29-26 Raiders lead.

The Cougars quickly pushed the ball into the front court. Closely guarded by Sonny, Miller missed a shot from fifteen feet. Willburn controlled the rebound and handed it off to Bathwaite.

As Morgans Awe set up its offense, Wells sagged off of Jake in case Bathwaite got by Marty and penetrated the middle of the Cougar defense. Instead, Bond dribbled casually toward Jake, gave him the ball, then set a screen on Wells. Trailing the play, Miller couldn't catch Skoon, who was now driving hard toward the basket.

Weatherford was again forced into a choice: either pick up Skoon and leave Seaberg, or sag back, hoping a teammate would recover to stop Skoon. Weatherford selected door number two. Seeing Dewitt retreat, Jake made good on an unmolested jump shot from the free throw line.

Now at the other end, DeVreaux spotted Hankins cutting back door. Josh moved deftly to intercept the Cougar center's bounce pass and tossed it to Bond. Crossing the center circle, he passed to Sonny Watkins, whose defender was stationed at least ten feet from him. When Hankins moved out to put pressure on Sonny, he shot a pass to Josh in the corner. Josh returned the ball to Watkins, Watkins fed Bathwaite, Bond quickly passed to Jake, and Jake pushed the ball back to Bathwaite who sank an eight-footer.

O'Ryan's team was running "North Carolina" to perfection.

After Weatherford missed a short jumper, Saul sensed his dilemma. If Morgans Awe didn't get careless, they could stall the rest of the half, then put up the last shot without his Cougars touching the ball again.

When Miller moved up to pressure the ball, Bond again drove to the middle toward the basket. This time DeWitt and Karl lay back, allowing the Raider guard to put up a short floater. The shot bounced off the rim. Josh screened out Hankins and tipped the errant shot in.

Another Miller miss led to an easy basket for the Raiders. Willburn again corralled the rebound to start the fast break. Speeding into the front court, Bond snapped a pass to Jake on the side, who sank a fifteen-foot jumper.

After Madison misfired again, the Raiders ran a full minute off the clock. As his team worked the ball flawlessly from player to player, O'Ryan noted the obvious frustration in the expressions of the Cougars. Finally, Sonny found himself open on the baseline. As the senior forward drove for a lay-up, Miller slapped futilely at the ball. As the shot slid through the net, the official slashed his arm downward. Whirling to the scorer's bench, he soberly uttered, "Foul on number three. Basket good. One free throw."

THE HOOSIER GAME

Watkins's attempt was true, giving Morgans Awe its biggest lead, 40-26, with only forty-four seconds remaining in the first half.

On the ensuing possession, Weatherford tried a sweeping hook shot, hitting the front of the rim. DeVreaux tipped it once, twice, missing both times. Miller snared the rebound and passed to Wells, whose shot fell short. Again, DeVreaux was well-positioned to pull down the rebound, but his frustration continued as his short shot rolled off the rim into the hands of Seaberg. Five shot attempts, five failures.

Only seconds remained as Bond moved swiftly into the front court. Finding Jake unguarded in the corner, Bathwaite fired a sharp pass to Jake. From twenty-five feet away, Skoon launched his high-arcing jumper. The net hardly rippled. Raiders 42, Madison Central, 26.

Before Wells could inbound the ball the loud report of the scorer's gun ended the first half.

Madison Central rooters were stunned. Approximately seven of every ten onlookers in the building screamed with delight at the startling turn of events. Spectators were sensing an upset of historic proportions.

The loudest sustained cheers any of the Raiders had ever experienced washed over them as they bounded off the court.

Friday, March 6, 1959

The Raiders' varsity had won their final four games of the season by impressive margins. Hopes were high that the team would make a good showing in the sectional, hosted by Madison Central High School. They drew the Pristine Lake Lions in the opening game of the tournament.

Morgans Awe advanced to the second round with a 44-41 win over PLHS. Jake contributed twelve points, including two key free throws in the last ten seconds to put the game out of reach.

Dreams of a sectional title were dashed Friday evening when a veteran Sycamore Creek High School team routed Morgans Awe, 83-67. The outcome was never in doubt as Sy-High raced to a 24-9 lead by the end of the first quarter. Jake, stifled throughout the game by the more experienced Eagle defenders, scored only four points.

MAHS finished the season with a record of 13-9. Jake averaged fifteen points a game, second-highest on the team.

On Saturday, the sectional hosts sponsored a sock hop in the Madison Armory between the afternoon games and the championship contest that evening. The dance provided students from all over the county opportunities for mixing and meeting their counterparts from other schools.

Packed into the tile-floored hall were cliques of teenage girls and boys dressed in school colors and trying to impress others with their "cool." The phalanx of hyperactive, gum-chewing teens of all shapes and sizes created an open-air market filled with flirting, bragging, and at least one fairly dramatic stand-off between self-perceived tough guys from rival high schools. These dramatic interludes usually ended with a few shoves, snarls and insults before chaperones stepped in to break it up.

Freshmen, of course, roosted on the lowest rung of the teenage ladder. For Jake, Josh, and the others it was an opportunity to observe and learn from older students. Their obscurity among the mass of teens rendered them spectators to the social interactions taking place.

A strikingly attractive cheerleader from Madison Central appeared, strolling through the parting crowd like a queen at court. Dixie Jo "D.J." Stiles was high school royalty, a well-known and much-admired accoutrement of the MCHS basketball program.

D.J. was petite, cute, and curvy. Her deep-set, almond-shaped brown eyes glistened beneath perfectly arched eyebrows and long lashes. She wore stylish earrings that complemented her short dark-brown hair. The Madison senior had a wickedly enchanting smile. Responding to a compliment, her nose crinkled, dimples deepened, her eyes disappeared beneath enticing narrow lids, and her mouth parted to reveal perfectly aligned teeth, white as snow.

She was a girl accustomed to male attention and female envy. Her natural beauty and flirtatious nature were like iron filings to a magnet for hormone-hyped teenage males.

A crowd began to gather near the middle of the floor as the strains of a particular pop song floated downward from the sound system in the ceiling. D.J. and a fellow senior from MCHS began to swing to the tantalizing beat of "Shimmy, Shimmy, Koko Bop," by Little Anthony and the Imperials. As she and her male partner swayed and twisted in a modified jitterbug, her short cheerleaders skirt swished to and fro, revealing perfectly proportioned legs and a round, compact posterior. Other dancing couples quietly exited the floor until only D.J. and her much-envied companion remained in a tightening circle around them.

THE HOOSIER GAME

Dixie Jo Stiles, "...a body like Sandra Dee and a smile that could charm a cobra."

Shimmy shimmy koko bop, shimmy shimmy bop (aah!)
Shimmy Shimmy koko bop, shimmy shimmy bop (aah!)
Sittin' in a native hut, all alone and blue,
Sittin' in a native hut, wonderin' what to do,
Along came a native girl, did a native dance,
It was like a paradise, put me in a trance,
Goin' shimmy, shimmy koko bop, shimmy shimmy bop (aah!)
Shimmy shimmy koko bop, shimmy shimmy bop (aah!)

Jake, Josh, Sonny, Mark, and Bobby Mack Deal, along with the rest of the male population there, ignored the Tenth Commandment as they ogled the Teen Angel. When the song ended, loud applause erupted from the males gathered round. Envious girls clapped to be polite, but not nearly as raucously as the boys.

While the five MAHS frosh were regaining control over their involuntary gaping, one of them mumbled something barely audible. To Josh, it sounded like Bobby Mack Deal whispered, "I'm gonna ask D.J. to dance."

Yeah, and a heifer can do a triple back flip.

Apparently delirious, Bobby Mack repeated his intention to pursue the unattainable.

"I'd stay and watch you, Bobo. But Brigitte Bardot just called ta tell me she's curlin' up naked on my couch, awaitin' on me," Arnie sneered.

Piling on, Sonny added, "You git a dance with Dixie Jo an' I'll pay for the wedding."

Dripping with sarcasm, Mark offered, "There's only 'bout twelve senior studs standin' around 'er right now. Go on over there an' tell her yer the man of 'er life."

Bobby Mack replied confidently, "I will."

As Deal began walking in the direction of D.J., his buddies knew he would chicken out. But, as they watched, the derisive laughter of the boys turned to stunned silence, then disbelief, then undisguised envy.

"Daa-yam, he's really gonna try it!"

Still unconvinced, Mark grinned, saying, "Bobo doesn't have the walnuts."

Standing 5'4"—at least five inches shorter than any of the Casanovas surrounding D.J.—Deal elbowed his way to the front of the group. Josh could see his lips moving as he confronted the teenage beauty. At first, she seemed a bit bewildered, her brow wrinkling, and her demeanor cautious. Then, with a

THE HOOSIER GAME

bemused smile, she took Bobby's hand and strolled toward the dance floor, leaving the surrounding male admirers gawking covetously after her and her bold young suitor.

The opening lyrics of the most romantic song of the year, "Smoke Gets in Your Eyes," sung by the Platters, had already begun when Bobby Mack placed his right arm around D.J.'s waist, took her right hand in his left, and began to slowly lead her around the dance floor.

"Bobo went 'n dunnit. I don' bleeve it," mumbled a shocked Mark, saying aloud what the others were thinking.

They asked me how I knew, my true love was true,
I of course replied, something here inside,
Cannot be denied.
They said someday you'll find, all who love are blind,
When your heart's on fire, you don't realize,
Smoke gets in your eyes.

All eyes were on the couple. While the sight of a pint-sized fifteen-year-old spinning determinedly around the floor with the Queen of the Hop was amusing, it seemed in the expressions of the observers that they were silently saluting the young whelp's audacity.

"Who the hell is that little piss-ant?" muttered one handsome senior from Madison Central.

"I don't know, but he's got my vote for havin' brass ball-bearings," answered a friend.

For her part, D.J. was classy, snuggling closely and adoringly, as if Bobby Mack was Adonis to her Venus.

With their mouths agape, Deal's teammates stood in unvarnished amazement.

So I chaffed and I gaily laughed,
To think they would doubt my love,
Yet today, my love has flown away,
I am without my love,
Now laughing friends deride, tears I cannot hide
So I smile and say, when a lovely flame dies,
Smoke gets in your eyes.

While he remained relatively cool as an entire hall of teenage boys and girls watched his every move, Bobby had the presence of mind to aim a quick wink and a devilish grin over Dixie Jo's shoulder toward his drooling teammates.

When the song finally ended, D.J. gave Bobby Mack a quick peck on the cheek and a smile that could've charmed a cobra.

Deal nonchalantly rejoined his mates where an extemporaneous celebration erupted as if Bobo had hit the winning basket for the state championship.

Veni, vidi, vici.

Friday, August 21, 1959

The summer before Josh's sophomore year was rapidly dwindling. On this day Hawaii officially gained statehood, joining Alaska as the second territory to become part of United States in this year. Prior to now, the latest expansion of the country was when Arizona and New Mexico became states in 1912. Also this month, David Carr, a British printer, had become the first person to die of a strange new disease. On a visit to the Congo, he had contracted the human immunodeficiency virus, later known as AIDS.

Josh, Jake, Sonny, and Bobby Mack were sleeping over at Arnie's home this evening. While eating popcorn and sipping eight-ounce Cokes they listened to Arnie's collection of hit tunes. His record player had a plastic spindle that held several 45 rpm records.

Connie Francis's lament about a best friend smooching her boyfriend hung in the air.

When you left me all alone at the record hop,
Told me you were goin' out for a soda pop,
You were gone for quite a while, half an hour or more,
You came back and man, oh, man, this is what I saw:
Lipstick on your collar told a tale on you.
Lipstick on your collar said you were untrue.
Bet your bottom dollar you and I are through,
'Cause lipstick on your collar told a tale on you! Yeah!

Always up for a new experience, Arnie had planned a special adventure of the clandestine kind for his guests tonight.

THE HOOSIER GAME

Around ten o'clock, the boys snuck out of the house. They moved quietly through the dark to a place behind the old shed out back. There, Arnie had buried a small burlap bag in a shallow hole. Retrieving the hidden treasure, he held up for all to see a Mason jar filled with clear liquid.

Arnie's Uncle Stitch was known among relatives and close friends for concocting his own home brand of country hooch. The young Packard heard the adult men in his family refer to the brew as "Hell's honey." Arnold had managed to swipe one of the jars during a recent visit.

The host unscrewed the lid and offered the libation to the innocents surrounding him. As the jar passed hands from boy to boy, each sniffed the contents. An odor like that of diesel fuel offended the nostrils.

Arnie challenged his buddies. "Okay, who's gonna go first?"

No one leaped at the invitation. Breaking the awkward silence, Arnie snarled, "You buncha' women!"

With that, he raised the jar to his lips. Arnie didn't sip. He gulped. Suddenly, his eyes bugged out. Tears rolled down his cheeks. As the fiery liquid headed south his esophagus rebelled, leaving him gagging and gasping for breath. Arnie's face contorted into a fiendish glower. His arms went numb. He emitted a guttural growl.

With a final, violent shudder, Arnie sat expressionless.

Seeing the catatonic gaze, his friends weren't sure Arnie was still conscious. Then, beginning at the left corner of his mouth, the impish Arnie grin spread across his face. Without warning, his eyes disappeared, his mouth flew open, and he emitted a full-throated, maniacal laugh. No longer were the boys concerned about his consciousness. Now they feared he was crazy.

"GREAT STUFF!" he announced, as he began to goad each of the others to take a nip. And so, each, in turn, tasted the brew. Only one—Bobby Mack—tossed his cookies. For Josh, that one foray into bootleg "licker" would count as two—the first time, and the last.

In mid-October the glorious color wheel of autumn's trees, shrubs, and flowers had reached its peak in southern Indiana. A panorama of vivid shades of gold, red, orange, green, and violet contrasted with the dying leaves of brown. The nostalgic, pungent smell of burning leaves at the street's edge was yet another reminder of the inevitable approach of winter.

It was eleven o'clock in the evening. Josh had passed on his friends' invitation to drive into Madison for a movie, preferring to rest after a demanding week of basketball practice.

DOGS DON'T BARK AT PARKED CARS

Propped up in his bed, Josh was reading his favorite book, *The Adventures of Huckleberry Finn*. As a sixth grader Josh had delighted in the light-hearted antics of Huck and his friend, Tom Sawyer. This time, he clearly discerned the underlying, sometimes dark, adult themes subtlety woven within the silliness and wild imaginations of Twain's fabled duo.

The radio-alarm clock by the bed was tuned to WAKY in Louisville. Popular DJ "Jumpin' Jack" Sanders played Top 40 rock 'n roll tunes while entertaining his listeners with humor and wit. Occasionally, Jake would pause in his reading to listen to a favored song.

> *Put your head on my shoulder,*
> *Hold me in your arms, baby,*
> *Squeeze me oh so tight, baby,*
> *Show me that you love me, too.*
> *People say that love's a game,*
> *A game you just can't win,*
> *If there's a way,*
> *I'll find it someday,*
> *And then this fool will rush in.*

The achingly maudlin lyrics and Paul Anka's pleading angst was ideal for slow dancing. Josh's eyelids began to droop. He turned the covers down and the light off.

As he lay awake, the curtains fluttered as a gentle breeze wafted through the open windows of his bedroom. Miles away, a train sounded its mournful whistle. Closer, a neighborhood dog barked with some complaint until whatever disturbed him moved on. Night sounds of insects, birds, frogs, and other small animals were more subdued than in summer.

In the distance, Josh could hear the soft rumbling of an approaching storm. Outside, as the wind swelled, leaves shimmered, turning over to show their undersides before the rain arrived. Scattered rain drops began to flick the leaves, a most relaxing sound to Josh. He drifted off into a peaceful sleep.

Like hundreds of small schools across Indiana, Morgans Awe was a non-football-playing member of the IHSAA. The Association allowed these schools to begin practice two weeks earlier than those involved in football.

Coach O'Ryan had posted the final varsity cut-list after practice yesterday. Both Josh and Jake had been shocked to find that no member of the junior

THE HOOSIER GAME

class had made the team, not even the three who had earned varsity letters last season.

The Raiders would begin the 1959-60 season with a roster of two seniors, eight sophomores, and two freshmen.

Ordinary news travels fast in small towns. Controversial events regarding the local high school basketball squad spread roughly at the speed of light.

Over the next few weeks O'Ryan's surprising move would be the principal topic of conversation among Morgans Awe residents. Upset parents sent him nasty letters or made heated phone calls to his home. Katie O'Ryan had been confronted in public by a few incensed friends of mothers who were furious that the coach had cut their sons. Even the O'Ryan's eleven-year-old daughter, Cara, had been harassed by classmates who were related to boys who had not made the team.

Principal Otis Oberfeldt and athletic director Rufus Gottschalk received impassioned complaints from irate fans. Among the most vocal in his fury was County Sheriff Thurl Burton, who had expected his son, Grey, to be on the starting five.

As usual, ground zero for quarreling between zealots on both sides of the dispute was the Totem Pole. Saturday morning found thirteen locals sprawled in the pews or leaning against a wall inside the small shop, jawing about community topic number one. Kettle Gut Harper was in the barber's chair.

"What in hell was he thinkin', cuttin' all the juniors?" an angry Muck Wiley asked. "Two seniors and a buncha freshman and south-mores?"

"I'll tell ya' this," snapped Harper. "I never seen Sheriff Burton with his dander up so. O'Ryan better not let Thurl ketch him speedin'. He'll throw 'eem in jail and hide the key."

"He only won thirteen games last year with a veter'n team," added Gizzard Smith. "He sure ain't gonna do any better with a pack 'a greenhorns."

"I heard about some high-falutin' ideas he's got about coachin'," sneered Muck. "Wally Schaff's kid that got cut, he says O'Ryan spends twice as much time teachin' *de*-fense than he does *off*-ense. How'd ya' 'spect to score if you work on guardin' all the time?"

"He's even got 'em liftin' weights!" Smith continued. "Anybody smarter'n a pawpaw knows that'll make kids muscle-bound. Them boys'll be bustin' the back-boards on ther lay-ups if he keeps that up."

A stranger who had entered the shop earlier sat quietly, listening to the banter. Breaking his silence, he said, "Boys, I ain't got no dog in this fight. But have you considered maybe the young kids he picked might be better than the ones he cut?"

Chief Treecat, who had been uncharacteristically reserved throughout, spoke in agreement with the unknown customer.

"We've all known Skoon and them tenth-grade kids since they started playin' in elementary school. Skoon may be the best shooter we've seen in these parts fer awhile. And the rest of 'em have a lotta talent, too. O'Ryan might be wantin' to throw 'em in the fire this year, so they'll git the experience they need the next two seasons."

Kettle Gut interrupted. "Them boys'll git crushed against the likes a' Hillcrest and Sycamore Creek, let alone Madison. It'll ruin ther confidence so's they'll never reach ther p'tential."

"That's the truth and then some," echoed Crumb Wakeland. "We was better off when ole' Rufus was coachin'. At least you knew—"

The bell on the door tinkled. Recognizing the flaming red hair and military bearing of the entrant, Crumb halted his harangue in mid-sentence. He had the look of a guy caught without a fishing license.

Michael O'Ryan strode in. He stopped near the door, glaring icily at the startled malcontents. Several seconds of uninterrupted silence followed as the coach moved his eyes from one to another. A few of the men met his glower, trying to appear un-intimidated. After a brief interval, however, the coach's piercing stare unnerved them. The men lowered their eyes or looked away and shuffled their feet or fiddled with the keys in their pockets.

Hoping to ease the tension in the room, Earl Barnett, with an unconvincing smile, said, "Hey, coach. How ya' doin'?"

His contrived greeting sounded tinny and shallow.

O'Ryan offered no reply. He just stood rigidly by the door, searching the faces of the customers there.

"Well, coach, are the boys ready for the opener against Jericho Friday? We were just talkin' about how this year's team could have a great season."

Coach O'Ryan dismissed Barnett's lame attempt to break the ice.

"Don't piss down my leg and tell me its rainin', Earl."

The coach spoke deliberately, sarcasm dripping from every word.

"It's apparent that you gentlemen feel you know more about the Morgans Awe basketball program than I do. A couple of you have even come to my office, under the guise of being a friend, wanting to warn me about people in town who are upset with how I'm doing things with the team. I figured they must be talking about you barber shop coaches.

"The idea of *you* having the gall to question my program makes me laugh. What all you people, together, know about coaching basketball wouldn't fill a tick's ear. I hear you'd just as soon have the coach back that you ran out of this job before I came.

"You're nothing but a pack of cowards, do you know that? Do you think you have a right to hold me up to ridicule, to make my wife uncomfortable at the grocery store, and open the door for junior high kids to humiliate my daughter?

"Well, here I am. Let me hear you say to my face what you've said behind my back. I want a man to step forward and tell me what he doesn't like about me, my team, or my family. Not that I give a shit about anything you think or say.

"This is your one shot, because I won't be back after today. So come out with it."

Stone cold silence. Shamed, the men just stared at the floor, looking cheap and sneaky.

"I thought so. The best thing you boys can do is to show up on Friday nights with your families, sit your ass on a wooden bleacher and support these teenagers as they deserve. We don't need your advice on basketball. But your support during the games would be welcome."

As coach turned to leave, Homer Norton, a retired firefighter and one of the few men present that O'Ryan respected, attempted to put things in perspective, saying, "Coach, dogs don't bark at parked cars."

"No. And a gnat doesn't try to shit like an elephant, either."

With that, the coach strode out the door, past the peppermint pole, and into the sunshine.

The love-hate relationship between Hoosier high school basketball coaches and fickle fans in small Indiana communities hinged on a simple formula: win and you're beloved. Lose, get out of town.

Saturday, March 19, 1960
Indianapolis, Indiana

Three weeks ago the sophomore-laden Morgans Awe squad had been eliminated from the sectional tourney by the Pit "Stonemasons," 45-41. The Raiders had won sixteen of twenty-two games, the best record an MAHS squad had had in twenty years. With three starters returning, plus several able candidates to fill in for the graduating seniors, Raiders fans were already looking eagerly to next year.

The Indiana High School Athletic Association provided every basketball-playing member school with the opportunity to purchase tickets to the state finals for coaches and players. The highly sought admissions were distributed in proportion to a school's enrollment, with Indiana's largest high schools receiving a greater percentage of the tickets.

Being among the smallest high schools in the state, Morgans Awe was entitled to buy only five tickets. Coach O'Ryan had invited assistant coach Barnhard plus Jake, Josh, and Mark to attend the Final Four event in Indianapolis.

When Arnie Packard learned that his classmates were going to the state finals, he excitedly told them about his older brother's trip as a former Raiders player.

"You guys have *got* to find a way to sneak into the Fox Theatre downtown. Pat told me the strippers there are purtier'n movie stars. And they take it all off! You gotta go. It's tradition!"

The Fox Theatre was a "don't-miss" venue for many teenage boys who came with their coaches and teammates to the tournament, especially for country rubes visiting the big city for the first time. Actually, the entertainers at the sleazy strip joint were generally aging, homely sorts, and they didn't take it *all* off—only enough attire to arouse the imagination of horny teenage males.

Between sessions, the coaches would have lunch and talk basketball with colleagues from other schools. The boys were trusted to go off by themselves. The Raiders teammates passed on the strippers. Coach's honor system, and the consequences of not abiding by it, overrode any temptation to risk going to the skin show.

Instead, the boys caught a cab to go downtown, where they took in the sights. At the appointed time, they returned to the Fieldhouse.

From their seats in the upper rows of the arena, the players had no problem recognizing Ron Bonham, considered the best player in the state. Bonham had scored forty points in Muncie Central's 102-66 mauling of Bloomington's Panthers in the afternoon game. The top-ranked and unbeaten Bearcats were a solid favorite to win the championship.

That evening, before the usual 14,983 fans in the capacity crowd, Coach John Baratto's determined Senators upset Muncie, 75-59, despite twenty-nine points from Bonham.

THE HOOSIER GAME

The excitement and atmosphere at Butler Fieldhouse added more fuel to the dream shared by the young men from Morgans Awe of playing for the title in the magnificent, tradition-filled arena.

Over the next two seasons Michael O'Ryan and his teenagers would provide entertainment and winning at a level never witnessed before in the town of Morgans Awe.

16

DON'T CALL HIM A COWBOY 'TIL YOU SEEN HIM RIDE

Jourden Arena
8:48 p.m.

The family and friends surrounding Katie O'Ryan in the frenzied Morgans Awe crowd were basking in the glory of the moment. A cautious Katie, however, wouldn't allow herself to think about Morgans Awe actually beating Central.

She was a typical coach's spouse. This game was only half over. Far too many times she had watched her husband's teams fight to the brink of victory only to have their hearts broken in the final minutes or seconds.

While Michael's squads would emerge victorious far more often than not, it was only natural for Katie to recall the agonizing losses rather than to relive triumphs of the past. Winning provided temporary elation and a sense of satisfaction. The torment of losing left permanent scars.

As the coaches and players in both locker rooms prepared for the second half, the Raiders-Cougars contest already had caused quite a stir in places far from the river town of Madison. One-hundred forty-five miles north, at the intersection of Superior Street and Apperson Way in Kokomo, a standing room-only crowd of 4,300 at the Memorial gymnasium heard the public address announcer fairly shout this update:

"At halftime, at the Madison Central sectional, the score, Morgans Awe forty-two, Madison Central twenty-six—"

Shocked Kokomo fans met the news with a prolonged cheer like the roar of a high-speed train passing. The Kats' major obstacle on their road to a state title might be eliminated by a new Milan.

THE HOOSIER GAME

Along the Jourden Arena press row excited writers chattered among themselves about the magnitude of the upset occurring before them. If Morgans Awe held on to beat Madison Central it would be the biggest shocker of the sixty-four elimination games being played this evening.

Veteran sportswriter Ernie Stoddard of the Louisville Daily News *had already begun to formulate the first line of what would be a front page account of the historic contest:*

> **David felled Goliath for a second time last night. The slingshot marksmanship of a frail, teenage cherub named Jake Skoon slew undefeated and second-ranked Madison Central in a morality play more shocking than the time that the first David cold-cocked a nine-foot tall Philistine with stone.**

Broadcasters Peck and Hollings were raving about the grit of the Morgans Awe cagers. Back in Morgans Awe, a gathering of regulars at the Totem Pole hung on every word spoken by the veteran announcers.

Chief Treecat had invited the usual gang to the shop to follow the broadcast on his battered Zenith "Owl Eye" radio. Everyone there had thrown two dollars into a basket to offset the cost of bags of popcorn and Chesty potato chips that Dull Knife had provided as well as the refreshments brought to the Pole by the proprietor of Morgans Trail Bar, John Coleman. As the men arrived, each dunked his hand into a zinc tub brimming with ice to grasp bottles of Hudepohl, Blatz, Carlings Black Label, or Falls City beer.

Police Chief Roy Ladysmith was among the partisan listeners drawn to the Pole. Tonight, within the confines of the barber shop, he had quietly suspended town ordinances that required a license to serve beer in the quantities the men would consume during the course of the game.

The men followed closely the lively commentary of Peck and Hollings. Occasionally, static—skaaarrakkkkkeeeeeearakkkk—interrupted the flow of information, at which time each of the listeners derided the Chief for having such a cheap radio.

"Will, I thought this game was over three minutes after the tip-off. Morgans Awe is down 11-0, reeling from Madison's overwhelming show of strength and power. Completely overmatched and no signs of life."

"You're right, Merle. I'd already stuck a fork in 'em, too. And now *look! Morgans Awe scores the last 13 points of the half and has Central tryin' to figure out where that truck came from that ran over 'em."*

DON'T CALL HIM A COWBOY 'TIL YOU SEEN HIM RIDE

"Those listening tonight on WKIN are probably as dumbfounded as you and I are that the game little Morgans Awe squad has turned the tables on the second-ranked team in Indiana. Let's talk about how they've done it, and if they can keep it going."

"My guess is that Coach O'Ryan sprinkled pixie dust or something magic on his team. They came out of that first timeout ready to skin a grizzly."

"I'm not sure that pixie dust had much to do with the big Raider center Danner man-handling DeWitt Weatherford. My daddy used to say, 'Don't call him a cowboy 'til you seen him ride.' Folks, Morgans Awe's got an hombre in the middle."

"There's no doubt that the key play of the first half was when Danner decked the Cougar center. After Madison had pretty much had their way physically with the Raiders, that strapping farm boy picked the biggest banana in the bunch and just flattened him."

"Seems like Danner marked his territory and the Central lads have begun to respect the boundaries."

"I agree. Mark let 'em know there was a man in the paint and he was takin' no prisoners. That seemed to boost the confidence of his teammates. That's leadership."

"Let's not forget to credit Michael O'Ryan for his part in the turnaround. Madison was just mauling his team. Then Danner floors Weatherford. I have a sneaky suspicion Mark's play wasn't by accident. The old Marine understands the nature of a street fight."

"That he does, Will. Usually, when you stick your hand in a bee hive, you get stung, big time. But after that incident, you could virtually see the shift in mood and body language of both teams. Morgans Awe began to force the action and seized the momentum."

"Let's talk a bit about that mysterious, unseen force we call 'momentum,' Merle. I mean, we talk about a player having a 'hot hand' or being 'in the zone.' The basket just seems bigger. Or we say a team 'catches fire,' and everything seems to go right for them. How do you account for, how do you know when a team has grabbed the momentum?"

"I can't define it, Will. But I know it when I see it. The fans sense it. A loud, partisan crowd helps to lift the players. Their adrenalin is sustained through the energy of their supporters."

"Some coaches will tell you that the home court is worth 10 points, for a number of reasons. The foremost advantage is the home crowd. Even though Madison is playing in their own gym, the Raiders are definitely the crowd favorite."

"I think Saul Fortune is getting beat in the game of X's and O's, too. When it looked like Madison had righted the ship, O'Ryan went to that semi-stall offense that Dean Smith runs at North Carolina. It confused the Cougars."

"Yeah, Bond Bathwaite is clever with the ball. He'll drive, suck the big boys to the middle to cut him off, then he finds the open guy for a bucket or foul shots."

THE HOOSIER GAME

"*Now let's acknowledge, too, Will, that havin' a dead-eye shooter the likes of Jake Skoon can offset a host of shortcomings. Lemme look. Yep, the kid has scored a sweet twenty-one in one half against one of the best defenses in the state.*"

"*O'Ryan keys his offense around setting a series of screens for Skoon. When that reed-thin kid finds an opening, he's deadlier'n grandma killin' snakes. You'd have to go way back to find anyone who scored twenty-one points in one-half against a Saul Fortune defense.*"

"*We need to pay the bills, folks, so let's take a brief commercial break. From courtside, the score, again, is Morgans Awe 42, Madison Central 26. We'll be right back with the second half, and I can't wait to see it. I gotta feeling it's gonna be all-out war from here to the end.*"

Saturday, May 5, 2012

As with typical reunion conversations, the participants' memories emphasized the pastoral, seemingly untroubled times of their shared youth. The anguish and hurt of families in need, of losing loved ones, and of innumerable other perceived or real suffering remained, for the most part, unexpressed in the minds and hearts of those gathered.

Josh continued the trend with another story of Arnie's outrageous behaviors.

"Do you guys remember the time Arnie wised off to the state trooper on the way to Kentucky?"

The event had certainly made an impression on Mark Danner.

"You almost got us all throw'd in jail that night, Fries."

"Aww, I was just makin' polite conversation with the honorable lawman. You buncha wussies got your shorts all in a wad."

"Hey, Fries, I hadn't heard that one. What happened?" Elmer asked.

Bear Billings jumped in. "Josh had just got his driver's license. Jake, Mark, Fries, and me were crammed in the car on the way to Lull-ville to see a movie."

"It was 'Summer Place.' I fell in love that night," Josh gushed. "Sandra Dee."

"Anyway, Josh sees a red light in the mirror. He was speedin'."

"I wasn't either, Bear."

"You was guilty as O.J., Seabird," Arnie reminded him.

Bear again. "So he pulls over and the state trooper comes up 'n says, 'Got any I.D.?'"

"Before I could get to my wallet," Josh continued, "I hear Arnie say, ''Bout whut?'"

DON'T CALL HIM A COWBOY 'TIL YOU SEEN HIM RIDE

Mark picked up the story. "The cop stuck his head in to see who the smart-ass was. Fries acted innocent as a preacher. Josh got out his license and registration real quick.

"We was two shakes of a frog's leg from gittin' hauled off. I think he took a look at Bear 'n me and decided he didn't have room in his cruiser for the pack of us."

Arnie grinned. "Just havin' a little fun, boys."

As the laughter subsided Josh noticed time had slipped away. Following the initial party at the Billings' home, the plan for the Class of '62 included wine-tasting and a catered dinner at the Lanthier Winery in Madison. Looking at his watch, Josh decided to return to his motel.

"Guys, I hate to leave such an august body of philosophers, but I need to get back to the room to take a shower before dinner."

"Aw-gust, my keister," Moon laughed. "More like Robin Hood's thieves."

"I better head out, too," sighed Mark.

"You're comin' to the dinner, right Mark?"

"Wouldn't miss it fer a Bill Clinton hand-me-down."

"See you all, later."

"Later, Josh."

After a shower and a change of clothes, Josh went into the tiny hotel bar. As he sipped a glass of Merlot, memories resurrected by his old teammates prompted him to delve further into the past.

Saturday, July 16, 1960

It was a sultry summer afternoon when Josh, Mark, Sonny, Bobby Mack, and Arnie sat eating pizzas at Hawkins General Store. The group was filling the jukebox with nickels to hear the latest top ten tunes of the day. As Roy Orbison sang about a crushed romance—"Only the lonely, a-know the way ah feel tonight"—the lads were hatching a plan that would take them to the Starburst outdoor theater later in the evening. They had little interest, however, in the featured movie "Ladies Man," a Jerry Lewis farce.

The unwritten code among members of the Raiders' inner circle allowed dating on Friday nights and Sunday afternoons. But Saturday night was strictly *no permite las niñas*—no girls allowed. Group pressure was enough to enforce this unwritten rule. One's first loyalty was to his teammates.

Arnie Packard had received some intelligence on Thursday that Moon was taking his new girlfriend to the passion pit tonight. When confronted, Jamie

205

THE HOOSIER GAME

had made a lame excuse that he couldn't make it because he had to go with his parents to see relatives over the weekend. They knew he was lying through his teeth.

Bobby Mack was elected to make a call to Moon's home to confirm their suspicions. At 7:30 p.m., Deal left his seat to go outside where the Indiana Bell pay telephone booth was located. He pushed aside the sliding glass doors and plopped down on the cushioned seat.

After putting a dime in the slot, he dialed Moon's number. A busy signal indicated that someone was home. As he hung up the receiver, the dime dropped into the coin return. Waiting a couple of minutes, he tried again.

"Hello. This is the Ross's residence."

"Hi, Mrs. Ross. This is Bobby Mack."

"Why, Hi Bobby! If you're calling for Jamie, he's already left to pick up his date. I think they're going to the movie in Madison."

Outed by his own flesh and blood!

"Thanks, anyway, Mrs. Ross. I'll see him tomorrow. Bye."

"Goodbye."

As Bobby Mack reentered the restaurant a wide grin told the gang all they needed to know.

"Moon's goin' to the Starburst."

"I cain't believe the rat would try to pull this on us."

The five immediately set out for the theater.

Whenever the boys went to the outdoor, they always arrived slightly after dusk, just before the movie started. On most occasions, Mark didn't have the twenty cents admission, so the driver of the evening would stop a couple of blocks from the entrance and open the trunk. Mark Danner then crammed his seventy-six inches of legs, torso and head into a space not much bigger than a foot locker.

When Sonny pulled alongside the ticket booth, the muted sound of rattling tools and thumping noises could be heard from within the trunk. The bored, grizzled old ticket seller looked at the driver oddly, curious as to the origin of those strange sounds. The legitimate paying customers in the passenger seats coughed loudly, crunched papers, and turned the radio up, trying to drown out the noisemaking of the stowaway.

"I'm takin' a tire iron to Danner when we get away," Watkins mumbled.

Arriving in the darkening night, near the back row, Mark popped the trunk lid, rolled out, and slid into the back seat.

DON'T CALL HIM A COWBOY 'TIL YOU SEEN HIM RIDE

Moon Ross would not be hard to find, for two reasons: first, he drove a canary yellow 1954 Plymouth. Hard to miss. Second, he would be parked in the row of cars farthest away from the giant screen.

Sonny steered his car, lights off, into the lane between the last two rows. They soon spotted Moon's vehicle. His windows were already steamed up. As they passed slowly by, Ross's freshman cutie, Margie Weathers, waved meekly from the back seat. There was no Moon in sight. The little worm had ducked down when he saw Sonny's car coming.

Turning at the end of the lane, Sonny drove to the vacant spot directly in front of Moon's. Urged on by his hooting companions, Watkins maneuvered his car into the parking space with the rear bumper *toward* the movie screen. Facing Moon's car, he switched the headlights on high beams, flooding the little love cubicle as if it were high noon.

With windows cranked down, the fivesome shouted to everyone in the area that the *real* show was taking place in the banana-colored sedan.

Finally, the degraded Moon came out of hiding, looking sheepish.

The ambushed couple endured the cat-calls, until Jamie's teammates decided he had suffered enough for his egregious flaunting of team etiquette. The harassers thought it was great fun. The victims not so much.

Tuesday, September 6, 1960

For the past two weeks cross-country coach Herman Booseman had been driving his team in preparation for their first meet in mid-September. For the purpose of building their stamina for the upcoming basketball season, Bobby Mack and Sonny had joined the team.

To keep tabs on his runners during practice Coach Booseman rode a bike around the three mile course. Among his favorite spots to catch and prod scofflaws at the back of the pack was a niche behind the huge smoke stack at Bergland's bucket factory. From there the coach would suddenly jump out to scold the laggards.

Usually, the chastised ones would break into a sprint, running as far as they could until they fagged out and starting walking again. More than once it was Bobby Mack and Sonny who received Booseman's tongue-lashing.

As the gang sat together in the lunchroom this first day of school, Mark asked, chuckling, "How's the daily ten-mile run to nowhere workin' out guys."

THE HOOSIER GAME

Attempting to convince Mark, Jake, Jamie, Josh, and Arnie that he was enjoying the experience—a blatant lie—Bobby Mack replied, "I love it. I'm in the best shape of my life. Really, it's fun."

"If you're havin' so much fun why don't I ever see you smilin' when you're runnin'?" Arnie asked.

"Yeah, Bobo," interjected Mark. "I was at the finish line the other day when you ralphed yer lunch."

"You guys'll be sorry when practice starts and we're runnin' circles around you."

Watkins had made no comment to this point. Josh now addressed him. "How 'bout you, Sonny? You love it as much as Bobo?"

He paused. With a sullen look on his face, Sonny snorted, "Deal's fulla' crap. Cross-country ain't a sport, it's a Chinese torture. I'll jam bamboo slivers under my fingernails afore I ever do this again!"

As Josh and the rest bent over, cackling, Watkins continued.

"If the 'ministration is really serious about stoppin' the teenage prag-nancy problem they oughta require ever' guy in high school to run cross-country, like gittin' a driver's license. Everybody'd be too tired for sex."

Saturday, October 1, 1960

The teenagers trying out for the Morgans Awe varsity basketball squad reported at ten o'clock sharp for the first practice today. As Betty Seaberg drove Josh through a chilly rain, the plaintive lyrics of tiny, fifteen-year old Brenda Lee's most recent hit filled the car.

Alone, so alone that I could cry, I want to be wanted,
Alone, watching lovers passing by, I want to be wanted,
When I am kissed I want his lips to really kiss me,
When we're apart I want his heart to really miss me,
I want to know he loves me so his eyes are misting,
That's the way I want to be loved.

Arriving a half-hour beforehand, Josh was dressed and on the court before most of the others got to the gym. He was so keyed up to begin the season he'd hardly slept last night.

DON'T CALL HIM A COWBOY 'TIL YOU SEEN HIM RIDE

After calling the thirty-three hopefuls together, Coach O'Ryan went over general guidelines and expectations for the first few weeks of practice. Every boy would have a fair chance to make the team.

"We'll post final cuts two weeks from today. I wish you all good luck."

Coach had added a new, surprise wrinkle to the practice ritual this season. All the boys were directed outside into the biting October air for a two-mile run. As they gathered at the starting line of the cinder track, smug grins crossed the faces of Bobby Mack and Sonny.

"Let's see how that *not* runnin' cross-country works for ya' now, Josh," Deal whispered sarcastically to one of his previous tormenters. Josh lowered his head, wondering how it would feel being a tortoise to Bobby Mack's hare.

A little over thirteen minutes later, Josh slogged across the finish line. He was the fourth to complete the circuit, well ahead of both Deal and Watkins. After completing the run players were allowed to go inside to shoot around. Practice had already begun when the last of the group straggled in.

No time was wasted as the coaches put the players through fundamental training. They continually shouted encouragement and correction as the players raced from drill to drill. There would be no scrimmages the first week. Players had to demonstrate mastery in the basic skills of basketball before being tested in live action.

Practices always ended with a series of "gassers." To the players the ritual was simply known as "O'Ryan's Hell." No conditioning drill was more beneficial to building stamina. And none was more despised by the players.

Team members lined up along one end line, facing the opposite goal. At the sound of the coach's whistle all twelve boys dashed as quickly as they could to the near foul line, stopped, bent over, touched the floor, and then hustled back to the base line. Without pause they repeated the stop-touch-turn sequence at the end line and then sprinted to the ten-second line. They continued at top speed, replicating the drill at the opposite foul line and end line, before returning to the original starting point. After a brief rest, the team repeated the ritual.

During very brief rest periods Coach O'Ryan constantly stressed the importance of unglamorous hard work in becoming the best.

"Do you want to be winners?" he'd yell.

"Yes!" team members would respond, between gasps.

THE HOOSIER GAME

"Well, gentlemen, let me tell you that everyone *wants* to win. But it's the guy who has the *will* to *prepare* to win that succeeds. At this very moment, players over at Sycamore Creek and Hillcrest and Madison are practicing just like you are. They all want to win. Are we tough enough, dedicated enough, brave enough to outwork all of 'em?"

"Yes!"

"Do we have the guts to lay it all on the line to be the best?"

"Yes!"

"Back on the line, gentlemen!"

Generally, Coach O'Ryan called for twelve to fifteen successive sets of the brutal conditioning regimen. If he surmised that a player or players were not putting forth their best effort the entire team faced additional gassers.

As the sprints piled up, pain coursed throughout the boys' bodies. Lactic acid seeped into stressed muscles. Once-fresh legs became heavy, making players feel as if they were running in deep sand. Sharp pains attacked their sides. Lungs felt as if there were blow torches in their chests.

Finally the coach announced that if everyone hustled this would be the last gasser.

"That's your reward for working hard, men."

The brash Mark Danner, shoulders heaving, panting for air, couldn't let the coach get by with that malarkey.

"Coach, you could—lay a—thousand dollar bill—in my locker—ever day—after—practice—an' I still—wouldn't see—no—*reward*—in it."

"Aah, Mr. Danner. Your reward will come in the fourth quarter of every game the rest of the season. Guys, if Mark has air enough to have a conversation, then all of you must still be fresh. Because every one of you is in better shape than Danner, let's do three more gassers. On the line!"

Every bleary-eyed Raider who toed the line for additional trips up the floor had homicide in his heart. His teammates would have strangled him then and there if they'd had the strength.

The players completed the run. Fully exhausted and sweating profusely, each filed slowly off the floor and down the stairs to the locker room below. Steam arose from heated, aching bodies. With every step, they cursed Danner in low growls.

DON'T CALL HIM A COWBOY 'TIL YOU SEEN HIM RIDE

Mark, of course, just grinned, because, as he shouted to his teammates, "I know y'all was wantin' a few more trips to git in better shape. No need ta thank me."

Sitting alone in front of a locker was Bond Jordan Bathwaite, a sophomore transfer from Tishomingo, Mississippi. His family had moved to Morgans Awe only weeks after his father purchased a large lumber company in Madison. A product of southern gentry, Bond's ancestors had been prominent state legislators, congressmen, and judges in southern states since the eighteenth century.

Bond's lazy drawl was even more pronounced than the languid, nasal dialect of the natives of southern Indiana. With a face like Frankie Avalon and thick, jet-black hair, the Mississippian had gained immediate notice from the town's teenage girls.

Slender and quick of foot, Bond had been the high scorer and star of his Tishomingo High School basketball team the previous year as a freshman. He was high-strung, a fearless player who rivaled Jake in his ability to score.

However, in pre-season practice Bond was reckless and undisciplined, often missing opportunities to pass to teammates with better shots as he barreled toward the hoop.

The Raiders offense was keyed to Jake Skoon, of course. Bond, the excitable young guard, chafed at Coach O'Ryan's unbending resistance to his wanton style on the court.

Acceptance among his male peers was not immediate. A few of his new teammates resented him. Teenage boys who were secure within themselves were not bothered by a move-in. It was those not so self-assured with their status in the athletic or social pecking order who felt threatened. Some of the guys wanted to make certain he was aware that he didn't fit in with their particular clique.

As a result, the newcomer had difficulty making friends.

Coach O'Ryan noticed one day that Bond was eating alone in the cafeteria, while the rest of the basketball team members sat together, ignoring him. The following morning, Coach called the team leaders into his office.

"Hey, guys, how's the new kid from Mississippi doin'? You've met him and welcomed him here, right? Where did you take him this weekend? Did you show him around town? Madison?"

Senior co-captain Ronnie Simpson, along with Jake, Josh, Mark, and Sonny began to squirm uneasily. Not one offered a reply.

THE HOOSIER GAME

"No? Well, let me tell you *why*. *None* of you have taken that first step toward helping a shy, probably frightened kid, who is fifteen-hundred miles from his home, eats by himself at lunch, and walks all alone to his house after school—not one of you have introduced yourself to a boy who will probably be your teammate in a month.

"You all should be ashamed. How would you feel being treated like a leper by the same guys you'll be passing the ball to this season?"

He dismissed the chastised five. The boys slunk out of the office, each one embarrassed at his behavior.

At lunch the next day, Bond was surprised to be sitting amidst a table full of Morgans Awe basketball players.

17

ELEEMOSYNARY

Jourden Arena
8:49 p.m.

Just inside the dressing room door coaches O'Ryan and Barnhard quickly analyzed the first sixteen minutes of the game. The elated assistant was caught up in the moment.

"Look at 'em, coach. I've never seen a bunch so fired up."

As Arnie distributed fresh towels to the players, Michael surveyed the body language of the members of his squad. On the surface they were excited, smiling broadly, and celebrating the fact that they were beating the second-rated team in the state.

After decades of coaching, O'Ryan recognized the double-edged sword now facing him. Initially filled with self-doubt, his players' unbridled joy was premature. Dangerously so.

He knew that when complicated hormones rule the emotions of adolescents, teenage self-confidence rises and falls like a yo-yo, depending upon the circumstances. A Raiders balloon inflated by the dizzying success of the moment could be punctured quickly by a determined Cougar rally in the third quarter. O'Ryan expected Madison to come out with all guns blazing in the third quarter.

O'Ryan's team was accustomed to winning, but the boys were now in unknown territory. Morgans Awe had never defeated Madison in a basketball game, ever.

Without diminishing their enthusiasm and growing confidence, the coach had to bring his players deftly back to reality. Walking this perilous balance beam would require an experienced and steady hand.

Coach O'Ryan now squatted before his flush-faced players. His chin rested between thumb and forefinger. Did his team believe *they would beat Central, or* hope *to? Confronting the anticipated all-out effort of the Cougars, would they play to win or play not to lose? Did they really want the rewards and accompanying responsibilities of victors? Did they possess that unsympathetic, foot-on-throat killer instinct?*

THE HOOSIER GAME

As he called the boys together, he chose his words carefully.

"I expect ole Saul's over there right this minute, lightin' a nifty blaze under his boys' be-hinds. They didn't expect to be in the situation they are. Madison is convinced that they are better than you in every way. And they're not used to losing, especially to a team they think are a buncha hicks.

"Men, champions are not satisfied with coming close. Champions find a way to win. I've always preached to you that athletics is ten percent talent, ninety percent between the ears and in the chest cavity.

"You've shown you can play harder, smarter, and with more will to win than the other team. But the job is only half done. The first half is history. The next sixteen minutes will be the toughest fight you've ever been in on a basketball court. You have to believe what I already know. You are worthy of being champions."

A collective cheer and loud clapping filled the locker room. The boys were believers.

"Get a drink. Rest a bit. Then we'll go finish the job."

In Madison Central's locker room, Saul sat in a folding chair, facing his discouraged squad. He knew they hadn't attained a spotless record on skill alone. The veteran Cougars had been to this dance before. Saul's team was a proud bunch, intensely competitive. Their swagger had been tested severely in the first half.

It is during times of adversity that outstanding coaches perform at their best. The record of success Saul Fortune had built over two decades attested to his skill in motivating high school players.

Part of his genius was assessing situations and responding in unpredictable, often surprising ways. When his team was winning he could always find something it could do better. If he felt that the team appeared to be playing with indifference, too casually or carelessly, Saul could suddenly explode like a volcano, ascribing every wrong move to their selfishness and lackadaisical attitudes. He might kick the whole team out of practice, as if they had concocted a giant conspiracy to play beneath their talent.

Despite knowing the coach's overreaction was his way of keeping the team grounded and humble, the players always responded as if they were guilty of all charges.

But now, facing his despondent teenagers, Saul stared at the ceiling, a quizzical expression on his face. He then addressed his Cougars in even, almost soothing tones. Saul's calm, expressive eyes moved from boy to boy as he spoke, softly:

"Of all the high school teams I've coached, you guys are not the most talented. But you are the most cohesive, the most team-oriented, the most unselfish group, which makes you the best team I've ever coached.

"And I owe each of you an apology."

ELEEMOSYNARY

Saturday, November 5, 1960

In one week Morgans Awe would face Zephersville to open the 1960-61 basketball season. Betty Seaberg dropped 16-year old son Josh off at the Totem Pole.

Josh arrived just in time to hear Crudd Lucas tell his latest Indian joke. Crudd was always on the lookout for a funny story about Native Americans, hoping to provoke the Chief.

"So this cowboy was ridin' the prairie when he come across an Indian a-layin' on the groun', face down, with his ear to a wagon track. The Indian sez', 'Wagon. Two horses. One white, one gray. Driver-man smoke pipe. Woman wear blue dress. And bonnet.'

"The cowboy sez' 'You mean you can tell all that by listenin' to the groun'?' Indian says, 'No. Run over me. Half hour ago.'"

The men guffawed, hollering, "Good one, Crudd!" and "That musta been yer great-grampa, Knife."

Ten-year old Timmy Martin sat on the wooden plank the Chief used to raise small children up to hair-cutting level. Timmy's mother accompanied him, sitting primly among the gathering of men. In respect to the child and feminine presence the magpies toned down their normal crudity to the merely mildly offensive.

As he took his seat, Josh received the usual congratulations and flattering comments that always greeted the ballplayers. Adults, especially the uptown coaches, showed deference to members of the Raiders squad.

It was inflating to a teen to have elders in town asking about the game strategy, the "inside dope." The high-schooler was not eligible for membership in the group, of course. But one's relative status on the team gave him an air of authority to which the adults in the room acquiesced.

"What's it look like for this season, Josh?"

"Uh, I think we'll be pretty good. Practice has gone well so far. We're all anxious for a game."

Speaking of the newcomer, Bond Bathwaite, Chief asked, "Who's this Bathwaite kid? Tenth grader, ain't 'ee? We heard he can play."

"Yeah, he's a transfer from Mississippi. I haven't gotten to know him that well yet."

"He better not be a shooter. He'll have to pry the ball outta Jake's cold, dead han's if 'ee's a mind to chuck one up," Crudd commented.

THE HOOSIER GAME

"What about you, Josh? Purty girls don't kiss the passers. It's the shooters they go for. Average fifteen or twenty a game this season and you'll have a passel a' fine fillies to choose from."

"Yeah, Josh, you cain't have Jake claimin' all them ladies."

"Someone has to throw the ball in from out of bounds," Josh retorted, laughing.

Earl Barnett, who only a year before was one of the loudest critics of Coach O'Ryan (as long as the coach was out of sight), spoke up.

"You know, O'Ryan did a great job coachin' last year. To take a bunch of south-mores like Josh here and win sixteen games, well, that was durn good."

Snickering, Doc Gentry asked, "Hmmm. Wasn't it you, Earl, that wanted to run O'Ryan outta town on a rail because he cut all the juniors?"

"Don't listen to that, Josh," Earl said in his defense. "I knew you boys was capable of playin' winnin' ball. It was just the way he went about it."

The crowd responded with mocking laughter.

Adding salt to the wounds, Chief added, "Yeah, as I 'member, Earl, you invited the coach to yer house that very night fer steaks'n ale."

"Now come on, fellers. I tole you all along he made the right move—"

"You're lyin' like a used car salesman, Earl. Wait. By damned, ya' are one!"

"Whadda you expect out of a guy who grad-je-ated in the upper half of the lower fourth of his high school class?"

"Yeah, it's no accident you always got that stupid grin on yer face, Earl."

As the boys continued to hoot, Barnett just shook his head and gave up the fight. As he headed for the door he told the chief over his shoulder, "I'll come back later, Knife, when there's fewer drunks and horse thieves takin' up space in here."

When the doors closed behind him the rest engaged in self-congratulations for chopping down the sometimes haughty Earl Barnett.

"Ole Earl didn't wait around long, did 'ee?"

"He was off faster'n prom dress."

"He ditn't know whether ta scratch 'is ass or wind 'is watch."

At that, Mrs. Martin cast a frigid scowl at the profane merrymakers.

Being so chastised, the raucous bunch toned down their coarse language, but continued to make fun of their latest victim. Of course, each knew that tomorrow it could be one of them facing the jaded humor of the Totem Pole's ornery curmudgeons.

ELEEMOSYNARY

Friday, November 11, 1960

Today, Josh found it difficult to focus on dangling participles or algebraic formulas, what with the first game of his junior year less than seven hours away. The Raiders would open the basketball season tonight at home against the Zephersville Cyclones.

After what seemed an interminable wait, seventh period finally arrived. All junior and senior high students assembled in the gym for a pep rally. Sixteen folding chairs were set up at center court, where the coaches, student manager, and varsity players would be seated. Josh was proud to be one of twelve boys representing not only the high school, but the entire community.

As Coach O'Ryan led his team onto the floor, the pep band struck up the Raiders' fight song. Members of the cheer squad led the student body in singing,

On, you Raiders! On, you Raiders!
Stand up fans and sing,
Onward is our driving spirit,
Let our voices ring
(Rah! Rah! Rah!)
Win or lose, we'll ne'er forsake thee,
We'll rise from every fall,
Stand now, ye' loyal legends,
For dear old Morgans Awe!
(Go! Fight! Win!)

Standing, cheering, and whistling, the students appeared to be as energized as the players in preparation for the game. Cheerleaders now spread around the gym floor to lead the traditional "line-up" cheer. In numerical order, every player was introduced.

"Bobby Mack, Bobby Mack, he's our man, if he can't do it, Jake can."

"Jake, Jake, he's our man, if he can't do it, Jamie can."

"Jamie, Jamie—," and so on through the entire roster.

After the twelve varsity players had been introduced came, "Coach, Coach, he's our man, if he can't do it—*nobody* can!"

THE HOOSIER GAME

The students rose as one, applauding as Coach O'Ryan stepped to the microphone. His remarks were brief. He thanked the students for their enthusiasm and support for the team. The Zephersville squad would be "no pushover. They're well-coached, and they hustle."

Michael did not single out any Raider player.

"It takes more than just the players to be successful on the floor. We coaches have to do our jobs. Our administration and faculty must hold each boy accountable in class and away from the gym. Parents have to instill in their sons the importance of playing as a twelve-man unit, to be supportive of teammates, and to respect the opponents. We have a loyal following among our townspeople and for that we are grateful."

From high in the crowd, a student yelled, "How many we gonna win this year, coach?"

After the laughter subsided, O'Ryan replied, "I can't predict that. But if these guys play to their potential, if they listen to the coaching staff, and if you students give them your full support, we'll represent this high school and this community to the best of our ability. Thank you!"

Cheers rained downward as the rally ended.

Josh arrived home at a little after four o'clock. Betty Seaberg had prepared his traditional pre-game meal. The light fare included broiled ground beef, a baked potato, green beans, and toast with honey.

Despite jitters, Josh lay down for a nap. Betty woke him at 5:45 p.m. After cleaning up, putting on his Sunday trousers and a tie, Josh donned his knitted stocking cap and letterman's jacket.

A short time later, Jamie Ross knocked at the door. The two walked together to the gym at each home game.

The sun had fallen below the horizon. A sharp wind blew tiny crystals of ice that stung cheeks, noses, and ears. The dull glow of amber streetlights illuminated the path. The pair ambled through darkened streets, past houses, and always took an unnecessary detour through an alley near the school, a superstition adopted for reasons now forgotten.

Approaching the MAHS gym on game night always triggered within Josh a special excitement. His pace increased as he and Jamie neared the weathered, imposing red brick edifice. The ceiling lights inside shone brightly through the windows around the top. Muffled shrieks of the crowd reacting to the action of the Junior Varsity contest reached their ears. Hundreds of cars and trucks filled the parking lot adjacent to the building.

Typical of so many small-town gyms—called "band boxes" because of the tiny interior dimensions—that were constructed by the Works Progress Administration during the Great Depression, the Morgans Awe facility was a symbol of community pride.

While most gymnasiums built by the WPA had similar architectural plans, each differed somewhat in its construction and peculiar idiosyncrasies. The MAHS playing floor was 66 by 40 feet, shorter and narrower than a regulation high school court, requiring two dotted lines four feet on either side of the center circle to provide additional playing space for the front court at each end.

Raiders players had an advantage as they became familiar with dead spots or slight warps in the floor that would cause the ball to take unexpected, bizarre bounces.

Along the home crowd sideline two permanent, padded steel poles supporting the balcony stood within two-feet of the floor, even with the first row of the bleachers. Players sometimes stepped on the shoes of rooters or tripped over their extended legs (intentionally, some visiting players and fans would insist).

A small stairway led to the balcony, which hovered directly over the sideline. The phrase, "…fans were hanging from the rafters" likely owed its origin to the tightly packed high school gyms of rural Indiana.

Located at one end of the playing floor was a set of double doors with panic bars on the inside that were only eight feet from the end line. Periodically a careening player would crash into the doors, sometimes ending up outside on the steps. Last season, a visiting player who flew through the door was temporarily locked out as the action on the floor continued.

Above the doors were three large paned windows that provided natural light during daytime. At the opposite end of the building was a stage, elevated four feet above the court.

Folding chairs provided enough seats for the school band (eighteen members) and additional room for an overflow crowd.

Identical electric-powered scoreboards were mounted on the walls above at each end. The backboards hung from steel girders riveted to the network of beams that supported the roof.

Two large blowers located just above the north backboard stanchion dispensed heat from the boilers in the basement. With the gym filled to capacity, the piped-in heat, combined with the number of bodies in a relatively small space, sometimes made the area stifling hot for players and fans.

THE HOOSIER GAME

The gym capacity was 684, or about three-quarters of the town population. Parents and followers of opposing school teams would snap up the fifty or so tickets reserved for visitors. Late-coming fans sat in the aisles. As the tip-off for the varsity game neared, late-late comers would fill every standing space.

Morgans Awe rooters arrived especially early for the season opener. Prior to the tip-off of the JV contest, the bleachers were filled. Every seat on the stage was taken and standing room only slots were disappearing rapidly.

Sound echoing off the wooden ceiling and walls seemed to double the decibel level of the packed crowd. The noise generated by seven-hundred screaming fans in the Morgans Awe bandbox seemed louder than the sound of 10,000 rooters at the IU Memorial Fieldhouse. The local fire marshal conveniently overlooked the fact that the number of people in the building exceeded, by a large margin, the number of seats available. After all, this *was* Hoosier basketball.

Arriving mid-way through the third quarter of the Junior Varsity game, Josh and Jamie entered through the lobby area. Ticket-takers and local fans rushed up to shake hands and wish the boys luck.

Walking around the edge of the court, Josh and Jamie acknowledged friends and fans in the stands. The boys joined their teammates in bleacher seats behind the JVs. At the beginning of the fourth period, the team arose as one, to a loud, standing ovation. Both the JV and the varsity cheerleaders led the home crowd in the chant,

"That's our team, the best in the land, c'mon fans let's give 'em a hand!"

Down the stairs and into the locker room the team members changed into their uniforms and gathered around the coaches for pre-game instructions. After a brief talk and a hearty "Let's go!" players gathered at the top of the steps to await the end of the curtain raiser.

The gun cracked. Uniforms soaked, the JVs began to file down the stairs. They were visibly upset, having lost by three points to the Junior Cyclones. As the downcast players passed by, members of the varsity offered encouragement.

"That's okay, guys, good game."

"Keep your chins up. You'll be ready for Mainport next week."

Someone hollered, "We'll get 'em for ya!"

Jake now led the team onto the floor to the thunderous roar of the crowd. The band struck up the fight song and the home crowd joined in.

ELEEMOSYNARY

"On, you Raiders! On you Raiders!
Stand up fans and sing—"

Morgans Awe controlled the opening center jump. Seconds later Sonny Watkins scored the first basket of the season, slipping behind his defender and laying the ball in on a nifty pass from Josh. By halftime, Morgans Awe held an eighteen-point lead over Zephersville.

In a scene common throughout the season, Grover Willburn stayed on the court at the halftime break to play cornet in the school band. As with many small schools, students were often involved in more than one extracurricular activity. With a hastily donned band jacket covering his jersey and a plumed shako adding to his height, the 6-3 junior was conspicuous wearing his basketball trunks and shoes. Grover towered over his band-mates. Some students made fun of the basketball/tuba player.

Coach O'Ryan and teammates fully supported Grover's avocation, briefing him on game strategy when he returned to the locker room just minutes before the second half began.

Coach O'Ryan was eager to see how the Mississippi transfer, Bond Bathwaite, would perform in a regular game. O'Ryan had not been pleased with the sophomore's tendency to force ill-advised shots and over-dribble, rather than pass to the open man. When he did pass, Bathwaite often attempted high-risk, fancy throws, when a simple fundamental pass would suffice. Defensively, he was quick, but relied too much on daring attempts to steal the ball rather than playing straight-up, hard-nosed defense. To date, Bond had not altered his style of play, much to the coach's dismay.

Bond entered the contest four minutes into the second period. Holding the ball at the top of the key, the determined soph drove to the basket and, ignoring a wide-open teammate, threw up a wild shot that missed everything. Subsequently, he threw two passes away, lost his man twice on defense, and cranked up three more field goal attempts while being closely guarded. He was removed from the game at the end of the quarter and did not see action again.

The talented young player would come to understand that he would play Coach O'Ryan's way, or not at all.

Friday, December 16, 1960

Topping the pop charts this day was Elvis's melancholy ballad of longing for a lost love.

THE HOOSIER GAME

Are you lonesome tonight,
Do you miss me tonight,
Are you sorry we drifted apart.
Does your memory stray to a bright sunny day,
When I kissed you and called you sweetheart.
Do the chairs in your parlor seem empty and bare,
Do you gaze at your doorstep and picture me there.
Is your heart filled with pain, shall I come back again,
Tell me dear, are you lonesome tonight.

Morgans Awe had jumped off to a blazing start to the season, winning seven of its first eight contests by comfortable margins. The team was averaging over seventy-five points per game as their fast break style led to easy baskets against most of the opponents. Jake Skoon averaged more than thirty points a game, with a high of 41 against Corydon Ford High School.

However, in the latest two victories over Pit and Jericho, the Raiders were sluggish and mistake-prone. Their normally solid defensive effort broke down too often as they seemed to underestimate lowly regarded high schools that were even smaller than theirs.

Josh was soon to learn that Coach O'Ryan believed that playing poorly and winning was a worse sin than playing well but losing. Despite winning easily, his team's ragged, uninspired play had the coach fuming.

When the Raiders reported for practice Monday, student manager Packard informed the players to get into uniform, then to remain in the locker room until Coach O'Ryan came in.

Sober faces greeted an obviously displeased O'Ryan as he entered. The only noise evident was the door slamming behind him and the drip of leaky showers. Players noted curiously, Coach carried a dictionary in his hands. He pulled up the lone folding chair in the room and handed the tome to a surprised Sonny Watkins.

"Look up the word *dismal*, Watkins," the coach snarled.

Sonny dived into the Webster's, flipping quickly through pages until his eyes rested on the word between *disloyalty* and *dismantle*."

"Read it out loud."

"*Dismal*. Showing or causing gloom or depression. Lacking interest or merit. Disastrous. Dreadful."

ELEEMOSYNARY

"Sonny, would you agree that your play on Friday night fits that description?"

As he lowered his eyes to study the concrete floor at his feet, the junior forward replied meekly with the only answer the prickly coach would accept: "Yes, sir."

"Pass the book to Seaberg. Try *listless*, Josh."

Josh dutifully found the adjective, though he knew well what the word meant.

"*Listless*. Characterized by a lack of inclination or impetus to action. Languid."

"Say that in words even Grover will understand."

"Uh, it means being lazy?"

"No, Seaberg, it's worse than that."

Coach O'Ryan fairly spat the words out. "*Listless* means being lazy—on *purpose*!"

Bobby Mack Deal was next to be subjected to the piercing vocabulary lesson. Coach O'Ryan's intimidating stare bore in on his playmaker.

"*Frenetic*."

"*Frenetic*. Marked by extreme excitement, confusion, or agitation. Wild. Mad."

"Six turnovers, Deal! In less than half the game!"

Everyone began to catch onto Coach O'Ryan's latest tactic meant to call attention to the team's basketball crimes of three days past.

Now the sizzling spotlight fell on Jake Skoon.

"Look up *eleemosynary*."

All twenty-four eyes looked up. "*Ely* what?" was the unspoken response.

After a pause, Skoon asked, "How do you spell it, Coach?"

"I'll give you a hint. It starts with an 'e.'"

The flummoxed guard groped in search of this foreign word.

"Try *e-l-e-e-m-o-s-y-n-a-r-y*!"

Finally, after an uncomfortable length of time, Jake found the elusive noun.

He stumbled over the pronunciation. "E—lee—e—m-m-moz—un—ary. Relating to charity. Alms."

Silence prevailed as the downcast team members thought, "What does charity have to do with basketball?" The answer came swiftly.

"Your effort was downright pitiful on the defensive end, Skoon. You score eighteen—and your man gets twenty-eight! You gave away points like Carnegie built libraries!"

THE HOOSIER GAME

The analogy was a stretch. But none of the teenagers volunteered to split hairs, even if one understood what the hell Coach was saying.

"Danner, since you won't find '*lard-ass*' in Webster's, look up *obelisk*."

"*Obelisk*. A tall, four-sided, taperin' monument that ends in a peer'mid-like shape at the top. Use'ly permanently fixed."

"In other words, it's a fancy post that has no life. It just stands there for people to admire. Well, son, you played *obelisk* defense against Farmersburgh. You rebounded like a man with both feet in concrete."

That took care of the starting five. Coach didn't spare the subs. They were equal-opportunity recipients of Coach O'Ryan's stinging rebuke. His steely eyes bore through the rest of the team. When he wrapped up his scathing critique, even the guys who never got off the bench in that game were ready to admit their guilt for the poor effort.

Except for Mark running his cuss-laps, coach never punished the individual. Everyone paid for the lack of effort or sloppy play of a teammate. Somehow coach could always find a way to connect one player's sins with the negligence of the entire squad.

It was his way of telling the team that they all win together and all lose together. Everyone has some responsibility in both outcomes. Like marines in foxholes, he taught them that each guy was not only accountable for his own performance but was answerable for every other member of the unit.

18

FER A TEN MINUTE NAP

Jourden Arena
8:52 p.m.

The Cougar players were surprised at Coach Fortune's conciliatory tone. This was a side of the stern mentor they had not seen before.

"I want to apologize to you for being thoroughly out-coached up to this point. It's my fault that I didn't prepare you properly for a dangerous team like the one in the other locker room. I didn't show Morgans Awe the proper respect. Because of that, neither did you.

"But we still have two quarters of basketball left to change that."

The hushed players leaned slightly forward in anticipation.

"First, forget about all the people in the stands. Forget the referees, your opponents. Forget all the X's and O's I've scribbled on this chalk board. Let's all stop being angry, embarrassed, or scared—right now. Let's remember why you play this game. For the sheer fun of competing, to be part of a team working together toward the same goal. Just go out and pit your talents against the guy in the other uniform.

"There is nothing wrong with our offense. Just stop thinking and play to your instincts and abilities. Run the offense, take shots with confidence. If you miss your first, don't hesitate to shoot the next one. They'll start falling, I guarantee you."

One could feel the tension in the room evaporating.

Saul turned to his captain, who'd had a miserable first half trying to stop Jake Skoon.

"Cole, Skoon shoots pretty well, doesn't he?"

"When he's open," Wells growled.

"Exactly!" the cagy coach replied. "So how do we go about stopping a guy who got twenty-one points off of us in the first half?"

"Deny him the ball!" volunteered DeWitt Weatherford.

THE HOOSIER GAME

"Sounds pretty simple," the coach responded. "But not so easy to accomplish. So here's how we're gonna stop number five and beat that team down the hall."

Coach Saul Fortune would now spring a surprise on Morgans Awe that Michael O'Ryan didn't see coming.

Coach O'Ryan's confident but restrained message had calmed the euphoria his players felt earlier. He began to prepare his team for an expected rejuvenation of Madison Central in the third quarter.

"They're gonna bust out of that locker room like a rabbit in a forest fire," Michael warned his team. "It'll be a test of our will and toughness against theirs. Be calm. They'll play hardball and try to rattle you into mistakes from the git-go. We can turn their aggressiveness against them. Just run our offense with confidence, take care of the ball, and play them tight defensively.

Arnie answered the knock on the door.

"One minute, coach."

"It's time to get upstairs. Gentlemen, when you reach the court, do not run. Do not jump. Do not display any sign that we are happy with our position. Strut like champions, men.

"Strut—like—champions."

During the final minutes of the intermission, Saul stepped to the chalkboard to review his box-and-one defense, one specifically designed to take a high scorer—particularly an outstanding shooter—out of his rhythm. Months ago, scouting the Raiders at Hillcrest, Coach Fortune decided he needed to devise a special defense to hinder Skoon's spectacular shooting, should his team play Morgans Awe in the sectional. Without fanfare, Saul had introduced the defensive tactic, spending at least fifteen minutes of practice daily to prepare for just this situation.

Four players lined up in a 1-3 zone, with a "chaser" shadowing Skoon wherever he went on the court. DeVreaux was stationed in front of the basket with Weatherford positioned at the free throw line. Wells and Donel Satterwhite, a junior forward replacing Hankins, would flank Weatherford on either side of the free throw line extended. The chaser's job was to deny Jake Skoon the ball with tight, man-to-man defense, ignoring every other Raider player. When Skoon had the ball the nearest teammate to the chaser would shift over to help, meaning the Raiders star would be constantly doubled and often triple-teamed.

Coach Fortune now played his hole card. Turning to a rarely used member of the Cougar squad, the wily coach said calmly, "Clay, you'll start with the first team in place of Miller. You're on Skoon."

Clayton "Clay" Childs was a senior who was not a skilled basketball player. The Cougars coach had added Clay to the tourney roster over a couple of better basketball players for just this circumstance.

FER A TEN MINUTE NAP

Childs was a superb physical specimen. He was muscular, quick, and athletic. A three-day growth of facial hair framed his pocked face. His eyes were coldly expressionless, like a gunslinger. In short, Clay Childs was a man.

Fortune had waited intentionally until the halftime break to set the trap. He was gambling that the surprise defense would confound Skoon and his teammates at least temporarily. If Saul's team could accomplish that, he was confident they would regain control of the game.

"Clay, you make life miserable for Skoon. Do not give him a free look at the basket. You have five fouls, Clay, so don't worry about too much contact.

"Karl, DeWitt, Donel, Cole—if Childs gets screened out or loses Skoon on the dribble, there are to be no lay-ups."

Saul's last instruction before his team left the locker room was to order a "hit"—not to injure the Raiders star but to try to intimidate him.

"Clay, first time Skoon starts to shoot," Saul said menacingly, "put him on the floor."

The newly energized Cougars gathered in a circle. The earlier attitude of arrogance had changed to icy determination. There would be no puffed-up posing, no pretentious bluster from Saul's Cougars. To a man, these fellows were going to wage war.

As the teams warmed up prior to the start of the third period an unfamiliar face caught the eye of Coach O'Ryan. Having scouted Madison numerous times over the past two seasons, he thought he knew everything about the Cougars. The Coach didn't recall seeing number fifty-two in any previous MCHS games. Quickly checking his game program, Michael found Clay Childs, senior forward, 6-2, 205 pounds.

O'Ryan had an ominous feeling in the pit of his stomach. Who is this guy? And why is Saul putting him in the game?

Wednesday, January 3, 1961

On the first day back from Christmas vacation, a rowdy pep session was held in the Morgans Awe gymnasium. That afternoon the whole school celebrated the Raiders team for earning its first holiday tourney championship trophy. In the Bloomington West Invitational Tournament on December 27, MAHS had defeated host Bloomington, 80-69, to advance to the title game against Scottsville. In a thriller, Jake Skoon drilled a shot from the corner as the gun sounded for a 78-76 victory.

It was the first time Josh and the team had cut down the nets, a privilege reserved for the tourney champs. Every member of the squad had watched others mount a ladder to claim the spoils of victory. Now it was their turn.

THE HOOSIER GAME

The history of claiming the nets was a ritual with Hoosier roots. A revered name in Indiana basketball is that of Everett Case, who coached Frankfort High School to state titles in 1925, '29, '36, and '39.

Following his sterling career with the Frankfort Hotdogs, Case was hired at North Carolina State University. Recruiting Hoosier high school stars, Case's teams dominated the Southern and Atlantic Coast conferences from 1946 to 1964.

Following one conference championship victory, his Indiana players found a pair of scissors and summoned a ladder. The Hoosier boys each rose to cut one piece of the net, just like back in Indiana. Their teammates from other states, including New York, refused to take part, feeling it was unsportsmanlike, an unnecessary slap in opponents' faces.

However, cutting down the nets—first done in high school celebrations in Indiana—soon caught on, becoming a rite of NCAA conference and national tournaments.

The six-inch piece of twine Josh Seaberg had clipped from the Scottsville net—kept in a small, Lucite display case—still occupied a prominent spot in his den fifty years later.

The Raiders beat Sycamore Creek and Cross Tracks before busing to Seymour for the much-anticipated contest against Jefferson High School's Big Green, a school with a student body seven times larger than that of Morgans Awe.

Seymour was rated 17th in sportswriters' polls, having won all twelve of their games thus far. Based on strength of schedule—despite its winning record—unknown Morgans Awe was considered a huge underdog.

To the dismay of the partisan home crowd, the Raiders were leading by four points going into the final two minutes of play and on the verge of a surprising upset.

Disappointingly, O'Ryan's team buckled. Morgans Awe players missed six of their last twelve free throw attempts, while Jefferson rallied to send the game into overtime. Given new life, the Big Green escaped with a 93-90 win. Skoon led the MAHS attack with 37, followed by Mark Danner, who tallied 26, along with 18 rebounds, and Josh Seaberg with 22, the trio scoring all but five points of the team total.

The MAHS team bus did not leave on time following the game. The prevailing attitude of his players in the locker room galled Coach O'Ryan. While some team members were generally downcast in losing, several players exhibited satisfaction, if not pride, that they had given Seymour a scare. Michael listened to the lighthearted banter coming from the shower area. A few of the guys were talking about their dates for the upcoming weekend. After everyone had dressed, a seething O'Ryan ordered them to sit.

For the next thirty-five minutes he delivered a searing tirade about their lack of concern about losing a game they should have won. The coach was not interested in moral victories. O'Ryan spared no one—including high-scorer Jake Skoon—in his rant about their pathetic response to the will of the Big Green team.

It would be an agonizing thirty-two-mile bus ride home. The contrite teenagers uttered not a word the entire trip. No one wanted to rekindle the righteous wrath of the coach.

This team would never again celebrate coming close.

Friday, January 5, 1961

Following the tough loss to Seymour, the Raiders seemed to lose their way. Before a sell-out crowd of 3,200, Morgans Awe fell to a powerful Cincinnati Archbishop Manyan squad by a score of 84-71. Cade's Lick, Kentucky proved to be equally harsh hosts, holding Jake to only 10 points in a 66-56 triumph.

O'Ryan's commitment to being in better physical condition than any of the opposition continued throughout the season. That meant an everyday dose of the merciless gassers and other fiendish conditioning drills conjured up by the dark side of the coach's soul.

Daily, when the exhausted teens staggered downstairs to the locker room to assess the damage to their bodies, one player usually remained upstairs. Unfortunately, Mark Danner's tendency to voice his frustrations with colorful profanity was undiminished. Today, Arnie Packard had dutifully recorded Danner's frequent indiscretions and reported them to Coach O'Ryan. Mark had racked up a total of thirty penalty laps for his swearing. A penchant for shouting his favorite expression—"Helly-be-damned"—was especially costly, as he was assessed two tours for each word, including the verb.

After showering, Josh slowly mounted the steps to courtside, where he saw his junior buddy slogging mechanically up and down the bleachers.

"You doin' okay, Mark?"

"Josh, if Mair'lun Munroe was a-layin' buck nekkid on the locker room floor, I'd leap right over her fer a ten-minute nap."

THE HOOSIER GAME

"How many tours have you done?"

"'Bout half."

Without another word, Josh returned to the locker room to put his sweat-sopped gear back on. A couple minutes later, Seaberg joined his surprised teammate, accompanying him until all laps were completed. Finally, they left the court, Big Mark with his arm around Josh's shoulder.

"Thanks, Sea-bird," Mark replied with gratitude. "You didn't have ta do that. I 'preciate the company."

"You can pay me back by learning to shoot free throws, Goom-bah," Josh teased. "Every time you miss, I catch more hell from Coach for not getting the rebound than you do for clankin' the shot."

Watching from a darkened hallway, unbeknownst to either boy, Coach O'Ryan had viewed the entire scene. Observing his co-captain display such loyalty to a teammate had touched him deeply. Before practice next day, the coach spoke about leadership, using Josh's action of the afternoon before as an example. Thereafter, whenever Mark accumulated laps to run after practice, his mates would take turns running with him.

With only two regular season games remaining before the sectional tournament, Coach O'Ryan had a growing concern about Danner. He had noticed that Mark had been sluggish and his play lackluster during the past couple of weeks. His junior center's normally dominating presence in the post had slipped noticeably. Mark seemed to be sapped of energy, becoming exhausted early in practice and games.

When the coach's usual sarcastic or humorous quips failed to motivate Mark, O'Ryan had become alarmed.

Prior to practice on Monday, Coach asked, "Mark, are you okay? You move like you're strapped to a plow. What's up?"

"Aw, nothin', coach. Dad and me's been workin' extra hours in the barn. I'm just tired from that."

O'Ryan wasn't buying Mark's attempt to downplay his debilitated condition. That evening the coach called the Danner home to talk with his parents. Mark's father listened as Coach O'Ryan aired his concern regarding Mark's health.

"Since you mention it, Mr. O'Ryan, we noticed Mark ain't eatin' much and he's been goin' to bed early ever night. The boy never complains, but Lucille and me have wondered what's wrong with him."

FER A TEN MINUTE NAP

At the close of the conversation Coach O'Ryan and John Paul Danner decided to take Mark to Doc Gentry. After examining the boy, who had a fever, sore throat, and swollen glands, and admitted to a lingering fatigue, Doc Gentry recommended a visit to a specialist that he knew in Louisville.

Dr. Lewis Wellstone, chief of staff for infectious diseases, immediately ordered Mark to be hospitalized. After further tests Danner was diagnosed with mononucleosis, a common but very contagious viral illness. The treatment called for lots of rest and little physical exertion.

It was apparent that Mark would be out for the rest of the year.

At practice that afternoon, Coach O'Ryan informed his team of Danner's condition. The next morning, a Saturday, the whole team piled into three cars for the forty-mile trip to the Kosair Childrens Hospital in Louisville.

As the thirteen members of the party entered Mark's room, his mother, Lucille, arose from her bedside chair. Acknowledging Mrs. Danner, Josh spoke for the group first.

"How're you doin', Hoss? Coach says you've got mono."

"Don't believe that rumor. I'm fine as frog hair. Just got the eppazootic or sumpin'."

"Yeah, sure."

"Ain't mono that kissin' disease?" inquired Arnie, coyly. "I seen you eyin' old Miss Holt in jography class. Makin' out with her, was you?"

"C'mon," Jamie Ross responded, "She's uglier'n you, Fries."

Bobby Mack Deal chimed in with, "I swear, that ole biddy taught Tommy Jefferson before the Loosiana Purchase."

"She wuz alive when the Dead Sea was only sick," Sonny added.

Mrs. Danner laughed as heartily as the rest at the outrageous claims.

"I'm glad you guys showed up," the lanky patient went on. "I need you to sneak me outta here. These nurses keep pokin' holes in me. If I had as many needles stickin' outta me that's been stuck in me, I'd look like a porky-pine. I need some relief, boys."

"Seriously, Mark," Josh said soberly. "What does the doctor say? How long before you can get back up to snuff?"

Lucille answered for her son. "It could be a few months til Mark can do anything strenuous."

"There goes the season," Joe Cotter muttered.

THE HOOSIER GAME

"That's crap, Joe," growled Mark. "The last thing I want to do is hurt you, Cotter. But that's still on the list. I don't wanna hear anymore a' that. You guys pull together and we can win the sectional.

"Tell the ole man I'll be at practice Monday."

From the rear a familiar voice responded, "Why don't you tell me yourself, Danner?"

Every teen froze. No one had seen Coach O'Ryan slip into the room. Each one was doing a mental retreat, trying to remember if he'd made some remark that could put him in front of Coach's firing squad.

"Uh-oh," whispered Jake, who hadn't said a word until now.

Momentarily silenced, Mark quickly recovered. "Hey, Coach. I was just askin' someone to tell you I'm comin' to practice on Monday."

"Better let sleepin' dogs lie, Mark," O'Ryan said, grinning, after which Mark replied, "Guys, to hell with the mono. I think I'm havin' a heart attack."

Everyone roared at their flustered teammate.

Just then a nurse nudged her way through the crowded room, hypodermic in hand.

"Better clear out, boys. It's time for the four o'clock run of horny nurses. They all-ways take a detour through my room, a-hopin' I'll—"

"That's enough, Mark," his mom chided. "You won't be getting out of the hole you've dug anytime soon."

Friday, February 16, 1961

As his 19-4 team prepared for the tournament without their big man in the middle, Coach O'Ryan allowed no excuses.

"I want no alibis, no woe-is-us talk," he challenged his squad. "Bad breaks, bad calls, 'We lost Mark,' or 'My big toe was hurt' are excuses for losers. Winners do not look for reasons to feel sorry for themselves. We play the games with whoever shows up. So let's get on with it."

Behind Jake's twenty-eight points and a solid defensive effort from the entire team, MAHS defeated Mainport in the first round, before being eliminated by Sycamore Creek, 58-54.

It was the first time since 1947 that a Raiders team had won 20 games in a season.

FER A TEN MINUTE NAP

Saturday, February 17, 1961

From Berry Gordy's Motown sound came this popular hit by the Shirelles:

Tonight you're mine completely,
You give your love so sweetly,
Tonight the light of love is in your eyes,
But will you love me tomorrow?
Is this a lasting treasure,
Or just a moment's pleasure?
Can I believe the magic of your sighs?
Will you still love me tomorrow?

The 1961-62 Morgans Awe basketball season began the day after the loss to the Eagles. Teams eliminated from the state tourney were allowed supervised practices until the championship game. After that, organized practices were forbidden by the IHSAA. Coaches were barred from any participation in summer pick-up games involving their players.

On Saturday morning all ten returning team members gathered at the home of Michael and Kate O'Ryan for a team breakfast. The coach reviewed the past season, stressing the importance of improving as individuals during the upcoming summer.

"Our goal for next season is to win the Madison sectional championship. To achieve that we can't wait until practice starts next fall. We can't wait until summer starts. We're too late if we wait until tomorrow. The pursuit of that goal begins right now.

"Great things can happen for you next year, but only if you are willing to put in the necessary work in the next eight months to be a better player and teammate. A lot of players 'light up' when the game starts, the crowd is cheering, and news guys are singing your praises. But to be a champion, you have to work hard to improve a little bit every day—when there are no stage lights, no pretty girls screaming your name, no outside observers boosting your ego.

"You have the tools to be a really good team next season. But talent alone won't be enough. The opening tip in our first game against Zephersville is exactly 261 days from today. As coaches, we are responsible for having each of you prepared, to be in top physical shape to compete with the best. I think we do a pretty good job of that, don't you?"

Players chuckled as Bobby Mack compared O'Ryan's conditioning drills to "that Bat-man death-march."

"It's Bataan, you dope," whispered Jamie.

"Yeah, that one, too," Deal hissed.

After completing his remarks, Coach O'Ryan dismissed the team. The Raiders' players were inspired. The boys who would represent Morgans Awe on the basketball court next season were determined to be more than a good small-school team. They intended to be a great team that would be remembered in the community for all time.

The final official team activity was attending the 1961 state finals. Athletic Director Gottschalk had managed to purchase enough tickets for coaches O'Ryan and Barnhard and all ten of the returning players to attend the Final Four.

Indianapolis Manual, featuring identical twins Dick and Tom VanArsdale, met Kokomo's Kats in the final game.

With Dick VanArsdale scoring twenty-six points and his brother Tom seventeen, the Redskins led by seven points with only 1:07 to play. Incredibly, Kokomo rallied to tie the score, 62-62, sending the game into overtime. With only three seconds remaining, Ronnie Hughes of Kokomo made two pressure-packed free throws allowing the Kats to defeat the Redskins, 68-66 to claim the state championship.

As they filed silently out of the arena into the cool March air, each of the boys from Morgans Awe vowed to come back to Butler Fieldhouse next year at this time—not to be in the stands, but as players on the floor.

Sunday, April 16, 1961

World-altering events marked the spring and summer of 1961.

Stirring the embers of the Cold War standoff between communist nations and the USA, President John Kennedy approved a plan to support Cuban natives with the ultimate objective of removing Fidel Castro from power. It was quickly foiled by the Cuban army, and the ignominious action, which became known as the Bay of Pigs, humiliated the United States on the international stage and further damaged relations between the world's superpowers, Russia and the USA.

FER A TEN MINUTE NAP

In May, Yuri Gagarin of the Soviet Union became the first human to enter space. Less than one month later American Alan Shepherd matched the Russian feat as he rode the 83-foot Mercury Redstone rocket into orbit.

In the Deep South, activists of all creeds and colors joined black civil rights leaders in the fight for equal rights. Peaceful marches and other protests turned violent as committed racists held their ground against integration. Many blacks—and whites—were beaten savagely. A number were slain, including activist Medgar Evers, bringing the world's attention to the plight of America's black citizens.

Unmindful of the historic events swirling around them, members of the Morgans Awe varsity traveled to the outdoor asphalt courts in Scottsville, Madison, and Louisville where they could find top competition. Jake, Josh, Mark, Sonny, Bobby Mack, and Bond Bathwaite were the equal to the stars of many of the larger high schools.

At the end of last season, Coach O'Ryan had a blunt but instructive conversation with Bathwaite. Essentially, the coach told his talented young sophomore that he could play a key role for the Raiders in the coming season, but only if he was prepared to sacrifice his personal style for the good of the team.

Bond would ultimately accept his diminished scoring role, stifling his instinctive scorer's mentality in deference to Jake and the rest of his teammates. During the summer months Bond had completely altered his devil-may-care approach to basketball in order to become a true team player.

Bond became the team's best backcourt defender. On offense, his ball handling and passing skills made each of his teammates better. His ability to take over the offense kept opponents' defenders honest when they tried to double-team Skoon.

Bond would prove to be a catalyst that blended ideally within the team chemistry. Coach O'Ryan had found and developed the final ingredient in the Raiders' future success.

Wednesday, July 19, 1961

I'm a travelin' man and I've made a lotta stops, all over the world
And in every port I own the heart of at least one lovely girl.
I've a pretty senorita waitin' for me, down in old Mexico
And if you're ever in Alaska stop and see my cute little Eskimo.

THE HOOSIER GAME

It was a typical summer in Indiana in 1961—hot and humid—when Ricky Nelson recorded his latest hit. The sultry climate only accentuated the commitment Josh and his mates had made to becoming better basketball players. Nearly every weekday the boys showed up at Memorial Park courts. Play usually began at six o'clock and continued until 10:30 p.m., when the lights were shut off.

Many weekends, Arnie Packard drove his six friends to Madison in his 1954 Ford Crestline convertible. The first time they came to Madison, players from MCHS and St. Isadore's, Madison's private Catholic school, recognized the Raiders. Central's team members were obvious in their haughty attitude toward the country bumpkins from Morgans Awe.

Madison's players felt justified in their disdain for the MAHS players, consistently beating them in the full-court, five-on-five scrimmages. Josh overheard one of the mouthier Central boys—later identified as Marty Miller—brag to his teammates that "Me and DeWitt could beat those clodhoppers, two on five."

The Morgans Awe boys would remember that comment down the road.

The Catholic kids from St. Isadore were warmer in their embrace of the new competition. While Cougars players stood aloof, the Saints' boys were congenial, engaging the newcomers in normal teen conversation.

Over the summer the hicks from Morgans Awe, while scorned by the elite cagers from Madison Central, gradually gained respect among players from other schools in the surrounding area.

19

B.O.B.

Jourden Arena
9:04 p.m.

 Jake lay flat on his back on the hardwood court, wincing, as his teammates gathered around. Only twelve seconds into the third quarter, Clay Childs had undercut the Raiders star as Skoon left his feet on a drive to the hoop. He landed shoulders first, then struck his head frightfully on the hardwood.

 Jake's teammates and Morgans Awe fans were incensed.

 The referees quickly stepped between members of the two teams, several of whom had moved angrily toward one another. The potential for violence was real.

 Oddly, Coach O'Ryan remained calm despite the blatant attack on his best offensive player. He walked slowly toward his fallen guard.

 As he came onto the court O'Ryan noted Mark and Karl DeVreaux were jawing angrily, faces only inches apart. From behind, Coach grabbed Danner around the waist and spun him away from the husky Cougar center.

 "Calm down, Hoss. There's a half of basketball yet to play."

 Mark nodded, and the other Raiders, following the example of their coach, held their tempers in check.

 Jake was sitting up when O'Ryan kneeled down and asked, "You okay?"

 "Sure, coach. Just need to clear my head a little bit."

 As Jake was helped to his feet, the Raiders cheerleaders led their rooters with,

> "He's a man. He's a man. He's a Morgans Awe man!
> Yay, rah, Skoon!"

THE HOOSIER GAME

With an uneasy peace restored, head official Norm Blaise moved toward the scorer's box.

"I have a foul on number fifty-two in the white. Act of shooting, two free throws for number five in the orange jersey. Also, an intentional foul on number fifty-two, resulting in a technical foul and an additional free toss."

Michael was certain Fortune had instructed his player to foul Jake hard. Saul held back when Danner ran over DeWitt Weatherford earlier in the game. O'Ryan understood. The rough foul was a message to the young Raider that there would be no easy shots the rest of the way.

Coach O'Ryan detoured slightly on his path back to the Raiders bench, slowing as he approached his counterpart near Madison's huddle.

"That undercut wasn't necessary, Saul. Foul him hard, no problem. Injuring Jake is another thing altogether. I'll call us even, but if Jake lands on his back again, you'll hear from me."

Fortune stared blankly at his accuser, then turned toward his team's huddle.

Jake would attempt all three free throws. He was alone at the line to shoot the technical foul as players from both teams fanned out behind him.

Mark sidled over to stand beside Cougar captain Wells. Looking straight ahead, the sturdy center offered the senior guard a bit of advice.

"What yer buddy just did didn't do you no favors," Mark said in a low, ominous voice. "I'll give you that foul, since Jake's okay. But you tell yer boys that the next time one of my teammates gits mawled like that, it's your ass I'm comin' after, Wells. When you come into the lane, count on me to find yer mouth with my elbow. Now, the refs'll prob'ly kick me out. But I'll still have my teeth."

The casual seriousness of Mark's demeanor and the tone of his voice hinted of real danger. Beneath his veneer of bravado, Cole felt sure Danner was a man of his word.

"Damn," thought the young guard, "that sonuvabitch ain't kiddin'."

Jake missed the free throw for the tech. He drained the next two to give Morgans Awe its biggest lead, 44-26. Then the bottom fell out.

Madison brought the ball quickly up court. Weatherford broke free at the baseline to sink a ten-foot jump shot.

As expected, Central then set up in what appeared to be a standard zone defense. But as Jake cut through the key, Coach O'Ryan noticed that Childs was sticking tightly to Jake while the four other Cougars held their positions. Saul was using a box-and-one zone designed to shut down the high-scoring Skoon.

Numerous times O'Ryan had found it necessary to respond to unorthodox defensive tactics intended to corral his star player. During the regular season at least four coaches had tried various atypical defensive schemes to try to contain Jake. While some of the unusual tactics had slowed Jake to some degree, none had completely shut him down.

Anticipating during the regular season that Saul would have in his bag of tricks some form of defense customized to stifle Skoon, Michael had designed a different offensive attack specifically for the Cougars. He now signaled the team to go into the offense they had spent ample practice time in preparing for opponent's defensive gimmicks.

Jake moved immediately to the foul line, his back to the basket. He became the fulcrum of a 2-1-2 offensive set, with Bond and Sonny on the perimeter and Josh and Mark flanking the basket near the end line. From his position in the middle, Jake could run off a series of screens by teammates on both sides of the foul line extended or he could drive into the defense, freeing up his teammates for shots from the perimeter. But the simplest and most effective maneuver was to face up to his single defender and launch fifteen-foot jumpers that were like lay-ups to a shooter of Jake's caliber.

However, Coach O'Ryan hadn't accounted for the superior athleticism and strength of Childs in contrast with Skoon's physical limitations. When Jake posted up at the foul circle, Childs fronted him, making it difficult for Skoon's teammates to pass him the ball. Clay's extraordinary quickness enabled him to seal off Jake and deny the Raider scorer the entry pass. The sturdy sophomore leaned on Jake, subtlety pushing him further from the basket. From his solid shoulders and torso to his muscular thighs and legs, Childs was simply too stout for the slender Raider guard.

The Madison defender was unrelenting in his determination to force Jake out of his comfort zone. Jake became frustrated and impatient with his inability to counter the rough play. He began to force shots and throw careless passes that the Cougars found easy to intercept.

At the other end, fired with fierce resolve, Central staged a furious rally. With the Raiders faltering, Madison Central began to find openings in the Morgans' defense. The Cougars scored nine straight points while allowing only one basket to their opponent to draw within seven points at 44-37.

Making matters worse, Mark had picked up fouls number three and four on consecutive plays, sending him to the bench. Without their only big man, Morgans Awe was overmatched underneath as DeVreaux, the towering sophomore Donel Satterwhite, and Weatherford controlled the boards.

Jake managed to hit two free throws before Madison scored the last sixteen points of the quarter. The Cougars simply overwhelmed Morgans Awe, outscoring them 26-4 since halftime. With only eight minutes to play in the sectional title game, Morgans Awe was behind, 52-46.

THE HOOSIER GAME

Childs finished the quarter with three fouls. Despite taking not one shot from the field and missing the only two free throws he attempted, Clay Childs was clearly Madison's most valuable player to this point in the game.

The box score for Jake Skoon in the preceding eight minutes? Zero for six field goal attempts, 3-4 free throws, and five turnovers.

Hanging their heads as they trudged off the floor, the Raiders were on death row. There was no stay of execution in basketball. Their defeat seemed inevitable.

As Jake passed by the Cougars' bench, Marty Miller couldn't help himself. He muttered to the senior star, "Are you in 'awe' yet, 'Morgan-boy?'"

Saturday, May 5, 2012

As he quietly sipped his glass of wine, Josh noted a man at the opposite end of the bar.

"Your name wouldn't be Seaberg, would it?"

Surprised, Josh turned to the man who had spoken his name. He had no idea who this person was.

"Yes. Do I know you?"

"You may not remember me, but I sure as heck remember you. I went to school at St. Isadore. You broke my heart in the '62 sectional."

Still unable to recognize the man, Seaberg probed further. "That's the first time I ever heard that from a grown man," Josh joked. "I remember playing St. I in the tourney. But—I'm sorry—I don't recall your name.

Thrusting forth his hand, the stranger introduced himself. "I'm Matt Rushton."

"Josh Seaberg. Very nice to meet you."

"I was a senior on the Saints team that you guys eliminated in the sectional. We were lookin' forward to playing Madison Central for the championship that year. We had you guys down by eight with five minutes to go. You made a run and tied it, 53-53. Then I stole the ball from one of your guards, Skoon, maybe."

"Anyway, I'm drivin' to the hole, wide open. I go up to lay it in for the lead when all of sudden this long arm comes outta nowhere and slaps the ball off the board, rebounds it, takes it to the other end, hits a shot, and gets fouled. You made the free throw, too."

"Man, you brought back a memory I'd forgotten all about."

"I'll never forget it, dang your hide. We fell apart after that play. Lost by six. I was never so down in my life. I still remember it every year at sectional time."

"Well, I guess the least I can do is buy you a beer."

"You couldn't begin to make up for that awful day—but I'll drink a Bud Lite on your tab. Do you still live in Morgans Awe?"

"No, when I went to college, my folks moved to Ft. Wayne. I live in Oxford, Ohio. I'm here for my fiftieth class reunion."

"Too bad the old Morgans Awe high school is gone. Consolidation swallowed them and about three or four other little county schools, didn't it?"

"Yessir, it did. We have a lady who keeps the class connected by e-mail, so the '62 grads have reunions every five years. What did you do for a living, Matt?"

"You mean, still doing. My two sons and me farm 340 acres up at Smyrna. They do all the work and I act like they couldn't do it without me. As long as Luke and Matt Jr. don't catch on, I'm golden."

"Ha! I wish I had your gig."

Josh found conversation with his new friend delightful. For the next half-hour the veritable strangers laughed with one another, sharing stories of a special era in both their lives.

Finally, Rushton reached to shake Josh's hand.

"It's been a real pleasure talkin' with you, Josh. Hope our paths cross again someday."

As he gripped his new friend's hand, Josh echoed the sentiments. "The pleasure has been all mine, Matt. Best of luck to you."

As the man walked away, Josh, eyes misting, asked the bartender for his bill.

Josh returned to his room to wash his hands and brush his teeth before leaving to join classmates at the Lanthier Winery. His mind was churning, stimulated by a multitude of recollections triggered by conversations of the past several hours. Vestiges of events and persons recalled today had long lain dormant. Now, like a mountain stream in springtime, nostalgic thoughts of the past rushed through his head.

Saturday, August 13, 1961
Richmond, Indiana

On the second Saturday of August, the IHSAA sponsored its annual conference of the Indiana High School Coaches Association. Hoosier basketball coaches, athletic directors, and basketball officials gathered to discuss rules

THE HOOSIER GAME

changes and new regulations. Additionally, selected coaches held clinics or made speeches about various aspects of the game.

On the program today, along with three legendary high school coaches from Lafayette, East Chicago, and Columbus, was Michael O'Ryan.

Coach O'Ryan was a respected elder among his peers. Indiana high school coaching contemporaries who were considered among the finest in the state recognized the gift Coach O'Ryan had in developing winning programs. That Michael coached at one of the smallest high schools in Indiana made no difference to knowledgeable counterparts. Great coaches held no prejudices against those teaching at other levels.

O'Ryan had brought seniors Josh, Jake, Mark, and Sonny with him to expose them to the wisdom of other Hoosier basketball mentors.

After his introduction, Michael carried a folding chair to center court of the Richmond High School gymnasium, straddled the seat, and placed his forearms on the back of the chair. Without notes, O'Ryan delivered an extemporaneous, thirty-minute monologue to the two-hundred-plus coaches facing him from the bleachers. His unwritten remarks focused on great leaders, including several military icons.

O'Ryan spoke first of Lieutenant General Friedrich Wilhelm Ludolf Gerhard Augustin von Steuben, a Prussian military strategist who volunteered to assist George Washington with a dispirited, starving Continental Army during the cruel winter of 1776 at Valley Forge.

"Von Steuben brought order and military discipline to the citizen soldiers," O'Ryan noted. "He told Washington bluntly that both his army of professional soldiers and members of the Patriot militia knew nothing of waging war as a unit.

"You see, the Prussian understood that experience can be a negative value. He unleashed a flurry of drills designed to break them down as individuals," continued the coach, "Then, he put them together again as soldiers by instructions in the manual of arms.

"His was the basic unlearning-learning process characteristic of modern armies, and teams, in every profession."

"In my view, building a cohesive unit begins with a realistic assessment of talent. Finding the players who have the attitude and skills to compete is the first responsibility of the coach.

"As the head of the Allies during World War II, then-General Eisenhower stressed the need for total objectivity in evaluating officers.

"He said 'considerations of friendship, family, kindliness, and nice personality have nothing to do with competence.' Ike believed that by nature, everyone wanted to be liked. He stressed that mental toughness was crucial in making sound but unpopular decisions."

O'Ryan then quoted a Pulitzer Prize-winning journalist, Herbert Swope, who said, "I can't give you the formula for success, but I can tell you how to fail. Try to please everybody."

"The second challenge, in my view, the real art of successful leadership," the coach continued, "is in molding individuals, with their wide range of skills and personalities, to work together toward a common goal.

"I'll bet every coach at one time or another has repeated the old adage, 'The whole is better than the sum of its parts.' How you make that happen is the genius of successful coaches.

"At Morgans Awe, no one is bigger than the team. We demand that, first, you show up on time for practice, meetings, bus trips, and when the team volunteers in the community. Second, you better know your job, on the floor, in the locker room, and in class.

"Finally, you're going to play hard, *all* the time. I don't believe in situational effort. If we can't depend upon a player for consistent performance, we'll find somebody who will. No exceptions.

"We've all had kids with great ability, unlimited potential, who just weren't motivated. He might amaze you with a lights-out performance one night and then disappear the next game. He teases you with his great talent but is frustrating to the max. You keep trying to get a consistent effort out of him, but in the end, he just never becomes the player you know he could be.

"I've found that rather than go through a season of hell, believing that 'if he only would do what we say,' you're better off to cut the ties at the start. He'll only end up being a detriment to the team and you'll waste too much energy on one guy at the expense of the rest.

"Getting players to buy into the roles the coaching staff determines for them can be a tough job. Telling a player who has been a scorer all his life that his value to the team is in assisting others to find shots may go against his strongest instincts and selfish interests. Behind him he often has parents and family, friends, and, yes, the uptown coaches, convincing him the head coach is wasting his talent. You have to trust your judgment and put that player in the role in which you feel he is best suited. If he won't adapt, he won't play.

THE HOOSIER GAME

"You make a fatal mistake if you leave players confused about their roles. Some coaches, faced with a player who won't accept his job, just cuts him or ignores him. If you don't take time to be certain the kid knows what you want and why he is not meeting your expectations, you're not being fair to him. His frustrations may carry over to other members of the team. Don't forget, these teenagers have more loyalty to one another than to you.

"One of the greatest coaches in history was George C. Marshall. He was chosen to be the top man to bring the political, cultural, and competing natures of the Allied armed forces—navy, air, and ground—to work together to win War World II. He had the task of convincing men of great courage and stern convictions to sacrifice their individual agendas, war materiel wants, and competing strategies into a unified whole. He's a hero who should never be forgotten.

"Well, I don't know if you've gained any special insights into leadership in the last fifteen minutes. But let me open it up for questions, now. I'd rather listen than talk, anyway."

Before anyone ventured a question, the coaches heartily applauded their colleague.

"Thank you, Coach O'Ryan," one of his contemporaries responded. "It's obvious you pay attention to the details. Regarding that, how much time do you spend in practice on fundamental drills versus scrimmage time?"

"The first twenty minutes of every practice we drill on the basics: dribbling, passing, offensive screens, defensive positioning, blocking out. Gentlemen, you know as well as I do that the fundamentals of the game don't change. But over time, we tend to change our attention to them. The result can be careless, sloppy play that gets you beat.

"We spend more time on half-court offense and defense than on full-court scrimmage. But we do work on keeping the boys in shape. Condition-wise, we believe in shared suffering. If a guy dogs it, everybody runs the extra sprints. If his teammates have to run extra because he messed up, he's less likely to repeat his poor effort. I believe, too, that it helps pull the team together. Every player is interdependent on the others."

"Coach, you've always been known for your high-scoring, fast-break offense. What's the key to your success?"

With a twinkle in his eye, Michael smiled. "I must be a distant cousin to that Confederate General Nathan Bedford Forrest. As to battles, he always tried to get there 'the fastest, with the mostest.' When we get the ball, that's what we try to do."

Following up, a young coach asked, "The fast break starts with rebounding. Do you have any special drills that can help a team with a lack of size compete with a bigger team on the boards?"

"You know, I recall, as a young coach, attending a conference like this. The speaker, who was raised in the barren hills of Kentucky, was asked a similar question to yours. He said (at this, O'Ryan tried his best impression of a slow Kentucky drawl), 'Ah all-ways found that the bess' *re*-bounders and *de*-fenders were the boys who hepp'd ther' daddies scratch a livin' outta dry and rocky Kentucky marl. They was a lot hungrier'n them boys who grew up on fancy horse farms. Those skinny fellers fought for every missed shot, kinda like a shark at feedin' time.'"

Returning to his normal manner of speech, O'Ryan concluded, "So, I don't think it's the drill that's important. Rebounding is in the 'want to' of the player. Of course, it helps if you have a front line averaging 6-5."

Another coach raised his hand. "Over the years, I've attended probably fifty coaching clinics like this. Sometimes, I think we coaches have too high an opinion of ourselves when it comes to winning games. Isn't the plain truth that lucky breaks and officials' calls decide as many games as clever coaching does?"

Michael paused. With a slight grin, he replied, "Albert Einstein made a lot of interesting observations in his life. The one I remember best is when he said, 'I am convinced that God does not play dice.'"

The assembly laughed appreciatively.

"Preparation in anything helps to remove fear of the unknown. Pressure is something you feel when you haven't fully prepared. In my experience, the best coaches do the *least* coaching from the bench during games. They're the same ones who have the team ready from great practice habits and a solid game plan."

"Speaking of fear, Coach O'Ryan, you have had great success in your career. What is it you fear as a coach?"

"The only time I tend to panic as a coach is watching a sixteen-year-old dribblin' into a double team—with my paycheck in his mouth."

Hardy laughter followed that image.

"Coach, is your offense geared to any one player or do you try to distribute the ball equally to all your players?"

THE HOOSIER GAME

"Our offense at Morgans Awe isn't a democracy. The best shooters are going to take the most shots."

High in the bleachers, Sonny Watkins whispered to his teammates, "That would be me."

Each rolled his eyes at that comment.

The coach continued. "That doesn't mean just any shot. Different players shoot best from different spots on the floor. Mark Danner, our center, for example, can shoot from anywhere he wants—as long as its not more than three feet from the basket."

"Good call, Coach!" Mark's teammates giggled.

"Each guy has to know his limitations, where he can make a high percentage of his attempts and where he can't.

"By the way, I'd like to introduce four members of the Morgans Awe basketball team. Stand up, guys. That's Josh Seaberg. Next to him is Jake Skoon. And that tall lad, there, you won't see firing up twenty-foot jumpers. That's Mark Danner. And that slight one, Sonny Watkins, plays hard-nosed defense—of which the others have little familiarity."

The foursome received welcoming applause from the coaches.

"While you're standing, fellas, do you have anything to add about our practices? Don't be afraid. If you say anything I don't like, I'll only run you extra laps—depending on the degree of the insult you think you can risk."

The chuckles from the audience helped the boys relax.

Sonny spoke first. "Coach, you didn't tell 'em about your "BOB" theory."

"Go ahead, Sonny, you explain it."

"If you're not playin' all that well, Coach yells 'BOB' at you when you run by him."

"What's that stand for, Mr. Watkins?" his coach asked coyly.

"Butt-On-Bench, Coach."

"It's funny what a piece of plank beneath your fanny will do to help you figure out what you're not doing right," said the coach, cannily.

Josh joined in the fun. "We came to practice one day and there was a stop sign stuck in a big old milk can at one free throw line. That was Coach's way of telling the middle man in our three-lane fast break to stop there, so one or two men couldn't cover all three of us."

Mark added this kicker: "We never did know where you stole that stop sign from."

"At halftime of one game, Coach asked me what time it was," Danner went on. "The clock in the locker room showed it was half past eight, so I told eem that. He said, 'No, Mark, it's not eight-thirty. It's time for you to git your ass in gear and rebound!"

The coaches roared.

"Okay," O'Ryan said, "I think that's enough of this portion of the program. You people up there are having way too much fun. And doing a good job of sawing that limb off behind you, too," Coach O'Ryan grinned as the coaching fraternity applauded enthusiastically.

The boys were the hit of the session.

The clinic director now stepped in to say, "Okay, guys, you'll have time to talk further with Coach O'Ryan afterwards; but we're out of time. One more question. Yes, you in the front."

It was a newswriter covering the conference who shouted, "Coach O'Ryan, do you think you have a prayer of beating Madison Central this year?"

In the audience, Saul Fortune grinned as several coaches seated around him looked to see his reaction.

"I've found my prayers work best," O'Ryan quipped, "when I have good players. Thanks, gentlemen. It's been a pleasure."

The spontaneous, extended ovation from his colleagues demonstrated their appreciation for his lively, penetrating remarks.

20

MOON RIVER AND ME

Jourden Arena
9:21 p.m.

"I guess it's true, Merle, that the cream does *rise to the top. Inside, we all root for the underdog. And this gritty little bunch from Morgans Awe made a great go of it for a half. But the horse is back in the barn. The Cougars are clearly in charge."*

"Yeah, partner, you gotta hand it to Coach O'Ryan and the Raiders. But a good big team will almost always beat a good small team."

"Wasn't it Tony Hinkle who said, 'A big guy has the advantage over the little guy, cause he's closer to the rim?'"

The veteran broadcasters chuckled at how the sage Butler mentor wrapped profound wisdom in simple jargon.

"Actually," Hollings continued, "that first half was a good thing for Saul Fortune. He'll be able to pull this lesson about overconfidence out of his pocket if he needs it further along in the state tournament."

"Madison separated the wheat from the chaff in that third quarter. Outscoring Morgans Awe, 26-4, demonstrated how dominant the Cougars can be. It sure looks like Saul Fortune's lads are only eight minutes of basketball from their ninth sectional crown in the past ten years."

"Well, it was fun while it lasted."

Up in the Morgans Awe crowd a startled Carol Bassman turned to her close friend.

"What's he doing?"

Mrs. Coach O'Ryan had no idea.

Michael O'Ryan and his entire squad were hurrying to the ramp that led downstairs to the locker room. The players' curious expressions suggested that they didn't know what

THE HOOSIER GAME

the coach was up to, either. Official Garry Worden moved next to the coach as the Raiders mentor reached the ramp.

"Hey, Mike, what's goin' on?"

"Is there a rule that says I have to hold my team huddle up here?"

"Not that I know of. But you've got a minute before the tip-off. I'll have to assess a team technical if you aren't on the floor."

"We'll be there, Garry!"

No coach in anyone's memory had left the arena proper during a quarter break. O'Ryan had often pulled creative coaching tactics out of his bag of tricks. But this one wasn't even in the satchel.

Reaching the bottom of the ramp, out of the glare of the lights, away from the buzzing of the puzzled crowd, and out of sight of the opponents, the Raider players gathered around their coach.

O'Ryan had recognized the critical juncture his team now faced. If he didn't get the boys refocused on playing as they were capable, Madison Central would continue the rout sparked in the third period. The next sixty seconds could determine whether his players would compete or if they would concede to the inevitable.

The coach's voice was hoarse as he addressed the team.

"Right now, for the next sixty seconds, close your mind and listen only to me. Can you do that?" *Nods all around. During this memorable season Jake, Josh, Mark, and the rest of the team had experienced the high and low moments of victory and defeat. Coach O'Ryan had bred them through years of coaching to understand that those accomplishments that are special are the hardest to achieve.*

"Before any of you start to give in to your doubts about whether you can beat Madison, I just want you to think of what you've sacrificed to get this far toward a goal we set and have prepared for the past three years."

Michael smiled. "Fellas, believe that you can beat this team, and you will."

Curiously, as the coach continued his encouragement, Josh's mind shifted to thoughts of the stinging, bloody open cracks in his palms and fingers from playing in freezing weather on dirt courts and of blisters on top of blisters from the asphalt on sweltering summer days. He was yanked back to the present when Arnie yelled from the top of the ramp, "Madison's on the floor, coach!"

As the coach ended his remarks, Josh and his teammates shouted and bounded up the ramp, scrambling together as a school of guppies evading a predator.

The crowd greeted the re-entry of the Raider players to the court with an odd mixture of shouts and muffled, almost polite applause.

Coach O'Ryan's next move added to the bizarre atmosphere surrounding the appearance of his squad.

He called his third time out—before the tip-off to begin the final quarter.

As the two teams gathered before their respective benches, the bewildered witnesses in the crowd looked on in unmistakable amazement.

Saul stood, looking at the officials with arms spread. "Are we going to play the rest of the game, or not?"

Will Peck tried to describe for his listeners the peculiar scene taking place before him.

"This is one for the books. First, Michael O'Ryan looks like he's raisin' a white flag, leading his team out of the arena. Then they come back and with Madison Central and the referees ready to start the fourth quarter, he calls another consecutive timeout! What do you make of this, Merle."

"I've been watching high school basketball for over thirty years and I've never seen anything like this. And through it all, O'Ryan's cool as a cucumber. Unbelievable!"

Having addressed in a dramatic way the mental attitude of the players, O'Ryan now used his extra minute to revise the team's tactics on the court.

"Okay, guys, we're going into our 'scoring' four-corner offense. Bond, you're on top. Jake, you move to the left flank and Sonny to the right side. Mark, Josh, move to the corners. I want you to spread out, with your heels almost touching the out-of-bounds lines. We've got to get Jake some space.

"When Jake has the ball on the side, Mark, Josh, you swing out your positions toward Jake. Mark, you set a screen on Childs's left hip and Josh, set yours on his right hip. Go either way on the pick, Jake. If you have the jump shot, take it. If not, drive the ball. Mark and Josh will roll to the basket. Penetrate the zone and try to create a three-on-two situation. Drive it to find an open jumper or feed one of the big men.

"Now, no standing around! Bond, Sonny, don't crowd the foul circle. Stay on the perimeter in case they sag back to cover Jake. Knock down the shot if you're open. We've got plenty of time, men. No reason to rush. Be smart. Find the open man.

"On defense, we'll play our four-one, switching man-to-man. Mark, you play the one-man zone in the middle. The rest of you play tight, switching man-to-man, just like we've done before. In their faces, guys, in their faces! Let's go!"

The ten combatants gathered at the center circle to begin the final period. After claiming the jump ball, Madison misfired on two tries. Sonny rebounded and Bond brought the ball down the floor. Just as coach had diagrammed it, Mark and Josh set a double pick on Childs. Jake cut quickly to his right as both teammates pivoted toward the hoop. The Cougar front line stayed back, leaving Skoon with an open twelve-footer. Swish! Morgans Awe now trailed by only four, MCHS 52, Raiders 48.

Saul rose immediately and signaled for a timeout.

THE HOOSIER GAME

Saturday, May 5, 2012

Arriving at the site of the Class of '62 reunion banquet, Josh stepped out of his car onto the gravel parking lot. A soft breeze rustled the leaves of the sycamore and cottonwood trees. Skies were now clear. The warm afternoon sun had dried the landscape as quickly as the brief spring shower had dampened it.

A glance to the south revealed the brown Ohio River flowing toward its inevitable convergence with the mighty Mississippi. Time had not altered the ancient path of the river, nor the stately mansions dotting its banks.

The city of Madison had changed noticeably since Josh's last visit decades ago. Decorative period lampposts, newly paved streets, and gentrified shops provided a quaint, retro ambience to the town. He felt comfortable here.

"H-Hey, J-J-Josh!"

Grover Willburn and his wife, Shirley, stepped to Josh's side. Coming up behind them were Jamie and Clair Ross. The men introduced their spouses.

"So nice to meet you both. Obviously, Grover and Jamie both over-married," Josh teased.

The pebbled path of the Lanthier Winery wound through a large garden of colorful flowers, shrubs, and trees. It was a beautiful setting for the event. Linen-covered tables and folding chairs were arranged in a wide space where the catered *alfresco* dinner would be served. A dais and microphone stood at one end of the garden.

A disc jockey had set up his equipment on the small outer stage, playing CDs of fifties and sixties music.

Beneath a tent, three long tables were crowded with memorabilia from high school days. Filling the available space were editions of Morgans Awe yearbooks and the school newspaper, *Awe Struck*; newspaper clippings from the Madison and Louisville media; sports trophies; an orange and black letter sweater and jacket; megaphones and pom-pons; and hundreds of black-and-white period photos. Resting on an easel was a large and yellowing class picture, the 1962 graduates beaming with smiles of hope and enthusiasm. Jake stood beside Josh in the top row.

Josh paused to gaze into Jake's eyes, trying to decipher from his friend's stolid countenance some hint of the demons that had beset him. But the photo elicited no evidence of unhappiness that would hound Jake into a premature death. Except for being a high school basketball legend in his hometown, he was just Jake Skoon, normal teen, with every hope for a productive life.

His reverie was interrupted by Jamie, who had noted Josh's fixed stare on the class photo.

"How many points do you think Jake would have scored in high school if we'd had the three-point shot back then?"

"Probably about half-again as many as he did," Seaberg answered wistfully.

"Yep, at least that," Ross agreed.

Classmates were milling around, flutes of red and white wine in hand. About half the alumni had brought their spouses. Pat approached Josh and the two couples.

"Pat Sargossa, I swear, you look as beautiful today as ever," Shirley gushed.

"Thank you, Shirley, for that kind fib. You always knew the right thing to say."

Arnie Packard was seated at a table near the speaker's platform.

"Arnold, I'd get you a glass of wine. But I see you've already been taken care of."

"First in line, Josh. Sit down."

Tuesday, August 29, 1961

With school opening the day after Labor Day, Josh had come to the bookstore to purchase textbooks and supplies. He waited in the short line at the table for seniors to rent robes for graduation.

Pat Sargossa was assisting the representative there, a measuring tape in hand. As Josh approached she greeted him warmly.

"Hi, Josh! Have a good summer?"

"Yeah, Pat, it was great. What did you do over the break?"

"I had the best time. I got a job as an intern at WAKY radio in Louisville. Actually, I was sort of a gofer. But I did get the chance to fill in a couple of times to read the news and weather report. It was the ten to midnight slot. That was a good thing, because I made all of my mistakes when nobody was listening."

"Are you planning on majoring in communications in college?" Josh asked, noting her glistening dark eyes and captivating smile.

"I'm not certain," Pat replied. "I've always thought I'd be a teacher when I grew up."

"Whatever you decide, you'll be good at it," Josh concluded.

THE HOOSIER GAME

The two continued their pleasant chat until Pat noticed the four in line behind Josh were shuffling and glancing at wristwatches.

"Uh-oh. I need to get back to my job. It was really good to see you!"

"Me, too. We'll have to get together sometime."

"I'd like that, Josh."

Representatives from Herff-Jones, Inc., had set up a table outside of the principal's office to distribute senior class rings ordered last spring. Josh had left the bookstore, joining Sonny to wait his turn behind Arnie Packard. Alongside Fries was his current girlfriend, sophomore Veralyn Carter. Arnie received the box containing his brand new treasure. As he admired the shiny band, Veralyn reached down and deftly removed it from its small case. Her assumption, of course, was that Arnie would present her with this token of his affection, as steady boyfriends tended to do. Taken aback by Veralyn's bold seizure of the prize, the befuddled Packard quickly realized his choice was to lose the ring or the girl. His attempt at an approving smile—as if he really intended to allow the tiny brunette to wear it—came out, instead, as a pained grimace.

Veralyn didn't notice Arnie's wry response to her aggression. She was already visualizing the senior ring on her finger or on a chain around her neck, symbolizing a meaningful bond with her senior beau. She showed up next day with the ring on her tiny finger, smothered in strands of Angora to make it fit.

It wasn't until they broke up over Christmas that Arnie would wear his class ring for the first time.

That following Friday night, Josh and Pat would go out on their first date together. The pair attended a back-to-school party at Sheila Brouwer's house as the first day of their senior year approached.

At the sound of "The Twist" blaring from Sheila's new stereo record machine, Pat pulled Josh out of his seat, laughing at his reluctance to try the popular, hip-swiveling dance craze introduced by Ernest Evans, alias "Chubby Checker."

Come on baby, let's do the twist,
Come on baby, let's do the twist,
Take me by my little hand, and go like this.
Ee-oh, twist baby, twist,
Oooh-yeah, just like this,
Come on little miss, and do the twist.

MOON RIVER AND ME

Pat took a position, feet apart, one slightly ahead of the other. With her arms spread away from her body and elbows bent she began to gyrate at the waist to the beat of the music. Shifting her weight from her right leg to her left, leaning forward, then back, she was doing "The Twist."

Befuddled, Josh shouted above the clamor, "Pat, I don't know how to do this."

Josh never was comfortable on a dance floor. But Pat was persuasive, so he tried to contort his body in the bizarre manner of the new phenomenon. His Twist was a bit awkward; but he had to admit, it *was* fun.

"That's it! You've got it! Now dip down like me. See, you're doing it!"

Later, dancing to the plaintive sound of Henry Mancini's "Moon River," Josh held Pat closely as each contemplated the strong feelings growing between them.

Moon River, wider than a mile,
I'm crossing you in style, some day,
Oh, dream maker, you heart breaker,
Wherever you're going, I'm going, some day.
Two drifters, off to see the world,
There's such a lot of world to see,
We're after the same rainbows end,
Waitin' 'round the bend,
My Huckleberry friend,
Moon River, and me.

Tuesday, September 5, 1961

On the first day of their senior year of school, Mark picked up Jake, Josh, Sonny, and Arnie in his '59 emerald-green Chevy Impala hardtop with its distinctive tailfins protruding outward and unusual "teardrop" tail-lights on each side.

Entering the building, students greeted friends they hadn't seen since last May.

Minutes later the bell rang, calling them to the fifteen-minute homeroom session for announcements, attendance-taking, and other odds and ends.

Josh and Arnie's home room teacher, Mr. Landwear, filled out his attendance book during the period. To keep his charges busy, he assigned a student to read from a list of silly questions meant to entertain for the short duration.

THE HOOSIER GAME

Fries Packard volunteered to come to the front for this annual exercise. He began, earnestly.

"Why does 'slow down' mean the same thing as 'slow up?'"

"Why are the odds equal whether you have a 'fat chance' or a 'slim chance?'"

"Why are they called 'the stands,' when they are made for sitting?"

With Mr. Landwear engrossed in his task, Arnold deviated from the script: "Why is a bra singular and panties plural?"

A collective gasp and stifled giggles of the students stirred the teacher from his task. With everyone wondering if Mr. Landwear had heard Arnie's bold witticism, the instructor looked up to ask, "What's wrong?"

The uneasy silence was broken by the adventurous Packard.

"These things are *really* funny, Mr. Landwear."

Obviously pleased that his inventive exercise was entertaining the students, Landwear smiled and hovered again over his business.

Arnold returned to reading the quaint observations, with no further divergence from the original script.

"Why do we drive on a parkway, and park on a driveway?"

Morgans Awe had a number of outstanding teachers on the faculty, contradicting the general reputation of small, rural schools as inferior to large metropolitan institutions. Among those was the very prim and proper spinster, Miss Flossie Wilright.

Tiny—standing 4'10"—never married, solemn of demeanor and severe in the classroom, Miss Wilright was determined to fill the empty vessels that were her young students with knowledge and culture. Despite her diminutive frame, her intense, no-nonsense presence was imposing, effectively suppressing normal teenage antics.

Upon entering Miss Wilright's classroom, students noted a quotation above the chalkboard that epitomized her passion for learning. It read, "*THE LARGER MY ISLAND OF KNOWLEDGE, THE LONGER MY SHORELINE OF WONDER.*"

She announced her expectations for the class by referring to an Indianapolis school that was considered among the elite public secondary institutions in Indiana.

"You will be better than those seniors at Shortridge High School!"

She seemed incapable of letting pass even the slightest misstep concerning language. On one occasion a student delivered to Miss Wilright an invitation to his piano recital. Noting the card requested that the recipient "R.S.V.P., please," a familiar frown of disapproval creased her face.

MOON RIVER AND ME

Monday
Hawthorne Quiz
Chapters 5-8

Miss Flossie Willright, "...the larger your island of knowledge, the longer your shoreline of wonder."

THE HOOSIER GAME

"You must correct this monstrous mistake appearing on your kind invitation!" she scolded the student for his dubious use of the common abbreviation of the French, *Respondez, s'il vous plait.*

"In plain English," she informed the bewildered bearer of the offending card, "R.S.V.P. means 'Please reply.' 'R.S.V.P, please' is an unnecessary and incorrect 'echo,' asking, in essence, "Please, reply, please."

The chastened student apologized for this intolerable breach of etiquette (thus falling on the sword for his mother, who authored the invitation) before asking meekly, "Can you still come?"

The following weekend she graciously attended, to the delight of her student's family and friends.

Not surprisingly, it would be Mark Danner who would test Miss Wilright's temper and patience. During the initial class meeting, that guardian of the present, future, and past tenses of fluent English asked Mark if he had completed the student questionnaire that had been circulated to members of the class. At his reply—"I done did dat"—the horrified linguist practically swooned.

Recovering her composure, she approached Mark's desk and directed him to rise out of his chair. Standing toe to toe with the 6-4 mass of muscle, the petite spinster looked upward until her snood pressed against her neck. Miss Wilright proceeded to hew him down to her size with one word—"Savage!"

The matronly English teacher would introduce Josh and his classmates to Twain, Frost, Emerson, Longfellow, Poe, Hawthorne, Whitman, Hemingway, and Hoosier James Whitcomb Riley over the course of the fall/winter term. She was passionate about feeding a banquet of America's greatest writers to her callow teenagers.

As able as he was as a basketball coach, Michael O'Ryan was even more effective as a teacher. One never referred to Mr. O'Ryan as "Coach" in the classroom. He demanded a clear delineation between his persona on the basketball court and that of the devoted teacher. Although he was a history instructor, Mr. O'Ryan often stepped outside the curriculum to challenge his students on a wide variety of issues of the day. He didn't stand or sit as he taught, but instead walked slowly up and down between the rows of desks, continually drawing students into discussions about current events that might significantly influence the future.

Entering his classroom, students noted that all five chairs in the front row near his desk were empty. Mr. O'Ryan intentionally kept those vacant. In succeeding days and weeks, those desks would be filled as he identified the class clowns, the scofflaws, and other disturbers of the classroom environment. No one wanted to sit in the "DMZ" (Dumb and Mouthy Zone) within easy reach of the strict mentor.

On one occasion, Mr. O'Ryan was lecturing on the difference between a democracy—"Two wolves and a rabbit deciding what to have for dinner"—and a republican form of government, when he noticed Mark Danner had nodded off at his seat in the back row of the room. Farm boys like Mark toiled long hours during the fall harvest, often coming to school physically exhausted.

As he came abreast of the unsuspecting dozer, Mr. O'Ryan pulled a small squirt-gun from his pocket and proceeded to douse Danner liberally with the contents of the toy. His classmates burst into laughter as the burly teen awoke with a start.

"Are you too tired to stay awake in my class, Mr. Danner?" O'Ryan challenged.

"No, Sir. I'uz just checkin' my eyelids fer holes."

Even the formidable teacher joined in with the rest of the class, chuckling at Mark's quick-witted reply.

"Select a desk in the front row, son. You'll be able to see perfectly from there."

Monday, October 16, 1961

Today, Josh could hardly focus on anything except the opening of basketball practice. After the last period bell clanged, Josh hurried to the gym. The varsity hopefuls took a seat in the bleachers. Coach O'Ryan went over general team rules of conduct and his expectations of those who would make the final roster.

After receiving his practice gear and new pair of size 10½ Converse All-Star shoes, Josh dressed hurriedly, then joined his mates shooting randomly until the coach blew his whistle to begin drills. The routine was a familiar one. The fast-paced hour-and-a-half practice of fundamentals, shooting drills, rebounding, and an especial emphasis on defensive positioning and movement went smoothly. Josh felt at ease on the court. Running, jumping, cutting sharply were involuntary movements developed over years of training.

One phase of the workouts never varied, however.

Practice closed with the dreaded gassers. The unrelenting pace was gruesome. Coaches yelled spiritedly, "Run hard until you feel that sharp pain in

THE HOOSIER GAME

your side. Then run harder! Pain is nature's way of testing your courage! Your manhood! Fight through it, men. To make this team, you have no choice. Fight through it!"

As the number of sprints increased, Josh wondered how long he could hang on. A few boys had already gotten sick. It seemed as if when a kid hurled, it was like an insult to Coach O'Ryan. He just poured it on harder, pushing those trying out well beyond what each thought he could endure.

Finally, when Josh was certain he would go into shock, Coach O'Ryan's whistle blast signaled a halt to the suffering.

"Practice Monday after school. Three forty-five. Be on time."

The weary lads careened downstairs into the dressing quarters.

"Ming the Mercilous," gasped Bobby Mack as they limped back to the locker room.

Flopping down on the bench in front of his locker, C.C. predicted, "They'll call me the Martyr of Morgans Awe. When I die tonight they'll remember my name. My tombstone'll say, 'Here lays C.C. Aguirre. Died heroically, at the cruel hand of the gassers.'"

Josh didn't try to talk. His head hurt. His hair hurt. Even his *teeth* hurt. Like zombies, he and his mates shuffled slowly toward the poorly lit shower room. A roughly paved cement floor helped keep the barefoot teenagers from slipping and falling. Six showerheads, at least two of which were often faulty, sufficed for the twelve-man squad.

Younger players deferred to the veterans, who always showered first. Soothing fatigued bodies, upperclassmen often lingered in the hot spray for extended periods. Overstaying a reasonable time in the shower would result in clamors of protest from those still waiting their turn. Hot water availability depended on aged, capricious boilers that many times malfunctioned. Consequently, those further down the line of seniority had to settle for a hurried, bone-chilling cold shower.

Another hazard of the ancient water system caused dread among the users. When a toilet was flushed, the water in the shower pipes would turn scalding hot. Angry victims promised a grisly death to the perpetrator seated on the john.

Toweling off after a shower, one experienced the "second sweat." As pores opened from the effects of the steaming shower, the body began to perspire again. The cool, clammy sweat saturated the player's clothing. When the boys left the building in soggy clothing and with hair dripping, the icy wind and chill of outdoors penetrated to the very marrow.

MOON RIVER AND ME

By the time practice ended, the late October sky would be approaching darkness. Exiting the gymnasium door, Josh would hear the familiar rhythmic series of clinks as the wind tossed the metal clasp of the rope holding Old Glory against the school's flagpole.

A soft, amber glow of streetlights marked the way as he walked the four blocks to his home. On a night with a brilliant full moon, ghostly shadows danced on his path. Prodded by an increasingly bustling breeze, trees dispatched hosts of dying leaves, wafting downward to the street below. The rattling of dry leaves scurrying across the pavement, pushed here and there by the wind, always touched Josh with feelings of melancholy. Such nostalgic images kept old men connected to their youth.

When it came to internal problems within the team, O'Ryan handled them deftly and creatively, disarming player squabbles or personal troubles with a minimum of drama. Josh thought of the time a player came to the coach after discovering his wallet missing from his locker.

Coach directed everyone to finish dressing, then to take a seat. O'Ryan sent a message to junior varsity coach Barnhard to halt practice. The JVs were to join the varsity players in the locker room.

Without fanfare or recrimination, the coach addressed the twenty-six young men surrounding him.

"One of our number is missing his wallet. I'm disappointed that someone in this room got confused and mistakenly took it. I want all of you to lower your heads, close your eyes, and keep them closed.

"Starting with Josh, at this end of the bench, each of you will do the following. Arnold will give you a towel. Go to your locker, find your billfold, cover it with the towel, walk behind the chalkboard, and drop it into the box. Even if you don't carry a wallet, do the same thing. Tap the next guy on his shoulder when you're done. Arnie, you and Krebs will go last, then come to the coaches' office where coach Barnhard and me will be waiting.

"Before we leave, everyone, in single file, will fetch his wallet out of the box. I expect the missing one to be in there with the rest."

The lost wallet turned up. Coach never mentioned it again.

21

JAKE'S COON

Jourden Arena
9:23 p.m.

Coach Fortune now adjusted his zone defense, keeping Clay Childs on Jake while directing his four other players to mirror the four corners. The box-and-one zone would match up better against the Raider offense than their 2-2 defense with Childs hawking Skoon.

"Now, no silly fouls, gentlemen. Get rebound position and go hard to the boards."

After inbounding the ball, Madison boosted its advantage to six on a short jumper by Wells. Two baskets by Marty Miller sandwiched around a traveling violation committed by Sonny gave the Cougars a 58-48 edge with 5½ minutes remaining. MC's rooters were breathing easier.

Following yet another Raiders turnover, Madison worked the ball into Weatherford. The graceful forward pivoted and shot past Danner on the dribble. Sonny shifted quickly into the Cougar star's path. As DeWitt began his leap toward the hoop, he and Watkins collided sharply, knee to knee. The ball skittered out of bounds. Weatherford buckled and fell heavily onto the court's surface. Central's star player grasped his left leg, writhing in pain. His teammates quickly gathered around him.

"Uh-oh, Merle," rasped. "We have a problem."

Will Peck described the scene, in lowered tones, to his radio audience. "Coach Fortune is standing over his star center as the team doctor examines him. DeWitt is obviously in great distress. He is now flat on his back, hands covering his face. They're checking his knee. It doesn't look good from here."

As the alarmed Madison crowd looked on, Merle Hollings groaned, "Oh, my. What a shame it would be if DeWitt Weatherford can't finish this game. What an unfortunate turn for Saul Fortune and his highly favored Cougars team."

THE HOOSIER GAME

Will Peck could only shake his head in response.

"Let's return to the studio for a quick commercial. When we return, I hope we'll have a further report on the condition of Madison's key player, DeWitt Weatherford."

Following the timeout, a relieved Will Peck informed his audience that Weatherford was up on his feet, but walking haltingly, favoring his right leg.

"DeWitt Weatherford is being assisted to the bench with a teammate under each arm. He's limping noticeably. Cougar fans are saluting their hero with a loud ovation. The sportsmanlike rooters for Morgans Awe are also standing and applauding with gusto in tribute to this fine young man."

"Wait, Will. Weatherford and his two teammates are passing by their bench, following team doctor Lance Morin down to the locker room. It remains to be seen whether DeWitt will be able to return to the game," Merle mused. "This is an unfortunate incident, but an unexpected opportunity for Morgans Awe. They're down eight with less than five minutes to play. But Madison could be without its best player—"

"—maybe the best in the state," interjected Will.

"—for the rest of the contest. This could be the break that puts the Raiders over the hump."

A brooding Saul Fortune stood frozen on the sideline, chin in hand, forehead crinkled in thought, staring grimly at the floor.

What now?

Darrell Bratton checked in to replace the Cougar star. He missed both free throws that Weatherford would have attempted.

On the ensuing possession, the clever Wells zipped between Bond and the pass, flicking it away. Jake reacted quickly, retrieving the loose ball. Jake drove into the front court. Childs tried to fight through a solid screen, bowling Josh to the hardwood in the process. Referee Norm Blaise whistled a foul on the Cougar defensive stalwart, his fourth.

Saul now faced a thorny decision. Up to now, Clay had done just what his coach had asked. He had slowed down Morgans' offense with his hard-nosed defense of Skoon. By leaving Childs in the game, Fortune would risk his fouling out. If he removed the sturdy guard now, Skoon might regain his rhythm and start another scoring binge.

Central's coach signaled his athletic sophomore to the sideline for a brief word.

"Clay, you're staying in. But don't commit a silly foul. Stay on Skoon tight, but avoid fouling him. We need you in there."

"Yes, sir."

The Raider senior guard hit both ends of the one-and-one.

JAKE'S COON

Cole Wells fed a nice pass to DeVreaux, open under the basket. DeVreaux sprang upward, but Josh leaped high and his hand grazed the ball just enough for the attempt to fall short. Sonny Watkins grasped the rebound.

Bond received the ball from Sonny on the run and dribbled quickly into the middle. Jake sped down the left side while Mark filled the lane on the right. Bond made a sharp cut as if to drive to the hoop. When Wells stayed with him, Bathwaite whipped a sharp pass behind his back to Jake, who nestled a soft shot into the net.

Wells retrieved the ball to toss it inbounds. Bond had turned as if to get back on defense. Cole hadn't noticed that Bathwaite had reversed himself, and when Wells lobbed the ball to Marty Miller, casually standing at the free throw line, Bond shot between Miller and picked off the pass. The Raider guard easily laid the ball over the front of the rim as a panicked Wells launched himself, too late, in an attempt to block his opponent's shot. His momentum carried him into Bond's orange jersey after the shot. The shrill bleat of the referee's whistle was drowned out by the bedlam erupting from the orange and black rooting section.

"Foul on number 10 in white—after the shot. Basket is good. One and one free throws for number 11 in orange," Garry Worden yelled authoritatively.

Cole's carelessness on the throw-in, combined with Miller's lackadaisical effort, was made even worse by his unnecessary foul on the Raider guard. Bond now had an opportunity to make a four-point play if he could connect on the one-and-bonus free throws.

And he did exactly that. Madison Central's lead was cut to only two, 58-56, with 4:48 to go in the game.

Monday, October 23, 1961

There were no surprises when those hoping to make the Raiders squad scanned the roster for their names. Of the eighteen hopefuls still practicing last Friday, Coach O'Ryan had selected twelve boys for varsity positions. They were:

Aguirre, C. C.	Mannheim, Orson
Bathwaite, Bond	Ross, Jamie
Cotter, Joe	Seaberg, Josh
Danner, Mark	Skoon, Jake
Deal, Bobby Mack	Watkins, Sonny
Freebolt, Elmer	Willburn, Grover

THE HOOSIER GAME

After the final practice on Thursday before the season opener, Coach O'Ryan called his team members together. His remarks were not about tomorrow's clash with Zephersville, as the team expected. Instead, the coach challenged the players to consider his approach to the upcoming season and the opportunity each had to achieve something special.

"Last March, we met with each of you to discuss what you needed to improve at if you are to reach your capabilities as a player. It's evident that most of you have worked on your individual strengths and weaknesses that we talked about.

"You reported in reasonably good physical condition. You showed last year you were an unselfish bunch. Athletic Director Gottschalk has worked hard to upgrade our schedule to challenge your abilities.

"Now let me advise you of something very important. This is for each of you, not for me or Coach Barnhard. Not for your parents, your friends, or the coaches at the Totem Pole. Dedicate yourself from this moment on to give your best effort at all times. This is you seniors' last go round. The worst possible thought you can have when you've played your last game at Morgans Awe, is 'If I'd only.' Once this year is done, it's done, forever.

"It all starts tomorrow night with Zephersville. I'll show up ready to coach. I expect you to be ready to play. Any questions? Anybody have anything to say?

"Okay. Be in front of your locker at 7:20 sharp."

Generally, larger high schools refused to play in such a small bandbox gym as that of the Raiders, so games against stiffer opposition would require O'Ryan's squad to play on foreign courts. The coach believed that such competition in hostile circumstances would inure his players mentally, emotionally, and physically. By the time sectionals rolled around, O'Ryan wanted to have his kids "tournament tough."

Upper-level teams from Indiana, Kentucky, and Ohio had replaced less-competitive schools that Morgans Awe had played in the past. Blue Union, Shelbyville Prep, and Cade's Lick were highly rated teams among Kentucky high schools. Coach had lobbied for three years to enter his team in Kentucky's esteemed Pleasure Ridge South holiday tourney, with powerhouses Ferrin Creek and Shepherdton competing. Morgans Awe would play the host Thoroughbreds in the first game.

Among newcomers to the 1961-62 docket were Indianapolis McCormick and Jeffersonville Roosevelt, both high schools with a rich basketball tradition.

JAKE'S COON

Sitting among his teammates as the coach discussed routine procedures, Josh Seaberg felt a rush of emotion. He would be one of approximately 8,000 teenage boys populating the rosters of the 662 high school teams in Indiana who would be taking the court to begin the season. Every boy dreamed of standing at center court in Butler Fieldhouse in March, holding aloft the IHSAA state basketball championship trophy.

Firmly embedded in Josh's memory was that night in March 1954 when a school even smaller than his had triumphed against all odds to win the state title. That he could visualize himself and his teammates, with conviction, as the last team standing was precisely the attitude Coach O'Ryan had worked so diligently to embed in his squad.

Friday, November 3, 1961

Today, the student body was excused from last period for the traditional pep rally prior to the opening game of the season. Cheerleaders exhorted the crowd into a frenzy. In unison, they began to chant,

> *"Where, O where, is our team?*
> *Down in the dressing room, pickin' up steam.*
> *Where, O where, is our team—"*

Suddenly, the door that led downstairs to the locker room flew open, with Jake leading his teammates in single file up the steps. The students burst into loud cheers as the players, dressed in white shirts and thin ties, formed a line at center court. Coach O'Ryan approached the microphone stand where he would introduce each boy and make a few comments about the importance of the support of the student body to the success of the team.

Elected captains by their teammates, Jake Skoon and Josh Seaberg each made brief remarks about the team's resolve to have an outstanding season. Following the dismissal of the students—twenty minutes early, to the delight of the flock—the team members went below to don practice gear. A light run-through of offensive and defensive tactics ended with Coach O'Ryan praising the players for the work they had put into the preseason drills.

MAHS was sharp from the opening center-jump against the Cyclones of Zephersville High. The hugely partisan crowd greeted every Raider score with roars of approval, particularly as Morgans Awe scored the first eighteen points

THE HOOSIER GAME

before allowing a ZHS basket. Jake dropped in a long jumper to end the first quarter, giving Morgans Awe a 23-2 lead.

Behind Skoon's thirty-three points, the Raiders handled the Cyclones with surprising ease, an 88-60 triumph. As anticipated, Jake thrilled the home fans with a variety of medium and long jump shots, hitting on 12 of 20 field goal attempts and going nine-for-nine at the free throw line. Mark (15), Josh (12), and Bond Bathwaite (10) also scored in double figures and defended and rebounded very well.

Veteran Raider observers left certain they had witnessed the beginning of what could be a record-breaking basketball season.

Saturday, November 4, 1961

The jangling of the bell interrupted the lively discussion of the previous night's basketball game. Yozsef Czarnecki, a Slovenian immigrant, entered the establishment. His pocked face featured a perpetual smile of bad teeth. Yozsef, known as Joe, wore a dirt-stained denim jacket. His casual wave revealed rough, tobacco-stained hands. He offered his customary greeting, ""Co szia, hogy vagy," which to the assembly sounded like Ko-see-ya-hoya vahga.

"Hunky!" the occupants yelled as one.

A new member of the Totem Gang, Vince Roe, turned to the venerable Muck Wiley to ask, "What did he just say?"

"Well, it all depends on the dy-lek," Muck replied. "If Hunk's usin' the high Slovenie, he said I was the finest stud in southern Indiana. If it was the low version, he just called you a low-life gas bag."

All enjoyed Muck's rejoinder to the neophyte. Hunky joined in immediately with a comment on the local five's big win over Zephersville.

"I theenk ve vuss looky. No goot, dem Zeffers."

"Now, Joe, you jus' don't git it," Whitey Evans shot back. "You need ta stay outta argy-ments that shows yer ig-neerns."

"Yep, Hunkster. You bess leave the coachin' to us whut knows what we're talkin' about," followed the smug retort of Hick Brice.

"As I was sayin'," Earl Barnett injected, "I swear their center must a' been a Korea veter'n.

He sure wasn't no high school kid."

Others agreed.

"I'm bettin' he was ther bus driver," Whitey put in.

Vince added his take on it. "I heard Z'ville's coach had to pay ees bail in time to git him on the team bus."

The tinkling overhead announced the approach of two more clients coming in the door.

"Here come the Ass Twins—Jack n' Dumb," chortled the Chief.

Identical twins Arlo and Harlo Cartwell were born and bred in the hills outside of Morgans Awe. Both worked as maintenance men in the local school system. The men had looked like clones until Harlo got his face re-shaped in a knife fight with a Kentuckian at the Morgans Trail Bar. Subsequent attempts by Doc Gentry to return slices of Harlo's cheeks and nose from that nasty clash to their natural landscape resulted in a curious mosaic of scar tissue. Locals no longer had difficulty telling which was which. Chief claimed that Harlo's love life took off afterwards because he was less ugly carved up than he was before.

"Howdy, Chief. Ain't you s'posed to be back on the res-avation?" Arlo replied. George "Greasy" Smith was beneath the sheet in Treecat's barber's chair. He was the lone attorney in the small village. His clientele were mostly local drunks and chronic traffic offenders, with a few B & E specialists and small-time embezzlers, "for the flavor," as he had it. Beady eyes, a sneaky scowl, and thin mustache contributed to his reputation as an untrustworthy manipulator. His success in the court system seemed to be in direct proportion to the number and seriousness of indiscretions he knew about the judges who tried his cases.

"I hear you guys's other brother, Marlo, is with the FBI now," Greasy smirked. "They caught up with him in Luh'ville, didn't they?"

Arlo shot back, "I hear you lawyers wuz all bottle fed when you wuz babies. Shows even your mothers didn't trust you."

The Totem crowd hee-hawed loudly.

Harlo jumped in. "Yow, Greasy, the only thing you wouldn't steal is a red-hot stove."

The laughter climbed a few decibels as Smith, esquire, absorbed the abuse. They loved it whenever a rube threw the smug attorney Smith for a loss.

Wednesday, November 22, 1961

It was Thanksgiving break when Jimmy Dean's new hit had everyone humming "Big Bad John." His Raiders teammates adopted the song for Mark Danner.

THE HOOSIER GAME

Ev'ry mornin' at the mine you could see him arrive,
He stood six foot six and weighed two forty-five,
Kinda broad at the shoulder and narrow at the hip,
And everybody knew, ya didn't give no lip to Big John,
(Big John, Big John)
Big Bad John
(Big John)

The Raiders followed the easy victory against Zephersville with similar wins over their next four opponents. Coach O'Ryan's squad set a school record for points in one game in a 103-69 rout of Blue Union High. In another first, all five Morgans Awe starters tallied at least twenty points against the Bluegrass lads, led by Jake with 30, followed by Bond (24), Josh (21), and Mark and Sonny (each with 20).

After a high-scoring victory over Corydon Harrison (91-66), the Raiders traveled to well-regarded Bedford Adams. A last-second field goal by Jake Skoon gave the Raiders an impressive 81-79 win over the Miners on their home court.

On Thanksgiving holiday eve, Jake Skoon shattered his own school single-game scoring record with a forty-six-point tour de force against St. Isadore High School. Jake's amazing display of shooting included making 19 field goals in twenty-four attempts—most coming on jump shots far from the hoop—and eight straight free throws. Following the game, as Coach O'Ryan was interviewed by a sportswriter, he offered rare praise for an individual.

"Jake took full advantage of his teammates' great screens and sharp passes. Skoon was as efficient on the offensive end as any boy I've ever coached. He was nearly unstoppable."

Oddly, Jake's personal joy from his singular achievement would be short-lived.

Against the Saints, the great majority of Skoon's points came against St. Isadore's only black player, sophomore Willie Marston.

After the game, Jake and Josh emerged from the locker room together, short hair still dripping slightly from their recent showers. The pair moved toward the main exit where Jake's dad and several cronies stood reviewing the game. Norval Skoon's wide grin, watery eyes, slurred speech, and distinct odor of alcohol was a familiar condition. Other parents mingling nearby acknowledged him as the star player's father but were uncomfortable and embarrassed for him, and for Jake.

Mr. Skoon embraced his son, who, noting his dad's unsteady posture, unenthusiastically returned a brief hug of recognition.

Coach met Mrs. O'Ryan nearby. As they passed by, the elder Skoon remarked, "Man, Jake. You sure made that brillo-head eat your jock tonight!"

"Yep," Norval's friend agreed, "That boy was Jake's 'coon,' awright," making a pathetic play on the Skoon surname.

"I swear that jiggaboo was pale as a ghost by the end of the third quarter," said another, as all laughed jeeringly.

Coach O'Ryan froze in his tracks. He nodded to Mrs. O'Ryan, who urged Michael to let it go. She knew her request was in vain. She continued on her path to the parking lot.

Michael O'Ryan was ardently prejudiced—against rude and racist behavior. Having fought side-by-side with brave black soldiers in the South Pacific during World War II, Coach O'Ryan never made racist remarks or tolerated anyone in his presence who did.

Pivoting slowly, Coach returned to where the group was still engaged in their polluted humor. Jake stared at the floor in humiliation as the coach cast a withering look at the elder Skoon and his friends.

"Jake, you go on out and wait for your dad in the car."

Josh didn't need to be told to leave. He quickly exited the premises with Jake.

The adults' expressions turned somber at Coach O'Ryan's intrusion. The four men visibly squirmed and randomly shuffled their feet. Adam's apples bobbed nervously. They looked away to avoid the laser beam of contempt in the eyes of the outraged coach.

He began to speak with a calm but firm voice.

"Norval, your son played well tonight. As good offensively as any boy I've seen in a long time. And I salute you, too, for the wound you carry from fighting for your country."

The men relaxed a bit.

"I was twenty-five years old in March of 1945, with the Marines 5th Division, spending a little time on a placc you may have heard of—Iwo Jima. I was scared shitless, but stupid enough to have the 'gung-ho' piss and vinegar that got men killed on that awful rock. We were in a serious firefight with a bunch of damnnasty Japanese, when I somehow got out ahead of my unit. Before I realized it those Japanese boys had me in a comfy little crossfire. The only protection I had was my khakis and an ability to ooze down into the sand I was layin' in."

THE HOOSIER GAME

The men listened intently, wondering why Coach O'Ryan would be telling war stories after the ballgame.

"At that point I didn't give myself too much hope of spending the next Christmas holiday with the family. All of a sudden this black kid—I later learned his name was Arthur Maxey—slid in next to me, firing continuously at the source of the incoming rounds. We both jumped up and ran like hell back to our line where the rest of the guys—all of 'em white—were hunkered down, some cryin' and pissin' their pants.

"I jumped in safely. Arthur almost made it.

"Now this black teenager—who was not even supposed to be fighting on the front—saved my life freely and with no obligation, with courage a lot of the white boys lacked. His mother received the Purple Heart he earned with the wound that took his life.

"My oldest son is Max O'Ryan. That's short for his full name, Arthur Maxey O'Ryan. From what I've overheard from you, Norval, and your buddies, I doubt if anyone will be honoring a child with any of your names."

The coach made an about-face and strode briskly away, leaving four degraded men looking cheap and forlorn as he left the building.

22

HE'S NOT JIMMY RAYL, BUT...

Jourden Arena
9:29 p.m.

The Cougars appeared discombobulated as they brought the ball up the floor. The Raiders had picked them up with a soft press to try to force MC into an error. Wells barely got the ball across the midline in the allotted ten seconds. Sonny cleanly stole a pass from a harried Miller intended for Wells. Speeding down court all by himself, Watkins went up for the lay-up—and missed.

Coach O'Ryan pirouetted as if he was dodging buckshot. A collective gasp went up from the Morgans Awe stands.

Back on offense, the Cougars' Bratton brushed by Danner to receive a pass from Donel Satterwhite. The sophomore hesitated, then saw an open lane to the hoop. Sweeping through the Raider defense, he approached the basket only to lose control of his dribble and the ball, which bounced out of bounds.

Saul turned agonizingly and muttered to no one in particular, "Three thousand square feet of basketball floor and Bratton dribbles it off his foot."

Only 3:15 shown on the scoreboard. Tension in the building lay heavily upon everyone with a pulse. Marshall Seaberg had chewed his nails down to the quick. Betty missed half the action, dropping her head and eyes during especially critical moments.

Bond brought the ball slowly up the court, holding one hand aloft to signal an isolation play for Jake. Childs slipped between Skoon and the screener to slap the ball away. Five players in the vicinity threw themselves onto the floor in an attempt to secure the loose ball. At the bottom of the pile, both Watkins and Donel Satterwhite had their hands wrapped around the basketball.

"Jump ball," cried Blaise, both thumbs pointing skyward.

THE HOOSIER GAME

Satterwhite easily controlled the tip over Sonny. As Wells dribbled into the front court, the diminutive Cougar captain spotted Childs, fifteen feet to the left of the basket with no one guarding him. Seeing the breakdown in the Raiders' defense, Cole rifled a pass to his muscular teammate. Up to this point, Childs had attempted only one shot, an embarrassing clunker off the under edge of the backboard.

Reacting instinctively, Childs drove the ball hard for an open lay-up. As he started to leave his feet, Clay uncharacteristically stumbled, plowing headlong into Mark Danner, who had belatedly rushed to cut off Child's path to the hoop. Both players sprawled onto the floor, their limbs interlocked as if they were wrestling.

Referee Worden hesitated slightly before he would disqualify one of the two for the rest of the contest. Both coaches stood on tiptoes, awaiting the most critical referee's decision of the game.

Garry suddenly raised his left hand and placed it above the nape of his neck. At the same instant he thrust his clenched right fist dramatically forward, like a boxer punching his foe's solar plexus.

"Charging! Personal foul on number 52!" screamed the ref.

Clay Childs had committed his fifth foul. And Mark Danner hadn't.

Fortune's gamble had failed. Childs was disqualified for the final two minutes, twenty-nine seconds of the game. Saul used his team's fourth timeout to reconsider his options to defend Skoon.

On the sideline, O'Ryan had shed his sweat-soaked sports jacket and tie. In contrast, despite the heat generated by the lights and seven thousand screaming fans, Saul looked composed in his tailored suit, matching tie, and red boutonnière. Not a bead of perspiration dampened his brow.

Commentators Merle and Will could hardly believe what was taking place before their eyes.

"Every time the Raiders from Morgans Awe look as if they've used the last of their nine lives, they arise from the grave again! Merle, I feel privileged to be in this house tonight to witness two teams of teenagers battle as these kids have."

"This game has had more dips and turns than a switchback road in the Smokies. Against all odds, the spirited kids from Morgans have fought back. And guess what? They actually have a good chance to do the unthinkable by beating one of the favorites to win the state title!"

After Danner missed the first of the one-and-one free throw penalty, Satterwhite secured the rebound.

Cole Wells brought the ball into the Cougars' front court. His intended pass to Miller was deflected by Sonny into Jake's hands. Skoon dribbled the ball all the way to the

HE'S NOT JIMMY RAYL, BUT...

Raiders hoop and banked a scoop shot high off the backboard and into the net. Worden saw Satterwhite's slap on the shooter's wrist. Whistle and a foul.

In excess of seven-thousand fans were in a full-throated frenzy.

The Raiders regained the lead, 59-58, as Jake hit the free throw with only 2:18 to go.

Madison worked the ball around the perimeter of the Raiders' zone. Receiving a pass in the high post, DeVereaux spun quickly around Mark. In his rush to the hoop, the big center collided with Mark. No foul was called and Sonny was quick to recover the ball. He passed sharply to Josh, who was already sprinting up the left sideline. Seaberg found Jake at the center circle, who whipped the ball to Bond. Bathwaite received Jake's toss on the right wing of the developing three-lane fast break and rifled a pass to Josh, who immediately snapped it right back to the junior guard. When the lone defender, Miller, chose to cut off his path to the basket Bond hit Jake in stride with a perfectly timed pass. Skoon laid it in.

The basketball had not touched the floor on the sequence. Raiders by three, 61-58.

Morgans Awe fans were delirious with excitement. Raw emotions welled up from some primal place within the spectators. Throats were raw and eardrums were on overload from the continuous din. On the opposite side, Madison's faithful pleaded for their boys to rally.

This *was bona fide, 24-carat Hoosier Hysteria.*

Above the deafening roar, Will Peck observed that "Expressions on Cougar faces are sober, in the sense of a defendant anticipating a guilty verdict. This game has turned on the loss of their star, Weatherford. Central looks like a ship without a rudder."

Merle shouted into his microphone to his radio audience, "No question. DeWitt provided not only scoring, rebounding, and defense, but also quiet, determined leadership. Morgans Awe is now in complete control of this game!"

Just as Peck closed his remarks, Donel Satterwhite was called for traveling. The Raiders again capitalized on the unforced error when MAHS boldly attacked the basket. Josh made good on a short jumper on a pass from Sonny.

When Watkins knifed between Miller and DeVereaux to steal the errant pass and lobbed the ball to Bathwaite for the easy score, the Raiders seemed unstoppable. MAHS led 65-58 with exactly one minute left to play. The impossible had suddenly become probable.

"Time out, Norm!" Coach Fortune hollered to stop the action. He was down to his last timeout. His players returned to the sideline with heads hanging on their chests.

Abruptly, at the opposite end of the floor, a growing ovation from the Madison Central cheer block interrupted action on the floor. The noise grew in magnitude as the crowd followed a lithe figure with a heavily taped right knee striding toward the Cougars' huddle. Suddenly every MC rooter in the hall was standing, applauding wildly, as in a Saturday matinee when the cavalry suddenly shows up to save the wagon train from encircling Indians.

THE HOOSIER GAME

Coach O'Ryan looked up from his seat as the wounded DeWitt Weatherford strode gingerly past the Raiders' bench. Morgans Awe fans stood dumbfounded as the Cougar star rejoined his teammates.

Saturday, May 5, 2012

Rob and Margaret Dunfy walked up to greet Josh, Pat, Arnie, the Rosses, and the Willburns. All shared handshakes and hugs.

"Rob, your cologne smells so good, and familiar, too." Shirley remarked. "What is it?"

Margaret answered for him. "You won't believe what he did. Rob found a bottle of English Leather in an old box he'd saved from high school days! I was amazed that it held its scent."

"Now I remember where I'd smelled that before!" Pat giggled.

Clair, whom Jamie had met in college, had attended high school in Illinois. She laughed as she remembered that very popular gift for teenage males at the time.

"Our senior year, when we got back from Christmas vacation, every other boy smelled like he had been embalmed in English Leather!"

"My Lord, that overpowering odor really takes me back. For years, whenever the slightest trace of English Leather was in the air, I immediately thought of Christmas. No offense, Rob."

"None taken. Glad I could bring back some memories for ya'."

Arnie recalled another Christmas present every parent seemed to purchase for their teenage sons. "Mom got me one of those soap-on-a-rope gadgets."

"I g-g-got one of th-th-them d-d-dopey soap-ropes, t-t-too," Grover chimed in.

"He still had that thing when we got married," Shirley scoffed. "Hung it on the shower spigot. Seemed like it lasted for years!"

From Bear's speaker system flowed the sweet sound of Connie Francis's greatest hit, "Where the Boys Are."

Where the boys are, someone waits for me,
A smilin' face, a warm embrace,
two arms to hold me tenderly,
Where the boys are, my true love will be,
He's walkin' down some street in town,
and I know he's lookin' there for me.

HE'S NOT JIMMY RAYL, BUT...

"Whoa, hear that, Mother?" Rob said enthusiastically to Marge. "Let's dance!"

Like so many popular tunes of the sixties, Connie Francis's "Where the Boys Are" epitomized a teen's unrequited longing for true love. Its dreamy tempo made it perfect for slow dancing.

"You ole fool. We haven't danced in years."

"Yeah, but slow-dancin' always made you hot ta trot. I might git lucky in the motel t'night."

Marge rolled her eyes. "You orn'ry pup."

"Hey, Jock. Turn that up way high," Rob shouted to the DJ as he grabbed his wife and hurried toward the dance floor.

"Rob hasn't changed a bit," offered Josh.

"H-h-he's s-s-still p-plum c-c-c-razy," commented Grover.

"Fries!" a voice from behind shouted. "You're still alive. I thought you'd a' been shot n' kilt by a jealous husband by now."

Dwight Foster had been one of Arnie's best friends in high school. Packard didn't recognize the bent and wizened former classmate at first.

"Well, I did have a close one last week. But I outrun the crippled old codger."

As Dwight engulfed Fries in a bear hug, Arnie realized who the hoary character was.

"Dwight Foster, when the hell didja git outta prison?"

"Ever since that time I tried to strangle you, Fries, I've got a thousand cards and letters of congratulations, except they was upset I didn't finish the job. How ya' been, buddy?"

"Better'n I deserve, Dee, better'n I deserve."

The others agreed unanimously with Arnie on that note.

"Hey, Foster, don't you still owe me money?"

"Fries, you're the chinchiest ole fart—'scuse me, ladies—that ever walked upright. Tell 'em, Josh. Fries threw nickels aroun' like manhole covers."

Arnie and Dwight badgered one another to the utter delight of those at the table.

That scene was repeated over and again as others stopped to chat with Fries, the most popular scamp in the class of '62.

Sonny Watkins and his wife, Sherry, and Mark and Aura Lee Danner ambled over.

They borrowed chairs from the adjacent table and sat down.

THE HOOSIER GAME

Sonny fired a shot across Arnie's bow.

"Fries, you sure ain't changed in all these years. You're ugly as a goat's be-hind."

"We were just talkin' about you, too, Sonny. Josh tole me you're wicked, stupid, and obnoxious. I think you're just the opposite. You're obnoxious, stupid, and wicked."

"I might be all that stuff. But I could still beat any of you guys in a dash, with my good leg tied behind me."

Shirley turned to Sherry: "I apologize for these Cro-Magnons, Sherry. Shake the head of any of 'em and it'd sound like a BB in a boxcar."

Saturday, December 9, 1961

In an 81-59 thrashing of the Christian Soldiers of Jericho High School on December 1, Josh Seaberg had played the best game of his high school career thus far, scoring twenty-nine points and grabbing 12 rebounds. Afterward, in the dressing room, Josh was serenaded by his teammates with a playful rendition of "Joshua fit the battle of Jericho and Christian Soldiers came a-tumblin' down."

After defeating Bailor's Corner (75-61) and the Pit Stonemasons (77-60), Morgans Awe began to draw the notice of sportswriters and coaches around the state. Having won each of its nine games, the Raiders shot up to 18th in the week's statewide poll, the highest ranking in the history of the school.

Local scribe Ernie Stoddard noted in his latest game story that Morgans Awe had played every game thus far in the season before capacity crowds. In every town to which the Raiders traveled, friend and foe packed the house to see these remarkable lads play the Hoosier game.

Friday, December 15, 1961

Morgans Awe's success prompted a visit from one of Indiana's renowned sports scribes, Mac Barker. Along with peers such as *Indianapolis Star* writers Harrison Howard, Ray Marquette, and Bob Williams, and Jimmie Angelopolous of the *Indianapolis Times*, Barker had earned the respect and admiration of fans throughout the state. His daily column in the *Indianapolis Sun*—"Hoosier Hoops"—was must-reading for any follower of high school basketball.

Mac Barker was an old-fashioned reporter who sought and dwelled on the positive in sports. He loved his family, his church, and a bawdy joke, and had a

HE'S NOT JIMMY RAYL, BUT...

penchant for Kentucky bourbon. Mac delighted in the Indianapolis 500-mile race, but his full-time obsession was reserved for Indiana high school basketball.

During the basketball season Barker regularly traveled to any city, town, or crossroads where he might find a hot-shot teenager who was exciting the local populace with uncommon basketball skills. Often Mac's traveling partners would include Hoosier college coaches scouring the state for recruits.

He emphasized the charm and the natural innocence of high school sports and its players and coaches. Acclaimed as the dean of sportswriters in Indiana, Mac Barker coming to your school to see a game was tantamount to a visit from royalty. Fans everywhere recognized the portly Irishman with the beet-red face and beaming smile as he entered the gym. School officials, coaches, and admirers would descend on him prior to tip-off, some to express gratitude for his mere presence, some to shamelessly promote the local high school star, and others to listen as he spun yarns from a deep well of Hoosier basketball history. Mac loved to entertain others, always punctuating his tales with a contagious roar of laughter.

This Friday night he appeared at the tiny Morgans Awe bandbox to see for himself what all the noise was about. He had come to observe the 9-0 Morgans Awe Raiders—and Jake Skoon. The Raiders did not disappoint, dispatching Milton's Marvels, 79-72, in a surprisingly close contest.

Josh awoke early on Saturday morning as usual. Despite the rigors of a Friday night basketball game, he was normally out of bed by seven. He arose and slipped quietly to the front porch to retrieve the *Indianapolis Sun*. Turning straight to the sports section, he read what Mac Barker had written about the previous night's game.

KEEP YOUR EYE ON THESE COUNTRY BOYS; THEY'll STEAL A WALLET FROM A PICKPOCKET
By Mac Barker

There is no way to explain to the uninformed about the mass insanity that engulfs Hoosiers every November through March. Like the first lap of the Indy 500, Indiana High School basketball is something everyone should see at least once. The alien must travel to small towns to begin to understand how the game of basketball transforms normally civil Indiana citizens into a state of semi-lunacy every Friday and Saturday night in the tiny gyms dotting the landscape.

THE HOOSIER GAME

Your fat friend, who was inducted as an honorary member of the Morgans Awe pep club before the start of the game, once again witnessed a maelstrom of emotions in a classic barn-burner. It was bedlam from tip-off until the final gun.

Backroad Hoosier hamlets are peaceful and hospitable places—until game time. Last evening, two tiny communities who embrace one another like the Hatfields and the McCoys lined up before a frenzied crowd in the Morgans Awe gym. A citizen in a striped shirt stepped between two gangly teenagers and tossed a ball into the air. Mayhem followed.

It should be noted here that the town's fire marshal tried being inconspicuous at his post near the doors beneath the north basket at the 2nd Street goal-hall. They told us the gym capacity was 684. Perhaps he didn't notice that every square foot of space not occupied by the basketball court held one or more fire-breathing fans. Counting babies on mom- mas' laps and a few stray dogs wandering around, I'd put a bundle on my estimate of the crowd at 800 present and unaccounted for.

In a fiercely fought scrap, a game bunch of hustlers from Milton unexpectedly pushed the undefeated Raiders to the limit, finally succumbing, 79-72, to Coach Mike O'Ryan's lads and his spellbinding scoring machine, Jake Skoon.

At 6-2 and maybe 150 pounds—with a pocketful of rocks from Brushy Creek in his trunks—Skoon dazzled the crowd and this humble observer by consistently canning high-arching jump shots that nestled into the net as soft as a cat with sore paws.

Two things you can't coach in basketball: to be tall, and to have a great shooter's touch. A player can become good—even very good—through hard work and passion for the game. But great natural shooters of a basketball are a breed apart. God-given, superior hand-to-eye coordination is at the core of the gifted scorer, just like Ted Williams hitting a baseball or Minnesota Fats handling a pool cue. Practice, practice, and more practice hones the craft.

Innate forces of competitiveness bring out the best in a gunslinger like Skoon. He's fearless, bred not to dread missing a few, because he knows he can hit the next five from the same spot. A boy doesn't average

HE'S NOT JIMMY RAYL, BUT...

27-plus points a game if he's shy about lettin' her fly. Jake Skoon is just such a talent.

He can score in a variety of ways. But the accuracy of his picture-perfect jumper is remarkable. I swear he smoked a couple from Scott County. From fifteen feet in, his jump shot is as good as a layup. The Raider Rifle finished with 35 points on the evening.

Skoon isn't Jimmy Rayl—but you have to look twice to tell the difference. The rainbow arc of his jumper and that special "pop" as ball meets twine is reminiscent of the Splendid Splinter from Kokomo, who is now wearing out the nets at Indiana University.

And Skoon's teammates understand who butters their bread. Jake's coterie does a yeoman's job of peeling defenders off of his uniform with an intricate maze of brutal—but legal—screens devised by the canny O'Ryan.

This old Navy vet wouldn't care to crash amain into the Raiders 6-4, 210 pounds of blue steel named Mark Danner. Trust me, if he's wearing basketball duds instead of bib overalls, beware. He'll take your breath away if you are brave, or silly enough, to risk running through one of his lamppost picks. Aside from discouraging opponents from guarding Skoon too tightly, he protects the lane like it's his farmland and anyone in a different color jersey is a squatter.

It would be heresy to suggest that the currently undefeated Madison Central Cougars might fail to win their sectional tourney this year. But a word to the wise—any team that tangles with these Ohio Valley boys better bring its "A" game. Morgans Awe is a skillful and hungry bunch of Raiders.

Mac's column provided fodder for commentary by Morgans Awe uptown coaches for weeks afterward.

23

BOMP-BA-BA-BOMP-BA-BOMP-BA-BOMP-BOMP

Jourden Arena
9:30 p.m.

With sober expressions the Morgans Awe players reacted to Weatherford's dramatic reappearance. Sonny found himself scanning the overjoyed Madison crowd. Jake stole a worried glance at the scoreboard.

To regain his unsettled players' attention, O'Ryan shouted in his hoarse, raspy voice, "Hey! You guys are acting like we're behind instead of ahead by seven! LISTEN TO ME! We're where we are because you've earned it. Everything they've thrown at us, we've handled. You've played better, smarter, and tougher than Madison in every way."

The Raider mentor continued as the scoreboard buzzer sounded.

"Nothing's changed. Maintain the pace of our offense. If you have a good shot, don't hesitate. Stay aggressive at both ends of the court. Now is not the time to be timid or to play scared. Go right at 'em! Reach down deep! This is YOUR moment!"

The Raiders broke the huddle with the confidence that they could—no, that they would—finish the job.

During the timeout Saul had designed a play for Weatherford. He needed to see how his 6-6 star would respond to his injury. Cole Wells took the inbounds toss and drove into his frontcourt. Receiving the ball near the free throw line, DeWitt patiently maneuvered Mark backward, closer to the basket. The smooth senior center then canned a beautiful fall-away jumper as Mark backed away to avoid fouling.

Madison Central now employed its stifling full court press. Inspired by the return of Weatherford, the Cougars displayed renewed energy as they hounded the Raiders. Battling to get the ball across the centerline before 10 seconds had expired, Jake saw Sonny break

THE HOOSIER GAME

loose near the free throw line. His pass was on target, but as Watkins went up for the shot, Satterwhite shot like a blur out of nowhere, smothering Watkins's attempt and snatching the ball out of the air.

Wells barreled down the court and delivered the ball to fellow guard Miller, who drove to the hoop as Bond retreated on defense. Both leaped at the same time and Miller's lay-up was too hard, caroming high into the air off the back of the rim.

Trailing the play, DeWitt timed his jump perfectly and with one hand jammed the ball ferociously through the basket. The volume of sound reverberating off the ceiling and walls was ear-spitting. The Cougars were back to within three, 65-62.

It was hand to hand combat on the court. These impassioned teenagers were leaving nothing in reserve. The fight was too momentous, the victory so crucial that every player refused to give an inch.

With forty-three seconds remaining, Satterwhite fouled Mark, who hit one of two free tosses.

It was Madison's turn. The ball again went inside to Weatherford. This time, however, his shot bounded off the back rim. Mark retrieved the ball, but as he attempted his two-hand, overhead pass to Bond, Weatherford deflected the ball from behind. An alert Marty Miller snatched the loose ball and laid it off the glass. Morgans lead was down to a slim two point margin.

Twenty-seven seconds remained when Coach O'Ryan called time. Norm Blaise leaned over to remind Michael that he had called his final timeout.

"That's five, Coach. You're out of timeouts."

This was a pivotal moment, when victory or defeat hinged on what would happen in the next few seconds. If Morgans Awe failed to score, Madison could tie the game.

Michael designed a play to get the ball into Jake's hands. His teammates would set a progression of screens to get him an open look at the basket or to force the defense to foul.

When the ball was put into play, the plan immediately broke down. Miller tipped the inbounds pass and a wild scramble found players from both teams diving for the loose ball. At the bottom of the scrum, Sonny had the ball in his grasp, with Karl DeVreaux wrapped around him. Referee Worden signaled a held ball, Sonny to jump for possession against the brawny DeVreaux.

Madison controlled the tip. As the clock wound relentlessly downward, Cole Wells dribbled to his right and handed the ball off his outside hip to Miller, blocking Sonny. As Wells rolled toward the basket, Bond was slow to switch, leaving Cole unguarded under the hoop. With no Raider defender within ten feet of the senior he waved his hands frantically, calling for the ball. Marty finally saw his wide-open teammate and delivered a

BOMP-BA-BA-BOMP-BA-BOMP-BA-BOMP-BOMP

sharp pass. Wells banked the ball easily off the glass as a flailing Seaberg arrived too late to help.

Tie game, 66 all!

The amber lights on the scoreboard showed fifteen seconds remained when the ball dropped through the net. Sonny stepped out of bounds and tossed the ball to Jake. As he dribbled up the court, Skoon was dogged step for step by Wells. Miller rushed over to help Cole double-team Skoon, forcing the Raider ace to pick up his dribble. Both pressed closely to Jake, entangling legs and arms as the Raider star looked frantically for someone to pass to. As the Cougar guards hacked Jake's arms and hands in trying to dislodge the ball, Jake fell to the floor. Wells landed on top of the sprawling Jake, as the Morgans Awe rooters screamed hysterically for a foul. But no whistle had blown. Miller grabbed the ball as it slipped from Skoon's hands and raced up the court.

As the final seconds ticked away many in the crowd chanted, in unison, "Ten—nine—eight—" Weatherford sliced through the lane and Miller delivered a perfect bounce pass to the onrushing Cougar center. DeWitt caught the ball, put on the brakes and leapt upward, softly shooting his dependable jumper, only to see it tick the rim. DeVreaux muscled over Mark to tip the ball up. Too long.

Weatherford swooped in from the right side, leaped and desperately tipped the ball off the backboard.

The ball caromed off the glass, lipped the inside of the front rim, and began to roll, slowly, agonizingly around the hoop. Players from both teams froze.

It slithered around the rim and—dropped through!

At some point during that interim, the report of the gun blasted in the background. *Did the shot count?*

Saturday, May 5, 2007

Class president Roger Cordell led the chorus of tinkling wineglasses to gain the attention of the attendees.

"I want to welcome graduates and members of their families to the fiftieth reunion of the greatest class ever at Morgans Awe!"

After a few requisite stale jokes, Cordell rose to introduce "Miss Ima Spinster," former Morgans Awe teacher. Disguised in an ankle-length, faded brown granny dress, with long sleeves, a high neck, and laced collar, Miss Spinster was actually Susan Jonquin. Her hair was wound in a tight bun and she wore no makeup. Ima wore plain, rimless glasses on the end of her nose.

THE HOOSIER GAME

Her classmates welcomed Miss Spinster with hearty laughter and prolonged applause. In a harsh, screechy voice, the schoolmarm immediately admonished the students for bad behavior. The old bag decided that what these incorrigibles could use was a good pop quiz of historical "facts" pertaining to their high school days.

She directed her wooden pointer at Randy Marks and growled, "Who was voted most likely to end up in a penitentiary?"

Among several recalcitrant boys at MAHS, Randy was known for his rebellious ways.

"I guess that'd be me, Miss Spinster," he admitted.

Arnie Packard immediately arose to protest.

"I was robbed when they put that in the yearbook! Because Randy won, my parents raised their expectations. I had to lead an upstandin', pure Christian life after that."

Fries' confession produced the hoots it deserved.

When questioned about how many presidents class members had lived under, no one came up with the right answer. Most claimed it was twelve (Truman, Eisenhower, Kennedy, Johnson, Nixon, Ford, Carter, Reagan, Bush 41, Clinton, Bush 43, and Obama). The correct answer was thirteen. The grads had been toddlers at the end of Franklin D. Roosevelt's third term.

"Who was the most annoying teacher? Excluding present company, of course."

Several answered in unison, "Genghis Stroop!"

Marvin Stroop, a math instructor was known for swilling Pepto-Bismol to calm his constantly irritated bowels and for his loathing for any male person between the ages of 13 and nineteen. More than one boy (never a girl) felt the sting of Stroop's sturdy paddle. If he detected any suspicious shenanigans taking place behind his back while diagramming formulas, he whacked first and asked questions later.

Max Williams was quick to provide the answer to another query, "What was the first 3-D movie we ever saw?"

"*Bwana Devil*! All I 'member was these wild-eyed nateeves throwin' spears and me a-duckin' em."

Susan continued with, "Who was chosen as Most Likely to Succeed—and did?"

BOMP-BA-BA-BOMP-BA-BOMP-BA-BOMP-BOMP

All eyes shifted in Pat Sargossa Randell's direction. She blushed as her classmates extended a warm applause recognizing her award-winning career in broadcasting.

The entire class stood and clapped enthusiastically for Sonny Watkins when Susan asked who in the 1962 class was an American hero.

The schoolmarm next asked Bear Billings to stand and sing the meaningless opening syllables of a popular 1961 song. Adapted to modernize Rogers and Hart's 1934 classic, *Blue Moon*, the Marcels had added a unique refrain. In his baritone voice, Bear blasted out, *a cappella*:

> *Bomp-ba-ba-bomp ba-bomp-ba-bomp-bomp-bomp*
> *ba-bomp-ba-bomp*
> *a-dang-a-dang-dang, a ding-a-dong ding,*
> *Blue moon, blue moon, dip-da-dip-da-dip,*
> *Blue, blue, blue moon, dip-da-dip-da-dip,*

Then the class joined in, gaily recalling,

> *Blue, blue, blue moon, dip-da-dip*
> *Bomp-ba-ba-bomp, a-ba-ba-bomp-ba-ba-bomp*
> *a-dang-a-dang-dang-dang, a ding-a-dong-ding,*
> *Blue moon, you saw me standing alone,*
> *Without a dream in my heart,*
> *Without a love of my own.*

After the rowdy rendition, Miss Spinster asked who had traveled the farthest to the reunion. Mark raised his hand to say, "I drove here from China. Anybody beat that?"

Since China, Indiana, was less than ten miles north, Susan quickly dismissed Mark's claim. Wanda Jones won the prize by revealing she had journeyed from Kwigillingok, Alaska, population 354.

The final question of the quiz was the requisite standard, "Who has the most kids and grandkids, combined?"

Married 44 years with eight grown children and nineteen grandkids, Bobby Mack and Sue Deal proved to be the most prolific of those present.

Before allowing the class to turn attention to table conversation, it was Roger's final duty to read the dreadful necrology report. One by one, classmates who had gone to their greater reward were named, accompanied by a brief moment of silence. Why this ghastly tradition survived as a reunion staple, nobody seemed to know. But no one ever suggested, at least publicly, that the appalling practice die a death of its own.

Roger Cordell returned to the microphone. He asked that each class member stand and take just a few minutes to introduce themselves and tell a few things about their lives. This is always dangerous business, especially when someone begins with the phrase, "Well, the first year after graduation. . ." because that usually means a long, tedious soliloquy, touching the highlights of all subsequent fifty years. Fortunately—except for one noted instance—classmates generally stayed within the limits of three or four minutes of self-indulgence.

It was Dale Lammers who tortured his increasingly squirming fellow graduates with a creative twist on recounting his life events. Opening his narrative, Dale explained he would use the individual letters of Morgans Awe to convey what their school had meant to him.

"M is for the *many* blessings attending our school brought to me." Lammers spent a minute and a half elaborating on the advantages of an education at MAHS.

"O is for the outstanding graduates gathered here tonight," burned another 180 seconds.

By now his wary classmates began to do the math. Let's see. Ten times two-to-three minutes—this could go on for half-an-hour! Oblivious to the audience's increasingly restless deportment, Dale slogged on.

"And, lastly, E stands for…"

Finally, nineteen minutes, thirty-five seconds later—by Shirley's watch—the oration came to a close.

Arnie broke the complete and awkward silence that followed, rising to exclaim, "Dale, I'm damned glad we didn't go to the Massachusetts Institute of Technology, or we'd all a-died a' old age by now!"

"Just Arnold being Arnold," Josh whispered, as the house roared.

Friday, December 22, 1961

The next opponent, Shelbyville (Kentucky) Prep, was another worthy foe from south of the Ohio River. Unexpectedly, Jake ran into a dogged defender who accomplished what other teams focused on stopping MAHS's star had failed to do—he held Skoon below double-figure scoring for the entire game.

BOMP-BA-BA-BOMP-BA-BOMP-BA-BOMP-BOMP

The determined, physical Thoroughbred senior guard Pat Lair—playing Jake straight up man-to-man—harried a frustrated Skoon into a horrid 2 for 17 shooting performance. Before fouling out in the final quarter, the stocky Lair allowed the Raiders' prolific scorer only eight points. Taking up the offensive slack, Bond had his best game with 24 points and Mark Danner dominated the boards.

A relieved Coach O'Ryan observed afterwards that "If you'd told me before the game that Jake would score only eight points and we would still win, I would have very much doubted your prediction."

Despite missing Jake's firepower, Morgans escaped with a 65-59 triumph.

Thursday, December 29, 1961

Last July, when athletics director Gottschalk informed Coach O'Ryan that the Raiders' bid to play in the Pleasure Ridge (KY) Holiday Tournament had been accepted, the coach was ecstatic. Three highly rated teams from the Bluegrass State—Sheperdston (currently 11-2), host Pleasure Ridge (13-1), and Ferrin's Creek (9-3), ranked 16th, 9th, and 18th, respectively—would comprise the opposition in the one-day event.

Although Morgans Awe (12-0) was unbeaten to date, the only Indiana school in the tournament field was still a decided underdog. Measured against the three Kentucky powerhouses, O'Ryan would learn if his squad was talented, poised, and tough enough to play with top-notch competition.

The Raiders had drawn the Colonels from Ferrin's Creek in the tourney opener. Despite the fact that the MAHS student body was off for Christmas break, two busloads of teenagers crossed the Ohio River to support their team. In addition, parents and a high number of Morgans Awe resident fans made the eighty-mile trip to Pleasure Ridge.

After Morgans Awe—led as usual by Jake Skoon with 25 points—defeated the Colonels, 80-67, Sheperdston scored a mild upset over the host team, 76-72. Immediately after the final gun, the sporting press and knowledgeable fans began to speculate on the potential for a shootout between Jake (averaging 27 points per contest) and the current Kentucky high school scoring leader Billy Don Darvin (38 per game) of the Rebels. Darvin had hit his average on the nose in the afternoon triumph over Pleasant Ridge.

In the tourney title game that night the two sharpshooters didn't disappoint. Skoon poured in 40 points, while his counterpart, Billy Don, put on an astounding offensive display, hitting twenty-one field goals on 25 attempts.

THE HOOSIER GAME

It took an extra period for Sheperdston to finally subdue the Raiders. Billy Don's 48 points made the difference as Morgans Awe suffered its first loss, 92-89.

In brief remarks to his team in the dressing room afterward, Coach O'Ryan praised them for their gutty performance against the tough and talented Rebels. Rarely did the coach find anything pleasant to say after a loss, but tonight he'd seen his group of teenagers outplay a formidable foe for much of the game, equaling the intensity and skill of the Sheperdston five. Only the extraordinary play of Billy Don Darvin enabled the Rebels to win in the final minute.

In his post-game remarks to the media, O'Ryan saluted Sheperdston Coach Bob Maxville for a very effective game plan and his on-the-court adjustments that made the difference in the contest. Teasing the journalists, Michael referred to Darvin as "*rarissime.*" Trying to avoid being shown up by a hick school coach, sportswriters from major newspapers in Louisville and Lexington simply nodded in agreement, even though none knew whether the Morgans Awe coach had praised or belittled the Rebel star. Less-erudite colleagues looked askance until, to the relief of those present, an innocent writer from tiny Gap Knob asked what that meant. O'Ryan merely chuckled, awaiting the next question.

Saturday, January 6, 1962

Sitting behind bus driver Clem Marshall, Michael O'Ryan shifted uneasily as he contemplated the Raiders' first game of the New Year. Traveling to play Indianapolis McCormick High School on West Washington Street—his team's longest road trip of the season—the coach was concerned about how his squad would respond after its loss to Sheperdston. Although the team had excellent practices this week, O'Ryan would be on alert for signs of doubt and wavering confidence.

McCormick's roster included seven players from their city championship football team. Like most schools on the Morgans Awe schedule, the Redskins would have a distinct advantage in height and strength.

As a result of the recent defeat at the hands of Sheperdston, MAHS had dropped out of the sportswriters top twenty. The game tonight would give them the opportunity to show the Indianapolis media that their 13-1 record was not a fluke. Sitting near the scorer's table, Mac Barker was telling his counterparts along press row that they were about to see a team from one of the

BOMP-BA-BA-BOMP-BA-BOMP-BA-BOMP-BOMP

smallest schools in the state beat McCormick, one of the largest Hoosier high schools with an enrollment of 2,120 students.

The skeptics became believers when Morgans Awe exploited the Redskins' fatal weakness—lack of foot speed—to win, 79-60. Time after time the Raiders raced up the court for easy fast-break baskets. MAHS still looked fresh when the final buzzer sounded while McCormick's bulky players looked dead tired.

When asked by reporters why his team had lost, a disgruntled Redskins Coach Maury DeLaun responded tersely: "Lactic acid. Morgans Awe was simply in better condition than we were. I can promise that won't happen again," he said for his players' benefit.

Jake's twenty-nine points led the Raiders but sportswriters there wanted to know about Mark Danner, who dominated his bigger foes in the white and crimson jerseys.

One Indianapolis radio broadcaster spoke for others when he posed the question, "We've heard a great deal about Skoon and he certainly lived up to his reputation. But what about this Danner kid? He was a man among boys under the hoop. Grabbed twenty-one rebounds, scored 15 points, and taught a lesson about unsavory play to a huge Redskin!"

Laughing gently, Coach O'Ryan answered the query with, "I guess you noticed that Mark takes great offense when any teammate of his is abused."

The Raiders' pivot man had caught the eyes of the press media during an incident early in the contest. McCormick had seized the opening tip and moved the ball into the frontcourt where Marvin Scotie, the Redskins' leading scorer, nailed a fifteen-foot jump shot. The boys from Indy immediately set up into a tight man-to-man full court press.

Josh Seaberg trotted up the court, looking back over his shoulder in case the guards needed help against the pressing defense. Thurman Janovich, who at 6-4 and 220 pounds had been named to the All-State football team, crouched at the midcourt line directly in Seaberg's path. With both referees focused on the action in the backcourt, Janovich suddenly launched a forearm at Josh, who hadn't seen the burly Redskin in his path. The unexpected shot to his chest dropped Josh to the floor, desperately seeking oxygen.

The refs hadn't seen the crime—but Mark had. Following two exchanges of possession, Scotie attempted another shot. All ten players collapsed into the key area, battling for the rebound. Josh snared the missed try and whipped a pass to Bond to initiate a Raider fast-break. While nine players retreated to the opposite end, one lay in a fetal position near the McCormick basket, holding

THE HOOSIER GAME

his groin. The refs had missed this foul, too. After he recovered, the contrite Janovich had learned what many players in similar circumstances already knew. One didn't mess with a teammate of Mark Danner.

Generally, post-game meals consisted of a sack lunch, with each player receiving a cold cut sandwich, an apple, and a small carton of milk. Mark always engaged in bargaining for another teammate's sack, for he would snarf his own, which didn't nearly satisfy his voracious appetite.

Tonight there would be no sack lunches. Departing from the norm, Athletic Director Gottschalk directed Clem to turn into a parking lot on South Madison Avenue at a restaurant with a giant replica of an Indian tee-pee on the roof.

The victorious Raider team would dine at the popular Tee-Pee restaurant. Gottschalk smiled as he handed each player, cheerleader, and manager a five-dollar bill—an amount that would buy a substantial meal by the standards of the day. Josh and Jake laughed as Mark Danner pulled an extra $2.50 from his pocket to purchase a second huge cheeseburger and two slices of pecan pie.

Friday, January 26, 1962

Returning to the home court for relatively easy wins over the next three foes—Sycamore Creek (90-75), Cross Tracks (74-48), and Jeffersonville Roosevelt (80-63) high schools—Morgans Awe had begun to draw notice and respect from other coaches and writers across the state.

Tonight the Raiders had an opportunity to avenge a loss from last season that they believed they gave away. The taste of the bitter 93-90 defeat at the hands of Seymour Jefferson had lingered. The Big Green had returned all of its starters, had beaten 17 of nineteen foes thus far, and was rated 14th in the state rankings.

Because of the demand for tickets from Seymour Jefferson's rabid fans, Morgans Awe followers were allowed only 100 tickets—and those were in the highest row in the arena. So when the Raiders took the floor to warm up, they faced a sold-out audience of 4,100, all ardently partisan for the Big Green.

As tournament time approached, Michael O'Ryan left no stone unturned in preparing his squad for the sectional. He had called a trusted friend, Herschel Johns, who was a successful coach in the Illinois high school ranks. Coach O'Ryan, seeking an independent view of his squad's strengths and weaknesses, asked Johns, who had not previously seen Morgans Awe play, to scout the Raiders. Athletic Director Gottschalk had reserved a ticket for Johns, who sat with the Morgans Awe crowd, taking notes on the action below.

BOMP-BA-BA-BOMP-BA-BOMP-BA-BOMP-BOMP

The contest was, like last year, a hard-fought struggle. With a comfortable 14-point lead at the end of the third quarter, the Big Green appeared to have thwarted MAHS again. However, a disrupting full court press allowed Seymour only seven points in the final quarter and Jake Skoon shot lights out to rally his team to a 65-62 victory.

The small contingent of Morgans Awe fans who witnessed the comeback would tell friends and neighbors back home that this was the Raiders' greatest win in memory.

Staying overnight at the O'Ryan's home, Johns and Michael stayed up well past midnight as Herschel delivered his report. Much of what was revealed affirmed what Coach O'Ryan already knew about his team. Hearing it from a credible peer only made Michael more confident that his high opinion of his players' skills and character was legitimate.

Herschel Johns' overall impressions proved to be complimentary of his coaching friend. Among his observations was that squad members all seemed to understand and accept their roles within the team concept.

"While the offense is, in my view, tilted a bit too much toward Skoon, your boys do an excellent job of screening and passing to open up shots for him. Jake's a pure shooter but isn't naturally athletic. He's only an adequate ball handler, but he moves well without the ball to find screens to get open.

"Bathwaite and Seaberg are capable scorers within limits. Watkins is a good garbage man. With everyone focused on Jake, Sonny often finds himself roaming free near the basket. He gets open looks by being clever and by coming up with a surprising number of rebounds. I'm impressed with Bond Bathwaite. He's what I call an 'obstinate' competitor. He's fully dedicated to winning.

"I really like Josh. He's a steady, heady, all-around solid player, with a nice 10-to-15-foot jumper. He rebounds and handles the ball well and is totally unselfish.

"Danner is the true leader of the team. He is strong-willed and tough, and his high energy and competitive nature makes your other players better. He keys the defense in the middle and controls the defensive board. His outlet passes to start the fastbreak are exceptional. Unfortunately, he is your only physical presence. If Danner stays out of foul trouble you've got a real shot at tournament time.

"Your team had trouble figuring out Seymour's zone. Frankly, I was surprised that their coach stopped playing it. You'll need to do a better job of attacking the zone concept."

THE HOOSIER GAME

Here, Coach O'Ryan interrupted.

"Herschel, we have a zone offense that we've only used in practice. It's a variation of Dean Smith's four corners. We've not shown it in a game so we can use it in the tournament, hopefully against Madison. It's a gamble not working on it under game conditions. But I don't want Saul getting a sneak preview."

"Good. I should have guessed you were hiding an ace up your sleeve," Johns replied.

"Defensively, both Watkins and Seaberg are tenacious man-to-man defenders. Sonny plays bigger than his size and does a good job blocking bigger men off the defensive board. But it's his fearlessness as a competitor that caught my eye. Has he punched anyone this season?" Johns laughed.

"I think the guy he'd most like to punch is yours truly," O'Ryan answered. "Sonny backs down to no one."

Returning to the report, Herschel pointed out that "Bathwaite takes too many risks on defense, especially when he leaves his man to try for a steal. But he generally uses good judgment when he does.

"As to Skoon, what can I say? He is a real detriment to your team defense. I'm impressed with how you manage to hide him. Your players are quick to react when Jake loses his man, switching off and sliding into the lane to cut off his man's path to the basket.

"Your trapping press defense caused panic in Seymour's guards. It helped that their big men failed to come to the ball to help out. Once your guys smelled blood, they became even more intense.

"In a nutshell, Mike," Johns summarized, "I think you have a special group of kids. They have above average quickness, but lack of size will be trouble against a tall, athletic team.

"Your first five can play with anyone, in my judgment, but you have no depth. Except for Willburn and his size, the bench contributes little. Fatigue can have a major impact if you can't afford to rest the frontliners.

"But the bottom line is this: your kids know how to win. They play as hard and as together as any team I've seen this year. That includes the state of Illinois and what little I've seen of Indiana teams we've played.

"And one last thing I'm certain of—they have the best damn coach in the Hoosier state."

That was a high compliment coming from a veteran, very successful high school basketball coach. Michael O'Ryan was grateful for his longtime friend's personal comment and gained even more faith in the teenagers he was coaching.

BOMP-BA-BA-BOMP-BA-BOMP-BA-BOMP-BOMP

Friday, February 5, 1962

Morgans Awe School District bus #16 bumped and swayed along U.S. 50 on its way to Cincinnati. The outside temperature was below freezing. Inside, the ancient heating system rarely reached sixty degrees on chilly winter trips. Bus driver Clem Marshall constantly fought against frost forming on the windshield, as the heat from the defroster was a hit-and-miss proposition.

Tonight the team would meet highly regarded Archbishop Manyan, a Catholic high school in downtown Cincy. To pass the time on lengthy road trips, a favorite form of entertainment for the boys was making top ten lists, such as best movies, worst team nicknames, top teen idols, sexiest actresses, ugliest dogs—basically any theme or subject they could disagree on.

Coach O'Ryan didn't insist on absolute silence on the bus as some coaches did. Quiet conversation was acceptable as long as it stayed below an acceptable decibel level.

Sometimes, in lowered voices, the boys would mock, in jest, Coach O'Ryan's homespun platitudes, adages, and malapropisms. The coach quoted poetry, historical references, military leaders, Martha Raye, and philosophers—ancient and contemporary—along with cab drivers, barmaids, and plumbers.

Orson Mannheim could do a spot-on impersonation of the coach. His teammates had to stifle their laughter on the bus when Mannheim would mimic the coach's knitted brow, serious demeanor, and husky voice, and say things like, "There's always free cheese in a mousetrap, Deal," or "You can't make pigs by runnin' the sausage machine backwards, Willburn," or "Pair off by threes, men," and Orson's personal favorite, "You don't attend many MENSA meetings, do you, Danner?"

Debating the worst songs of the day, Arnie Packard and Bobby Mac Deal were deadlocked over whether Tab Hunter's rendition of "Young Love" or Fabian's "Turn Me Loose" was the biggest insult to popular music.

"Hunter had the looks of Adonis and the voice of Cheeta," Arnie argued.

Bobby Mac countered with "Fabian was some fool a record exec pulled off the streets of Philly to prove he could make a teenage idol out of *anyone*. He was dead wrong on Fabian."

Jamie Ross interrupted to guide the conversation to another favorite category.

THE HOOSIER GAME

"Okay, okay you guys. Let's name the best belly-rub songs," referring to slow-dance tunes.

"'Smoke Gets in Your Eyes!'" led off Sonny Watkins.

"'Sleepwalk,' by Santo and Johnny," offered another.

"Anything by Johnny Mathis."

"'A Summer Place.'"

"No way, Jose. Nothin' tops Anka's 'Put Your Head on My Shoulder,'" Mark said emphatically.

"'I Can't Help Falling in Love' by Elvis gets my vote," Josh remarked of the song he and Pat Sargossa had adopted as their own.

C. C. Aguirre asked, "What about Connie's 'Where the Boys Are?' Great movie, great song."

"You guys are all wrong. Best ever was 'I Only Have Eyes—'"

At this point, the bus turned into the parking lot at Manyan, ending for now the light-hearted banter. It was time to focus on basketball.

When the Raiders trotted out for the pregame warm-up they were met with a chorus of derisive cat-calls, boos, and abusive language from the all-boy student body. The ancient gym—filled to the rafters—held fewer than 500 fans, but this would be the loudest venue the Raiders had played in this season.

The Irish rooters came in all manner of dress, some with hilarious, mismatched clothes, others with bare chests painted in the kelly green colors of the school, and at least one ape costume.

The boys were rowdy and ready to rumble. A group of boys within the crowd would shout a creative, but generally humorous, insult at the opponents. Another group would try to top that with an even more derisive put-down of the enemy.

The school band added to the raucous atmosphere, playing the fight song during every break in the action. Cheerleaders from nearby Saint Mary of the Woods brought high energy and spirit to the constant noise. And the PA announcer was shamelessly partisan, urging the home crowd to cheer ever louder during the contest. Lost in the clamor was the handful of spectators who had driven up from Morgans Awe.

Even fans of the Raiders had to admit that some of the antics of the Irish students were clever. During a timeout near the end of the first half, one of the officials stood holding the basketball under one basket when the Manyan band struck up a lively tune. The Morgans Awe crowd was astounded when that referee dropped the ball and met one of the Saint Mary's cheerleaders in the middle of the floor to engage in a vigorous jitterbug!

BOMP-BA-BA-BOMP-BA-BOMP-BA-BOMP-BOMP

Like most of the people in the arena, the visitors had not seen a Manyan student—complete with whistle, striped shirt, and black pants—trade places with the real ref, who had disappeared beneath the bleachers. As the couple danced feverishly, the crowd finally caught on to the deception. Loud cheers followed the routine as the professional official returned to the court.

The very physical game ended in a rout, with the Raiders playing *toro* to Manyan's *torero*. The final score was Irish 72, MAHS 55. Josh, Mark, Sonny, and Bond got into early foul trouble, each ultimately fouling out of the contest. The discrepancy in the number of free throws made and attempted—Manyan's 28 of 42 to 6 of 9 for Morgans Awe—was significant enough that O'Ryan was ejected for only the second time in his coaching career.

It occurred with two minutes remaining in the game. Danner, Josh, and Sonny had already been disqualified by the two officials. Now a delayed call sent O'Ryan into orbit.

Near the ten-second line, Bathwaite had flicked the ball away from his opponent, racing alone to the Morgan basket. Clearly there was no contact on the steal. As he went up for the lay-in, the referee at mid-court blew his whistle, calling an unseen personal foul, Bond's fifth. Normally self-composed, Bond turned to see the ref with his fist in the air, pointing at him. The Raider guard wheeled and threw the ball half the length of the court into the vicinity of that official. Immediately the signal went up for a technical foul.

Coach O'Ryan rushed to confront the ref, protesting with one word: "WHAT?"

The official wasted no time, turning to the scorer's table and practically hissing, "Personal and technical foul on number 11. Technical foul on the coach."

Michael approached the scorer's table furiously, snatching the game record book from the unsuspecting official scorer. Stomping toward the grim-faced referee, the coach jammed the open book under his nose to point out the clear discrepancy in the number of fouls assessed to his players.

"This is ridiculous!" O'Ryan shouted "You two are a coupla' homers! Worst I've ever seen!"

Staring coldly, the official assessed a second technical on Michael O'Ryan and ordered him to the locker room. At that, the coach burst into laughter, shaking his head from side to side. He merely nodded at Assistant Coach Barnhard, who would become the Raider authority for the balance of the game.

THE HOOSIER GAME

As he strode before the jeering home crowd, Michael paused, smiled, and pointing to a boy in the stands with "HOOZIER HICKS PREPARE FOR LAST WRIGHTS" painted on his torso, shouted, "Next time we come here to play, do two things for me. First, I want you to ref. Nobody could be as bad as those two. Second…learn to spell."

24

OFF TO SLAY THE DRAGON

Jourden Arena
9:31 p.m.

As Madison fans erupted in wild celebration, Norm Blaise stood alertly in his spot beneath the basket. Given his line of sight to the hoop and the scoreboard clock, it was the responsibility of the outer official, Garry Worden, to determine whether the basket was made before the pistol sounded. As Blaise looked to fellow official Garry Worden for a decision, his partner froze, as if cast in bronze, a blank look and widened eyes revealing his uncertainty. With a slight, subtle shake of his head, Worden looked to the senior official to make the call.

Without hesitation, Blaise bounded toward the scorer's table. With arms outstretched horizontally before him, the man in stripes slashed his arms decisively.

Though it was impossible to hear above the pandemonium, both coaches could read Blaise's lips.

"No basket! No basket!"

Saul fell to his knees as if he'd been shot. Despite feeling as if his heart was in his throat, O'Ryan calmly motioned his now jubilant teenagers to huddle up. The Raiders still had life.

Fortune leaped up to confront the referee, his face only inches from that of Blaise. The incredulous Cougar coach made his case that the ball had been tipped before time had expired.

"Norm! Norm! The ball left DeWitt's fingertips before the gun! The ball rolled around the rim and went in after the gun! It's not when the ball goes into the net! It's when the shot leaves his hand!"

THE HOOSIER GAME

His was a sound argument. He may have been right. But despite his vehement protestations, Blaise stood by his call. The veteran in the striped shirt leaned over to speak directly into Saul's ear.

"Coach, I had a perfect look at the shot. Your player clearly tipped the basketball after I heard the gun."

"But it's not even your call! It's Worden's! And he still *hasn't said anything!"*

Without waiting for a further explanation from Blaise, Fortune sprinted toward the other official. Norm followed on the Madison coach's heels.

"What's the call, Garry? You know that basket was good! Make the call, now!"

Garry Worden stood mute, arms crossed at his chest.

Blaise stepped in to separate the coach from his partner. Finally, Worden spoke.

"Saul, Norm had the better view. He made the correct call."

Fortune stomped his feet and flailed his arms in disgust. His expression was that of a child forced to swallow caster oil.

The disbelieving Cougar rooters filled the hall with boos and invectives, encouraging their fuming coach to demand justice. The two officials allowed Saul to vent more than they ordinarily would have. The call was that close.

Finally, order was restored. Fortune turned toward his players who were milling around the MCHS bench. As he strode away, Saul fired several unkind salvos at the refs, who were, themselves, regaining their composure after the controversial turn of events.

Realizing that the call was final, the roar of the majority of the crowd—who moments ago were agonizing over the heartbreaking ending to Morgans Awe's hopes—easily drowned out the indignant protests of Central's faithful.

After thirty-two minutes of furious action the teams were back where they started—tied. In sixty seconds the three-minute overtime session would begin. Through his by now gravelly voice, Will Peck attempted to convey to his listening audience the chaotic scene transpiring in Jourden Arena.

"This, listeners, is Hoosier basketball at its finest, beautiful to behold," he croaked. "The players' gas tanks are nearing empty. They're competing with little more than heart and guts. The Raiders must not have been told that they didn't have a chance to beat Central. Every time we get ready to lower the casket, they virtually will *themselves back into the game. What a tribute to Coach O'Ryan and how he has prepared his team for heavily favored Madison."*

Merle Hollings matched Peck's hyperbole with his own. "What's so special about these two squads is how they have elevated their game, reacting instinctively to the unfolding

OFF TO SLAY THE DRAGON

drama. These young men have become lost in the flow, totally absorbed with a primal instinct to survive, to triumph. It's almost as if they are playing in an empty gym, oblivious to the constant roar of 7,000 spectators."

"Merle, it's like swimming the English Channel, headlong into wave upon cresting wave, stroke after weary stroke, refusing to give in."

"And both coaches have done an incredible job of keeping their respective teams from unraveling under intense pressure."

"Look at this, pardner. You talk about two kids who can fill up a basket. DeWitt Weatherford has poured in twenty-seven points. And in a spectacular shooting display, Jake Skoon, the gunslinger, has riddled the vaunted Madison defense for thirty-seven points!"

"This brings to mind one of the greatest two-man shootouts in the history of Indiana high school basketball. Do you remember it, Will?"

"Who could ever forget the 'Church Street Shootout,' the night Kokomo's legendary Jimmy Rayl scored 49 points, but Ray Pavy of New Castle hit twenty-three of 36 shots and five of 8 free throws for 51."

"I tell ya', I've gotta pull out my thesaurus to find some more superlatives for Weatherford and Skoon."

An incident in the stands drew the attention of the crowd. A brief skirmish broke out between two young men who apparently were rooting for opposite sides. Police quickly subdued the two rowdies. Boos from all sides followed them as they were escorted from the arena.

As his team huddled around him, Coach O'Ryan observed a subtle change in the demeanor of his boys. What he saw in his players' eyes was not satisfaction with competing evenly with the Cougars. They were angry and defiant that they'd let Madison off the hook.

He urged them on. "Nobody outside this huddle gave us a chance. But they aren't in this huddle. I have men surrounding me, unafraid. Now guys, they're tiring fast. You are better conditioned than them. They'll blink if you just keep the pressure on 'em, guys."

Back at the center circle Garry Worden stepped between Weatherford and Danner, both of whose jerseys were sweat-sopped. Again, the Central center easily out-jumped Danner. However, Sonny Watkins knifed in front of Marty Miller to steal the tip. Looking up the floor, Watkins found that Mark had slipped behind Madison's defenders. Sonny snapped a half-court pass to Danner as he sprinted to the Raider hoop. Mark caught the heave, gathered himself, rose high, and with both hands, jammed the ball ferociously down into the net.

Mark had given his sister Abby Danner her "dunt" and Morgans Awe the lead, 68-66. Raider rooters went wild.

When Cole Wells threw an errant pass intended for Donel Satterwhite, Bond Bathwaite hurried the ball upcourt. Spotting Jake in the right corner, Bond flipped a pass to him. Miller had quickly recovered, however. Jake leaped as if to shoot his deadly jump shot despite Miller's long arms obstructing his view. At the height of his jump, Jake rifled a pass to Josh, standing alone under the basket. Seaberg laid the ball softly off the glass.

Morgans Awe 70, Madison Central 66.

Undaunted by MA's two quick scores, the veteran Cougar squad rallied. Weatherford hit two consecutive jump shots on both ends of a traveling call on Skoon, evening the score at seventy all.

O'Ryan rose from the bench to direct his team to return to their spread offense. When Bond passed to Sonny Watkins deep in the left corner Weatherford and Miller rushed to trap the Raider forward. Watkins urgently looked for help from teammates, but before he could find anyone open Warden's whistle pierced the air.

"Five seconds! White ball!"

Central immediately took advantage of the Morgans Awe turnover, Miller banking in a short shot. The Cougars were back in the lead.

Less than a minute remained in the extra session. Coach O'Ryan chose not to use his remaining timeout, trusting his team to stay calm under pressure. With the clock winding down, Josh cut sharply off of a screen by Danner and swung into the foul circle. Bond bounced a pass to his willowy forward and when DeVreaux and Satterwhite collapsed on Josh, his quick toss to Sonny along the baseline found the hole in the MC defense. Sonny's left-handed jumper dropped through the net with only 48 ticks left on the scoreboard, which showed Madison and Morgans Awe tied again at 72.

Saul stood to call timeout. As his exhausted five squeezed around him, each boy was gasping for breath, bent over and grasping the hem of his shorts, a sure sign of fatigue.

O'Ryan's players were spent, as well. He reminded them of what they had sacrificed to be in position to defeat mighty Madison. He pleaded with them to make one more defensive stop to force a second overtime.

OFF TO SLAY THE DRAGON

With the last possession of the period and to the surprise of no one, Coach Fortune again would go to his money player. Using chalk on the court surface, he diagrammed on the floor a double screen for DeWitt to free him from Mark's tight defense.

Cole Wells received the inbounds pass and dribbled to a spot about ten feet above the free throw arc. There he carefully bounced the ball to the floor as crucial seconds ticked away. With 12 seconds to go he raised a clasped fist above his head, signaling to his teammates to initiate Saul's set play. Karl DeVreaux and Donel Satterwhite suddenly pivoted, setting a two-man wall to free Weatherford. As intended, Weatherford scraped Mark off the broad body of DeVreaux. Just as Saul had drawn it up, Cole tossed a perfect chest-high pass to DeWitt as he burst into the open. His feathery jump shot arced toward the basket. From his position in front of his team's bench, Coach O'Ryan thought the shot looked dead center.

Weatherford's try nicked the front of the hoop, caromed off the backboard, and dropped off the rim.

In what can only be described as a free-for-all under the bucket, six teenagers pushed, elbowed, and held opponents, frantically fighting for the rebound. Satterwhite was quickest off his feet, tipping the ball toward the basket. The sphere rolled off the iron. With arms interlocked, Danner and DeVreaux leaped as one. Karl managed to get his fingertips on the ball, sending it upward.

In one final, desperate move, Mark Danner swatted the ball into the backcourt.

The basketball fell to the floor as the scorer's gun cracked.

The teams were still even after thirty-five minutes of unrelenting action.

Saturday, May 5, 2012

As the hour approached midnight, many classmates rose to make their farewells before returning to their cars to head home. Among the dozen or so still reminiscing under the stars, Pat and Josh drifted away for a private conversation. Inside the winery they climbed the stairway to the loft where curios and other wine-related whatnots were displayed for purchase. There they found a makeshift booth in a quiet corner.

For the next couple of hours they exchanged views on life, laughed at themselves and their innocent dreams of long ago, shared one another's sorrows, and spoke of God's tender mercies.

THE HOOSIER GAME

Josh and Pat after fifty years—"*Ich liebe dich,*" my friend.

OFF TO SLAY THE DRAGON

Before descending the stairs to re-enter the real and present world, Pat and Josh held one another tightly and shared a soft kiss on the cheek. There was no insincere expressions like "When you're in the area, come see us," or false promises such as "I'll look you up." Both knew this was likely the last time they would be together in this way.

"What a joy it's been to see you again, Pat," Josh said with finality.

"You're an exceptional man, Josh," Pat murmured. "You've always been that way to me."

"All the best to you and your family, Pat."

"Likewise to you, Josh. *Ich liebe dich*, my dear friend."

With that, they turned away, each walking through a soft rain to their cars at a slow pace, both reluctant to let this evening end.

Saturday, February 10, 1962

The sun was peeking over the horizon as Josh stepped into the chill of morning.

He walked to Schoenkirche's Sinclair station, the only place in town one could buy a copy of the *Indianapolis Sun*. From the small radio behind the counter, Josh hummed softly to the enchanting sound of the Everly Brothers latest hit, "Cryin' in the Rain."

> *I'll never let you see,*
> *The way my broken heart is hurtin' me,*
> *I've got my pride and I know how to hide,*
> *All my sorrow and pain,*
> *I'll do my cryin' in the rain.*

Josh also purchased the *Louisville Courier-Journal*. He turned first, as always, to the scores from last evening's high school games.

Listed there he found the outcomes of the contests played February 9, 1962, including Morgans Awe's 81-60 win over Cade's Lick.

THE HOOSIER GAME

INDIANA HIGH SCHOOL BASKETBALL, FRIDAY GAMES

Anderson 63, New Castle 61
Ashley 52, Orland 42
Aubbeenaubbee 92, West 49
Auburn 94, Leo 71
Arcadia 39, Dillman 32
Bainbridge 82, North Salem 67
Battle Ground 75, Lauramie 65
Belle Union 59, Clay City 42
Boone Grove 56, DeMotte 50
Bourbon 63, Etna Green 48
Bristol 54, Middlebury 53
Center Grove 48, Edinburg 46
Charlestown 104, Vevay 52
Connersville 62, Franklin 58
Crispus Attucks 61, Cathedral 54
Decatur 87, Garrett 73
Delphi 49, North Judson 48
Economy 46, Boston 45
Ellettsville 77, Bloomfield 59
Eminence 104, Morgantown 65
Evansville North 82, Washington 54
Ft. Wayne Central 49, Ft. W. South 41
Gary Froebel 87, Hammond 65
Goshen 72, South Bend Riley 62
Howe 52, Manual 47
Hymera 54, Dugger 45
Ireland 88, Chrisney 64
Jasonville 73, Freedom 54
Knightstown 82, Batesville 63
Kokomo 80, Indpls. Tech 62
Lebanon 74, Crawfordsville 61
L & M 54, Edwardsport 52 (OT)
Loogootee 86, Switz City 65
Madison Central 103, Zephersville 47
Milan 68, North Dearborn 61
Mooresville 63, Clayton 59
Morgans Awe 81, Cade's Lick 60
Muncie Central 94, Frankfort 71
Nappanee 77, Manchester 64
New Albany 67, Bloomington 55
New Carlisle 76, Bremen 54
New Market 65, Patriot 34
North Liberty 63, Wakarusa 60

Ossian 69, Geneva 52
Otwell 60, Dubois 59
Paoli 66, Brownstown 65 (OT)
Patoka 59, Francisco 56
Peru 72, Monticello 61
Reynolds 72, Buffalo 28
Royerton 72, Fairmount 59
Russellville 55, Cayuga 45
Seeger 71, Montezuma 57
Shawswick 66, Needmore 34
S. Bend Adams 60, Elkhart 58 (OT)
Southport 83, Martinsville 66
Speedway 65, Decatur Ctl. 47
Stillwell 70, Hanna 69
Terre Haute Garfield 69, Brazil 53
T.H. Gerstmeyer 92, Bedford 61
Tippecanoe 69, Atwood 64
Tunnelton 91, Fayetteville 45
Tyner 74, Hamlet 58
Union City 81, Parker 49
Union Twp. 73, Monterey 58
Valparaiso 72, Gary Wallace 49
Vincennes 61, Huntingburg 52
Wabash 73, Tipton 60
Waldron 69, Hauser 37
Walkerton 66, Washt'n-Clay 59
Wallace 70, Mecca 58
Wanatah 73, Mill Creek 62
Warsaw 76, Columbia City 59
W'ton Twp. 62, Bunker Hill 58
Waveland 68, Hillsboro 61
Wawaka 59, Shipshewana 56
Waynetown 49, Kingman 26
Waysdale (KY) 45, St. Isadore 40
West Vigo 72, Rosedale 62
Whiteland 57, Greenwood 55 (OT)
White's Inst. 62, Park School 41
Whitestown 99, Alamo 57
Williamsburg 74, Greensfork 52
Winamac 71, Rensselaer 54
Winchester 53, Hartford City 39
Wolcottville 66, Riverdale 42
Zionsville 62, Danville 61

OFF TO SLAY THE DRAGON

At ten o'clock, Josh joined his teammates in the gym for the Saturday morning ritual of jogging and loosening-up exercises. Time was limited to a half-hour or 45 minutes. The coaches were present, but only in the capacity of chaperones, saving the review of the game until Monday's practice.

In the midst of stretching drills, Mark asked how Madison Central came out in their game.

"Slaughter," Josh replied. "Beat Zephersville by fifty-six points."

"Yer kiddin' me."

"Did I hear you say they beat 'em by 56?" a wide-eyed Orson Mannheim asked.

"103-47. Guess they're tuning up for sectionals."

"Speakin' of sectionals, ain't the draw this week?"

"Tuesday," Josh answered, still contemplating Madison Central's dominant performance.

Tuesday, February 13, 1962

On a day of anticipation for hundreds of thousands of Hoosiers, pairings for the IHSAA state basketball tournament's 64 sectional sites were to be drawn at the Office of the Commissioner in Indianapolis. Radio station WIBC and its statewide affiliates broadcast the event live into high school classrooms as 660 Hoosier high schools learned who their first opponent would be in the winner-take-all championship.

Originally scheduled for Wednesday, the 1962 draw had been moved up a day in deference to NASA's scheduled historic space launch of the first American to orbit earth. His launch postponed by bad weather, John Glenn finally blasted off one week later.

Beginning at 8 a.m., the tourney draw was completed in a record 54 minutes. As match-ups for the sectional in a school's area were drawn at IHSAA headquarters, learning was temporarily suspended.

It was a rare exception when Flossie Wilright's senior American Authors class would deviate from the staid, quiet atmosphere she carefully cultivated during the semester. There were very few reasons she deemed worthy enough to justify interrupting her teaching time. However, as always at this time of year, she suspended her standards to allow a ten-minute interlude for a tradition even more weighty than grasping the symbolism of the raven in Poe's classic poem.

THE HOOSIER GAME

Josh Seaberg sat nervously in Miss Wilright's class, until, at 8:54 a.m., the intercom crackled and the voice of Principal Oberfeldt made the announcement, "Teachers and students: Mr. L. V. Phillips, commissioner of the Indiana High School Basketball Association, is now drawing team match-ups for the Madison Sectional."

As the entire school listened in anticipation, a WIBC sportscaster relayed the news.

"In the first game at Madison Central, Hillcrest will oppose Madison Central on Wednesday, February 21, beginning at 5:45 p.m."

The classroom cheered when Morgans Awe drew Pit High School, whom the Raiders had beaten soundly in the previous meeting. More important was the fact that the Raiders and the Cougars were in opposite brackets.

Madison Central Sectional

Zephersville "Cyclones"

Hillcrest "Patriots" _____ (Fri., 6:00 pm) _____
    (Weds., 5:45 pm) _____
Madison Central "Cougars"

                                    (Sat., 1:00 pm)
Cross Tracks "Engineers" _____
    (Weds., 7:00 pm) _____
Sycamore Creek "Eagles"
    (Fri., 7:30 pm) _____
Jericho "Christian Soldiers"
    (Weds., 8:15 pm) _____   (Sat., 8:00 pm)
                                                (Champion)
Mainport "Rivermen" _____

                                        _____
Pristine Lake "Lions" _____
                        (Thurs., 6:00 pm) _____
St. Isadore "Saints" _____

                                    (Sat., 11:30 am)
Pit "Stonemasons" _____
    (Thurs., 7:30 pm) _____
Morgans Awe "Raiders" _____

OFF TO SLAY THE DRAGON

The draw for his team could not have been better, Josh felt, because Pit should be an easy contest. Morgans Awe would need to win only twice to reach the championship game, while Central would have three opponents to beat.

"We'll meet them in the final game," Josh said to himself, optimistically.

His thoughts were interrupted by a most unusual response from the prim and very proper Miss Wilright.

"Egad!" she said forcefully. "Can we beat that team, Joshua?"

The surprised students erupted in "All right, Miss Wilright!" It was assumed that she lived only to ponder sentence structure and force her rustic youth to drink of classical literature. This departure from her usually dignified, sober mien demonstrated she was actually human, after all.

As the only member of the varsity team in this class, Josh's peers looked to him for a reaction. He announced bravely, if not altogether convincingly, "The team is really ready to go. This means we will play Madison Central in the championship game—if they make it that far."

Again his classmates gave a rousing cheer.

The drawing of tournament pairings now completed, the intercom was silenced. In most classrooms, speculation about the team's chances to beat the opponent selected continued until the bell rang. Not in Flossie Wilright's class, though. Gathering herself after the momentary thaw, she ordered her students back to their texts.

Interrupting Josh's brief tournament reverie, Miss Wilright inquired about the main theme of Poe's cryptic poem, "The Raven."

"Joshua, tell me what the author's anguished central character communicates to the reader."

"His undying love for the lost Lenore?"

"Excellent, Mr. Seaberg. To the point of madness, actually."

It was apparent that the dedicated schoolmarm had quickly moved on from the fleeting significance of the sectional drawing.

Wednesday, February 14, 1962

From Scoop 'n Dollies to Williams's grain elevator, from Hawkins General Store to the Morgans Awe VFD, from the Farmers Savings and Loan to Morgans Trail Bar, and from Schoenkirche's Sinclair filling station to Earl Barnett's Used Cars and Trucks and Berglund's Cooperage, the citizens of Morgans Awe

THE HOOSIER GAME

were abuzz with the results of the sectional draw. Where two or more were gathered, people were debating the chances of the local five winning the school's first-ever sectional title.

Nowhere was the conversation more thoroughly thrashed about than at the Totem Pole. The men who arrived late found only standing room in the tight quarters of Owen Treecat's barber shop. Already regulars like Hog-Jaw Hinton, Kettle Gut Harper, Crumb Wakeland, Shifty Sparks, Wheezer Barnett, Hick Brice, and Old Whitey Evans were engaged in a lively exchange about the only topic that mattered in Morgans Awe today.

Some were convinced this could be the team and the year for MA's first sectional crown, while skeptics in the local crowd saw no hope of unseating Madison Central, who'd won eight consecutive sectional championships.

Wheezer Barnett had the floor, expounding with great enthusiasm his belief that the draw placing the Raiders and Madison Central in opposite brackets will be the key in launching the local squad into history.

"We got the best path to the championship game, playin' Thursday, then not again until Saturday morning. Madison has to play an extra game to git to the final game."

Hick firmly disagreed. "Wheeze, if you lost your mind you'd still have more sense than to pick Morgans over Madison. They're rated second in the state and playin' on their home court to boot."

"I'm with Hick. They'll eat us like a blue-plate special," Shifty Sparks offered.

"Swaller yer tongue, Shifty. We ain't never had a team as good as these boys are. I'm tellin' you, this is the year we cut them nets down. I swear I git chill bumps just thinkin' about it."

Crumb sided with Barnett. "We only have to win two games to get into the final, but Madison has to win three in four days to play us."

"I swear, Wheezer, you're usin' a nail to pound a hammer in the wall. Just how do you think we're gonna stop Weatherford? He's the best big man in the whole state."

"Mark Danner, that's how," Wheezer shot back. "He's more of a man than any of them big kids at Central—including DeWitt Weatha-ferd."

From the pool table in the adjoining room, a deep drawling voice from an unseen bystander shouted his opinion on the matter. "Th' only way Danner can stop Weth-ferd is to bring a wrench to loosen them bolts and take the basket off and hide it."

The next sound was a rack of balls being blasted and rattling around the billiards table.

"If you play pool like you make basketball perdictions," laughed Wheezer, "I'm bettin' you owe somebody a buncha money."

"He's just tellin' what the Lord knows," Whitey Evans piped in.

"Hey, that black boy ain't Superman. O'Ryan'll have some defensive concoction thought up to slow eem down. I'd take a poke in the eye with a sharp stick before I'd bet against our coach."

Crumb Wakeland again came to the support of Barnett. "All you guys can talk about is stoppin' Madison. What about them tryin' to shackle Jake Skoon?"

"I'll give ya' that," Frogwart Fenn said, closing the door behind him as he stepped into both the establishment and the debate. "It's easier nailin' jello to a tree than to shut down Skoon."

"Yeah, if Jake ever gits the ball. How we gonna git a rebound against their front line? Besides Weatherford, they got three or four other hosses tippin' 6-5 and two-hunnerd pounds! I swear, Frogwart, you only just got here and yer awready talkin' stupid."

The spirited squabble continued, the heat of the disagreement rising steadily. The tinkle of the doorbell signaled the entrance of yet another customer. Those in the shop briefly looked up to acknowledge the bony-framed Possum Trot Williams as he sashayed through the doorway.

"Hey, boys. What-chu talkin' 'bout? Youse musta heard Ollie Hornback's barn purt-neart burned to the ground lass night."

The men's astonished looks confused the innocent Williams, until Whitey Evans snorted, "Where the hell you been, Trot—Mars?"

Friday, February 16, 1962

On the night MAHS played its last game of the regular season against the Tractors of Farmersburgh, senior players, cheerleaders, and band members were recognized in a pre-game celebration. Walking onto the court, flanked by beaming parents, each senior received a rousing applause when his or her name was announced.

The game was the Raiders' final tune-up before the start of sectionals on Wednesday. After the starting five jumped out to a 26-9 first-quarter lead, every other Morgan team member saw substantial action. In the final minutes the home crowd focused attention on Jamie Ross. Jamie hadn't scored a point during the entire season, but his spirit and commitment to the team made him one of the student body favorites. With fans cheering wildly for Ross, the players intentionally gave him the ball and set screens in hopes of getting him a

THE HOOSIER GAME

good look at the basket. His teammates and fellow students in the bleachers groaned each time he attempted and missed a shot. Having misfired on his three field goal tries and the ball in possession of Farmersburgh, it seemed as if his chance to please the home rooters was not to be.

However, with only eight seconds left in the game, Elmer Freebolt stole the ball cleanly and raced down the court. With the final seconds ticking away, Elmer stopped at the free throw line and turned to find Jamie loping along behind him. Instead of shooting, Elmer tossed the ball back to Ross just as he crossed the center line. With the crowd screaming for him to shoot, Jamie launched a one-hander from the top of the key. The ball ripped the net as the final gun sounded. The students exploded as Jamie's teammates seized him and placed him on Mark Danner and Orson Mannheim's shoulders. What a great moment it was for Jamie and his teammates, as well as the admiring observers in the stands.

Final score MAHS 87, Farmersburgh 58.

Morgans Awe finished the regular season with 20 wins and two losses. Jake's average of 27.3 per game placed him among the top scorers in Indiana. The team had momentum and great confidence as Coach O'Ryan made final preparations for the game versus Pit.

Wednesday, February 21, 1962

A capacity crowd filled every seat and standing area in the Jourden Arena for the opening game of the Madison Sectional. Central's Cougars demonstrated why they were the odds-on tourney favorite. With stifling defense so characteristic of Madison Central, Hillcrest scored only four points in the entire first half as the Cougars coasted to a 61-17 victory.

Sycamore Creek slipped by Cross Tracks, 43-42, in the second contest, while Mainport bested Jericho, 44-29, in the final match of the evening.

Thursday, February 22, 1962

Following St. Isadore's easy 62-47 win over Pristine Lake's Lions in the initial game of the evening, Morgans Awe took the floor against Pit High School. Shooting a sizzling sixty percent from the field, Jake, Josh, and Bond scored almost at will, with a combined 63 points among them, in a 94-55 triumph. Despite playing only twenty-two minutes, Mark Danner set a school record with

OFF TO SLAY THE DRAGON

26 rebounds. O'Ryan had pulled his starting five early in the third quarter, giving the reserves plenty of action.

The Raiders' awesome offensive display in the 39-point blowout of the Stonecutters raised eyebrows along press row. This was a team to be reckoned with. Excitement grew at an impending clash between these swift and hot-shooting Raiders and the overwhelming favorite, Madison Central.

Following the game, Pat and Josh sipped sodas at Scoop 'n Dollies, when Gene Chandler's #1 hit, *Duke of Earl*, played in the background.

> *As I walk through this world,*
> *Nothing can stop The Duke of Earl,*
> *And-a you, you are my girl,*
> *And no one can hurt you, oh no,*
> *Yes, I, oh, I'm gonna love you, Oh, oh,*
> *Come on let me hold you, darling,*
> *'Cause I'm the Duke of Earl,*
> *So, yeah, yeah, yeah, yeah.*

"Our senior year has been like a dream so far, Josh," Pat said softly, "and I'm so lucky to be spending it with you."

"I'm the lucky one," Josh countered. "It's been the best time of my life.

Both hoped even better was yet to come.

Friday, February 23, 1962

On Friday night, MCHS kept the pedal to the floorboard, defeating Zephersville, 61-29, while Sycamore Creek took the measure of Mainport, 66-39. All but four teams had been eliminated from tourney play. Beginning at 11:30 tomorrow morning, Morgans Awe would line up against St. Isadore in the opening game of the sectional semifinal, with Madison Central and Sycamore Creek squaring off in the 12:45 afternoon contest. The two winners would meet for the sectional title.

Saturday, February 24, 1962

Tickets returned to the box office by followers of losing teams were gobbled up, resulting in another sellout crowd. Slanting shafts of midday sunrays streamed through the gym's large windows, creating a patchwork of dazzling luminescence on the burnished court.

Trailing most of the game by five to 10 points, Morgans Awe rallied in the fourth quarter for a 61-55 victory over St. Isadore. The Raiders would meet the winner of game two in the title match.

Coach O'Ryan and the team didn't stay around for the second game. As Madison and Sycamore Creek took the floor to loosen up, Coach O'Ryan had his team showered and back on the bus. The team had about six hours until it would be time to travel back to the arena. The coach had arranged with a 1951 Morgans Awe grad, Hubert Woodwynd, to rest between games at his farmhouse about a mile outside of Madison.

Coach Barnhard had remained behind to scout the two teams. He would watch nervously as Central dominated the Rivermen, 79-44. In three sectional victories thus far, the Cougars had allowed opponents a total of 88 points, an average of only twenty-eight points per contest.

The Woodwynds had sufficient room for every team member to lie down and stretch out. Most were too keyed up to nap. O'Ryan directed his players to talk quietly among themselves so that those able to calm the adrenalin high of the previous two hours could drift off.

Jake rested but didn't go to sleep. He always felt logy if he napped prior to a game. Mark Danner had no trouble dozing off. His light snoring began as soon as his head hit the pillow.

At precisely seven o'clock the boys arose, gathered their gear, and boarded the bus. It was a serious, confident crew that arrived at the snow-covered parking lot at Jourden Arena.

25

THREE SECONDS...TWO...ONE...

Jourden Arena
9:33 p.m.

At the crack of the scorer's pistol ending the first overtime, the frazzled onlookers—limp from the rising and falling emotions of the contest—responded with a collective and extended "Awwwww" mixed with a chorus of screams.

The ten teenagers on the floor were momentarily dazed by the prospect of having to play yet another three-minute period. The second conclusion of the game had been another non-conclusion. Bone-weary and emotionally drained, their uniforms soaked, players from both squads plodded back to form a circle around their respective coaches.

The emotional rollercoaster tossing the patrons in Jourden Arena had left many fans hoarse and most of them as sweat-soaked as if they were playing the game. School officials had ordered that the doors at both ends of the court be opened to provide relief from the stifling heat generated by those thousands of bodies, despite outside temperatures hovering around the freezing mark.

The voices of WKIN radio attempted to recreate the passions in the gym for their listeners.

"Well, Merle, for the third time we're starting over, the teams tied and fighting for the right to cut down the nets. Boys from both squads are running on youthful adrenalin and little else—except for their remarkable will to win.'

"Saul Fortune and Michael O'Ryan deserve great credit for the noble performance of their teams, which we are privileged to witness here tonight. I've been watching high school basketball for over thirty years, Will, and I don't think I've ever seen such tenacity in a high school game as these warriors are showing. Both teams simply refuse to lose."

"For you folks listening back home, I'm only sorry that what we're seeing here tonight is beyond my power to adequately describe to you. There is simply no way we can do justice

THE HOOSIER GAME

through our microphones. You have to be here to fully comprehend and appreciate the heart of these high school kids."

Huddled around the radio in the Totem Pole barbershop, the self-appointed coaches debated the odds that their Raiders would beat Madison Central.

"Well, boys, whatcha' think? Can we do it?" Muck Wiley inquired of no one in particular.

Still smarting from the stern lecture delivered by Michael O'Ryan in this very room months ago, Earl Barnett snorted, "As long as O'Ryan doesn't screw it up, I bleeve we can beat 'em."

"You still pricklin' about the coach callin' you out fer second-guessin' him on cuttin' the junior class, Wheeze?" challenged the Indian Chief.

"You're just fartin' in the wind, Wheezer," retired firefighter Walter Norton added. "O'Ryan is the best coach this one-horse town's ever seen."

"Sixty-nine and twenty-two. That's a 76-percent winning record in his four years here, Wheezer. Nobody else comes close," affirmed Whitey Evans.

"Better have another Carlings, Earl. Might clear yer head a bit. You won't be so surly, maybe."

Met with the overwhelming opposition to his remarks about the coach, Earl didn't attempt to persuade them further, but smoldered in silence at his seat in Dull Knife's pew.

Kettle Gut Harper said, "There's one reason I wish't I'd a bought a ticket to be there at Madison. Love to've seen the look on Weth'ford's face when Danner abused eem on that charge. That sure showed those arrogant sons-a-polecats we come to play."

The constant chatter flying about the shop tempered as the horn sounded, calling the players back to the playing area.

Halfway up the Jourden bleachers, drained of energy, too tired to be nervous, Kate O'Ryan acknowledged the encouragement of those seated around her. Under her breath, she quietly repeated her mantra of hope: "You can do it, Michael. You and the boys can win it."

Sitting in the row just above Mrs. O'Ryan, Betty Marshall turned to her husband and spoke pleadingly "The boys look so exhausted. Can they hang on?"

"Morgans Awe is the best-conditioned team on the floor, Bett," her husband offered, to calm her despair. "Count on that. If they just listen to the coach, stay poised, and keep playing it tough on defense, they'll beat Madison."

To the Seabergs' left and one row higher, Norval Skoon and his cronies sat glumly, fearing the worst.

"I tell ya', we just cain't stop that Wethaferd," shouted Oren Olstine.

Michael O'Ryan greeted his players with a reassuring smile, acknowledging the tough and tenacious performance of the boys in this dramatic battle of wills.

THREE SECONDS...TWO...ONE...

Bent over, sweat dripping from his forehead, and gulping air like a beached fish, Josh mentally levitated briefly above the frenzy that engulfed him and his teammates.

"'Fatigue makes cowards of us all,'" he silently pondered. "Who said that? Some football coach, I think."

That quote attributed to Vince Lombardi, coach of the NFL champion Green Bay Packers had seemed to foretell the painful exhaustion consuming the Raiders' senior forward.

It was for just this moment that Coach O'Ryan's agonizing conditioning drills had been a daily ritual during practice. That he was in excellent shape gave Josh confidence that in the next sixty seconds, his trained body would recover. He would be ready to return to the combat being waged within the four black lines framing the court.

With only sixty seconds to prepare his team for the second overtime session, O'Ryan didn't focus on the X's and O's of the sport. Nor did he waste valuable time criticizing player errors or missed opportunities of the previous 35 minutes. Instead, he attacked the mental and psychological enemies that could overwhelm the exhausted athletes.

Looking into their eyes with an upbeat, almost jaunty air, the coach lifted their spirits by downplaying the reputation that Madison brought to the arena.

"Men, I've never been more proud of a team than I am of you guys. You've handled everything that other team has thrown at you and now look at 'em. They're fighting for their lives over there. They CANNOT face losing to what they thought were a pushover. And that's just why we'll win this thing."

O'Ryan then reminded the players to maintain their focus, blocking out the crowd noise and concentrating on positive thoughts.

"The pressure is squarely on their shoulders. All we have to do is keep on doing what got us here. Take care of the ball! Work our offense and don't hesitate to shoot, don't doubt yourself when you have the shot. Stay down and dirty on defense, talk and call out screens, and rebound, rebound, rebound! Forget the crowd. Believe in yourselves."

As the horn sounded, calling the teams onto the court, O'Ryan closed by reminding them that each was one part of the whole.

"Now listen. I cannot win this game for you. Not one of you can win this by yourself. But together, you share an opportunity to achieve something never done by anyone who ever wore the Raider uniform. And you *can* do it! Go out there and take it straight at 'em!"

As the team members reached up to clasp hands, O'Ryan quickly scanned their faces, looking for signs of doubt or defeat in their eyes. What he saw left no doubt that his squad was equal to the challenge of beating Madison Central. Instead of false bravado, anxiety, or fear, Michael read in their expressions and body language a sense of purpose and belief in themselves. He smiled inwardly.

THE HOOSIER GAME

Shouting as one, "Win!" the Raiders broke the huddle and strode toward the center circle.

O'Ryan caught Danner by the elbow to remind him of his foul situation. "Mark, you got four fouls. Stay aggressive but be smart. No silly foul."

Sonny also had lagged behind to ask Coach Barnhard about tightness in his right calf.

"You'll be alright, Sonny," the assistant told him. "Just play through it."

That was the only advice Barnhard could come up with, as he suspected Watkins was suffering the onset of debilitating leg cramps.

In the other huddle, Saul had challenged his players to ramp up their intensity. They broke the huddle shouting, "Cougars!"

Officials Blaise and Worden checked signals at the center circle to ensure that they worked in tandem, maintained focus, and stayed alert to back one another up if his partner didn't have a clear look at a violation or foul. As the players approached, Blaise stepped into the circle, the ball held high on his fingertips.

At the apogee of the toss, Weatherford again outreached Danner, tipping the ball to Miller in the backcourt. Cole Wells found an opening and drove hard to the basket. Sonny cut him off, so Wells lofted a short jump shot that rolled off the rim. Mark seized the rebound.

Back into their four-corners offense, the Raiders patiently ran a half-minute off the clock before Bond passed to Jake cutting free on a screen by Josh. Jake set his feet for a 20-foot jump shot. As he released the ball, Miller partially blocked the try, but struck Jake's wrist, drawing a whistle from Worden.

Skoon netted both free throws, putting MAHS back into the lead, 74-72.

As Wells dribbled upcourt, Bond attempted to steal the ball and collided with the Central's captain, resulting in an unnecessary foul thirty-five feet from the basket. As Bond looked toward his coach, O'Ryan just shrugged his shoulders with an expression of "Why?"

Wells coolly tied the game, both free throws hitting nothing but net.

Seconds melted steadily off the clock. With 1:49 left, Bond sliced down the middle of the Cougar defense. As Weatherford and DeVreaux reacted to stop his drive, Bathwaite dropped a pass off to Sonny, who stood alone beneath the hoop. In his haste to score Sonny fumbled the ball out of bounds. The Raider faithful groaned.

"My fault," Sonny muttered as he trotted by Bond.

"We'll get it back, Wats. Don't worry."

Madison immediately took advantage of Sonny's mistake. DeVreaux set a crushing screen on Jake, allowing Wells to score unmolested from 10 feet. The Cougars had regained the lead, 76-74, at the 1:20 mark.

THREE SECONDS...TWO...ONE...

As Josh prepared to inbound the ball, Bond suddenly fell heavily to the floor, clutching his right calf. Coach O'Ryan rose to call timeout. Coach Barnhard trotted to the fallen player, who was now writhing in agony. Bond was suffering from severe leg cramps. His calf had contracted into a hard knot.

Barnhard quickly seized Bond's shoe and began pushing the fallen player's toes toward the knee. This generally helped the muscle to relax, alleviating the tightness, at least temporarily.

No sooner had Bond's condition started to improve than Sonny Watkins felt excruciating pain his lower legs. The team physician, Doc Gentry, quickly moved from his seat in the second row behind the bench to attend to Sonny, who now lay prone on the court.

Taking in the scene from the Cougars' bench area, Saul Fortune mentally thanked Madison's trainer, who had provided his players with salt tablets at halftime.

With his 60-second break running out, O'Ryan frantically diagrammed a play, using chalk on the hardwood, intended to free Jake for a shot. By the end of the timeout, Sonny had loosened up and returned to the huddle. Bond, his calves still painfully taut, remained on the bench as Coach O'Ryan directed Bobby Mack Deal to report to the scorer's bench.

Bobby Mack inbounded to Jake, who carefully brought the ball up-court. The play O'Ryan had drawn up would be no surprise. The ball would stay in Jake's hands. Three Raiders cleared one side of the floor as Mark set a screen at the top of the key. As Jake crossed the centerline, Josh, Sonny, and Bobby Mack raced to line up on the left sideline. Mark moved to Jake's right and positioned himself solidly.

Anticipating O'Ryan would try to free his best scorer for a shot, Saul had positioned Wells and Miller shoulder to shoulder just inside the ten-second line. If Skoon was going to score he'd have to do so with two defenders in his face.

Quickly recognizing the double team, Jake abandoned the set play and did what only one player on the court could do. Driving straight toward the two crouching defenders, Skoon suddenly elevated and launched his jumper from thirty-five feet away, well out of the range of most high school players. Startled at Jake's bold move, Miller rushed at the Raider star. Miller stumbled into Jake, knocking him to the floor. Skoon didn't see the ball go in, but the roar of the crowd assured him of the outcome.

As his shot nestled in the net, official Worden raised his fist and pointed to the hapless Miller.

"Foul. Number three!"

In a separate motion the ref brought his arm forcefully downward, indicating the shot counted. With a successful free throw, Jake could put the Raiders back in front.

THE HOOSIER GAME

The net barely rippled as his free toss slipped through, his twelfth of the game. With one minute, 12 seconds remaining in the second overtime session, Morgans Awe led, 77-76.

With the experience of the tested veterans that they were, MC worked the ball around deliberately. Miller broke free, but his jumper missed badly. Satterwhite controlled the rebound. His follow-up shot from close in was too strong. DeVreaux's tip-in attempt skipped off the rim. Finally, Weatherford yanked the ball off the board, gathered himself, and sprung up for what appeared to be an easy basket. In contesting the shot, Mark Danner bashed DeWitt hard from behind.

Blaise's whistle halted the action. Pointing at the Morgans Awe center, the ref made the call that O'Ryan had dreaded.

"Foul! Number fifty-one! In the act. Two shots."

The heart and soul of the Raider team had committed his fifth personal foul, disqualifying him for the remainder of the contest.

Mark made no complaint. The oxygen seemed to be sucked out of Morgans' dispirited fans. Without Mark's steady hand and physical play, the team was surely doomed.

As he slogged toward the bench, observers from all points of the arena arose to applaud the noble effort of the Raider star.

Courtside, broadcasters Will Peck and Merle Hollings saluted the performance of the Morgans Awe mainstay.

"That there is a real warrior, Will. Danner left it all on the court. Didn't back down once from that Cougar front line."

"Look at this, Merle. Charley Dain, our stat guy, had the big guy with 21 rebounds."

"And some intimidating defense against Weatherford, a young man not easily cowed."

"What a shame for the Morgans Awe team."

Taking in the scene stoically, Coach O'Ryan lifted his eyes from Mark to the scoreboard. His team would have to battle the final 53 seconds without their leader.

O'Ryan greeted his misty-eyed senior with a firm handshake and an embrace.

"God, if every kid I had played as hard as Mark…" the coach thought wistfully.

Hanging on every word of Peck and Hollings, the patrons at the Totem shook their heads in anguish.

"Kiss a' death," lamented the Chief.

Throwing up his hands in despair, Muck Wiley growled, "To come so close—!"

"Hey, it ain't over, boys," said Walter Norton, noting the Raiders still had the lead.

"Yer applaudin' with one hand, Norty," countered Treecat. "Losin' our only big man'll give Weth'ford and the rest of them roosters the key to the coop. We don't stand a chance, now."

THREE SECONDS...TWO...ONE...

"I tole ya' O'Ryan shoulda took Danner out before he picked up that third foul," Earl Barnett complained. "Any dope could see that."

Tiring of the constant sniping, Whitey Evans turned serious. "Wheezer. Just shut it."

Pondering his options, Michael initially thought to replace Mark with C. C. Aguirre to give the Raiders greater quickness and a stubborn defender. The coach felt that his obvious choice, 6-3 Grover Willburn, simply lacked the mobility to play Weatherford straight up. His hand was tipped by the difference in height.

"Grover, report in."

O'Ryan considered going to a zone defense, but decided to stick with his switching man-to-man. Willburn would guard DeVreaux, with Josh switching over onto DeWitt Weatherford. It was a challenge he welcomed.

Fortunately, Bond's cramps had abated, so he joined Willburn at the scorer's table, returning in place of Bobby Mack Deal.

Norm Blaise called the teams back to the floor. Sweating profusely, Weatherford called for a towel to dry his hands. His aim was true on both free throws. 78-77, Cougars.

On the ensuing possession, as Bond dribbled across the center line, Josh set a screen on an unsuspecting Wells, who collided awkwardly with the Raider forward. Seeing an open lane to the basket, Bathwaite drove hard to lay the ball over the front rim. As Bond left his feet to shoot, DeVreaux alertly slid over into the path of the junior guard. The Cougar center felt Bond's knee drive sharply into his chest. As Bond's floater fell softly through the net, Gary Worden's whistle halted play.

Charge or blocking? To Raider fans it was obvious DeVreaux had arrived a split-second late. The crowd froze, awaiting the referee's crucial call.

With his right fist in the air, Worden shouted, "Charging! Number 11! No bask—"

His words were drowned in the sea of shrieks and boos from the distraught partisan crowd. Lying on the court surface, Bond leaped up to protest the call. Sonny raised outstretched arms in disbelief.

"No!" screamed Josh.

Coach O'Ryan, enraged by the call, couldn't contain himself as he stomped vehemently along the sideline. Seeing the Raider coach's histrionics from the corner of his eye, Worden turned and glared at the coach, a tacit signal implying that O'Ryan risked a technical if he went further with his outburst.

Only 46 seconds remained when Wells crossed into the Cougars' offensive end. Donel Satterwhite received Wells's pass near the foul line and inexplicably launched a wild hook shot that caromed sharply off the backboard without touching the hoop.

Saul, irate, whirled in exasperation, flinging his neatly pressed jacket onto the floor in front of his bench.

THE HOOSIER GAME

Fortunately for Satterwhite, Weatherford was in position to snatch the rebound from Sonny and quickly called timeout, a heads-up play.

Saul Fortune strode onto the court to confront Satterwhite, who, with head lowered in shame, endured a scathing upbraiding from his coach. Scowling at the young sophomore, Saul angrily waved him to the bench.

After collecting himself, Saul made a tactical, potentially controversial decision. Coach Fortune directed senior guards Roosevelt Dime and Henry Fields to report into the game, replacing DeVreaux and Satterwhite. At 5-8 and 5-9 respectively, Dime and Fields had been dependable backups for Wells and Miller during the season. Both were excellent defenders and accurate free throw shooters. Having four good ball-handlers on the floor along with DeWitt, Saul would sacrifice height and bulk for the speed and quickness of his diminutive guards, creating match-up problems for O'Ryan during the final 39 seconds of the contest.

"We've got the ball and the lead, men. Run our weave, and force 'em to foul you. All we have to do is take care of the basketball! Do not shoot unless you are wide open near the hoop. Make them gamble. Let's not beat ourselves. If you get trapped, we've got one timeout left, so use it if you have to. If they foul, hit the shots and let's go home, okay?"

In the opposing huddle, O'Ryan stressed to his players to "overplay your man, deny him the ball. Double down and trap every time the ball changes hands. Don't foul. If we get down to 15 seconds or less, we'll have to put 'em on the line. But let's try to get the steal first! Let's go!"

When he spotted two fresh faces in Saul's lineup, Coach O'Ryan immediately grasped his opposing mentor's ploy. He thought it to be clever but risky. The Morgans Awe lineup would remain the same.

As Michael anticipated, Central immediately went into its stall-weave. But Miller's pass to Fields was deflected by Josh. A wild scramble ensued as the ball bounded toward the end-line. In a desperate attempt to gain possession, Bond dove to keep the ball inbounds. He grasped the ball but, as he did, slid over the black stripe. Madison retained control.

The crowd was on its feet and screaming continuously. Wells raised four fingers, signaling the out-of-bounds play to his teammates. Josh recalled practicing against the Cougar plays and anticipated that Weatherford was the designate to receive the pass-in. As the series of screens freed DeWitt, Josh cannily stepped between him and Wells's toss. Josh had guessed correctly, and the ball fell directly into his grasp.

He quickly fed Bond, who raced toward the Raiders' hoop. Miller cut him off at the midline, but Bathwaite deftly dribbled behind his back without losing a step. Speeding down the right side, Sonny caught Bond's bounce pass in stride and laid it off the glass. Raiders 79, Cougars 78, with but twenty-two seconds left to go!

THREE SECONDS...TWO...ONE...

Wells hustled the ball up to center court and called his team's final timeout. Morgans Awe needed only to make one last defensive stop to complete an amazing upset of the state's second-ranked high school basketball squad.

As Saul coolly addressed his team, setting up their crucial offensive play, Michael smiled at his players. After several seconds passed, the coach thrust his fist into the middle of the huddle. Twelve players stacked an open hand onto the coach's.

Looking into their eyes, Coach O'Ryan repeated a maxim he'd challenged his men with before the game had started:

"Ain't no bronc never been rode, ain't no cowboy never been throwed. One stop, men, one stop, and you're sectional champions."

Shouting in chorus, "Win," his five strode confidently onto the court.

Josh averted the temptation to picture himself, prematurely, jumping into his mates' arms in victory.

"Don't foul, Josh," he whispered, "Stay between Weatherford and the basket. Rebound, rebound."

Norm Blaise handed the ball to Cole Wells for the toss in. The Raiders tightly covered their opponents, attempting to deny the pass. Weatherford was supposed to receive the ball but couldn't break free as Josh draped him like a blanket.

As the ref's count reached four seconds, Wells was forced to throw a risky pass to Marty Miller along the sideline. Jake instantly closed on Miller, joining Sonny to double-team the 6-4 Cougar guard. Sonny and Jake blocked any avenue that Miller might try to dribble out of his dilemma. As he protected the ball from the slashing, clawing hands of his nemeses, Miller spotted Roosevelt Dime waving his arms frantically, all alone near Central's basket. When Jake jumped to help Sonny trap Marty, Dime had slipped behind the Raider defense.

Miller suddenly leaped, spun, and lofted a perfect pass to his teammate. Roosevelt secured the ball, dribbled once, and banked the ball softly into the net. However, in his haste under pressure, the speedy Dime took one step too many.

Garry Worden had seen the obvious traveling violation and made the call, negating the score that would have put MCHS back on top.

Morgans Awe now had possession of the ball and a one-point lead. The Raiders were only 11 seconds away from winning the sectional crown.

With no timeouts left, Michael O'Ryan could only watch and trust that his team would respond after their years of experience and handle the situation with poise and skill.

Jake positioned himself to make the pass in bounds. The Madison five clung to their assigned players in a desperate, all-court press. From the foul line, Bond broke sharply

THE HOOSIER GAME

toward Jake. Cole Wells was a step behind the fleet Raider guard, so Bond received his teammate's bounce pass in the clear. Jake swiftly ran inbounds and gathered Bond's return pass at top speed. Dribbling furiously upcourt, Jake's progress was halted as Henry Fields blocked his path near the center-line. Miller caught up and closed on the star Raider guard, and Weatherford arrived simultaneously to smother Jake in a web of flailing arms and flashing hands.

Jake spotted Bond by himself at the center circle, sprung upward, and launched a two-handed, overhead pass directly at his teammate. It was a pass Jake would forever regret throwing.

As the ball left his fingertips, a blur flashed into Jake's peripheral vision. It was the cat-quick figure of Roosevelt Dime. As the clock turned to 0:08, Dime slashed between the ball and Bond, intercepting the throw. Dime drove alone and laid the ball into the basket.

Bedlam followed as the scoreboard numerals showed the score: Cougars 80, Raiders 79.

Three seconds...

Trailing Dime to the basket, Sonny alertly grabbed the ball from the net and stepped quickly out of bounds.

Spotting Jake still standing near center court, Watkins made a strong, accurate throw to his teammate.

Two seconds...

In one fluid motion Jake caught the ball, turned, and heaved the ball in the direction of Morgans Awe's hoop. The desperation try had no chance, bounding off the top of the backboard and landing in the crowd behind the basket.

The sharp report of the scorer's gun resounded throughout the arena. The game was over.

Coach O'Ryan's shocked players hung their heads or collapsed onto the playing floor. O'Ryan stared at the floor, hands on hips, disbelieving the appalling final seconds of the game.

Pandemonium followed. Madison Central players leaped for joy, embracing one another as their fans flooded the court in ecstasy at the incredible outcome.

It was for that reason that Norm Blaise's whistle could not be heard over the unrestrained joy of those storming the court.

Racing to the scorer's table and dodging the delirious Cougar rooters, his fist clenched tightly above his head, the veteran official leaned over the bench to inform the official scorer that a foul had been called.

His face inches from the scorer, Blaise had to shout to be heard above the bedlam.

THREE SECONDS...TWO...ONE...

"Foul on Madison's number 13 in the act of shooting! Morgans number 5, two shots."

Henry Fields had done the unthinkable. As Skoon's shot left his hand, the Cougar guard had instinctively swatted at the ball. His momentum had carried him into Jake and his elbow struck Skoon in the face.

Blaise's whistle and the crack of the gun seemed to have sounded simultaneously. The veteran official's finely attuned eyes and ears convinced him that the contact had occurred a tick ahead of the gunshot. So sure was Blaise of his call that he didn't even confer with his fellow official, Worden.

Neither coach had seen the referee's dramatic gesture. Saul was first to spot Blaise, pinballing among players and fans as he ran to the scorer's bench. Fortune was dumbstruck as he saw Norm with a fist in the air and in an animated conversation with the official scorer.

Fortune then rushed to confront the official. Saul screamed, "NO, NO, NORM! My boy didn't make contact UNTIL AFTER THE GUN WENT OFF!"

Looking up to see his florid-faced, bug-eyed counterpart charging the referee, a flushed Michael O'Ryan finally became aware of what was taking place.

He could hardly believe what he was seeing. It was rare that an official would make a call in the waning seconds of a game that could dramatically change the course of the contest. The play was so close that the time between the contact and the report of the gun had to be a matter of milliseconds.

Many high school referees would have chosen to take the easy way out, avoiding controversy by overlooking the contact. But Norm Blaise was no ordinary official. His self-discipline and gift for blocking outside influence made him the highly esteemed official that he was.

He had made the right, the courageous call.

Fans of Madison Central plunged from the height of euphoria to the depths of agony. The effect on Morgans Awe rooters was the opposite. As ecstatic Raider supporters absorbed the elation of the moment, a few from the Cougar side threw cups and coins onto the floor.

Reacting quickly, the PA announcer warned vociferously that "Anyone caught throwing articles onto the court will be immediately escorted from the gymnasium!"

After order was restored and the hardwood was cleared of spectators, attention returned to the court, where Jake Skoon was slowly approaching the free throw line.

The scoreboard clock stood at 0:00. Except for the two referees, Jake was the only person standing within the 3,700-square foot playing area. Every person in the arena was on his feet. As he toed the black stripe, Jake tried to block out the deafening maelstrom swirling about him.

THE HOOSIER GAME

The official handed him the ball and retreated behind and out of Jake's sight line. The second official took his position beneath and on one side of the basket outside the endline.

As he had thousands of times before, Jake bent his knees into a slight crouch, the toes of his right shoe almost touching the black line, his left slightly behind. One, two, three bounces: then the ball nestled in his extraordinarily large hands, and the fingers of the right hand spread over the seams, the left lightly balancing the sphere. Eyes focused on the front of the rim, Jake raised the ball just slightly above and in front of his forehead. Shooting confidently, as a ninety-two percent free throw shooter would, he released the ball upward in perfect accord with the basket fifteen feet away. As he watched the shot on its downward plunge, Jake knew he'd tied the game.

The try was slightly long. Hitting first the back of the rim, the ball then caromed to the front rim and blew out of the cylinder as if a sharp gust of wind had spiraled upward from beneath the net.

A collective gasp from the Morgans Awe crowd was drowned out by a thunderous cheer from the MC backers.

Among a handful of spectators not standing, Kate O'Ryan sat head in hands and eyes closed. She couldn't bear to watch. The reaction of the crowd confirmed her worst nightmare.

Will Peck hoarsely responded to the crucial miss. "At this moment, Merle, you could knock me over with a feather."

"Oh, my," his partner replied ominously. "Skoon has to hit this one to get his team to overtime. Oh, my."

Jake had backed away from the free throw circle. He winced as the color left his normally rosy cheeks. Unseen by anyone more than a few feet away, Jake's eye sockets had filled with a thin mist. His throat constricted and his heart pounded.

Standing on the sidelines with a clear view of his best friend, Josh read the nearly imperceptible change in Jake's mien. He'd seen this reaction before. Josh felt a rock fall into the pit of his stomach.

"Oh, my God," he whispered to himself.

Visions of Jake leading a student assembly in the Pledge of Allegiance and forgetting the words, frozen until a sympathetic teacher jumped to his rescue and joined him at the podium to recite the pledge flooded Josh's memory. Josh recalled that day at the A&W Root Beer stand in Madison when Jake asked a girl there for a date, and she had humiliated him in front of his friends with a tart denial. Or that time he ran away when a school bully had challenged him to a fight.

THREE SECONDS...TWO...ONE...

Alone at the free throw line, no time remaining, with 7,000 pairs of eyes focused on one teenage boy: "It looked good all the way."

THE HOOSIER GAME

Jake's panic was undetected by nearly everyone but Josh. Josh understood that Jake's self-assured and gregarious deportment masked a vulnerable, fragile psyche. Jake's evident poise, born of and confirmed by success, could be shaken in adverse circumstances. Although Jake had developed a convincing aura of impenetrable poise, Josh could spot the subtle signs of fear Jake emitted in crisis.

The crowd noise was deafening when Jake returned to the line for his second attempt. His routine was nearly the same, except that he appeared to be overly anxious, in too big of a hurry to shoot to make up for his earlier miss.

His shot was a little flat but hit the front of the rim, then the backboard. The ball rolled tantalizingly around the iron hoop like a putt circling a golf hole, before dripping off the rim.

It was 10:27 p.m. when the ball dropped, cruelly, to the court below.

26

WHAT'LL I DO NOW? WHERE WILL I GO?

Jourden Arena
10:28 p.m.

As the chaos of an epic Hoosier high school basketball game boiled around him, Jake hadn't moved from the free throw line, staring at the hoop as if it had betrayed him.

His teammates were stricken in various poses, some falling to the court, sobbing aloud. Josh rushed to Jake's side. His arm around Jake's shoulder, Josh led the dazed player through the maze of jubilant Madison fans.

In a rare moment of humility, Saul sought out O'Ryan to congratulate his adversary. With genuine sincerity in his voice, Fortune said softly, "The wrong team won this game, coach. Your boys outplayed us—man for man—the entire 38 minutes. I'm genuinely sorry, Mike."

The coaches shook hands, Coach O'Ryan wishing Saul and the Cougars the best in their upcoming regional tourney.

Madison's players showed more relief than joy. Following the example of their coach, they demonstrated respect for their opponents by exchanging handshakes and words of condolence. Inconsolable, the Morgans Awe players trudged to the dressing room. They simply couldn't bear watching the victorious Cougars cut down the nets.

As Morgans Awe rooters around her offered words of comfort, Kate O'Ryan still leaned over, head in hands, crying softly. She ached all over from the stress.

Marshall Seaberg turned to Betty, sighing deeply. Betty could hardly stifle the tears stinging her eyes.

"We had 'em, Marshall," she whimpered. "We had Madison beat."

THE HOOSIER GAME

"The boys played the best they could, Mother. Just wasn't to be," Marshall replied, his voice trailing off.

Orange-and-black-clad Raider fans throughout the arena stood frozen, not yet accepting the outcome they had just witnessed.

The uptown coaches back in Morgans Awe argued among themselves, some blaming Coach O'Ryan for blowing what could have been a certain win, others countering that his steady control of the boys kept them in a game that no one expected them to come close in, let alone win.

Saul now sat between Peck and Hollings as they interviewed him for their listening audience. A small gaggle of reporters cornered Coach O'Ryan to record his thoughts on the game. When one scribe boorishly asked what he thought about Skoon "choking," O'Ryan reacted angrily.

"When have you ever stood alone in front of 7,000 screaming people and written a Pulitzer Prize-worthy sentence?" Michael retorted. "When you were 18 years old? How dare you question the courage of a kid who's probably done more in his young life than you have in all your years as a newspaper hack!"

With that, the coach stormed away from the startled reporters. Days later he would write a note of apology to the offending writer. But he was in no mood for foolishness at this moment.

The Raider locker room was a scene of crushed spirits, tears, and fury. With red-rimmed eyes, a few sobbed audibly. Others sat unmoving before their lockers, quiet as the dead. Mark was speechless. Sonny Watkins responded bitterly; as he removed each piece of his uniform, he slammed it to the concrete floor.

Jake was oddly stoic. It was if he were in a room filled with mourners, but he wasn't part of the contingent. He showed no emotion. Josh sat nearby, gathering his own thoughts about the devastating event.

The silence on the bus ride home was deafening. The only sound was occasional whispers between players sitting next to one another. The brooding coaches simply sat in the forward seats without comment. It was too soon for soothing words.

Upon arriving at the Morgans Awe school parking lot, Rufus Gottschalk boarded the bus and approached Coach O'Ryan.

"Coach," he whispered, "The students asked if they could have a pep rally to honor the team."

"I'll leave that up to the team," Michael answered, unenthusiastically.

A few male students had already begun to gather various pieces of wood to build a bonfire in the field adjoining the gym. As players stepped off the bus, their fellow students tried unsuccessfully to raise their spirits. The team members, heads hanging, staring blankly at the ground, filed toward the gym to return their gear to their lockers.

WHAT'LL I DO NOW? WHERE WILL I GO?

Players had no interest in the sympathy of the crowd gathered in the high school parking lot. Neither did the crowd, actually. The brief, vain attempt to breathe life into a celebration that no one really wanted had fizzled. Seeing the utter dejection on the faces of the players, students began to drift away into the darkness. Everyone went home.

Except for the opening and closing of lockers and the shuffling of equipment, the locker room was quiet as a tomb. O'Ryan gathered his players for a brief moment.

"Seniors, you'll meet with me at the usual practice time on Monday to turn in your equipment and to go over the season. Bond, C. C., Grover, you dress for practice with the reserves and freshmen. Coach Barnhard will go through drills until I get there."

With that, he nodded and the players moved off in different directions.

Josh found Pat Sargossa in the parking lot, sitting alone behind the wheel of her dad's car. Josh entered the passenger's front seat. Pat leaned over, kissed her boyfriend lightly, and drove away without saying a word. She respected his silence, speaking only when he spoke to her.

Pat drove aimlessly over country roads, the only sound coming from the tires droning on the pavement and the windshield wipers snapping in rhythm as they swept away the icy sleet. Josh's thoughts meandered as he tried to put a rational perspective on the grief that gripped him. Finally speaking in a low monotone, his first comment, oddly, referred to his practice routine.

"What'll I do now? Where will I go after school on Monday?"

There would be no practice, no quest, just an utterly empty sensation.

His generation was the last of the hero worshipers. Josh had grown up in a matinee cowboy culture where the cavalry arrived in time to save the wagon train and the lawmen in white Stetsons always prevailed over the robbers, reinforcing the message that ultimately the good guys do win in the end. He had been convinced that the team's moment had arrived, that they had earned the right to be champions. And now, the cruel truth. The painful reality of dreams shattered, that life isn't fair, that all men are not created equal.

Around midnight, Pat dropped Josh off at his home. In a fog of bewilderment, Josh lay awake for hours, contining to replay the game in his mind. Every missed shot, violation, and foul was magnified in his self-recrimination. While he wasn't fully prepared to digest what had happened a few hours earlier, he did accept that his modest, unstoried basketball career had ended.

Josh finally drifted off into a fitful sleep at about 4 a.m.

THE HOOSIER GAME

Sunday, February 25, 1962

Mr. and Mrs. Seaberg were still sleeping when Josh arose and came downstairs. In pajamas and bare feet he fetched the Sunday morning edition of the *Louisville Daily News* from the porch. At the breakfast table he turned directly to the game story. He looked first at the game box score:

Madison Central (80)

	FG	FT	FTA	TP	PF
Hankins, f	2	1	1	5	1
Weatherford, f	16	5	7	37	3
DeVreaux, c	1	1	3	3	3
Miller, g	7	3	4	17	2
Wells, g	5	3	4	13	2
Satterwhite	1	0	0	2	1
Childs	0	0	0	0	5
Bratton	0	0	0	0	1
Clendon	0	1	2	1	0
Dime	1	0	0	2	0
Fields	0	0	0	0	0
Totals	33	14	17	80	18

Morgans Awe (79)

	FG	FT	FTA	TP	PF
Watkins, f	4	0	1	8	2
Seaberg, f	7	2	2	16	2
Danner, c	1	1	3	3	5
Bathwaite, g	5	2	4	12	2
Skoon, g	14	12	14	40	0
Deal	0	0	0	0	0
Willburn	0	0	0	0	1
Aguirre	0	0	0	0	0
	31	17	24	79	12

Errors - Madison Central, 17; Morgans Awe, 14. Shooting Averages: Madison Central: 33 of 61 FGA, .541; 14-17 FTA, .824; Morgans Awe: 31 of 52 FGA, .596; 17 of 24 FTA, .708. Officials - Norm Blaise and Garry Worden.

Score By Quarters

	1	2	3	4	1OT	2OT	Final
Madison Central	15	11	26	14	6	8	80
Morgans Awe	20	22	4	20	6	7	79

A brief glance at the statistics suggested Morgans Awe could easily have been the winning team. The Raiders had committed fewer errors and fewer personal fouls, were more accurate from the field—an extraordinary 59 percent—and made 71 percent of their free throws. The smaller Morgans Awe squad had outrebounded its opponent by 37-30. Next Josh began to read Ernie Stoddard's summary of the action.

WHAT'LL I DO NOW? WHERE WILL I GO?

DAVID MISSES HIS MARK—GOLIATH STAYS UNBEATEN
By Ernie Stoddard

Madison—With no time remaining on the scoreboard clock and a shooter who had made better than nine out of every 10 free throws he attempted during the season on the line, it appeared reasonably certain the biblical story would repeat itself.

In what could have been a monumental upset on the level of Milan's epic defeat of Muncie Central eight years ago, Morgans Awe star Jake Skoon missed both ends of a two-shot foul attempt to allow 2nd ranked Madison Central to escape defeat by the thinnest of margins, 80-79. Skoon, who put on an astonishing shooting display, notching 40 points against every conceivable defensive strategy MCHS's Saul Fortune could throw at him, found a basket with a lid on it in the denouement of a classic contest.

This game will long endure as a heartbreaking end to Raider fans. The greatest team in the history of the small school fell just seconds short of what would have been one of the biggest upsets in the history of the state tournament.

With a huge sigh, Coach Fortune commented—

At this point, Josh abruptly dropped the sports section onto the kitchen table and returned to his room. He wanted to put the dizzying details of last night out of his consciousness response. It hurt too much.

Entering the school building on Monday morning, Josh found himself in the midst of a silence like that of a morgue. Students murmured in low, funereal whispers and shook their heads sadly. It was as if the faculty and student body had all dreamt the same nightmare. A number of his peers came forward to pat Josh softly on the back in sympathy. Others ventured clipped references of congratulations for the historic season just ended.

Jake Skoon handled the loss just as he always did—by shooting endless hours in the gym, alone, with only the sound of the splat of the basketball bouncing off the court echoing throughout the building.

Thereafter, his lost opportunity to validate himself as a high school legend would haunt him. He couldn't seem to grasp that the result was final, the game over, never to be replayed.

In time, others moved on. Jake never did.

THE HOOSIER GAME

Saturday, May 26, 1962

Come let us stroll down memory's lane,
Once more to sing our own refrain,
Though we must say auf wiedersehen,
Auf wiedersehen, to you,
Your love will cling to me through the lonely daytime,
Each night will bring to me the magic memory of May-time,
I know my heart won't beat again,
Until the day we meet again,
My friends, goodbye, auf wiedersehen,
Auf wiedersehen, to you.

The bright blue sky held no clouds on this perfect, sun-bleached day in May. Forty-one blue-robed members of the Morgans Awe class of 1962 sat in rows of wooden folding chairs on the front lawn of the school building, surrounded by faculty, parents, family members, and friends. The temperature was a pleasant 72 degrees with a gentle breeze as graduation ceremonies began at 2 o'clock p.m.

Seaberg, Joshua, and Skoon, Jacob, sat beside one another for the final time at an official rite of high school.

Deinde...

That summer the boys of the '62 sectional runner-up didn't see much of one another. Being together wasn't the same. In one another's presence, the reminder of the shared pain of losing the game of their lives was too much. Besides, they were no longer in high school. Each now was forced to look over the horizon at what the future held for them.

Josh had been admitted to Berea College in Kentucky. He had already decided not to play basketball, despite the earnest pleas of the coach. His separation from basketball had begun. His future included earning his bachelor's in Social Arts at Berea, plus master's and doctoral degrees at Ohio State University. He accepted an appointment to the faculty at Ohio's Miami University, the only job he would ever hold.

Jake Skoon expected to receive basketball scholarship offers from a number of major colleges. However, college recruiters who had followed the Morgans Awe star were not impressed enough to recommend Jake to their

WHAT'LL I DO NOW? WHERE WILL I GO?

head coaches. Scouts had concluded that his lack of athleticism—especially his slowness of foot—and frail physique would negate his extraordinary shooting ability when faced by superior athletes at the college level.

Bitterly disappointed, Jake turned down offers to play at smaller schools, such as Hanover, Indiana Central, and Franklin colleges. He determined to try out as a non-scholarship player at Indiana University, earn a place on the Hoosiers' roster, and prove that he was a Big Ten-caliber player.

After enrolling, he joined members of the varsity and other walk-on hopefuls in preseason scrimmages at the IU rec center. It was here that veteran members of the Hoosier squad, like Tom and Dick VanArsdale, Tom Bolyard, Jon McGlocklin, and Jimmy Rayl would test the mettle of the freshman hopefuls. No quarter was given to the newcomers; the IU men played brutal, physical defense, especially resenting high school hotshots whose overblown reputations preceded them.

Sylvester "Sy" Penniman, a junior guard for the Hoosiers, had assigned himself to guard Jake for the purpose of measuring the will and the skills of the country kid who would compete for Sy's place on the roster. Penniman's superior quickness and rough defense was so dominating that Jake could rarely break free to get the ball. When he did, Penniman regularly stole it from him, with the quickest hands the former Raider had ever seen. Skoon quickly discovered what the recruiters had known all along—he simply couldn't cope with the quickness and physical play of major college players.

Jake was not one whom head coach Branch McCracken invited to tryouts when practice officially began. An assistant coach approached Skoon to ask if he would like to be a student manager. Jake's pride wouldn't abide it. Instead, he dropped out of school and returned to Morgans Awe.

Jake began to play ball wherever there was a game in town—independent teams, pick-up games with high school players—as if by proving his superiority over the flotsam and jetsam of playground basketball he could somehow atone for his failure to make it at IU.

The peers, friends, and fans who admired and envied him as a teenager would have nothing of depth to say to him in adulthood beyond hackneyed basketball memories. Many of the same people who had placed him on a hero's pedestal now smiled to his face while whispering disparagingly behind his back. Some openly scorned him to others out of Jake's hearing. Others simply averted their eyes at the pathetic caricature Jake Skoon had become.

THE HOOSIER GAME

No one heard the report of the pistol shortly after midnight that frigid November evening in 1975. They found him next morning, a grimy basketball clutched in his left hand, beneath the goal on the barn where Jake had scored his first basket as a child.

Hoosier Hysteria had claimed another victim.

Made in the USA
Charleston, SC
17 December 2013